OPERATIONS STRATEGY

APICS SPECIAL EDITION

Taken from:

Operations Strategy: Focusing Competitive Excellence
by Peter W. Stonebraker and G. Keong Leong

PEARSON
Custom Publishing

Printed in the United States of America

10 9 8 7 6 5 4

ISBN 0-536-84973-0

2004160438

EH/JM

Please visit our web site at *www.pearsoncustom.com*

PEARSON CUSTOM PUBLISHING
75 Arlington Street, Suite 300, Boston, MA 02116
A Pearson Education Company

CONTENTS

PREFACE

ABOUT APICS

APICS Community Offers Certifications, Education, Online Resources, Networking

For more than 45 years, APICS has been on the leading edge in the production and inventory management arena with its certifications, educational programs, chapter activities, publications, and online resources.

CPIM and CIRM

APICS offers two internationally recognized certification programs, Certified in Production and Inventory Management (CPIM) and Certified in Integrated Resource Management (CIRM). A widely sought-after industry certification, CPIM has more than 74,000 certified professionals worldwide. The CPIM program provides a common basis for individuals to assess their knowledge of the production and inventory management field. After obtaining the CPIM designation, individuals are eligible to take their professional credentials to the next level with the Certified Fellow in Production and Inventory Management (CFPIM) designation, demonstrating their knowledge by presenting, publishing, teaching, and participating in APICS professional development activities.

The CIRM program explores how to achieve cross-functional management integration and leadership skills. Participants gain a clearer understanding of how the independent resources of an organization function together to achieve bottom-line results.

APICS prepares certification candidates for the exams through publications and review courses. The exam content manuals, reprints, practice questions, and resource texts are available from the APICS Bookstore. APICS chapters offer review courses, and Weber State University and Fox Valley Community College conduct online certification review courses.

Webinars

APICS Webinars provide specialized, convenient, and cost-effective education to solve everyday production and inventory management challenges. Each 60-minute online event features an educational discussion, case studies, and a Q&A session. With an Internet connection and a telephone, companies may educate a large number of individuals at once. Each APICS Webinar is archived and available for unlimited on-demand viewing as well.

On-Site Training

APICS brings education to a company's worksite for training of 10 or more employees. Programs fall into four general categories: manufacturing essentials, production and inventory management, integrated resource management, and topic specific. On-site training helps companies excel by providing uniform instruction; eliminating staff travel costs and minimizing the disruption in workflow by managing instruction schedules and locations.

APICS International Conference and Exposition

Each year, inventory and supply chain management professionals gather at the APICS International Conference and Exposition to learn about the most effective strategies, techniques, and systems and services to increase their companies' position in the market. Directors and managers attend who are focused on customer and supplier alliances to increase flexibility and improve the value-added chain in the following areas: materials handling and management, business process/change, IT, purchasing and procurement, transportation, distribution, warehousing, plant management, third-party logistics, customer service, sales and marketing, and e-commerce.

General session and featured speakers offer solutions to real-world challenges, highlighting their experiences and offering insights into the business world. The exposition provides exhibitors the opportunity to promote the value of their products and services. Leaders in software, systems, services and information technology for e-commerce solutions, supply chain management, MRP/ERP, automated electronic data collection, planning and scheduling, training, CRM, systems integration, RFID/wireless, logistics/distribution, and business consulting are showcased.

APICS—The Performance Advantage

APICS' award-winning magazine provides comprehensive articles on enterprise resources planning, supply chain management, e-business, materials management, and production and inventory management. APICS members rank the magazine as their number one resource for industry news and information.

APICS e-News—Your Solutions for Increasing Workplace Performance

APICS' semimonthly e-mail newsletter delivers quick reading, yet hard-hitting articles on inventory and supply chain management issues. Published the first and third Tuesday of the month, the newsletter also covers the latest products and services offered by APICS. To subscribe to this free electronic publication, go to the APICS Web site at www.apics.org.

APICS Online

The APICS Web site, www.apics.org, is the solution for finding critical production and inventory management information. This valuable online resource features the APICS Online Bookstore, the Publications Database, the APICS Career Center, the Online Buyers' Guide, and the Online Consultants Guide.

The APICS Online Bookstore is home for a collective source of more than 800 valuable publications, training tools, and other resources. The Publications Database is a searchable online tool to locate articles in *APICS—The Performance Advantage* magazine and the *Production and Inventory Management Journal*. The APICS Career Center is the premier resource for inventory and supply chain management professionals and companies seeking experienced specialists to meet enterprise needs. The APICS Online Buyers' Guide is a searchable database helping searchers find solutions providers and industry suppliers by company name, category, keyword, and location. The APICS Online Consultants Directory connects consultants, professors, interim managers, freelance specialists, or researchers with those who are searching for consulting services.

APICS Community

More than 270 chapters throughout North America offer educational and networking opportunities at the local level, providing workshops, seminars, and professional development meetings. The APICS electronic discussion lists provide an e-commerce community where industry professionals may network, discuss issues, and exchange ideas with others in their field via e-mail. The lists include Auto-ID; CPIM; CIRM; Constraints Management; Engineered Products, Aerospace, and Defense; Lean; Process Industries; Remanufacturing and Service Parts; Small Manufacturing; Service; and Textile and Apparel.

CHAPTER 1

DIMENSIONS OF OPERATIONS STRATEGY

*An organization can survive so long as it adjusts to its situation;
whether the process of adjustment is awkward or nimble
becomes important in determining the organization's
degree of prosperity.*
—James D. Thompson and William J. McEwen, 1958, p. 25

*The feasible alternatives range in one continuous space, which
is often as big as the business environment itself.*
—An Operations Planner

Objectives

After completing this chapter you should be able to:

- State concisely the original basis for strategy.
- Identify the dimensions of the domain and the environment.
- Elaborate the product/service- and process-focused models of strategy formulation.
- Describe the operations strategy development process.
- State the productivity paradox and suggest ways to address that paradox.
- Identify a hierarchy of actions to fit operations strategy.

Outline

INTRODUCTORY CASE: "THERE'S SOMETHING ABOUT A HARLEY!"*

Harley-Davidson can rightfully be called an "American legend." It is the only survivor among numerous domestic motorcycle manufacturers in the 1950s. The company has gone through several crises in its almost 90-year history; however, the crisis of the mid-1980s was perhaps the most difficult. Simultaneously, that crisis is the most significant because of the strength with which the firm recovered. Despite heavy U.S. Government tariffs on foreign competitors, in 1985, Harley-Davidson was only several hours from being required to file for bankruptcy or face court-directed liquidation. Harley's survival was due, in part, to dumb luck, but also because "there's something about a Harley."

Some products, and the Harley-Davidson motorcycle is certainly one, have a mystique, a special relationship with their customers that results from the nature of the product, the production process, or the marketing methods. Corvette automobiles, Apple computers, and L. L. Bean camping and outdoors gear may also have such an identity. However, few products in American history have been able to sustain this powerful, often personal, relationship of the product, its design, and the market as well as Harley-Davidson.

The Harley-Davidson Company visibly supports charities, such as the muscular-dystrophy foundation, and has numerous apparel and equipment franchises. However, there is more to the mystique than charities or clothing franchises. As a Harley-Davidson

---

*Materials drawn from Willis, 1986, and Reid, 1990.

T-shirt articulates: "Harley-Davidson—If I Have to Explain, You Wouldn't Understand." Though such visible activities help, the something about the Harley has more to do with product design (metal—not plastic—fenders, the vibrating "heart," and the throbbing "voice"), the process (a local job shop competing against the high-tech automation of imports), and the after-market services (Harley Owner's Groups—HOGs, tours, identity, and individualism). Though some of these activities may be perceived as marketing gimmicks, the design of the product and the nature of the manufacturing process give substance to the uniquely defined domain of Harley-Davidson.

In the mid-1970s, Harley came under pressure from imports as foreign companies started to build and export to the United States motorcycles in the "heavy" (greater than 750cc) classification. However, the company's difficulties also resulted from other factors, including quality problems, poor inventory management procedures, difficulties with dealership groups, product identity, and design questions. Simply, Harley-Davidson was losing its domain.

The revitalization of Harley-Davidson involved the identification and evaluation of these and other corporate assets, the buy-back of the corporation from a conglomerate by a group of dedicated executives, and support for rather extensive belt-tightening from unions, employees, management, and financiers—even the President of the United States. Harley-Davidson has survived this crisis; it has resecured its domain and its distinctive competence. Harley-Davidson is now expanding production because the company cannot build all of the motorcycles demanded by the market. The Harley is on a roll again.

Origin of Strategy

As the experience of the Harley-Davidson Company suggests, the definition and implementation of operations strategy are extremely complex and subtle processes, which vary extensively between industries and among competitor firms. The environment and the corporate self-definition contribute significantly to these processes. This chapter elaborates the definitional, descriptive, and environmental background of operations management. The origins of strategy are described, and several models of strategy are defined. The strategy dilemma is then presented, and a process to address that dilemma is considered. Subsequently, a model of operations strategy to fit the organization with its environment is developed.

Principle of Competitive Exclusion

Though the concept of operations strategy may appear to be a recent development, in fact, as Henderson (1989) comments, the origin of strategy is derived from life itself. In 1934, Professor G. F. Gause, known as the "Father of Mathematical Biology," proposed the principle of competitive exclusion, which states, "No two species can coexist that make their living in the identical way." When two species compete for the same resource, without constraints, one specie will eventually displace the other. Following Darwin's laws of natural selection, some species become extinct, while others adapt to their surroundings and survive. This process has bolstered the tremendous variety of life on earth. Each specie is encouraged to develop a domain or territory and several usable resources, which, taken together, constitute a distinctive competence. Thus, the concepts of the domain and critical resource of an operation, which define distinctive competence, are derived from a biological interpretation of the origins of life.

Though these evolutionary processes may take millions of years, active pursuit of a strategy can hasten the process. Strategy is directed toward identifying and evaluating a situation and developing a plan to create, hasten, or compound a distinctive competence or a competitive advantage. It is the commitment of resources to build the capabilities of the firm or to implement a value-adding transformation. As Thompson and McEwen note in the introductory quote, the nimbleness of the process is the key to assuring the prosperity of the firm. Such efforts would include investment in research and development of a new product or service, the discovery and implementation of a new process technology, or reorganization of sales regions to enter a new market. For example, in the late 1970s, Coors Brewing Company evaluated their regional distribution area (west of the Mississippi River) in view of the increasing threat of companies with powerful national distribution systems. Coors redefined its strategy toward the development of a national market domain.

Strategy—Applied Competitive Exclusion

For success, a strategy must overcome the inherent inertia of the environment and the advantage that naturally accrues to a defender. Military operations, a very measurable environment, suggest that a three-to-one advantage, or some other factor, such as a technological advantage, is necessary to overwhelm a defended position. In most other environments, however, success may depend upon less definable and less measurable cultural or behavioral factors and include, as in the case of Harley-Davidson, the mystique of the product.

Because of the difficulties of overcoming inertia or of gaining control of a hostile domain, the existing strategic relationships will likely continue for years with minor and often unmeasurable variations. Alternatively, if a strategy is either highly successful or a failure, change will likely occur rapidly. For this reason, most competitive environments typically experience long periods of relative stability during which organizations build capabilities (plan and fit) and develop their distinctive competence. For example, Lincoln Electric Company, a maker of transportable electric motors and welding equipment, has a very stable product, process, and market. After a strategic refocusing of the relationship of labor and management in 1934, the firm's strategy has since been relatively stable. Company energies are directed toward internal efficiency and growth through capability-building, including planning and fitting activities.

However, when risks of strategic change are reduced, such as by the emergence of an empty domain due to market or political collapse, a technical discovery, or mismanagement of resources, periods of rapid strategic development occur. Examples of such dynamic change include the emergence of the markets of Eastern Europe and the former Soviet Union, the North American Free Trade Agreement (NAFTA), the European Community, and the Pacific rim markets. Manufacturing and service delivery examples include the recent precipitous growth of computer technology, the emerging linkage of the communications and entertainment industries, the use of customer data bases, and the tremendous changes in process technology due to automated equipment controls and laser tools. Dramatic shifts in product/service definition, process technologies, or market penetration ensue. This pattern of long periods of stability followed by rapid and dynamic change is found in all areas of competitive interaction, including business, politics, military, and ideology. From a global perspective, Drucker (1992) suggests that business is entering a twenty- or thirty-year cycle of turbulence.

In summary, during periods of stability, capability-building activities predominate. The risks of change in the product/service, process technology, and market domains of the organization are high. However, during periods of turbulence, rapid and proactive implementation of change is necessary. The labor turbulence at the General Motors Lordstown assembly plant in the late 1960s is a classic example. Industrial engineers, using methods developed over the prior 40 years, refined assembly line operations to the point that a worker's task cycle repeated at 30-second intervals. But by the late 1960s and in the Lordstown situation, the needs of the labor force had changed. More educated workers rejected the monotony of a fast-cycle line, leading to a direct confrontation with management over job definition and production process management (Lee, 1974).

Thus, in strategy, the appropriateness of capability-building and implementation activities are, themselves, contingently dependent upon the dynamism and complexity of the environment. In one situation, capability building should be preeminent, whereas in another, implementation should be pursued. Carroll (1982, p. 17) acknowledges the importance of strategic capability-building activities, but concludes that "the cumulative effect of a successful performance (implementation) strategy is devastating, but is rarely accorded its due." More recently, Stalk et al., (1992) emphasize the very significant cumulative effects of capability-building efforts at Wal-Mart.

STRUCTURE AND PROCESS

A strategy contains elements of both stable structure and dynamic process, either of which, depending on the situation, may take precedence. These elements, in the aggregate, are called the *strategic architecture* of the firm (Kiernan, 1993). This dichotomy is expressed in the terms of the definition of strategy; that is, the stable nature of the "current domain and pattern of resource commitments" to transformation processes, contrasted with the "planned improvements to achieve the distinctive competence and goals of the firm." The organization preserve represents the stable component of strategy, which is often associated with implementation activities, and the planned improvements incorporate the dynamics of strategy, often of a capability-building nature.

Organization Preserve

The structural or stable approach to strategy defines the organization preserve as consisting of organization boundaries, within which are the domain, deployed resources, an area of distinctive competence, and the technical core. These and other parts of the organization preserve are shown in Figure 1-1.

The domain (the area within the organization boundary) is defined as an "environmental field of action" or an area in which the organization is committed. It includes the definition of products/services, process technology, markets, and mechanisms to inter-

FIGURE 1-1 The Organization Preserve

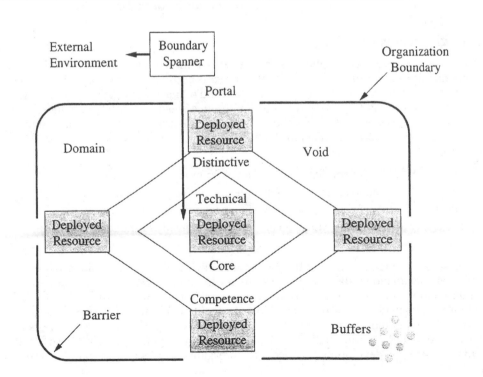

face with the external environment. The domain is defined by a boundary consisting of barriers, portals, and buffers. Barriers prohibit entry to or exit from the organization. Portals are designed to facilitate the flow of resources into and out of the organization in a controlled manner. An example would be the labor market portal to acquire appropriate labor resources, which is managed by Human Resources. Buffers are designed to establish a constant interaction with the environment, for example, sales representatives or automated bank teller machines. Boundary-spanning functions regularly interface in various functional areas with the organization environment. Many organizations, for example, are members of trade associations or interest groups to interact both informally and formally with industry and government.

The organization deploys its resources within the domain to protect its implemented transformation processes (the technical core) and its capability-building efforts (its distinctive competencies). Some areas within the domain may not be actively pursued due to constrained resources, and thus are "void." To avoid duplication of effort or failure to accomplish necessary tasks, interactivity and congruence of deployed resources are encouraged. The positioning of deployed resources may be structured or amorphous, but all resources are directed toward enhancing the distinctive competence and the technical core. Of course, the external environment contains other organizations with similar preserves.

A bank, for example, might define its domain as its services, the processes to provide those services, the market to which it caters, and the capability-building activities (such as investments, market research, design of quality services, and employee skills) that it undertakes. Within the bank, the deployed resources (tellers, and so on) implement the transformation process and various staff functions provide specialized services to this technical core. Distinctive competencies are used to build capabilities, such as the strength of an investment or resource portfolio. Boundaries, barriers, buffers, and portals ensure that interaction with the environment occurs in a controlled manner. Interactions with outside organizations, for example, with the government and banking community, are accomplished by boundary spanners such as lobbyists and information services. This description of the bank is a very physical representation of the organization preserve. However, most organizations, including banks, could use similar techniques to define their domain in terms of knowledge, capital, or specific labor skills.

Strategic Processes

The organization preserve emphasizes the implementation activities of strategy in a stable, unchanging environment. The alternative process approach emphasizes the dynamic capability-building activities of strategy definition and management. According to the process approach, strategy involves a series of congruence-seeking or fitting activities. These processes are addressed at the level of the individual, the group, and the environment.

At the individual level, Henderson (1989) has defined five "elements" of strategy. Those elements are

1. The understanding of competitive behavior as an interacting system
2. The use of this understanding to predict the outcome of a strategic move
3. The identification of resources available for permanent commitment
4. The ability to predict risk with sufficient accuracy to justify resource commitment
5. The willingness to act

These five elements represent the essence of individual strategic thinking skills. They emphasize that an individual must understand the interactive nature of the strategic environment and be able to assess the outcomes of strategic moves by others. Additionally, the individual must have resources available for deployment and must be willing to bear the risks of that deployment. Given the numerous possible individual contributors to a firm's strategy, and the potentially differing capabilities and perspectives of these five elements, the strategy development process in an organization is highly complex. Formal

FIGURE 1-2 Contributors to Corporate Strategy

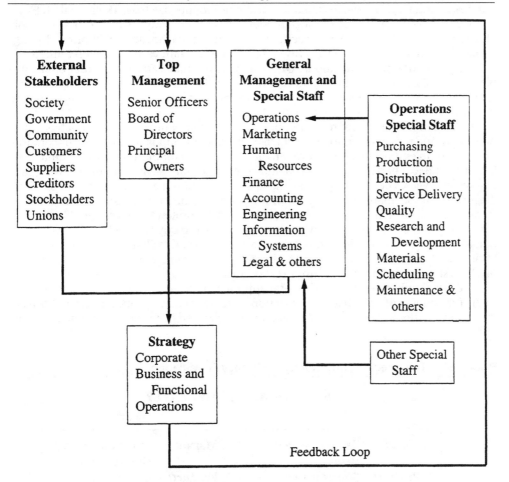

and informal interaction must be developed across organization functions, a process which involves information gathering, mechanical analysis and judgmental evaluation, organization and personal value systems, and intuition. Thus, the corporate strategy will be a composite of contributions from several functional areas, as shown in Figure 1-2.

Figure 1-2 identifies three primary contributors to corporate strategy: external stakeholders, top management, and, third, general management and special staff. The feedback loop provides interaction among these contributors. This interaction is both horizontal and vertical. The interaction of groups should be viewed as a system to evaluate resource commitments and the associated equilibriums and risks. Of course, contributions will vary from situation to situation, but most groups can be expected to participate extensively in specific parts of the corporate strategy, thus, the notion of "stakeholder."

The Japanese word *keiretsu*, meaning cooperative business groups, suggests a higher-level cooperation between companies. *Keiretsu* integrates customers, suppliers, industry groups, creditors, and other external stakeholders, with an emphasis on mutuality of interest, not individual self-interest or direct competition. Companies in the United States have recently developed their own style of *keiretsu*. For example, with assistance from the government, the big three automakers are jointly working on a new battery for electric cars. Many companies, including Ford, John Deere, IBM, and Digital Equipment are pursuing joint ventures that share technology with suppliers, and, in numerous cases, companies have taken joint equity positions in a supplier or a customer. United States companies are increasingly walking a fine line between effective horizontal and vertical integration of related businesses and illegal trusts designed to restrain or monopolize trade (Kelly et al., 1992).

The involvement of external stakeholders or *keiretsu* groups is of enormous importance in reducing the effects of uncertain environments. Duncan (1972) originally suggested that environmental uncertainty is the most important variable to differentiate the strategic response of organizations. Uncertainty is defined in terms of situational complexity (simple and complex) and the rate of change (stable and unstable). These dimensions may be used to categorize firms according to their markets, products/services, and process technologies, as shown in Figure 1–3.

In the simple-stable environment, there are few competitors, the product has a simple design, and process technology changes slowly. At the opposite end of the uncertainty axis, the complex-unstable environment, there are many competitors with dynamic market entry and exit patterns, short-lived and complex products, and rapidly evolving process technologies. The stable-complex and unstable-simple environments may be similarly diagnosed. In this manner, a range of product/service, process technology, and market situations is classified based on the amount of environmental uncertainty. Situational complexity and the industry rate of change contribute directly to this classification. Additionally, the myriad individual and group contributions and evaluations of dynamic equilibrium and risk are focused toward a situational definition, stated in terms of market, product/service, and process technology and market.

This section has defined two general approaches to strategy. First, the stable structural components of a strategic organization were defined and elaborated, emphasizing the current pattern of resource deployment and planned improvements. Then strategy

FIGURE 1-3 The Effects of Uncertainty in Strategy Formulation

SITUATIONAL COMPLEXITY

	Simple		Complex	
Stable	**1. Market**	Few competitors, stable	**1. Market**	Many competitors, slow changes
	2. Product/ Service	Simple design	**2. Product/ Service**	Complex design
	3. Process Examples	Simple, stable Container manufacturer, commodity processor	**3. Process Examples**	Complex, stable Universities, insurance, utilities
Unstable	**1. Market**	Few competitors, rapid entry, exit	**1. Market**	Many competitors, rapid entry, exit
	2. Product/ Service	Simple short-lived design	**2. Product/ Service**	Complex, short-lived design
	3. Process Examples	Simple, but rapidly changing Toy manufacturer, retail fashion, housing construction	**3. Process Examples**	Complex, dynamic technology Telecommunications, information processing, aerospace

RATE OF CHANGE

Increased Uncertainty

was considered as a dynamic process, initially at the individual level, then at the group level, and finally in environmental interaction. Congruence of individual evaluations of resource deployment and risk assessments with those of the group and organization and contingent on the environment is central to strategy development. A carefully defined and closely fit operations strategy ensures survival in the competitive environment; it involves the use of varying combinations of stable implementing activities and dynamic capability-building processes.

INTEGRATION OF STRATEGY

This section starts at the highest level of strategy definition, corporate strategy, and identifies the linkage to business strategy, then to operations strategy. These links may be uncharted and definitionally complex, particularly at the highest levels; but they give a necessary foundation for operations strategy. Unless founded on business strategy, and ultimately in the corporate strategy, operations strategy has little chance for success.

Corporate Strategy

Most businesses are responsive to an underlying corporate strategy, which, though often not clearly stated, links the corporation with its environment at the highest level. Because of the high level and inherent vagueness, the corporate strategy can be described as a mission or philosophy. Corporate strategy must embody the essential elements for corporate survival. The historical evolution of corporate strategy has been described (Steiner and Miner, 1977) in three stages: classical, balanced interest, and socioeconomic. The classical approach, preeminent until the early 1930s, required firms to efficiently use available resources to produce desired goods or services at acceptable prices. The management task was to maximize profits, with little concern for other needs. However, additional requirements were gradually placed on the firm by stockholders, customers, employees, and the general public. The firm's task became that of a trustee to balance or trade off specific interests. More recently, the third stage is gaining prominence. The socioeconomic approach states that the total physical and social environment of the company must be incorporated in management decisions. Though there is no consensus of what the socioeconomic philosophy should include, "safe" products, "fair" employment practices, "reasonable" profits, and "healthy" environments are often identified. The vagueness of the socioeconomic approach makes the management task difficult to define, yet gives management a flexibility and contingent basis for task definition. However defined—and today's corporate strategies are rarely explicit—the management task required for long-term survival is to reasonably respond to these socioeconomic issues.

Business Strategy

Porter (1980) generalizes three generic strategies that a firm can use to competitively distinguish itself: cost leadership, product differentiation, and focus. The focus describes the relationship of the firm with its market and may be further categorized as a cost focus (a cost advantage within a particular niche) or as a product differentiation focus (a product advantage that is directed toward specific characteristics of the targeted market segments). More specifically, the competitive differentiation of a firm must be based on the achievement of:

1. Cost leadership: low-cost, standardized, off-the-shelf products and standardized processes
2. Product differentiation: high-quality products and easily adaptable processes
3. Focus: cost advantage or responsive delivery and customization in response to targeted market segments

These three approaches emphasize that business strategies must be directed toward process technology, product/service, and market objectives. Lacking such emphasis, the firm becomes "stuck in the middle," without a clear business objective. By focusing attention on process technology, product/service, and market terms, the added value of the transformation activity is linked to the distinctive competence of the business.

These three business strategies are directly related to the four operations' competitive priorities. Cost leadership requires that the operations process achieve stable quality at low cost. Product differentiation requires that the operations process achieve high quality with some process flexibility. And market focus requires that the operations process achieve either cost and quality objectives or flexibility and delivery objectives. The definition of a clear linkage between business strategies and operations performance criteria is the key to effective strategy development.

Ultimately, the business strategy must address distinctive competence and the transformation processes whereby value is added to goods or services. It must link the general corporate strategy with the more concisely defined operations strategy. Business strategies may be defined in terms of the extent of vertical or horizontal integration of the transformation processes. Four types of integration, directed toward those value-adding transformations, are considered here:

Focused System.   Concentration on a single narrow product/service, process technology, and market domain. For example, a building contractor builds houses, but purchases materials from a supplier and sells the finished product through a real estate agency.

Vertical Integration.   Sequential linkage of the business along the chain of transformations toward either the raw material or the customer domains. For example, an automobile manufacturer owns an electronics assembly plant, a battery maker, and a network of dealerships.

Horizontal Integration.   Linkage of the business with directly related products/ services, process technologies, or markets. For example, a soap maker also manufactures paper towels, both of which involve basic chemical production processes and are distributed through grocery stores. Additionally, a soft drink bottler has a controlling interest in juice and energy-replacement drinks and a sports management business has franchises in several different sports leagues.

Horizontal Diversification.   Affiliation of the business with unrelated products/services, process technologies, or markets. For example, a major food processor manufacturers and distributes leather luggage, lamp fixtures, and a line of apparel.

Note that these four types of integration specifically identify the nature of the transformation relationship of the business, both within itself and with the external environment. Other types of integration describe structural or financial mechanisms but do not directly relate to the technological core, the distinctive competence, or the value-adding process of the organization.

Business strategy requires inputs from various general director functions, which would identify initiatives to reach those goals. Initially, a data-gathering effort, or strategic audit, would develop the foundation data for a thorough evaluation of the threats, opportunities, strengths, and weaknesses of the business. However derived, this evaluation of the corporate product/service, process technology, and market capabilities must be integrated across functions. Commonly, this is done through TOWS analysis (Koontz and Weihrich, 1990) of the external environment (**T**hreats and **O**pportunities) and of the company (**W**eaknesses and **S**trengths). TOWS analysis is called "WOTS-Up" analysis by Steiner and Miner (1977) and "S.W.O.T." by Wheelen and Hunger (1987). This process permits the company to focus on the desired strategic alternatives in terms of cost leadership, product differentiation, and market focus, and links the processes of corporate strategy definition with those of the operations function.

Operations Strategy

Operations strategy must be clearly linked with business and corporate strategies. Companies that develop this linkage tend to be more successful and profitable (Richardson, Taylor, and Gordon, 1985). Thus, a clear distinction between operations and business strategies is often not possible. Of course, operations and business strategies should be mutually consistent, but are often stated with different levels of specification.

Linkages with Business Strategy. In defining the linkage of operations strategy with business strategy, top management must decide whether operations strategy drives business strategy, or vice versa. In other terms, should the operations strategy be adjusted to achieve organization-level strategic requirements, or should the business strategy be constrained by operational capabilities?

The traditionally recognized relationship of operations and business strategies describes operations strategy as "richly and deliberately integrated" (Stobaugh and Telesio, 1983), though subordinate to corporate strategy. However, more recently, Hayes (1985) and others suggest that operations should define the distinctive competence and technical core, which is the foundation of business strategy. There is some evidence (Swamidass and Newell, 1987) that as the role of the operations manager in business strategy decision making increases, the economic performance of the company improves. This research substantiates the argument that manufacturing may be *the* key competitive variable, at least in some circumstances.

The distinctive competence of the firm, the nature of resource decisions, and the value-adding transformation process are central to this question. Additionally, the relationship of operations and business strategies is dependent on the product/service-process technology life cycle (operations might be predominant in new product or service development situations, while marketing may be more important as products or services mature) and dependent on the position along the chain of transformations (operations might be predominant in extraction through distribution systems, and marketing management more important in service businesses); however, there are currently no studies to clarify this issue.

The importance of the operations function to the technical core and the distinctive competence of the organization varies depending upon the organization and the specific environment. A fine university, for example, may rightly conclude that its distinctive competence results from recruitment and management of its faculty, not from the administration of the course offerings. Similarly, an importer of fine wines might conclude that its distinctive competence was in marketing (advertising and promotion) of the product, rather than bottling operations or shipping. In these environments the operations function likely is not *the* key contributor to distinctive competence, because the operations activities involve a relatively specialized and limited segment of the chain of transformations.

However, in other businesses, notably automobile manufacturing, air transportation, pharmaceuticals, food products, and furniture, consumers are increasingly cost and quality conscious. They are willing to pay for supplemental marketing differentiation only when there is tangible value added. "No haggle" fixed pricing, enhanced warranties, liberal return policies, and design of functional high-quality products all suggest that customers are increasingly looking beyond marketing or financial competencies to operations, both manufacturing and service, competencies (Power et al., 1991).

The criteria by which to measure the operations function are the performance of the transformation process, which are directly related to the competitive priorities of cost, quality, flexibility, and delivery. The definition of one, or possibly two, of these competitive priorities directs operations efforts to achieve the distinctive competence of the business, stated as cost leadership, product differentiation, or market focus.

Process- and Product/Service-Focused Strategies

These concepts, and several further and more general concepts suggest a difference between an organization that adopts a process-focused strategy and one that adopts a product/service-focused strategy. The process-focused strategy is applicable to a facility that produces a wide range of customized products or services at low volumes. A production system with a process focus is often called a job shop. Because each product is unique, it requires a different routing through the process and usually involves different processing at each work center. Similarly, in a service system, customers follow different routes. Management of the separate activities is decentralized so that the process may be flexibly responsive to individually supported market demands. This organization is suited to less complex, less capital intense technologies, such as metal fabricators, print shops, and many service providers.

Alternatively, the product/service-focused strategy is applicable to a facility that produces a narrow range of standardized products or services at high volumes. Because the products are standardized, they are most efficiently produced using the same routing through the production process. This type of production system is often called a flow shop because of the linear routing pattern. The product-focused strategy is concerned with the efficient movement of materials or sequencing of value-adding activities through several sequentially integrated work centers. Management is concerned with scheduling, capacity, and inventory management responsibilities. Product-focused strategies generally use technologies that have high capital requirements. Examples of the organizations with a product-focused strategy are petroleum refining, food production and processing, and automobile production.

The distinction between process- and product/service-focused strategies is important because it suggests further categories of strategic concerns that should be considered. At every level of management and in every functional area of operations, these two focuses require different management approaches, employee skills, and resource intensities. Various intermediate strategies may be defined which include aspects of both the process- and product/service-focused strategies. A production system that uses an intermediate strategy requires a combination of resources and methods.

Issues in Process- and Product/Service-Focused Strategies

After the process- or product/service-focused strategy, or an intermediate strategy, has been selected, several further issues must be considered. These concerns are generally applicable to both process-and product/service-focused strategic situations; however, they vary in importance, depending on the specific situation.

The first issue involves selecting the decision focus of the firm. For example, one situation may necessitate the smoothing of the schedule for the many different jobs so that each work center is permitted to run at or close to capacity. Alternately, other criteria, such as minimizing the cost of inventory, may be the critical strategic factor. In other situations, such as nuclear, space, or aircraft industries; the assurance of quality at each stage of production is of primary importance. Other decision focuses might include the linking of operations system design, just-in-time integration of facilities, or efficiencies of operations planning.

The second issue is the number of products or services a firm wants to produce/deliver and the range represented by the portfolio. A firm may decide to produce/deliver only one or two products/services or a broader or more customized line. Those products/services may be focused on one market, possibly a geographical area, or several markets. Often the products must be protected through patents, trademarks, and copyrights. Patents held by Xerox, the registered trademark Coca Cola, the copyrighted software used by consulting services, and the widely recognized Kleenex brand name are examples. However, such protections may also limit the market. For example, because it was difficult to copy the "pure" Rocky Mountain water, it was also difficult for Coors to find an acceptable source of water for brewing beer in the eastern United States. Similarly, a "kreuzened" beer (a specific mix of hops and barley) is popular in some parts of the upper midwest of the United

TABLE 1-1 Stages of the Product/Service-Process Technology Life Cycle

Stage	Some Strategic Concerns
1—Birth of the Production/Service Delivery System	A. What product/service will be offered? B. What is the design of the product/service? C. What is the expected market for the product/service? D. What is volume and what process capacity is required?
2—Product/Service Design and Process Technology Selection	A. What is the technology of the product/service? B. What are expected product/service costs at various volumes? C. What product/service safety issues should be considered? D. Does the prototype meet market expectations?
3—Design of the Production/Service Delivery System	A. What level of process technology is appropriate? B. What types of equipment and labor force should be selected? C. What organization of the production/service delivery system should be selected? D. What information system should be chosen?
4—Start-up of the Production/Service Delivery System	A. Is the production/service delivery system (training, maintenance) ready? B. Are resources available? C. How will the hand-off from prototype research to production/service delivery be handled? D. How will exceptions (problems) be handled?
5—Growth of Volume	A. What facility and process upgrades are required? B. How will production/service delivery be scheduled? C. How will performance be evaluated? D. How will the distribution system be organized?
6—Stable State	A. What process efficiencies are necessary? B. What product/service features are required? C. What market repositioning is appropriate? D. What follow-on product/service should be considered?
7—Decline and Renewal of the System	A. What is the salvage value of the facility? B. What repair parts stock should be produced? C. How to minimize the effects on employees? D. What are the long-range responsibilities for the product/service, process technology, and production system residues?

States, but that distinction would not likely be the basis for a mass market. Though a product or service may be protected, the protection can also limit market penetration.

Third, the life cycle classification defines development of a product or service from the initial concept (birth), through the product/service design and process technology design stages, to start-up, growth, and stable state, then to decline and renewal. Operations strategy must consider the stage of the life cycle, because an appropriate strategy for one stage might be disastrous for another. Companies that have products or services in stable state or declining stages of the life cycle should start product/service modification or a follow-on product/service which would permit leveling of operations resources, as well as company sales and profits. Table 1-1 lists several strategic concerns of operations managers during the seven stages of a product/service/process technology life cycle.

A fourth strategic issue, the product/service portfolio matrix, defines the dimensions of market share and market growth. Products and services are categorized as question marks, star performers, cash cows, and dogs. This model was originally defined by Tilles (1966) and associated with the Boston Consulting Group; it is still widely used to evaluate product/service growth and market share. The product/service portfolio matrix is shown in Figure 1-4.

FIGURE 1-4   Product/Service Portfolio Matrix

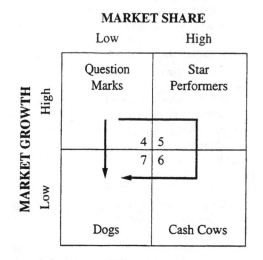

Reprinted with permission from Barry Hedly, "Strategies and the Business Portfolio," *Long-Range Planning*, February 1977.

The four product/service categories roughly correspond to the final four stages of the product/service life cycle, as shown by the numbers in each box. "Question mark" products or services are those in the start-up and early growth stage. The "star performers," "cash cows," and "dogs" respectively are found primarily in the growth of volume, stable state, and decline and renewal stages. Some products or services may never achieve market growth, but move from "question mark" directly to "dog" status. The arrows in Figure 1-4 note the relationship of product/service life cycle to product/service portfolio. The product/service portfolio strategy should define several different products or services, each at a different stage of the life cycle.

The fifth issue, originally identified by Hayes and Wheelwright (1979), considers market entry and exit timing. Traditionally, a manufacturing or service organization would manage a product or service, or range of products and services, through all phases of the life cycle. Although adjustments were required as the firm moved through the different life-cycle stages, in less turbulent times companies were able to easily adapt. Today, however, with increasing complexity and market dynamism, the adaption is more difficult, particularly with the socioeconomic philosophies of stabilized work forces, broadened community relations, and other constraints. The difficulty is that the management of products/services at different stages of the life cycle requires, as noted in Table 1-1, different strategic considerations and different professional skills. Thus, corporations often decide to enter the market at one stage of a product/service life cycle and exit at a later stage. Four generic entry and exit strategies are shown in Figure 1-5.

The traditional strategy, strategy 2, requires a firm to enter when the products/services, process technologies, or markets are new and evolve through stages of growth, stable state, and decline. A company with strategy 1 discovers and develops a process technology, product, or market, and then sells out as growth stabilizes. Recent examples are found in cable television, computer, and airline industries; earlier examples are the automobile and newspaper industries. Strategy 3 is exemplified by IBM, which delayed entering the PC market until the early 1980s, when the tremendous market potential became apparent. IBM then vigorously entered the market in the growth of volume stage. Strategy 4 is a mistake because entrance during the growth of volume stage incurs high costs, which are diffi-

FIGURE 1-5   Combinations of Entrance and Exit Strategies

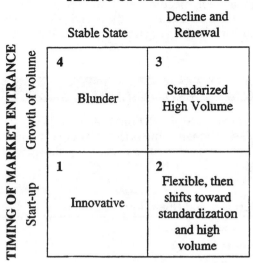

cult to recover in the relatively short time until the stable state market is reached. Strategies 1 and 3 require careful timing and rapid resource commitment. If a firm with strategy 1 held on too long, it might face a process-driven mass market that it was not prepared for. Alternatively, the difficulty of entering a market late (strategy 3) is that a large investment is required to decisively enter a rapidly changing market, and it may be difficult to "play catch up."

Strategy Development Process

Like all processes, the development of an operations strategy is an ongoing and iterative series of activities. It involves a regular and complex interaction of the operations manager with top management, other general managers, operations specialist staff, and operations activities. Figure 1-6 shows an operations strategy founded in the corporate strategy and on the survival needs of the firm. The operations strategy is further developed through the business strategy and the operations strategy to establish the distinctive competence by TOWS analysis. Figure 1-6 integrates corporate, business, and operations strategies.

The corporate strategy is the highest statement of the corporate philosophy, goals, and mission. If formalized, the corporate strategy will likely appear as a company credo, in platitudes by top management about the firm, or in stockholder materials. At the next level, the business strategy offers a much more detailed perspective of the organization, the formalization of which usually appears in the business plan, a document of some 10 to 15 pages, with more detailed appendices to elaborate on appropriate functional areas. Table 1-2 gives a general outline of a business plan. Of course, depending on the industry, the business plan might include other topics, such as emerging technologies, equal employment opportunity compliance, safety and contingency plans, and others.

To summarize, operations strategy, focused on one or two, or possibly more, of the competitive priorities (cost, quality, flexibility, and delivery), will likely be closely, even inextricably intertwined with the business distinctive competencies (Kim and Arnold, 1991). The operations capability-building (Stalk et al., 1992) and implementation activities use operations resources toward the specified competitive priorities, with emphasis toward either a product- or process-focused strategy. Several resources are integrated through the transformation process that is managed with structure and infrastructure decision focuses. The implementation of strategy is managed through a range of policy directives that specify the timing, actions, and measurement standards of management activities. Ultimately, a service-enhanced product must be delivered to a satisfied customer. Applications Box 1-1 gives an example of these activities. This process is the basis for the strategic focusing and fitting of the organization, the topics of the next two sections of this chapter.

"FOCUSING" OPERATIONS STRATEGY

The development of operations strategy is definitely an unstructured, dynamically shifting highly interactive process. Though some operations environments are more clearly defined than others and some environments are changing slowly while others are more

FIGURE 1-6 Corporate, Business, and Operations Strategies

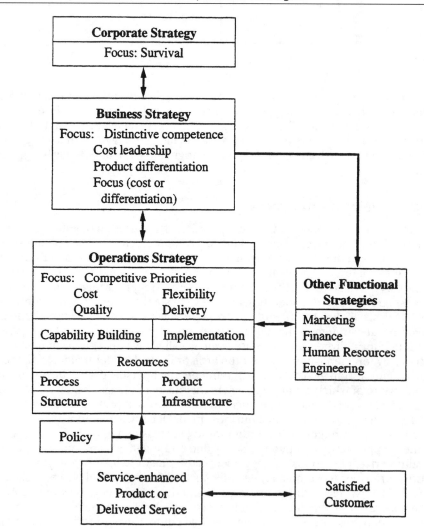

TABLE 1-2 Outline of a Business Plan

I. Introduction
II. The Firm
 A. Locations
 B. Organization and people
 C. Levels of process technology
 D. The nature of banking and consulting services
 E. Major suppliers
 F. Principal investors
III. Client Base
 A. Location
 B. Growth rates
 C. Changing client needs
IV. Geographic Area (global, regional bloc, national, state, and so on)
 A. Economic considerations
 B. Legal considerations
 C. Business conditions
 D. Major competitors
V. Business Climate
 A. Forecast projections of business growth
 B. Major variables
 C. Impacts of changes in regulatory legislation
 D. Impacts of changes in telecommunications and delivery systems
 E. Other potential changes
VI. Growth Opportunities
 A. Long-range growth in national/international markets
 B. Medium range by business area
 C. Short range by location
VII. Ownership Obligations
 A. Stockholder obligations
 B. Obligations to employees
 C. Long-range fixed obligations
VIII. Conclusions
IX. Appendices
 A. Human resources
 B. Finance
 C. Operations
 D. Marketing
 E. Legal
 F. Engineering
 G. Others

turbulent, operations strategy is at best a complex process. The function of an operations strategy is to focus (identify, define, and describe) several strategic alternatives, one of which is ultimately selected for fitting to the organization. Fitting is used to adjust the domain in order to achieve a more efficient congruence of activities and resources. Four general techniques of focusing have historically been developed. These are called the overview, trade-off, reductionist, and sequential methods.

The difficulty of focusing the operations strategy is that there are so many possible variables involved. Each of the operations strategy dimensions could be used to elaborate subsets of variables. In addition, the competitive priorities (cost, quality, flexibility, and delivery), process or product focus, the stage of the chain of transformations, and the product life cycle all suggest further variables.

APPLICATIONS BOX 1-1   Strategy Development at a Defense Contractor

1. *The Environment.* The environment of most defense contractors is somewhat different from that of other businesses. The principal defense contractors commit major portions of their operation (sometimes 80% or more) to one client (the U.S. Government Department of Defense). The standards of product and process design and the criteria for product acceptance often are not evaluated in the open market for reasons of security and proprietary technology. Additionally, the technologies of weapons systems and equipment are constantly changing and the manufacturing and service processes are often very costly and certainly unique in application. Though some products and the process to build them have corresponding or closely related nonmilitary applications, often the costs of conversion from a military to a commercial application are extremely high.

2. *Corporate Strategy.* To survive in such an environment, a contractor must ensure that it is not "blind-sided" by a change in technology or in the market. Redefinition of national defense policy and of technology can happen rapidly, and the contractor must be constantly prepared for such changes. Though contractors are usually bound by socioeconomic constraints of "fairness" in employment matters, historically, they have not been as tightly constrained by safety or environmental concerns. Because this nation, as reflected by political decisions, has traditionally placed a high priority on military preparedness, the costs for research of new technologies and for the development of applications have been accepted.

3. *Business Strategy.* The link of the contractor with the customer is often protected by long-term contracts and a bilateral monopoly relationship; thus, many defense contractors concentrate on production of prototypes of several models in a line of products using similar high-technology processes. Though the product and process development effort is ongoing, contractors must always be prepared to convert to high-volume production of the current prototype. Thus the firm must be able to move quickly from differentiation focus to cost leadership. The TOWS analysis is a particularly important and regular part of the contractor's corporate strategy development process. New technologies for product applications and production process modifications should be quickly evaluated and integrated. The company's strengths and potential weaknesses, in terms of product and process modification, should be carefully assessed in the process. Typically, the strength is in the technology, and the weakness is in the limited applicability of the process or product.

4. *Operations Strategy.* The specific operations strategy and the performance criteria of a contractor will likely vary over time, depending upon the number and intensity of conflicts throughout the world. During times of peace, the single most important goal would likely be flexibility; however, production volumes increase during periods of conflict and delivery would be more important. To achieve these operations and business objectives, many defense contractors maintain large research departments and numerous linkages with the environment through boundary spanners. The market is a niche, with two or three products in different stages of the product life cycle. Knowledge is the key resource. Most defense contractors, particularly those of ships, aircraft, and vehicles, are process-focused because of the necessity to integrate various resources into the product. However, some high-tech items, such as communications and vision equipment, may require a product-focused strategy. In peacetime, efforts are applied to product and process design; in wartime, scheduling issues would become more important.

Overview Approach

Though it is not possible to simultaneously evaluate all relevant contributions to operations strategy, the operations manager can identify a small but important subset of decision issues. Hayes and Wheelwright (1984, p. 31) have identified eight such core strategic focuses as: capacity, facilities, technology, vertical integration, work force, quality, production planning/materials control, and organization. This list has been aggregated by Anderson et al. (1989) to capacity/facilities; production planning, materials control, and quality; work force and organization; and technology.

Other discussions of strategic operations contain minor variations of this grouping; however, a high level of agreement has been found (Leong et al., 1990) among researchers that these are the important functional topics of an operations strategy. These classifications are particularly convenient, because they may be used as either a formal check list or a memory guide. The rationale of the overview approach is that an operations manager can substantively focus on one, or possibly two, of these issues, and on several important contributing subfactors. This categorization corresponds, with minor variations, to the decision focuses identified in this book. In that sense, the major issues discussed in each chapter can be used as a check list for evaluation of the operations strategy.

The limitation of the check list approach, however, is that it merely serves as a listing, or a definitional and descriptive assist; it does not show the relationship of these highly interactive variables. Skinner's "Productivity Paradox" (1986) documents the dilemma of identifying one or several variables in an attempt to improve the operation. Manipulation of the particular variable might reduce the cost of that specific variable, but might exacerbate other related conditions, resulting in little, if any, overall improvement and quite possibly an overall deterioration in productivity.

Trade-off Approach

The trade-off approach helps identify which of these variables and contributing factors are more important; and, for a specific situation, what interaction and possible impacts may result from those decisions. For example, a traditional operations approach viewed cost and quality as a trade-off. Higher costs must be incurred to ensure that a good would be of high quality, while lower-cost goods were likely of lower quality. A good, according to traditional operations theory, could be either high quality or low cost, but not both. Further elaboration permits application of this concept to each of the decision focus areas. Support for this approach of evaluating the patterns of priorities and trade-offs among operations managers is provided by St. John and Young (1992). Table 1-3 identifies some twenty-eight such trade-offs, generally categorized in the decision-focus areas.

The limitations of the trade-off approach are that a genuine trade-off may not exist, that the appropriate alternative may not have been identified or selected, and that the decision based on the trade-off may reduce the productivity of other selected variables. Recently many operations managers have found that there is not a trade-off between low cost and high quality. The contemporary approach suggests that, as volumes increase, experience increases and per-unit costs decrease. Because of familiarity, product variances are reduced as well. Thus, as the operations of many firms have shown, low costs are associated with high quality.

More importantly, with so many possible variables (and other possible trade-offs could be developed), the magnitude of the problem is uncontrollable. When a manager tries to evaluate and manipulate one trade-off, as Skinner (1986) suggests, the other related variables "explode." For example, changing the inventory level would likely affect the process and quality trade-offs, and possibly the facility, personnel, and capacity variables. Several mathematical models could be used to evaluate such a multidimensional problem, but they are not particularly helpful for several reasons. Initially, such algorithms are dependent upon possibly inaccurate and often changing input values. Further, some variables (customer satisfaction or employee safety) are difficult to measure. Third, although

TABLE 1-3 Common Operations Management Trade-Offs

Decision Focus	Variable 1	Variable 2	Common Name
Capacity	Fixed costs	Variable costs	Break-even analysis
	Build capacity before demand	Build capacity with or after demand	Capacity timing
Facilities	Lease facilities	Own facilities	Lease-own analysis
	Many facilities	Few facilities	Centralized/diversified
	Large plant	Small plant	Plant size decision
	General-purpose equipment	Specialized equipment	Choice of equipment
Operations	Line flow	Process flow	Process strategy
System	Make-to-order	Make-to-stock	Customization
Design/	Carry cost	Set-up cost	Economic lot size
Operations	Level production	Chase production	Operations planning
Planning	Labor intense	Capital intense	Resource allocation
	Preventive maintenance	Equipment failure	Maintenance strategy
Materials	Carry cost	Order cost	Economic order quantity
	Hold inventory	Backorder/stockout	Safety stock strategy
	Build part	Buy part	Make-buy strategy
	Direct ship to customer	Warehouse/service distribution centers	Customer service level
	Standard product	Custom product	Customer responsiveness
Quality	Quality of design	Quality of inspection	Product quality
	Reject rate	Warranty rate	Service quality
	Proactive quality	Reactive quality	Quality planning
Productivity	Safety program cost	Accident cost	Safety strategy
and Work Force	Overtime	New hiring	Employment
	Specialized labor	Generalist skills	Job specialization
	Close/direct	Loose/indirect	Method of supervision
	Authoritarian	Permissive	Management style
	Functional	Product	Organization design
Technology	Rapid production	Long-term process development	Research goals
	Develop own technology	Use technology developed elsewhere	Technological risk

Adapted from Fogarty et al. (1989, p. 645) and Skinner (1985, p. 61).

the model may be accurate mechanically, senior management may be uncomfortable with such formal computations, preferring intuition. The identification of a strategy to address competitive distinctness or productivity is just too complex and subjective for complete reliance on mechanical processes.

Reductionist Approach

A third approach, suggested by Skinner (1986), can be used to reduce the effects of such trade-offs. The concept is to address the root causes of the situation and thereby reduce its effect, rather than to trade off one variable against another. By concentrating on the exact "best" trade-off solution the operations manager may ignore the underlying conditions that drive those variables in the first place. The emphasis of the reductionist approach is on management and control of the underlying variables, not on the identification of a particular minimum cost of the variables involved.

Sequential Approach

The fourth approach, labeled the sequential approach by Ferdows and De Meyer (1990), rejects the possibility that a facility can simultaneously focus on multiple competitive priorities and reasserts that a facility should primarily address the priorities one at a time. The selection of the appropriate priority would be contingent upon the external environment and internal factors, such as technology and work-force characteristics. For example, the early Japanese entry to the U.S. automobile market was based on low cost; however, once that competitive priority was met, the subsequent effort was to improve quality. The results of this quality emphasis were felt in the mid-1970s, as costs increased marginally, but quality improved dramatically. By the mid-1980s, Japanese automakers concentrated on production flexibility, and, though quality was still high, costs began to rise. Thus, an operation can successfully concentrate on only one competitive priority at a time, but as the emphasis shifts over time, the residual effects of prior efforts will continue to be felt.

Empirical research (De Meyer and Ferdows, 1988) has found that companies believe that they can improve more than one competitive priority at a time. The predominance of respondents (40%) stated that they improved two of the four priorities simultaneously, though 22% claimed to be able to improve three or four measures simultaneously. The ability to effectively operate on more than one priority may result from what Ferdows and De Meyer (1990) characterize as the sand cone model. The first priority (likely cost or quality) must initially be clearly established, as is the compacted or wet core of a sand cone. This foundation is followed by sequential layers of other priorities. These subsequent efforts have the effect of reinforcing and building upon the foundation priority.

The operations strategist might focus operations strategy by using the overview, trade-off, reductionist, or sequential approaches. Though it is possible to jump directly to the sequential approach, that method requires that the definitional and structural foundations developed by the other methods be in place. The decision issues that most directly affect the particular manufacturing or service situation must be identified. A process of elimination is often helpful to aggregate the grouping to no more than two core variables and several additional contributing factors. Additionally, a manager might consider various trade-offs and compute several minimum values. However, those minimum values should be used only as a baseline for evaluating the effects of contributing variables. The reductionist process is directed toward the root cause of the situation, rather than playing one cost against another. Even so, the dynamism of operations situations is likely to cause the competitive criteria to shift over time. For this reason, effectively defined operations strategies must incorporate the sequentially developed priorities, like the layers of the sand cone. Because of these shifts in competitive priority, the operations manager must regularly address the concept of "fitting" the operations strategy to the organization.

"FITTING" OPERATIONS STRATEGY

Focusing operations strategy is primarily a definitional and conceptual approach to consider the strategic variables. Alternatively, fitting the strategy to the situation dynamically adjusts disjunct parts of the organization and thereby enhances operations congruence, either internally or with the external environment. Thus, focusing is relatively stable, while fitting is more dynamic. Unless there is a reasonably high level of fit among the divergent parts of the organization, inefficiency and waste result (Galbraith, 1986).

A typology of organization change and the mechanisms to adjust organization fit has evolved. The basis for the typology was originally suggested by Leavitt (1964), Steers (1976), Nadler and Tushman (1977), and Galbraith and Nathanson (1978), who, with minor definitional differences, develop four primary organization variables: people, task, design, and technology. Figure 1-7 represents these dimensions.

FIGURE 1-7 The Multilevel Typology of Fit

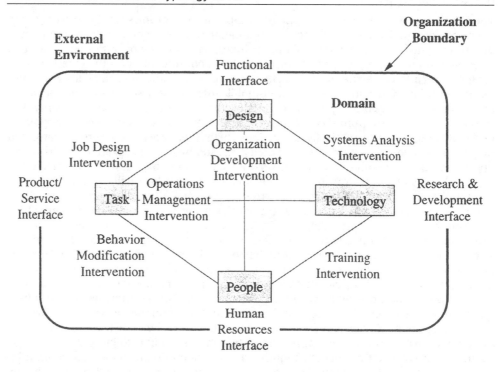

This approach is useful because it defines several principal staff activities as components of the external interfaces of the organization and emphasizes the strategic structure and processes of the organization. Additionally, the key organization variables (technology, people, task, and design) are shown. Fitting the organization is accomplished in three ways (Stonebraker, 1986). A manager can *intrude*, or directly change a variable; intrusion is appropriate only in extreme situations because of the potential for serious side effects. Intruding upon the organization design, as did John Reed of Citibank, would likely cause serious perturbations to the tasks, the technologies, and the people. Intervention is a less direct and more effective method of enhancing the fit of an organization because it simultaneously interacts between two variables to further their congruence. As Figure 1-7 shows, the training intervention enhances the fit between people and technology, and the related behavior modification intervention enhances the fit between people and task. *Interfaces* are used to link key organization variables to the external environment. The product/service interface links the organization task (broadly defined, operations activity) with the consumer; the human resource interface links employment needs with the labor market, and so forth. Interventions and interfaces can be used simultaneously. For example, the contracting with an outside group for a new information system likely would include hardware, software, and training, as well as follow-on consulting.

The multilevel typology of fit provides a framework for diagnosis of the organization; it permits operations managers to adjust their focus either to the organization or to the external environment. Though the notion of fitting is described here in terms of lateral interaction at the general management level of the organization, it can also be applied at higher or lower levels, for example, to the interactions of operations area specialists. Fitting defines three levels of action, intrusion, intervention, and interfacing, which can be contingently used to adjust resource commitments in the domain. Increased congruence within the domain, and, if desired, externally, is an outcome of these focusing and fitting activities, and a requirement for efficient management of both the firm's distinctive competence and technical core.

SUMMARY

The origin of strategy is best explained by a corresponding concept from biology, the principle of competitive exclusion. This principle provides a foundation for the notions of domain and resources, which, taken together, are the basis for distinctive competence. The principle also suggests the importance of strategy as a means of understanding and potentially hastening evolutionary processes. Strategy was then considered from a stable perspective by describing the technical core, boundaries, deployed resources, and interaction mechanisms with the environment. Strategy can be further considered as a dynamic process, with individual decision-making elements, group interaction, product/service, process technology, and market links of corporate strategy and the environment. Although operations strategy is likely different from corporate strategy and is separately defined, there is increasing support, based on the relationship of competitive priorities and value-added transformations with distinctive competence, that operations, business and corporate strategies are inextricably entwined in many business environments. It is also becoming apparent that operations strategy may, in many businesses, be the key determinant of the business strategy.

Operations goals are measured in terms of productivity, with focus on how well the company has been able to achieve one or more of the four competitive priorities: cost, quality, flexibility, and delivery. The strategies to achieve these competitive priorities, however, involve numerous variables. An interactive process was defined to identify the horizontal and vertical relationships of strategy formulation and the primary variables were briefly elaborated. Because of the complexity, the operations manager must focus those variables, using a strategic overview perspective, followed by the trade-off, reductionist, and sequential approaches. As these underlying factors shift over time, further fitting activities, such as intervention, interfacing, and—rarely—intrusion, should be used to enhance the congruence, and thus efficiency, of the organization. Though these processes are very abstract, they must be thoroughly conceived and carefully managed; if they are not, the viability of the organization will be threatened and certainly the prosperity of the organization will be reduced. To compete in the increasingly global, dynamic, and complex business environments of the 1990s, operations management must develop an effective strategy, as defined by these dimensions.

DISCUSSION QUESTIONS

1. Explain, in your own words, the principle of competitive exclusion.
2. How does the principle of competitive exclusion relate to strategy? From your readings or experience, give an example of how strategy uses the principle of exclusion.
3. Describe the parts of the organization preserve. Give an example that exemplifies the various parts.
4. Why is strategy considered both a state and a process?
5. Differentiate the product-focused organization from the process-focused organization. Give an example of each.
6. What is the role of corporate strategy? From your readings or experience, give an example.
7. Why are operations and business strategies inextricably entwined? State and support an example.
8. What factors define business focus and what factors define operations focus?
9. Describe and exemplify the product/service-process technology life cycle approach to strategy definition. How does this approach relate to the product/service portfolio model and to entrance and exit timing?

10. Describe the rationale of the overview, trade-off, reductionist, and sequential approaches to operations strategy. Give an example of a product for which the strategy has shifted.
11. Why is the trade-off approach insufficient as a mechanism to develop operations strategy?
12. Differentiate the "focusing" and the "fitting" processes of operations strategy.
13. What is the difference between intrusion. intervention, and interfacing? When are these fitting activities used? Describe an example.

STRATEGIC DECISION SITUATIONS

1. Prepare a business plan for a product that you are familiar with. Consider the outline in Table 1-2 as a general format, and elaborate on appropriate areas. Note that the value of the business plan is that it provides a "formal and specific focus of the company."
2. Prepare an operations appendix to the business plan called for in Strategic Decision Situation 1. Consider, as an organizing basis, the bottom portion of Figure 1-6 and the discussion in the "Operations Strategy" subsection of this chapter.

REFERENCES

Anderson, John C., Gary Cleveland, and Roger G. Schroeder. "Operations Strategy: A Literature Review," *Journal of Operations Management.* April 1989, pp. 133–158.

Carroll, Peter J. "The Link between Performance and Strategy," *Journal of Business Strategy.* Spring 1982, pp. 3–20.

De Meyer, A., and K. Ferdows. "Quality Up, Technology Down." INSEAD Working Series No. 88/65, 1988.

Drucker, Peter F. "The New Society of Organizations," *Harvard Business Review.* September–October 1992, pp: 95–104.

Duncan, Robert B. "Characteristics of Perceived Environments and Perceived Environmental Uncertainty," *Administrative Science Quarterly.* Vol. 17, No. 3, 1972, pp. 313–327.

Ferdows, Kasra, and Arnoud De Meyer. "Lasting Improvements in Manufacturing Performance: In Search of a New Theory," *Journal of Operations Management* April 1990, pp. 168–184.

Fogarty, Donald W., Thomas R. Hoffmann, and Peter W. Stonebraker. *Production and Operations Management.* Cincinnati, Ohio: South-Western Publishing Co., 1989.

Galbraith, J. R., and R. K. Kazanjian. *Strategic Implementation: Structure, Systems, and Processes.* St. Paul, Minn.: West Publishing Co., 1986.

Galbraith, J. R., and Daniel A. Nathanson. *Strategy Implementation: The Role of Structure and Process.* St. Paul, Minn.: West Publishing Co., 1978.

Hayes, Robert H. "Strategic Planning—Forward in Reverse?" *Harvard Business Review.* November–December 1985, pp. 111–119.

Hayes, Robert H., and Roger W. Schmenner. "How Should You Organize Manufacturing?" *Harvard Business Review.* January–February 1978, pp. 105–118.

Hayes, Robert H., and Steven C. Wheelwright. "The Dynamics of Process-Product Life Cycles," *Harvard Business Review.* March–April 1979.

Hayes, Robert H., and Steven C. Wheelwright. *Restoring our Competitive Edge.* New York: John Wiley & Sons, 1984.

Henderson, Bruce D. "The Origins of Strategy," *Harvard Business Review.* November–December 1989, pp. 139–143.

Kelly, Kevin, Otis Port, James Treece, Gail DeGeorge, and Zachary Schiller. "Learning from Japan," *Business Week.* January 27, 1992, pp. 52–60.

Kiernan, Matthew J. "The New Strategic Architecture: Learning to Compete in the Twenty-First Century," *Academy of Management Executive.* Vol. 7, No. 1, 1993, pp. 7–21.

Kim, Jay S. and Peter Arnold. "Competitive Priorities, Manufacturing Objectives, and Action Plans: Constructs and Linkages." Boston University School of Management Working Paper Series 91–66, 1991.

Koontz, Harold, and Heintz Weihrich. *Essentials of Management.* New York: McGraw-Hill, 1990.

Leavitt, Harold I. "Applied Organization Change in Industry: Structural, Technical and Human Choices," in William L. Cooper, *New Perspectives in Organization Research.* New York: John Wiley & Sons, Inc., 1964.

Lee, Hak-Chong. "Lordstown Plant of General Motors (A) and (B)." State University of New York at Albany, 1974.

Leong, G. K., D. L. Snyder, and P. T. Ward. "Research in the Process and Content of Manufacturing Strategy," *Omega: International Journal of Management Science,* No. 2, 1990, pp. 109–122.

Nadler, David A., and Michael L. Tushman. "A Congruence Model for Diagnosing Organizational Behavior," *Perspectives on Behavior in Organizations.* New York: McGraw-Hill, 1983.

Porter, Michael E. *Competitive Strategy: Techniques for Analyzing Industries and Competitors.* New York: Free Press, 1980.

Power, Christopher, Walecia Konrad, Alice Z. Cuneo, and James B. Treece. "Value Marketing: Quality, Service, and Fair Pricing are the Keys to Selling in the 1990s," *Business Week,* November 11, 1991, pp. 132–140.

Reid, Peter C. *Well Made in America: Lessons from Harley-Davidson on Being the Best.* New York: McGraw-Hill, 1990.

Richardson, P. R., A. J. Taylor, and R. J. M. Gordon. "A Strategic Approach to Evaluating Manufacturing Performance," *Interfaces.* November-December 1985, pp. 15–27.

Skinner, Wickham. *Manufacturing: The Formidable Competitive Weapon.* New York: John Wiley, 1985.

Skinner, Wickham. "The Productivity Paradox," *Management Review.* September 1986.

St. John, Caron H., and Scott T. Young. "An Exploratory Study of Patterns of Priorities and Trade-offs Among Operations Managers," *Production and Operations Management.* Spring 1992, pp. 133–150.

Stalk, George, Philip Evans, and Lawrence E. Shulman. "Competing on Capabilities: The New Rules of Corporate Strategy," *Harvard Business Review.* March–April 1992, pp. 57–69.

Steers, Richard M. "When Is an Organization Effective?" *Organizational Dynamics.* Autumn 1976.

Steiner, George A., and John B. Miner. *Management Policy and Strategy.* New York: Macmillan Publishing Co, Inc., 1977.

Stobaugh, Robert, and Piero Telesio. "Match Manufacturing Policies and Product Strategy," *Harvard Business Review.* March-April 1983, pp. 113–120.

Stonebraker, Peter W. "Managing Organization Fit in Times of Tumult," *The Journal of Management Development.* Vol. 5, No. 4, 1986, p. 24.

Swamidass, Paul M., and William T. Newell. "Manufacturing Strategy, Environmental Uncertainty, and Performance: A Path Analytic Model," *Management Science.* April 1987, pp. 509–524.

Thompson, James D., and William J. McEwen. "Organization Goals and Environment: Goal-Setting as an Interactive Process," *American Sociological Review.* Vol. 23, No. 1, 1958, p. 23.

Tilles, Seymour. "Strategies for Allocating Funds," *Harvard Business Review.* January–February 1966.

Wheelen, Thomas L., and J. David Hunger. *Strategic Management.* Reading, Mass.: Addison-Wesley Publishing Co., 1987.

Willis, Rod. "Harley-Davidson Comes Roaring Back," *Management Review.* March 1986, p. 20.

CHAPTER 2

OPERATIONS STRATEGY PROCESS

Content focuses on the specifics of what was decided, whereas process addresses how such decisions are reached in an organizational setting. That distinction is useful, in spite of the obvious interaction between the two in organizational life.
—Liam Fahey and H. Kurt Christensen, 1986

Flexibility is the key to success —and indecision is the key to flexibility. —A Cynical Operations Manager

Objectives

After completing this chapter you should be able to:

- Identify the content and process issues of operations strategy.
- Define operations strategy and show how operations strategy differs from operations planning.
- Describe four elements of the operations strategy process; then, for each element, elaborate several subelements or concepts.
- Use the operations strategy process to evaluate a particular plan and to consider contingently defined alternatives.

Outline

INTRODUCTORY CASE: OPERATIONS STRATEGY AT THE XYZ MANUFACTURING COMPANY*

Joan Schouten paused for a moment and looked out the window, reflecting on her seven years with the CRT Division of the XYZ Manufacturing Company. She had joined the firm during her last year at the University and stayed on after graduation. Her first job was as an expediter; then, when she completed her MBA with a major in operations management, she was promoted to Scheduling Manager. Joan was extremely proud of some of the innovations she had introduced, particularly a simple forecasting heuristic to manage returnable packaging for CRTs. Later, she was promoted to her current position as Purchasing Agent, working for Ed Lee, the Production Manager. She was concerned, however, with the lack of an organized planning process.

"Oh, they talk about business planning," she told a friend one day. "Even hired a consultant to give some classes, but then it sort of went away." Joan was then asked to spend more time working with suppliers to ensure effective communication on quality specifications, delivery dates, and lot sizes. The more Joan worked with supplier and customer representatives, the more she recognized the importance of planning, but when she discussed this with Ed Lee, he just shrugged his shoulders and said something about the turbulence of the CRT business.

Ed was right, she thought, because they both could recall many times when a customer canceled an order or changed the quantity, due date, or specification. Other divisions of XYZ seemed to be the most notorious. Possibly they thought that, because they were sister divisions, the cost of changes would be less. In those situations, Ed Lee could be very decisive. "I realized when I came here that this was not a leading edge company—and I sort of accepted that we have few information systems and planning structures. Most people here handle the product on a daily basis, even Ed Lee. We have a low-overhead operation." As Joan again looked out the window, her voice trembled a bit. "I've

---

*Though Joan Schouten is a real person, her employer, who has reviewed this case, requested that the company's identity not be specified.

learned to leave my MBA at home or to use it when I teach at the University. I don't expect anyone to implement computer integrated manufacturing, or even a materials planning system, but I think we should look into some planning and time fence management techniques."

Joan would quickly acknowledge that she was still young. She was gaining experience daily in a business which, though based on traditional CRT-making technologies, had become very dynamic, with global competition, an expanding computer market, and tight cost pressures. "All of this poses several rather interesting questions for me," Joan continued. "Should I shoot for top management or stay a technician? If I choose management, would I still see things the same way that I do now, as a series of simple problems, addressable with some basic planning guidelines, or would I see things as Ed Lee does—from a wider, less definable perspective? Where are this business and plant going to be in five years? If the business thrives, which direction offers more advancement opportunity? If the business fails, which background is more marketable? Should I spend my energies trying to educate my peers and persuade Ed Lee that planning problems are really opportunities to improve efficiency and reduce cost, or should I seek employment at a company that already has state-of-the-art planning techniques?"

"As a professional who thrives on problem resolution, where do the greater challenges lie? I have talked with Ed Lee on several occasions, but he sort of shrugs and says something like 'Give yourself time.' You know, sometimes I marvel at the patience of Ed Lee and at other times I worry about his indecisiveness and lack of structure."

EVOLUTION OF OPERATIONS STRATEGY

Though strategic management has been applied throughout history in various fields, its impacts have only recently become apparent in operations management. The history of military campaigns involves extensive strategy development followed by implementation through deployment and tactics. Similarly, strategy has played an important role in various political campaigns. However, for several reasons, operations strategy has been ignored in the business environments of the nineteenth and much of the twentieth centuries. Skinner first identified the issue in 1969. Drucker (1988) further explains this situation by his characterization of the organization until the 1960s and 1970s as managed by either owners or by bureaucracies, neither of which necessitated extensive use of strategic management processes. The owner-management structure established sufficient formal and informal power to assure owner control of the organization, while the bureaucracy provided a further, often redundant, control mechanism.

More recently, as Drucker notes, organizations have shifted from a command and control structure to an information-based structure. By its very nature, the information-based structure must achieve a common vision to integrate specialists from diverse professional fields in a highly dynamic, knowledge-oriented, and internationally competitive environment. Operations strategy provides the necessary mechanism to achieve this integrative vision. To paraphrase Joan Schouten in the introductory case, "What is operations strategy and how is it formulated and implemented?"

For organization survival, it is necessary to be effective, or to do the right things, but to prosper, it is necessary to do the right things efficiently. Organizations that use planning activities, as discussed in Chapter 1, generally survive because they are doing the right things, but organizations that prosper often supplement good planning with effective management of their resources and value-adding operations processes. Thus, while the thrust of Chapter 1 was to generally define the dimensions, variables, and content and process issues of operations strategy, this chapter details the process of operations strategy formulation. More specifically, this chapter briefly describes the historical development of operations strategy and elaborates content and process considerations. The four elements of operations strategy: impact evaluation, time dimensions, integrated operations decision-making, and focused operations, are then described.

TABLE 2-1 Operations Planning and Operations Strategy

Characteristic	Operations Planning	Operations Strategy
Orientation	Means oriented	Ends oriented
Focus	Greater detail	Conceptualizing overview
Objectives	Optimal but narrow decisions	Competitive advantage
Approach	Variable/Dimension identification	Systems integration
Method	Analysis	Action implementation
Components	Written plans	Intuitive sensitivity and risk assessment

The characteristics of operations strategy are clearly distinct from those of operations planning. This difference is important because planning positions are technical jobs, defined in support of senior executives whose more generalist functions entail development and management of operations strategy. Operations planning functions are generally characterized by means-oriented efforts, which are analytical, seek an optimal, but often narrow solution, are meticulous in descriptive detail, and are elaborately documented and presented. Alternately, operations strategy functions are characterized by ends-oriented efforts, directed toward a conceptualizing overview to produce satisfactory results through management of the dynamic operating system. Though there are numerous interactions and overlaps between operations planning activities and the operations strategy process, this distinction is useful in that it expresses organizational reality. There is a clear difference in perspective between an operations planning technician, such as Joan Schouten, and a more strategically focused operations manager, such as Ed Lee. As suggested by the introductory case, some technicians mature into operations strategists; some do not. Table 2-1 differentiates the characteristics of operations planning and operations strategy.

This distinction between the planner and the strategist is defined in various different ways. For example, Venkataraman and Prescott (1990) contrast the "reductionist planning approach" with the "holistic management approach." Similarly, Paine and Anderson (1983) emphasize the perspective and process of the strategic manager by differentiating "incremental planning" from "rational comprehensive evaluation." This fundamental dichotomy between the planner analyst and the conceptualizing operations strategist is highlighted by Ward et al. (1990), who suggest that the lack of conceptual synthesis is one reason why U.S. manufacturing capabilities have declined, relative to those of other nations, in the past several years.

Another way of viewing operations strategy is the "configurational" approach, which facilitates the synthesis of reductionist planning and holistic strategic management. Configurations are "commonly occurring clusters of attributes or relationships that are inherently cohesive" (Miller and Friesen, 1984, p. 12) or "tight constellations of naturally supportive elements" (Miller, 1986, p. 236). They are useful because they offer a systems perspective of the important mutually supportive and integrated elements, yet simultaneously give sufficient detail of key elements to permit some understanding of the subsystems and operation. By eliminating or aggregating the less important clusters and by identifying the dynamic interaction within and among the remaining important clusters, configuration theory is able to focus attention on both the content and the underlying processes of an organization.

The configuration approach identifies the few relevant organizational forms and concentrates on the interaction among them. Thus, while organizations undergo the inevitable long periods of relative stability, the focus of the strategic operations perspective is on adaptation of the operation to build capabilities through synergy and consistency. However, when these periods of maintenance give way to periods of intense and multifaceted turbulence, configuration theory captures both the process dynamics and the shifting substance of the organization.

Historical Growth of Operations Strategy

The importance of operations strategy has grown dramatically over the past several decades. This growth has occurred in four general phases, which roughly equate to the four elements of operations strategy. The phases are called *impact evaluation, time dimensions, integrated operations decision-making,* and *focused operations,* as identified in Figure 2-1.

The significance of Figure 2-1 is that it represents simultaneously the general historical development of operations strategy and a typical growth pattern of operations strategy activities in a firm. Additionally, the four phases of this historical evolution may be generalized to represent the growth of an individual from the technical perspective of operations planning to the overview perspective of the operations strategist.

In Phase I, which started in many firms in the 1940s and 1950s, the quarterly or annual budget drives the process. Functional sections bid for program lines; then performance is controlled to meet those lines. Additionally, some static resource allocation and simple forecasting are used. However, by the late 1960s, many firms defined and used time dimensions, growth planning, and advanced forecasting techniques, activities associated with Phase II, in an attempt to better manage uncertainties and project future requirements. During the early 1970s, high-cost labor markets, developing technologies, and

FIGURE 2-1   The Evolution of Operations Strategy

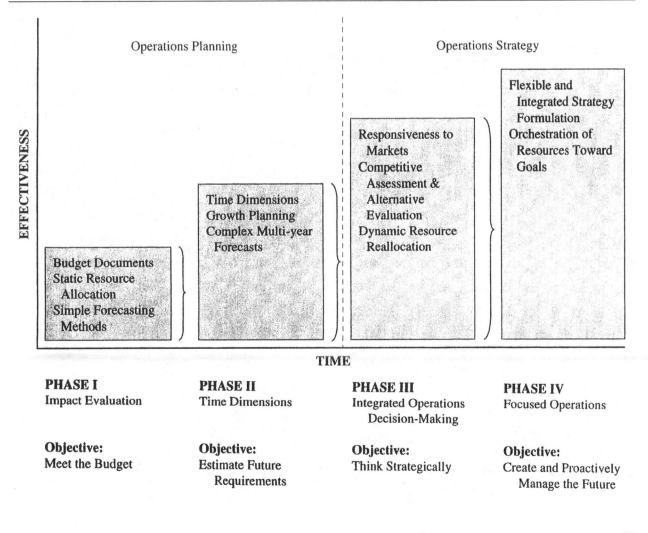

the dramatic growth of international trade encouraged the development of an integrated decision-making process in order to better respond to markets, to evaluate the competitive situation, and to reallocate resources. During Phase III, those companies which were not able to think strategically found themselves overtaken by competitors, often from other countries. Finally, Phase IV facilitates the further step of proactively creating favorable business conditions and managing those conditions as a strategic system. This is achieved by flexible and integrated strategic planning and orchestration of resources toward building capabilities to achieve competitive advantage. Note that these phases are cumulative and that the activities are both content- and process-oriented.

Content of Operations Strategy

The content approach of operations strategy identifies key variables of operations strategy, which may be further categorized as decision areas and competitive priorities (Leong et al., 1990). Those variables, initially set forth by Skinner, with subsequent elaboration by others, were introduced in Chapter 1 and are summarized in Table 2-2.

Table 2-2 elaborates the important dichotomy between the structural and infrastructural aspects of operations strategy. This distinction, originally defined by Hayes and Wheelwright (1984), is analogous to the distinction between computer hardware and computer software. It differentiates the fixed, long-term and often unrecoverable investments of the firm in durables or facilities from those "software" components that are more controllable by management. As previously noted, structure and infrastructure are central topics of this book.

TABLE 2-2 The Content of Operations Strategy

	Skinner (1969)	Hayes and Wheelwright (1984)	Buffa (1984)	Fine and Hax (1985)
Structure	• Plant and equipment	• Capacity • Facilities • Technology • Vertical integration	• Capacity location • Product/process technology • Strategy with suppliers, vertical integration	• Capacity • Facilities • Processes and technologies
Infrastructure	• Production planning and control • Organization and management • Labor and staffing • Product design and engineering	• Production planning and control • Quality • Organization • Work force • New product development[a] • Performance measurement systems[a]	• Implications of operating decisions • Work force and job design • Position of production system	• Product quality • Human resources • Scope of new products

[a]Addition by Hayes et al. (1988).

Source: Leong et al. 1990.

A second consideration of strategy content is the definition of competitive priority, which includes cost, quality, delivery, and flexibility. Those terms, which were introduced as part of Figure 1-6, are defined as follows:

Cost—The production and distribution of a product or delivery of a service with a minimum of expenses or wasted resources such that you have a cost advantage in the market

Quality—The manufacture of products or delivery of a service in conformance with specifications or meeting customer needs

Delivery—The dependability in meeting requested and promised delivery schedules or speed in responding to customer orders

Flexibility—The ability to respond to rapid changes of the product, service, or process, often identified as mix or volume

Thus, content approaches focus on "what is decided" in terms of both decision area and competitive priorities of the firm (Fahey and Christensen, 1986). However, the content approach disregards the processes of integration, interactivity, implementation, and performance measurement. As such, the content approach is a necessary, but not sufficient, contributor to the strategic management process. Companies that use a content approach survive, but they rarely prosper.

Many American companies, among them General Motors, American Telephone and Telegraph, International Business Machines, U.S. Steel (now USX Corporation), and Sears, Roebuck, continued to operate through much of the 1980s by refining the methods developed in the 1950s and 1960s. Those companies all survived, in part because of their tremendous size and market dominance. However, though they may have been aware of the changing competitive environment around them, there was little apparent response to those changes until the mid-1980s. In each of these firms, restructuring has resulted in a leaner organization. By implementing an effective operations strategy, these firms have developed the capability to deliver quality goods and services at competitive prices. These firms have repositioned and refined themselves to be significant factors in the global marketplace of the new millennium, just as many smaller, more vulnerable companies have done previously.

Process of Operations Strategy

Operations strategy activities are also a process, or "how operations decisions are reached" in an organizational setting. As might be expected, these processes do incorporate content considerations, but add the further strategic process dimensions of movement and dynamism. Hayes and Wheelwright (1984) identify four elements of an operations strategy formulation effort. Initially, operations strategy requires methods to *evaluate the impacts* of activities and accommodate higher levels of uncertainty. Second, the clear definition of *time dimensions*, including the time horizon and time fences, permits the specification of periods within which actions must be taken. Third, operations strategy must incorporate a *mechanism for integrating decisions.* There must be a change of perspective from a global, long-range, and broadly defined business plan to a focused, specific, and executable operations plan and shop order. Further, the operations strategy must be linked with higher and other functional area strategies. Finally, operations strategy must involve *focused transformation efforts.*

With this introduction, operations strategy is defined as:

The content and process of activities, directed toward distinctive operations competence, that evaluate potential impacts *of situations and alternatives in* structured time dimensions *and* integrate a pattern of decisions *to balance the resource commitments, output requirements, and risks in various* focused transformation efforts.

This definition incorporates the term "directed toward distinctive operations competence and goals," which is drawn from the definitions of operations management and of strategy. Recall from Chapter 1 that those definitions are

Operations management is the effective management of value-adding transformation processes to efficiently integrate resources and achieve specified performance measures toward product/service, process technology, and market goals.

Strategy is the current domain and pattern of resource commitments to transformation processes, and planned improvements, as a means to achieve the distinctive competence and goals of the firm.

The definition of *operations strategy* identifies content and process issues, highlights the four elements of operations strategy, and states the dependence of operations strategy on operations planning. These four elements, which correspond closely to the historical growth of operations strategy, are the major topics of this chapter.

As noted in Chapter 1, the content or structure of operations strategy involves the defined and established resource commitments in the domain. These would include definition of work activities and functions and the use of management policies in various areas. Operations strategy as a process involves interaction of the operations position or perspective in business strategy formulation and with the other functional areas. Additionally, the content and position of the primary operations activities, such as facilities management scheduling, inventory management, quality, purchasing, and shipping, should be included both in the development of the operations strategy and in the interaction with business strategy and with the strategies of other functional areas.

Typically, process models establish a hierarchy of plans based on specific time lines, integrated through key decision processes, and evaluated by performance measurement. Invariably, there is a feedback loop to permit interactivity of the model. Unfortunately, as Leong et al. (1990) point out, these models suggest a structural neatness that does not necessarily exist in reality. Additionally, implementation capabilities do not always follow from operations strategy formulation or plans. Operations planning efforts must balance implementation with an organized process of capability building. The process of operations planning places these analysis- and time-based activities in a dynamic pattern of integrated decision-making, directed toward a focused, executable operation. For clarity of discussion, the next four sections will artificially separate these elements of operations strategy, though they are, in fact, highly interrelated.

IMPACT EVALUATION

Operations strategy must identify the impact that intervening or expected future events or variables will have on the current situation. This process involves the analysis of current changes in competitive forces and the projection of those competitive forces based on one or several intervening events or variables. Of course, the projection of these competitive forces in an uncertain environment is tricky at best and necessarily involves some amount of error. Thus, formalized forecasting and error identification and reduction efforts are used to increase the predictability of future conditions.

Analysis of Competitive Forces

The operations strategy of the firm may be evaluated in terms of three separate competitive forces in a business environment, originally identified by Porter (1980). These three forces are the existing competitive rivalry, the bargaining power of both suppliers and buyers, and the threat of new entrants or substitutes in the product or service market. The importance of each varies among industries and businesses; yet, in sum, these three factors drive and shape strategic management at all levels. For example, competitive rivalry may be changed significantly by advertising methods or sales expenses, which, if effective, can significantly change profits. The bargaining power of buyers and sellers hinges on such things as the number of competitors and the differentiability of products or services in terms of cost, quality, flexibility, and delivery. For example, the emergence of a new competitor or substitute product would likely reduce prices and thus profits. The business environment, including political and social conditions, must be evaluated regularly for the effect on each of these factors. These competitive forces are shown in Figure 2-2.

An intervening event or variable, identified as the organization projects its situation into the future, can take several general forms. These are categorized as:

Random events

Planned for, yet difficult to predict, events

Planned, patterned events

Some business environments may be very stable but are seriously disrupted by a random intervening event. Examples include the effects of weather (tornadoes, hurricanes, and floods) and geologic conditions (earthquakes and volcanic activity), which, although they can be generally predicted, appear to strike at random times and locations and often with random effects. These intervening events cause effects that are unanticipated and appear to be random, although some might argue that such events may be better anticipated or that protective measures should be planned. These events clearly change the nature of the competitive rivalry, the relative power of suppliers and purchasers in the marketplace, and the potential for new market entrants or product substitutes. For example, the airline industry suffered from the turbulence of fuel prices and the loss of business from terrorist threats during the Persian Gulf War in the early 1990s.

Planned-for, yet difficult-to-predict, events are involved with many product/service, process technology, or market situations. The introduction of any change in product/service, process technology, or market situation is usually extensively planned; yet such situations, because there is a limited pattern to serve as a baseline for projection, are difficult to predict. Most forecasters would have projected rather good prospects for the personal computer, but few would have anticipated the tremendous growth and impact that it has had. The initial decision by IBM to enter the PC market was a carefully planned and organized decision, but the outcomes of that decision, including changes in the mainframe market, were, at best, hard to predict. The introduction of most new products/services,

FIGURE 2-2 The Analysis of Competitive Forces

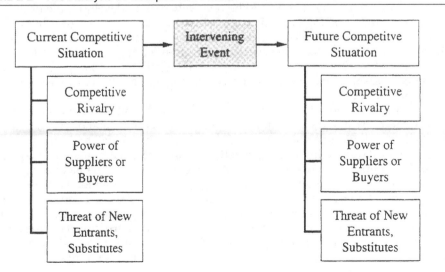

process technologies to build those products, or the entry into new markets are planned-for, yet difficult-to-predict, events.

The third type of intervening event is based on a pattern which, to a greater or lesser degree, integrates stable and definable plans or events. In many cases, the existing historical pattern will reflect the confluence of several different separately measurable and controllable patterns. For example, most retail goods experience higher sales in the prewinter-holiday period; however, such factors as market growth trends, economic conditions, weather, the number of days between Thanksgiving and Christmas, and the exact day of Christmas also have an effect on holiday retail sales. Similarly, greater volumes of retail sales occur during weekend and three-day holiday periods, and in response to national and international events.

Forecast Alternatives and Error Identification

Forecasting involves capturing, through a model, the inherent pattern or relationships of past observations, and simultaneously recognizing the limits of predictability. Though most managers realize that the "forecast is always in error," most managers also place limits on the amount of error or risk that they are willing to accept in a particular situation. Ultimately, a forecasting system is measured by the accuracy with which it identifies patterns and discovers relationships. However, as a manager repetitively examines a situation, he or she develops a greater understanding of the patterns and an intuition about the relationships. This appreciation goes beyond the forecasting method or tools used in the evaluation. Thus, a forecasting process uses both mechanical techniques to isolate a pattern or relationship and individual sensitivity and intuition to appreciate the effects of related factors. Forecasting is thus both a science and an art.

Quality information and structured process management are prerequisites of an effective forecasting system. Forecast errors directly cause higher inventory costs, schedule adjustments, and lost revenue. Selection of a forecasting method, including incorporation of judgmental processes, error identification, and carefully applied adjustments, are all required for a good forecasting system. General Electric found, for example, that a monthly two-day forecast review process reduced the cost of forecast error by between $80,000 and $150,000 each month. The identifiable quality of a forecast program increases confidence in the system and reduces the temptation among inventory planners to carry excess safety stock (Duncan, 1992).

Most forecasting texts note some twelve to fifteen qualitative and quantitative forecasting methods (ranging in complexity from simple moving averages to exponential, autoregressive and other methods), each with numerous methodological variants and computational factors. Thus, it would be relatively easy to develop three or four hundred different forecasts for a specified situation (for example, sales of product for the next 12 months). The definition and computation of these different forecasting models is the realm of the technician; however, the operations strategist must identify the need for the forecast, evaluate the contributory factors of the future competitive situation, and relate the associated error to the risks involved. Figure 2-3 gives an overview of the forecasting system.

Quantitative methods include time series, regression, and economic methods. Time series methods are designed to address level, trend, and seasonal or cyclic patterns of the data. For example, snowblowers are demanded in the late fall and early winter, and lawnmowers sell well in the spring and early summer. Regressive methods may be used to identify a simple trend relating external data patterns to a variable of concern, or to identify the pattern in a trend or cycle (autoregression). A weather forecast, for example, might be used as an external variable in a regression formulation to project the amount of heating gas (winter) or electricity (summer) demanded by utility customers. Economic multifactor methods, such as national income analyses or international composite models, use regression formats to integrate many factors (upwards of 300). Interested readers can pursue these topics in Valentine and Ellis (1991) or other forecasting or

FIGURE 2-3 An Overview of the Forecasting Process

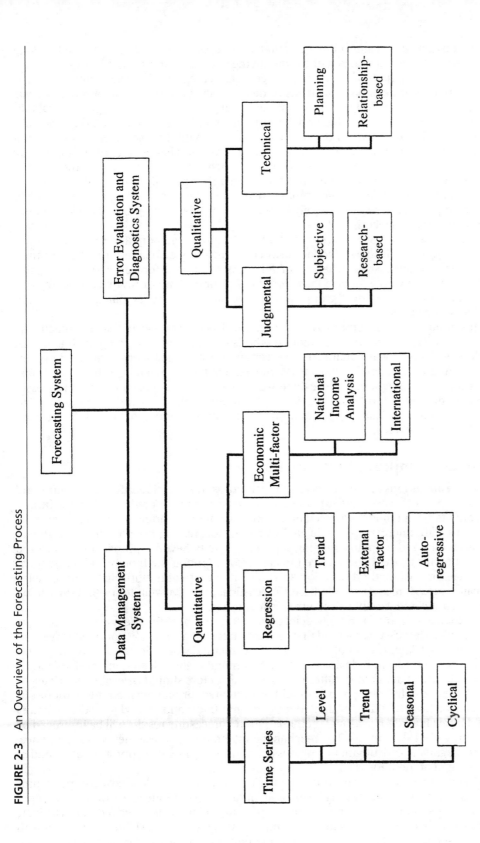

econometrics texts. In summary, quantitative models project a series of data by using the inherent pattern of the data or by identifying and using an external relationship.

Qualitative methods of forecasting are generally categorized as judgmental and technical, although there is no clear basis to distinguish these two. Judgmental forecasts include, according to Makridakis and Wheelwright (1989), executive opinions, Delphi methods, sales force composites, anticipatory customer buying surveys, market research-based methods, and a variety of other subjective probability assessments. Judgmental methods may be purely subjective or may incorporate varying degrees of substantiating research. Alternatively, many technical methods, including relevance tree methods, cross impact matrices, and prospective methods, are either planning-oriented methods or relationship-based. Qualitative methods range from purely intuitive judgments to highly structured plans and vary extensively in research- or relationship-based substantiation (Makridakis and Wheelwright, 1989).

The forecast process involves a system for data management and for error evaluation and diagnosis. The data used for the forecast must be stated in terms of the time unit, the entity that is forecast, and the level of detail. For example, a forecast may involve daily, weekly, or monthly time units of sales, profitability, or cost measures that are aggregated by component, item, product group, and product family. The data management system considers these issues.

Additionally, a forecasting system should involve an error evaluation and diagnostic system. A variety of error measurement methods may be used, including the bias, mean absolute deviation, mean square error, percentage error, standard error, correlation coefficient, and tracking signal. Choosing the measure of the error can be as tricky as choosing the forecasting method, because there are numerous different computational processes and each method of error computation has different limitations and advantages. Various of the references describe the computation and interpretation of these different evaluations of forecast error.

Methods to Improve Predictability

One of the limitations of most forecasting methods is that they identify past patterns and relationships, but an accurate explanation of the past may not predict well in the future. Even qualitative methods are based on an intuitive understanding of the past to predict the future. Particularly in dynamic environments, forecasting methods must be able to rapidly identify and adapt to emerging patterns or events. Several approaches can be used to facilitate this process and reduce forecast errors. Among the more widely used techniques are forecast method selection and adjustment, use of multiple forecasting methods (called focus forecasting), rule-based forecasting, proactive monitoring, internalization of the situation and variables, and error cost analysis.

Of course, it is appropriate to select a method that best fits the nature of the data. For example, a forecasting method that captures a level pattern might not be effective with highly seasonal data. The simple moving average method would likely not perform as well with cyclical data as an indexing method. Additionally, the selected method should be adjusted for the data. That is, different smoothing factors should be evaluated for exponential methods; different periods should be evaluated for moving methods; various differencing factors should be evaluated for trend methods; and several periodicity factors should be evaluated for seasonal methods. Often, forecasting results will be improved by combining several methods. The mechanical integration of these methods is a science, but the diagnostic and judgmental process of identifying the most appropriate method or combination of methods is an art.

One approach that has become popular with the advent of low-cost computer programs is called "focus forecasting." This simulation-like technique may involve 15 or more forecasting methods and several different exponents or factors for each method. The logic of focus forecasting is that it identifies the method that gives the least forecasting error with recent observations of a data series. That method is then used to forecast future events, using the rationale that because it was best able to capture some recent (though not necessarily understood) phenomena in the data, it should continue to do so in the near future. Focus forecasting methods are often evaluated and updated quarterly or annually.

A similar approach is used in rule-based forecasting, in which the forecasting process is monitored by a series of rules that are developed for each series. Rules can be defined to evaluate the domain and various features of the series and to adjust for short- and long-range levels, trends, and other patterns. Additionally, rules identify and manage extreme values, specify and vary the number of relevant periods, and manage discontinuities of data and unstable trends. In one study (Collopy and Armstrong, 1992), the use of 99 carefully constructed and validated rules resulted in a reduction of the forecast error of 42% over a comparable baseline method.

Monitoring the forecast for accuracy may involve one or more methods. Some measure of error must be selected; then the process is periodically reviewed. Following the Pareto Principle (which states that there are the critical few and the trivial many), the forecaster may desire to identify the series for which forecast errors are most costly. Those critical few items would be reviewed more regularly than others for which the cost of forecast errors is less critical. Additionally, defined limits of forecast error, however measured, might be used to assess the process periodically and to flag those items for which the forecasting process was getting out of tolerance. Numerous specific control-limit-definition, tracking-signal, and error management systems are described in the references.

Probably the single most critical impact evaluation issue for management is measuring the cost of forecasting error. Of course, if the costs of errors are low, then the selection of the forecasting method may be less important and the periodic review less regular. Ultimately, management will have to assess the risks of forecast error (stated in terms of product stockouts, slow response to product/service, process, or market changes, or inaccuracies in projecting quality or maintenance costs) against the costs of the improved forecasting methods. In today's automated environment, the additional computational costs of very complex forecasting methods are relatively small, compared with the costs of data entry and supervisor training. Though the human variable of forecasting likely is the most costly component, continued work with a data series encourages an internalization and sensitivity toward the factors that drive the series, thus facilitating an intuitive, judgmental, and strategic perception of the environment. Of course, as forecast error is reduced, the improvement is amplified throughout the scheduling, inventory management, quality control, and customer service systems, resulting in lower production costs (Jenkins, 1992).

TIME DIMENSIONS

The definition of time dimensions permits the differentiation of planning functions into long-range, mid-range, and short-range planning activities. Time, as well as product/service group categories and geographic areas, can be aggregated and disaggregated through a technique called pyramids of aggregation. Additionally, the long-range, mid-range, and short-range time periods permit the definition of specific time fences which are used to manage the finalization of certain decisions and activities.

Defining Time Dimensions

Initially, the time limit of interest, or time horizon, must be defined as the point of time beyond which it is not necessary for the planning or forecasting system to project. As the forecast projects a greater number of periods into the future, it will generally become less accurate; thus, at some point in the future, further projection becomes pointless. For example, the horizon must be defined at least as far into the future as the maximum order lead time, and it is usually a good idea to have some additional demand visibility beyond that maximum lead time. The time horizon thus is used as a bound for the long-range forecast. Once that time horizon has been specified, the periods of the long-, mid-, and short-range plans can be defined.

The three ranges of planning are described here sequentially from long-range to mid-range to short-range on the rationale, adapted from Plossl (1985), that if long-range planning is good, the mid- and short-range plans will be workable. That is, resources must be well-managed in the long-range aggregate before they can be controlled in detail in the mid and short range.

Long-range plans will rarely cover a period of less than six months and may extend ten or more years; short-range plans will rarely be less than two weeks or more than six months in length. Mid-range plans are in between. By convention, the long-range time frame is often defined as the time necessary to develop a new product and the production process to support it. In automobile building, for example, the long range may be the six or more years necessary for a manufacturer to design an automobile and then build a production process. General Motors took roughly six years to design the Saturn automobile and build the Spring Hill, Tennessee plant. Alternatively, the short-range planning period is often stated as the time within which changes in the production schedule cannot be made without substantial costs. It may correspond to the longest lead time of a procured component or the longest production time for an item that is built in house. Other situations might involve much shorter planning horizons and planning time periods. These relationships are shown in Figure 2-4.

The planning horizon in Figure 2-4 is set at a relatively short two years, with the long range of one to two years, the mid-range of three to 12 months, and the short range of 13 weeks. The reason for differentiating the long-, mid-, and short-range planning time frames and the planning horizon is that the planning activities in these periods have different characteristics, are used for different types of decisions, and involve different forecasting methods. These differences are shown in Table 2-3.

Generally, the long-range planning process is a one-time, high-level, and highly judgmental process. It usually involves more external data inputs and a more dynamic and

FIGURE 2-4 The Planning Horizon and Planning Time Frames

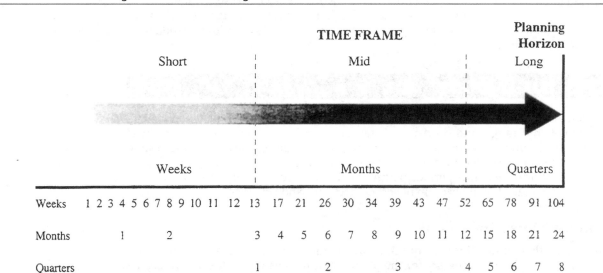

Note: The 4—4—5 method of adjusting weekly data to monthly data uses 4 weeks in the first month, 4 weeks in the second month, and 5 weeks in the third month of each quarter. This method permits the accurate identification of 13 weeks in each quarter or 52 weeks per year.

Reprinted by permission, APICS, *Master Planning CPIM Review Course,* 1991, Transparency 1-13.

TABLE 2-3 Long-, Mid-, and Short-Range Planning

LONG-RANGE	MID-RANGE	SHORT-RANGE
CHARACTERISTICS		
One-time analysis	Periodic (monthly/quarterly)	Recurring
Mostly judgmental	Both quantitative and qualitative	Quantitative
External data	Some external data	Internal data
High level	Mid-level	Detail level
Dynamic environment	Varying environment	Stable environment
Few products/families	Product groupings/families	Many items or SKUs
Quarterly	Monthly	Weekly/daily
DECISIONS		
Facilities analysis	Budgets	Inventory deployment
Long-range projects	Operations planning/ master scheduling	Operations scheduling/ final assembly scheduling
Capital investments	Blanket purchase orders	Material planning

Adapted by permission, APICS, *Master Planning CPIM Review Course,* 1991, Transparencies 1–14, 1–15, and 1–16.

unpredictable environment. The plan is stated in general terms, such as total sales or the sales of aggregated groupings of products or services. Such planning efforts are used in long-range decisions, including facilities or capacity analysis, long-range projects, and the development of new products or new markets. Invariably, long-range decisions involve large capital commitments and difficult to recover (or sunk) investments.

The corresponding characteristics of the mid-range planning period are monthly quantitative and qualitative data, usually mixed from both internal and external sources and conducted for product groupings and families at the middle level of the product hierarchy. Decisions involve budgets, operations planning, the initial master schedule and operations plan, and mid-range purchasing commitments, such as blanket orders.

By contrast, short-range planning efforts are recurring (daily, weekly), highly detailed, and quantitative in nature. Short-range data usually comes from reliable internal sources and presumes stability of the external environment. Large numbers of individual items are managed in the short range. Decisions often involve the scheduling and execution of the operations plan, and may integrate materials planning and purchasing decisions, scheduling, and inventory deployment through the distribution system.

Pyramids of Aggregation

The importance of defining these three planning periods is overshadowed by the necessity of integrating them. This is often done through a process of aggregation and disaggregation. Three frameworks are customarily used for aggregation pyramids: time, product group, and geographic area. In the time aggregation, data is collected by day; then days are aggregated into weeks and months and quarters by using a variety of calendar-based algorithms, including the 4—4—5 rule (explained in the note to Figure 2-4). Similarly, geographic pyramids involve aggregations of store, district, regional, and global (or like designations), and product group pyramids involve aggregations of stock-keeping units (SKUs) or components, product items, and product families. Aggregation and disaggregation techniques may be used for one, two, or all three of the pyramids of aggregation. Figure 2-5 shows the commonly used increments of aggregation for time periods, geographic areas, and product groups.

A rather widely used application of aggregation–disaggregation is the pyramid forecasting technique. In that application, product forecasts are "rolled up" from the lower level to the higher level. Then, at the higher level, an adjusted or planning value is specified and

FIGURE 2-5 The Pyramids of Aggregation

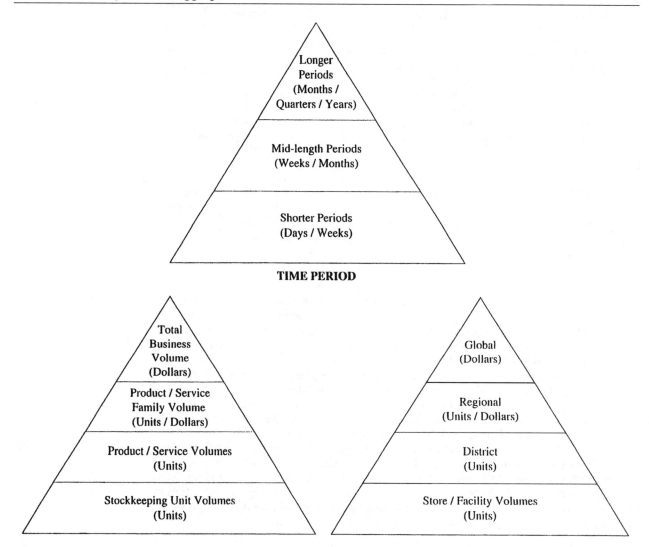

Reprinted by permission, APICS, *Master Planning CPIM Review Course*, 1991, Transparency 1-12.

"forced down" to the lower level. The adjustment may be determined by a variety of considerations, including the convenience of lot-sizing or bulk delivery volumes. A two-level example of the pyramid forecasting technique is shown in Decision Model Box 2-1. Note the products X_1 and X_2 are aggregated to the group level; then an adjustment is made at the group level (based, perhaps, on an intuitive evaluation) and the adjusted total volume is forced down to each of the two products, based on the prorated proportion of the initial forecasts.

Time Fence Management

The concepts of impact evaluation and time dimensions are drawn together by time fence management. Time fences are critical junctures in future planning periods. They specify the times within which certain operations-related changes must be made. Three fences,

DECISION MODEL BOX 2-1 Pyramid Forecasting at the Brand Central Retail Store

Brand Central, a national retail chain store, uses a pyramid forecasting process to integrate product item volumes for each product with the product family and total business volume forecasting process, and simultaneously to integrate geographic regions and time periods. The following data is a very small, but representative subset of Brand Central's forecasting process. Region forecasts of items X_1 and X_2 are given with the prices of those items. The number of units forecast is aggregated to a product family forecast, then adjusted, then forced back down in proportion to the original forecasts. The adjustment (in this case, to 15,000 units) may be purely judgmental, or based on some very mechanical consideration, such as efficient shipping lots, ranges of forecasting error, or seasonal demand. This example shows the integration of two levels of the product group pyramid, but it is common practice to simultaneously integrate several levels of two or three pyramids. Note that the slight difference between the adjusted dollar volume rolled up of $250,050.00 and the forced-down forecast of $250,041.69 results from a rounding variation.

Roll-Up

	Product	Units Forecast		Price
Product level forecast for 1 month	X_1	8,200		$20.61
	X_2	4,845		10.00
Product family forecast for 1 month	$X_1 + X_2$	13,045	Average	$16.67
Adjusted forecast for product family for 1 month		15,000		$250,050.00

Force Down

	Product				
Prorated forecasts from product family	X_1	$\dfrac{15,000}{13,045}$ (8,200) =	9,429 × $20.61 =		$194,331.69
to product level for 1 month	X_2	$\dfrac{15,000}{13,045}$ (4,845) =	5,571 × $10.00 =		55,710.00
					$250,041.69

the demand time fence, the planning time fence, and the capacity fence, are commonly defined (Greene, 1987). The *demand* fence is when physical or financial resources are committed to operations, and the *planning* fence is when planning effort is committed to operations. Inside the demand time fence (often the demand time fence corresponds with the short-range planning time frame), the schedule is "firm." No changes are permitted unless the cost of those changes is paid by the activity requiring the change. Between

FIGURE 2-6   The Use of Time Fences

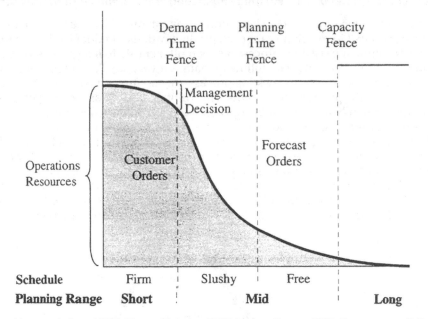

Reprinted by permission, APICS, *Master Planning CPIM Review Course,* 1991, Transparency 7-5.

the demand fence and the planning fence, the schedule is somewhat fluid (or "slushy") and beyond the planning time fence it is "free," or easily changed. Capacity changes can be made beyond the capacity fence, which often corresponds to the long run. Forecasting is used to project future resource needs, but, as customer orders are received, they "consume" the forecast. These relationships are shown in Figure 2-6.

Consider, for example, a make-to-order furniture factory that can final-assemble 1000 chairs per week. Because of variations in chair size, style, type of wood, finish, and covering, many components can be rough-cut and prepared for assembly, but not final-assembled. It takes eight weeks to dry the lumber and prepare the components, and an additional four weeks to assemble, finish, and cover a chair from components. Thus, inside the demand fence of four weeks, the schedule is firm; within the 12- (four plus eight)-week planning time fence, plans and materials are being prepared, but no resources (other than time) are *irrevocably* committed to final production. Beyond the 12-week planning fence, there is a period of visibility for planning purposes. The capacity fence, which might be defined at one year, is often defined between the mid-range and the long-range planning times.

In the mid- and long range, the firm uses forecasts to project the total number of chairs that will be demanded. A capacity increase is projected to 1200 units per week in the long range. In the mid-range, however, the forecast or current capacity of 1000 units per week is gradually absorbed, or "consumed," as customer orders are received. At the demand time fence, management must make the decision to produce at the level of existing customer orders or to produce to the forecast, hoping that subsequent orders will be forthcoming for the models that are produced.

Note that the demand time fence often coincides with a firm schedule and the short-range planning period, and that the long-range planning period defines the capacity fence and is driven almost entirely by the forecast. Capacity can be changed beyond the capacity fence, as shown in the diagram, for example, by adding more equipment or building an additional plant. Though time fences were initially designed as mechanisms to stabilize a production schedule, they are equally useful today as mechanisms to integrate and manage planning efforts.

INTEGRATED OPERATIONS DECISION MAKING

The operations planning cycle uses the concepts of impact evaluation and time dimensions to integrate operations planning activities from the long-range business plan to the execution of the operations plan and evaluation of that process. It is divided into three time frames, corresponding to the long-, mid-, and short-range plans. In the long range, the business plan draws together plans for each of the major staffs and is specifically focused toward the accomplishment of corporate goals. Forecasting is a strategic activity, defining the management objectives of the business plan as a detailed statement of future requirements that are usable by all operating departments (Artes, 1992). Operations planning defines the operations contribution to the business plan and identifies, often by product family, the appropriate requirements by month or quarter. Resource planning assures that all key resources required by the operations plan are available. Thus, at the capacity fence, the general availability of resources is confirmed.

In the mid-range, the master production schedule and rough-cut capacity planning processes create an initial working schedule; then, as the planning fence is passed, the schedule becomes increasingly firm. Subsequently, material requirements planning and capacity requirements planning, respectively, identify all of the specific requirements for the operations schedule and evaluate available resources to assure feasibility. Within the planning time fence, planning assets are increasingly committed; for that reason, it is important to avoid spurious changes and adjustments. Thus, costs are often charged for changes in this range.

At the demand fence, the scheduled plan is affirmed, and planning is accomplished for short-range activities such as purchasing external components, shop floor planning (for example, input/output planning) of internal production, and performance measurement. Within the demand time frame, changes in the schedule can be made, but usually only if committed resources are paid for and if top management approves. The operations planning cycle is shown in Figure 2-7.

The individual plans and activities of the operations planning cycle will be described in detail in subsequent chapters. The introduction of the operations planning cycle here suggests the importance of the cycle as an integrative operations strategy tool. Concisely:

1. The activities of long-range, mid-range, and short-range planning are specifically differentiated but integrated by management-defined evaluative time fences.
2. The planning time fences contain several feedback and feed-forward loops that are based on key decision junctures.
3. The process demonstrates the use of an aggregate long-range planning perspective which leads to disaggregated mid- and short-range planning processes.
4. The planning cycle is focused toward the execution of an operation and the performance measurement of that operation, stated in terms of previously defined competitive priorities.
5. At each step of the cycle, conceptual perspectives and inherent risk management activities can be identified.

Though the representation of this integrative operations strategy framework varies (Leong et al., 1990) and the importance of various components may differ among industries and certainly among specific operations, it is absolutely important that the operations manager master and intuitively use this or some variation of the operations planning cycle. This cycle provides a planning framework based on high-level and long-term plans, iterated sequentially to mid- and short-range activities in a constantly reviewed process. This framework also provides the operations manager with a mechanism through which to evaluate and manage the focus of operations resources.

FIGURE 2-7 The Operations Planning Cycle

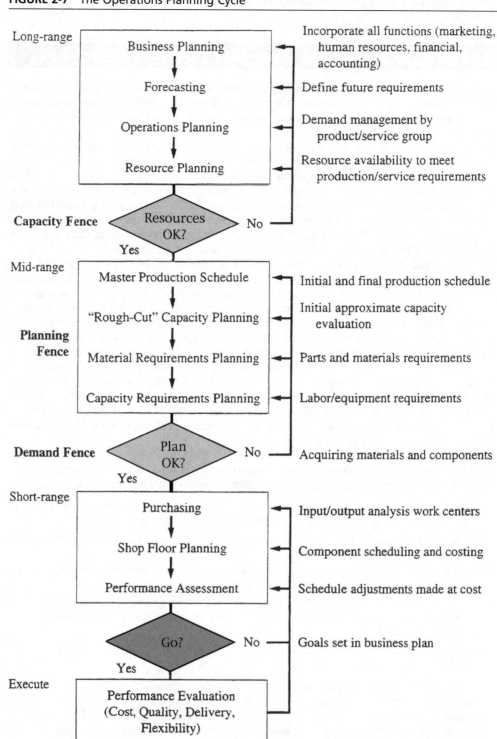

Reprinted by permission, APICS, *Master Planning CPIM Review Course*, 1991, Transparency 1-13.

FOCUS OF OPERATIONS

The final element of operations strategy is a measure of implementation, defined as the focus of operations resources. Skinner may have been the first to coin the term *focus*, meaning a clear and sharply defined set of products, technologies, volumes, and markets (1974). The operations planning cycle, because it integrates impact evaluation and time dimensions, should focus the requirements of the production or service system. What remains is the important task of concentrating resources toward those requirements and establishing a critical mass or focus of resources sufficient to achieve an effective and efficient operation.

Focused Resources

The three generic business strategies defined by Porter (1980) are cost leadership, product differentiation, and focus. Cost leadership is primarily based on process technology, process economies of scale, and linkages along the chain of transformations. Similarly, product differentiation relates to a unique aspect or characteristic of the product or service that is achieved in the value-adding process. Finally, focus is based on the selection of a narrower market segment or group of segments and tailoring the strategy "to serve that segment to the exclusion of others." Thus business cost strategies are primarily process technology-related, product differentiation strategies are primarily product- or service-related, and focus strategies are primarily market-related.

The operations manager must specify categories of those three dimensions. This is often achieved through project management techniques. For example, process technology groups may be classified as job shop through the discontinued line and fully automated line. Differentiated products may be defined as variations from the mechanical typewriter to the computer with word processing software. The customer or market for a product might be defined as "in house," local, regional, or international or by a range of segments or niches. Certainly more exact statements of these groups could be defined in specific businesses. This combination of product/service, process technology, and customer/market permits the company to define and focus one primary objective, with possibly a secondary objective for a particular facility—if not for the company. The selection of a specific product/service, process, and customer/market combination also suggests the competitive priority of cost, quality, delivery, or flexibility. For example, it would be difficult for most firms to have the same delivery capability for in-house and international markets. Cost, quality, and flexibility priorities would also likely differ between the in-house and international markets. The firm must concentrate its limited resources toward achieving competitive advantage in the market.

Within the specified distinctive competence, the operations manager should further classify the markets, processes, and products. For example, the models of an electronic typewriter might include those with a 24-character display, a 50-character display, a 3-line display, and a 10-line display. A regional market might be classified by major distribution zones, including states and cities, and the discontinuous-line process technology might involve several different production options, such as hot pressing, molding, and laser coring for the plastic liquid crystal display unit. These options, once selected, more specifically identify and constrain the cost, quality, flexibility, and delivery positions of the firm. A very fine discussion of this topic is offered by Sprague (1990). Figure 2-8 shows an application of the focus of operations resources.

When an operation is defined in these specific terms, it is much easier to understand the changes that would be associated with a proactive shift in strategy. For example, shifts in strategy such as the movement from the 24-character display model product market to a full 10-line screen display model, the opening of a new market region in Pennsylvania, or the implementation of a new process technology are all visualizable. Galbraith (1986) calls this the "population ecology" approach to strategic adaption and suggests a

FIGURE 2-8 The Focus of Resources

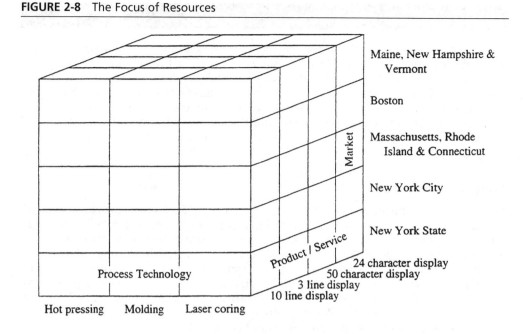

bio-ecological analog to the natural selection process. In operations strategy, such an approach would mean that the more costly, less efficient segments would be gradually replaced by better segments as market, process, and product conditions change.

Commitment Versus Risk

Ultimately, the focus of committed operations resources and the risks associated with various strategic changes must be assessed. This process involves identifying and projecting the direction of the operation under the present conditions and with several given contingencies, based on plans, forecasts, or a combination of both. The current direction of the operation then is compared with several alternative possibilities and under various conditions of intervening events (recall Figure 2-2). This contingency analysis approach permits an examination of specific measures such as product quality or cost, market penetration, delivery rates, process flexibility, or others, and to assess the present direction of the firm against one or several alternative plans. The variation between the current projection and the specific plan (the gap) suggests an increased or decreased focus of resources with the associated risks. This contingency analysis is shown in Figure 2-9.

The current projection suggests a stable resource commitment to focus, say, a quality control program. Of course, this measure can be stated in very explicit terms, such as dollars for a new quality measurement system, or in less-defined terms, such as the use of a training program to develop personal commitment to identify all quality problems. Two alternative plans show different amounts of either per-period or cumulative resource commitment. But these plans are simultaneously associated with different risks. Though it would be easy to conclude that the less the commitment, the less the risk, that may not hold in all circumstances. A lesser commitment may be associated with a greater risk. For example, if a company makes a small commitment to the development of a new technology, a competitor may be encouraged to enter the market with a greater resource commitment and gain a competitive advantage. A more elaborate example of contingency analysis is given in Decision Model Box 2-2.

FIGURE 2-9   Contingency Analysis

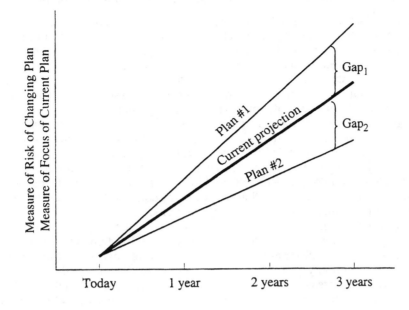

Flexibility as a Resource

The Bredemeier Company application emphasizes the importance of the earlier description of the competitive priorities of cost, quality, delivery, and flexibility, and particularly the importance of flexibility. The ability to respond to changes in customer requirements is more than just technique-based. As Plossl (1992) notes, a sound strategy directed toward flexibility is also needed. Flexibility may be classified as product/service- or process technology-related, and further defined in six different ways, as shown in Table 2-4. This approach incorporates the concept of innovation, which has been separately identified by some researchers (Maidique and Hayes, 1984; Gerwin, 1987) as a fifth competitive priority.

Flexibility is either product/service- or process technology-related. Product/service-related flexibility, such as changes in the volumes, mixes, or product/service design, is very important in terms of responsiveness to customer delivery and quality requirements. However, the related process technology flexibilities of changeover, scheduling, and process innovation are equally important because they ensure the process capability to produce the product or deliver the service flexibly at an acceptable cost, thus meeting delivery and quality requirements. A further description of different types of flexibility and a mathematical programming evaluation of the costs of trade-offs among those types of flexibility are provided by Ramasesh and Jayakumar (1991).

Because of the increasing dynamism of the global market, flexibility may emerge as the most important competitive priority of the 1990s and the first part of the twenty-first century. Over the past several decades, the key competitive priority in operations management has shifted. For example, in the decades of the 1950s and 1960s, many industries emphasized low cost with little flexibility of product or process, sometimes with a resulting subtle decline in quality. By the 1970s and 1980s, many American businesses were undercut by overseas producers who were able to produce higher-quality goods at low costs. Thus, quality became the critical production priority for many industries. However, as suggested by the Bredemeier application, high costs and the inherent risks of producing in increasingly dynamic international environments may increase the importance of flexibility as a competitive priority.

DECISION MODEL BOX 2-2 Contingency Analysis—Bredemeier Samples

Bredemeier Samples is a small (100-employee) family-owned business that makes sample swatch books and cards. Swatch materials are used by many furniture, automobile, appliance, fabric, and rug retailers to show available color, covering, or wood grain alternatives. Manufacturing the sample books requires printing, cutting, pasting, and binding skills, and is generally labor intensive. Small volumes of 2,000 books per job are typical. Bredemeier currently plans to purchase a swatch cutter-paster machine that will automatically cut and mount up to 30 cloth or color paper swatches per page. This technology has been used successfully by an overseas competitor, but Bredemeier managers have identified as potential risks the sensitivity of the equipment to humidity and dust and the high labor training and skills required. Though the company has a policy to protect employees against layoffs, employee frustration with the high technology may be reflected in lower than expected efficiencies. One benefit of the new equipment is that the company could reduce delivery times and thus be more responsive to customer requirements.

The current plan calls for purchasing one new machine per year at a cost of $100,000 per machine, for each of the next five years. Bredemeier managers have estimated that the additional responsiveness provided by the first machine will increase the company profits by $40,000 per year. The second through fifth machines would increase company profits by $30,000, $20,000, $10,000, and $5,000, respectively. Additionally, managers have estimated that because of variations in receptiveness of current employees toward the equipment, the first machine would result in a 150% efficiency improvement over current methods, and that the additional machines would result in efficiency improvements of 120%, 90%, 60%, and 30%, respectively. The following table gives several decision options, stated in current dollars.

Option	Description	Equipment Cost	Cost of Installation and Training	Benefit		Benefit/Cost Ratio
1	1 machine in first year	$100,000	$150,000	$5(40,000 \times 1.5)$	$= \$300,000$	$\frac{300,000}{250,000} = 1.2$
2	1 machine in each of first 2 yr	$100,000 \times 2$ $\overline{\$200,000}$	160,000	$5(40,000 \times 1.5) + 4(30,000 \times 1.2)$	$= \$444,000$	$\frac{444,000}{360,000} = 1.23$
3	1 machine in each of first 3 yr	$100,000 \times 3$ $\overline{\$300,000}$	170,000	$5(40,000 \times 1.5) + 4(30,000 \times 1.2)$ $+ 3(20,000 \times 0.9)$	$= \$498,000$	$\frac{498,000}{470,000} = 1.06$
4	1 machine in each of first 4 yr	$100,000 \times 4$ $\overline{\$400,000}$	180,000	$5(40,000 \times 1.5) + 4(30,000 \times 1.2)$ $+ 3(20,000 \times 0.9) + 2(10,000 \times 0.6)$	$= \$510,000$	$\frac{510,000}{580,000} = 0.88$
5	1 machine in each yr	$100,000 \times 5$ $\overline{\$500,000}$	190,000	$5(40,000 \times 1.5) + 4(30,000 \times 1.2)$ $+ 3(20,000 \times 0.9) + 2(10,000 \times 0.6)$ $+ 1(5,000 \times 0.3)$	$= \$511,500$	$\frac{511,500}{690,000} = 0.74$

This very basic example only minimally introduces the issues of forecasting future sales and projecting future performance. The timing of the investment must be considered in terms of the strength of the economy, the feelings of the employees about the equipment, and the possibility that if they do not offer more responsive delivery, a competitor will. Certainly the variables suggested by this situation can be extensively elaborated, as can the benefit/cost analysis. Of the five options, option 2 has the best benefit/cost ratio, yet many of the decision factors may change. Perhaps the least risky option is to purchase one machine in the first year, followed by a reevaluation of the plan.

TABLE 2-4 Operations Flexibility

Product/Service/Process Technology and Type	Definition and Examples
Product/Service-related	
Volume	The ability to respond quickly to changes in the amount of a particular product or service that is required. For example, a business card printer can easily respond to an order to print either 500 or 50,000 business cards, whereas the volume of an automobile assembly line is difficult to change rapidly.
Mix	The ability to react quickly to changes in mix or proportion of products of a product family that are produced. For example, a nut packaging operation can be changed to pack a different mix or product (100% peanuts to a cashew—peanut mix) more easily than a paint-can filling operation or a beer or soda bottling operation.
Modification	The ability to incorporate changes in product characteristics and to develop and produce newly designed products. For example, delivery of a redesigned automobile model would take a minimum of two years and as many as five years, whereas design and delivery of fashion clothing might take as little as several weeks.
Process Technology-related	
Changeover	The ability to respond rapidly to different production set-ups required for various products. For example, changeovers of heavy presses from one model of automobile fender or bumper to another may take 30 or more minutes, whereas changeover of a small drillpress can be done virtually without delay by computer-assisted-manufacturing systems.
Scheduling	The ability to vary the routing, sequence, or production lot-sizes to accommodate required production volumes. For example, a job shop typically has greater scheduling variability or flexibility than does an assembly line.
Innovation	The ability to define and implement new technologies in production processes with minimal disruption. For example, a firm with high employee skills would likely be able to implement a computer-assisted-manufacturing or material requirements planning system more rapidly than a firm with lower employee skills levels.

Adapted from Gerwin (1987).

SUMMARY

Ultimately, the operations manager, as a management strategist, must be responsible for defining and implementing a strategy based on four elements: impact evaluation, time dimensions, integrating operations decisions, and focused operations. The technical expertise and eye for detail of the operations planner, who defines the measures and time dimensions, are necessary, but not sufficient preconditions for the success of the operations strategy process. The strategic management of an operation requires further integration and focus. At many points, the process involves the evaluation of incomplete and dynamic data and judgmental assessment and risks. The operations manager develops, with extensive experience, an intuitive appreciation for the subtleties of the environment, the product/service, and the process technology. Such an appreciation is clearly an art form.

Though the ability to structure a problem and use a variety of tools to establish a baseline is an important first step, the judgmental process of integrating information from a variety of measurable and unmeasurable sources is even more important. It is for this reason that Skinner and Sasser (1977), Drucker (1989), and Brightman and Noble (1979), among others, have identified the importance of the judgmental and subjective skills, including perspective, versatility, and communications as the key abilities of the strategic manager. As with forecasting, operations strategy involves a not clearly definable combination of science with art, of content with process, and of scientist with humanist.

The configurational approach to operations strategy, applied contingently, offers an important perspective of the operations strategy process. It focuses on key content structures, yet also on the internal dynamics of those activities. The operations management strategist may desire, in relatively stable environments, to emphasize the content aspects more heavily than process aspects. Alternatively, in dynamic situations, the operations management strategist may choose to use more process-oriented approaches. As noted in the quotations at the beginning of the chapter, operations strategy relies on both content and on process; however, it also requires behavioral flexibility and an overview perspective.

DISCUSSION QUESTIONS

1. Identify the characteristic differences between operations planning and operations strategy. Identify (by position) and describe a manager who represents each perspective.
2. From your personal experience or readings, identify several structural and infrastructural aspects of operations strategy.
3. List and define the four competitive priorities of the strategic analysis of the operation of a firm. Give an example of each.
4. What are the three competitive forces involved in the analysis of the strategy operations of a firm? Give an example of each.
5. As an organization projects its situation into the future, the effects of intervening variables or situations can take several general forms, as follows: random events; planned, yet difficult to predict events; and planned, patterned events. From your personal experience or readings, briefly describe an example of each category.
6. Identify several limitations inherent in all forecasting methods.
7. List several general characteristics of long-, mid-, and short-range planning activities; then note several examples of long-, mid-, and short-range planning activities.
8. Identify the three pyramids of aggregation and briefly describe each pyramid.
9. With regard to impact evaluation and time dimensions, define the three time fences and describe the production schedule within each time fence.
10. How is the operations planning cycle important as an integrative strategic management tool?

11. Describe a method that assesses the pervasiveness of commitment and the risks associated with various strategic changes. Briefly assess an organization decision in these terms.

12. List, define, and give an example of each of the six categories of operations flexibility.

13. Which type of flexibility is most important in terms of responsiveness to customer delivery and quality requirements? Give an example to support your position.

14. What do process flexibilities of changeover, scheduling, and process innovation provide and permit?

STRATEGIC DECISION SITUATIONS

1. The Atlas Automobile Products Company distributes replacement automobile headlamps and taillight bulbs in a ten-state area in the mid-western United States. Dealerships and retailers are directly serviced on a weekly basis by several route trucks that carry an inventory of some sixty different regular and halogen headlamps and an assortment of some 100 taillight bulbs. Due to the growth of the business and the increases in the numbers of different headlamps and bulbs, several of the routes are starting to require more product to ensure that the trucks do not run out of stock before the end of their route. The following table gives the demand data for the H0184 headlamp, a representative model.

Average Weekly Demands by Month

	Jan	Feb	Mar	Apr	May	Jun	Jul	Aug	Sep	Oct	Nov	Dec
1989	232	247	219	211	199	183	167	174	170	169	187	213
1990	239	256	237	221	199	182	185	174	172	177	198	228
1991	241	258	248	246	217	203	189	181	184	179	188	219
1992	249	261	257	257	235	222	231	215	202	188	217	227

   a. Assist the operations manager to address this distribution situation. Note several operations concepts or theories that help explain how this situation relates to other operations variables. Consider the perspectives of the planner and the strategist. Which is more appropriate?

   b. Plot the data and intuitively define the appropriate components of a forecasting system.

   c. Using a computer program, establish a baseline forecast with a simple moving average and then define an appropriate measure of forecast error and evaluate several advanced forecasting methods to improve the accuracy of the forecast.

2. The Good Day Tire Company forecasts demand by company-owned and franchised retail outlets for approximately 90 different varieties and sizes of automobile tire. The tires are defined in three product lines which are stocked at seven local distribution centers throughout the state in standard tariffs (size mixes) based on the proportion of demand. Good Day wants to develop an effective, yet practical and easy way to understand and use a forecasting system for the distribution centers and keep inventory as low as possible. Since weekly demand for tires can vary positively or negatively by as much as 20% over the year (but generally is within ± 10%), depending upon weather and other seasonal factors, it is difficult to forecast appropriate stockage for the distribution centers more than roughly two weeks ahead. The average number of units per week and price per tire are shown. Use the concepts of product mix and the pyramid forecasting method to develop an analytic approach with the following data and advise the director of inventory planning on the implementation and use of your recommendation.

Product Line	Average Units/Week	Price/Tire
Ariba	4950	$40.00
GLX	2990	55.00
Quantum	1995	75.00
	9935	

3. The Watertown Toy Company builds plastic and composite rubber models and figurines for a variety of retailers, including Toys-R-You. They currently employ six people in their molding operation, and have six "flat pan" molding machines that they purchased in the 1970s. For efficiency, labor-machine cycles dictate that each machine be tended by an employee. The company wants to transition to an injection molding process because the new technology will eliminate the step of welding the two halves together and the unsightly seam in many, though not all, products. Each new machine costs $50,000 and installation and training is an additional $50,000 for any number of machines purchased. Management has estimated that the apparent higher quality of product produced by each new machine will increase company profits by $25,000, $20,000, $15,000, $10,000, and $5,000 per machine in each year of operation. The company expects to buy no more than one machine per year for five years.

   a. Recommend how many units Watertown Toy should purchase.

   b. Further situation: The vender has agreed to waive $30,000, which is the training portion of the installation and training fee if five units are purchased, one per year. Should the company take the offer? Consider the benefits of early payback and possible business condition changes.

REFERENCES

Adam, Everett E., Jr., and Paul M. Swamidass. "Assessing Operations Management from a Strategic Perspective," *Journal of Management.* Vol. 2, No. 15, 1989, pp. 181–203.

Artes, Richard. "Strategic Forecasting," *APICS: The Performance Advantage.* January 1992, pp. 33–38.

Brightman, Harvey, and C. Noble. "On the Ineffective Education of Decision Scientists," *Decision Sciences.* Vol. 10, No. 1, 1979, pp. 151–156.

Buffa, Elwood S. *Meeting the Competitive Challenge: Manufacturing Strategies for US Companies.* Homewood, Ill.: Dow, Jones and Irwin, 1984.

Collopy, Fred, and J. Scott Armstrong. "Rule-based Forecasting: Development and Validation of an Expert Systems Approach to Combining Time Series Extrapolations," *Management Science.* October 1992, pp. 1394–1414.

Drucker, Peter F. "The Coming of the New Organization," *Harvard Business Review.* January–February 1988, p. 45.

Drucker, Peter F. *The New Realities.* New York: Harper & Row, 1990.

Duncan, Robert M. "Quality Forecasting Drives Quality Inventory at GE Silicones," *Industrial Engineering.* January 1992, pp. 18–21.

Fahey, L., and H. K. Christensen. "Evaluating the Research of Strategy Content," *Journal of Management.* Vol. 12, 1986, pp. 167–183.

Fine, C. H., and A. C. Hax. "Manufacturing Strategy: A Methodology and an Illustration," *Interfaces.* Vol. 15, No. 6, 1985, pp. 28–46.

Fogarty, Donald W., John H. Blackstone, Jr., and Thomas R. Hoffmann. *Production & Inventory Management.* Cincinnati, Ohio: South-Western Publishing Co., 1991.

Fogarty, Donald W., Thomas R. Hoffmann, and Peter W. Stonebraker. *Production and Operations Management.* Cincinnati, Ohio: South-Western Publishing Co., 1989.

Galbraith, J. R., and R. K. Kazanjian. *Strategic Implementation: Structure, Systems, and Processes.* St. Paul, Minn.: West Publishing Co., 1986.

Gerwin, D. "An Agenda for Research on the Flexibility of Manufacturing Processes," *International Journal of Operations and Production Management*. Vol. 7, No. 1, 1987, pp. 38–49.

Greene, James H. *Production and Inventory Control Handbook*. New York: McGraw-Hill, 1987.

Hayes, Robert H., and Steven C. Wheelwright. "The Dynamics of Process-Product Life Cycles," *Harvard Business Review*. March–April 1979.

Hayes, Robert H., and Steven C. Wheelwright. *Restoring Our Competitive Edge*. New York: John Wiley and Sons, 1984.

Hayes, Robert H., Steven C. Wheelwright, and Kim B. Clark. *Dynamic Manufacturing*. New York: The Free Press, 1988.

Jenkins, Carolyn. "Accurate Forecasting Reduces Inventory," *APICS—The Performance Advantage*. September 1992, pp. 37–39.

Leong, G. K., D. L. Snyder, and P. T. Ward. "Research in the Process and Content of Manufacturing Strategy," *Omega: International Journal of Management Science*. Vol. 18, No. 2, 1990, pp. 109–122.

Leong, G. Keong, and Peter T. Ward. "Multifaceted View of Manufacturing Strategy." Columbus, Ohio: The Ohio State University: College of Business, Working Paper Series 90-50, June 1990.

Maidique, Modesto A., and Robert H. Hayes. "The Art of High Technology Management," *Sloan Management Review*. Vol. 25, No. 2, 1984, pp. 17–31.

Makridakis, Spyros, and Steven Wheelwright. *Forecasting Methods for Management*. New York: John Wiley and Sons, 1989.

Miller, D. "Configuration of Strategy and Structure: Toward a Synthesis," *Strategic Management Journal*. Vol. 7, No. 3, 1986, pp. 233–249.

Miller, D., and P. H. Friesen. *Organizations: A Quantum View*. Englewood Cliffs, N.J.: Prentice Hall, 1984.

Miller, J. G., and W. Hayslip. "Implementing Manufacturing Strategic Planning," *Planning Review*. July/August 1989, p. 22.

Paine, Frank T., and Carl R. Anderson. *Strategic Management*. Chicago, Ill.: The Dryden Press, 1983.

Plossl, George W. *Production and Inventory Control: Principles and Techniques*. Englewood Cliffs, N.J.: Prentice Hall, 1985.

Plossl, George W. *Managing in the New World of Manufacturing*. Englewood Cliffs, N.J.: Prentice Hall, 1991.

Plossl, George W. "Flexibility Is Now the Key to Survival for Manufacturing," *APICS—The Performance Advantage*. April 1992, pp. 37–42.

Porter, Michael E. *Competitive Strategy: Techniques for Analyzing Industries and Competitors*. New York: Free Press, 1980.

Ramasesh, R. V., and M. D. Jayakumar. "Measurement of Manufacturing Flexibility: A Value Based Approach," *Journal of Operations Management*. October 1991, pp. 446–468.

Skinner, Wickham. "Manufacturing—Missing Link in Corporate Strategy." *Harvard Business Review*. May–June 1969, pp. 136–145.

Skinner, Wickham. "The Focused Factory," *Harvard Business* Review. May–June 1974, p. 113.

Skinner, Wickham. *Manufacturing: The Formidable Competitive Weapon*. New York: John Wiley and Sons, 1985.

Skinner, Wickham. "The Productivity Paradox," *Management Review*. September 1986.

Skinner, Wickham, and W. Earl Sasser. "Managers with Impact: Versatile and Inconsistent," *Harvard Business Review*. November–December 1977, p. 140.

Sprague, Linda G. "Strategic Analysis for Global Manufacturing," in Patricia E. Moody, *Strategic Manufacturing*. Homewood, Ill.: Dow-Jones Irwin, 1990.

Stonebraker, Peter W. *Master Planning Certification Review Course*. Falls Church, Va.: American Production and Inventory Control Society, 1991.

Valentine, Lloyd M., and Dennis F. Ellis. *Business Cycles and Forecasting*. Cincinnati, Ohio: South-Western Publishing Co., 1991.

Venkataraman, N., and J. E. Prescott. "Environment–Strategy Coalignment: An Empirical Examination of Its Performance Implications," *Strategic Management Journal.* Vol. 11, No. 1, 1990, pp. 1–23.

Ward, Peter T., Deborah J. Bickford, and G. Keong Leong. "Configurations of Manufacturing Strategy, Business Strategy, Environment, and Structure." Columbus, Ohio: The Ohio State University: College of Business, Working Paper Series, 90–77. September 1990.

CHAPTER 3

EVALUATION OF CAPACITY STRATEGIES

*We can break production . . . management down into two
essential problems:* priorities *and* capacity. *Priorities in this
context implies something more fundamental than determining
which jobs are the "hottest." It means knowing* what *material is
needed and* when, *and keeping this information up to date. This
is what many people mean when they use the word
"scheduling." Capacity means knowing how much man and/or
machine time is needed to meet a schedule.*
—Oliver W. Wight (1984, p. 5)

Objectives

After completing this chapter you should be able to:

- State the importance of capacity decisions and identify three levels of capacity evaluation.
- Define capacity and show several applications of ways that capacity can be varied.
- Relate capacity costs to the best operating level curve.
- Differentiate required capacity and available capacity and show how the four-step process of resource evaluation resolves differences of required and available capacity.
- Identify and exemplify timing and size considerations of strategic capacity changes.

Outline

Introductory Case: Lordstown—A Historical Perspective

Capacity—A Costly Necessity

INTRODUCTORY CASE: LORDSTOWN— A HISTORICAL PERSPECTIVE*

There is nothing more awesome than a smoothly tuned automobile assembly line—and nothing more obvious when things have gone awry. The Lordstown Vega assembly operation of the early 1970s is likely one of the best examples of industrial anarchy and the woes of modern technology. Simultaneously, the experience and knowledge gained at Lordstown have been widely applied to revitalize assembly methods. Envisioned at the time as a "factory of the future," the Vega assembly operation was designed by engineers for maximum production and efficiency, with an average production time of 36 seconds per car, or 100 cars per hour and 1600 cars per day from two shifts. There were 43% fewer parts to assemble due to careful product design, which was required by high-speed assembly methods.

Unfortunately, the zeal for efficiency and productivity felt by the engineers was not shared by the workers on the assembly line. The younger, better-educated work force had difficulty with the 36-second repetitive-cycle tasks and the very tightly specified assembly procedures. By late 1971 and early 1972, absenteeism, tardiness, turnover, and defective production of the sort that suggested industrial sabotage were at such levels that plant management was concerned. Labor grievances were at a record 15,000 per month. Something had gone wrong with this state-of-the-art high-capacity process.

By March of 1972, after a three-week strike, General Motors and the United Auto Workers agreed upon a multipart resolution of the problem. Recognizing the widespread distrust and insecurity of labor, coupled with boredom and lack of information about jobs and company objectives, GM instituted an extensive communication program, including daily plant radio announcements, information meetings, and supervisor train-

---

*Materials drawn from "Lordstown Plant of General Motors (A) and (B)" by Lee (1974) and "How GM's Saturn Could Run Rings Around Old Style Carmakers," 1985.

ing programs. These programs gradually reduced the levels of hostility and improved most measures of productivity, including absenteeism, production efficiency, and warranty cost ratings.

The program stopped short, however, of the revolutionary automobile assembly processes pioneered by Volvo at the Kalmar and Uddevalla (Sweden) plants. There, independent assembly teams of 15 to 25 workers set their own work schedules and used an innovative battery-powered dolly to move the automobile to various assembly sites. This reduced the pressures of the automated line and made the process rather like a job shop; however, as planned, the facility was projected to produce at a lower rate than a conventional assembly line but with higher quality. Improvements in job satisfaction were immediately apparent. Though fixed costs of the Kalmar facility were slightly higher than those of a conventional plant, variable costs were lower due to reduced scrap, higher quality, and greater worker productivity. It is notable that the Volvo production design worked well with a relatively low-volume production facility, but may not be competitive with a higher-volume facility. In fact, in the mid-1990s, the Kalmar and Uddevalla plants were closed due to high costs and low volumes.

Saturn, the strategic successor to Lordstown, suggests that GM considers effectively managed, highly automated facilities to be the best method to produce automobiles in a high-capacity environment. Though the ultimate production rates and labor productivity are expected to exceed both Lordstown and Kalmar, Saturn is starting up slowly and is ensuring that the automation is correctly managed. Voluntary recalls are initiated for seemingly trivial reasons and the inconvenience of the recall is minimized by available loan automobiles and hospitality suites. While Lordstown may have been close to industrial anarchy, the experience gave GM valuable insights into how to manage a highly automated, high-capacity facility. Recently announced plans to close 21 aging and less productive assembly plants suggest the continuing need to integrate capacity, facilities, and operations system design decisions in an environment of changing market demand.

CAPACITY—A COSTLY NECESSITY

All manufacturing and service delivery organizations, regardless of the type of process, must consider available capacity and how they will use that capacity to produce the required goods or services. As the introductory quotation from Wight indicates, capacity and scheduling are closely interrelated and these, in turn, are driven by facilities and processes. This interrelationship is exemplified by the dilemma of General Motors noted in the Lordstown case. GM has excess capacity and expects to close 21 less productive automobile assembly plants over a five-year period; however, the high-tech Saturn plant does not presently have sufficient capacity to meet demand. Changes in capacity, either in volume or by product mix, are very costly because fixed assets must be reallocated, and, as shown by the Saturn example, quality, flexibility, and delivery are all affected. For this reason, operations capacity must be recognized as a strategic resource, and the effective management of capacity is a high priority for operations managers.

Capacity is a measure of the transformation process; it may be stated in volume (for example, units), time (hours or days), product range (number of products), process adaptability (rapidity of changeovers), or any combination of those measures. Though capacity is often thought of as a short-term or implementation variable, as in number of units per hour, it is even more important as a long-term planning variable. This is because today's capacity may require two or more years of planning lead time to ensure that all resources are available and efficiently integrated. Errors or failures of this process, if not quickly identified and corrected, can be extremely costly.

One of the most obvious distinctions between manufacturing and service businesses is the amount of flexibility in the use of capacity. As Bill Evans, general manager of the Bahia Resort Hotel in San Diego, states: "We have a commodity—a room—that's only got a one day shelf life, so we have to move it." This usually means that, as bookings drop, price breaks and promotions increase (Grover et al., 1992). Manufactured goods generally have a longer shelf life, which gives manufacturing greater flexibility in the timing of resource utilization.

This chapter introduces capacity as a necessary "cushion" to accommodate varying rates of the transformation process and of customer demands. The concern is not whether to have capacity, but rather how much capacity is necessary and at what cost. The importance of capacity decisions is noted and several levels of capacity decisions are described. Subsequently, cost analysis, economies of scale and scope, and the best operating level are related to strategic capacity analysis. These foundations are the basis for resource planning, which evaluates available capacity against required capacity. The final section applies these issues to the timing and extent of capacity changes. Capacity decisions are directly interrelated with facilities strategies, production system design, operations planning, materials management, just-in-time, and other subsequent topics of this book. Those relationships will be highlighted and pursued more specifically in subsequent chapters.

Capacity decisions may be considered to be more related to marketing or financial strategies; yet, as this chapter shows, the operations function makes a critically important, often overriding, contribution to capacity evaluation. The argument, simply stated, is that capacity decisions define the measure of the transformation process for which the operations manager is responsible and thus constrain the selection and pursuit of competitive priorities. Operations management must be directly involved in capacity decisions.

More specifically, capacity decisions involve fixed costs. The commitment to a particular level of technology requires a large and long-term investment, for example, in plant and equipment, which is not easily recoverable. Further, once such capacity commitments are made, they are difficult and costly to change. Consider, for example, the cost of reconfiguring a building to double loading-dock capacity. Thus, capacity decisions are costly because they cannot be easily recovered or changed. Further, from a practical perspective, once a particular capacity decision is made, managers usually do not want to readdress the issue for at least several years.

Additionally, capacity decisions set a limit on the ability to do a job by defining the primary costs of the operations process. The investment in a specific transformation process, such as capital equipment, commits the organization to a fixed cost and implicitly sets future per-unit costs, such as for labor or other variable-cost resources. For example, it is possible to build a road by using labor-intense methods and little equipment. The Romans built an extensive network of very fine roads, some of which are still used today. However, modern road-building operations use more capital-intense methods, involving expensive earth-moving and paving equipment, with a relatively lower contribution of labor to the production process. Once the specific technology is selected and the costs are committed, then the associated variable cost is also set. Additionally, numerous other capacity-related factors, such as the number of locations, the character of operations at each location, and the integration of facilities and processes, must be considered. Thus, the capacity decision involves a choice of technology, locations, process, and systems integration, all of which directly affect the fixed costs and the per-unit process time of the operation.

THEORY OF CAPACITY STRATEGY

Traditionally, capacity is defined in terms of the rate of output of a facility or process. However, that very general definition must be amplified to consider the levels of capacity planning and capacity analysis in an integrated process, the capacity activities at each level, the measurement of capacity, and the types of operations capacity. These dimensions are generally discussed here and are amplified in the following sections.

Levels of Planning and Capacity Analysis

Chapter 2 introduced the levels of the operations planning cycle from the long-range business plan, through the mid-range operations plan, to the short-range master production schedule and materials requirement planning activities (Figure 2-7). At each level, these planning activities should be evaluated by capacity activities to ensure that the plan is "doable." Additionally, capacity planning is directly related to the establishment and development of the distinctive competence of the firm. Generally, capacity strategy is defined as:

the process of identifying, measuring, and adjusting the limits of the transformation process to support competitive priorities such as cost, quality, delivery, and flexibility.

Planning efforts should proceed from the long range, to the mid-range, and then to the short range. Once long-range plans are in place, mid-range and short-range plans can be prepared toward those defined goals and directions. As Plossl (1985) comments, capacity should first be managed in the largest possible aggregations. At each level of planning, then, an appropriate capacity process is used to evaluate the plan for feasibility, efficiency, and acceptability. The capacity strategy answers the basic questions:

1. Is the plan feasible, or "doable"?
2. Is the plan efficient, measured in terms of resource utilization, costs, or other stated competitive priorities?
3. Is the plan acceptable, in terms of meeting operating schedule, delivery, quality, and other customer-specified requirements?

Of course, if the answer to any of these questions is no, then the capacity process may be used to define the necessary actions to achieve the plan or to suggest alternatives or adjustments to the plan (Greene, 1987).

At each level, a dialogue occurs between the planning proposals and the capacity constraints. When the plan satisfies each of the capacity constraints and, as planning time fences are reached, the higher-level plan is approved and the process proceeds to a lower, more disaggregated capacity planning level, where the evaluation continues. This capacity evaluation process using "finite" resources smooths the production schedule and permits a more accurate link of the demand forecast with materials requirements, often yielding significant efficiencies (Casella and Barnes, 1992). However, as Levenbach and Thompson (1992) note, this process puts greater pressure on the accuracy of the forecast. Finally, after all capacity issues have been resolved, the plan is executed and managed through input/output control and sequencing. These techniques will be considered in more detail in subsequent chapters; this chapter focuses on the capacity strategy process. The levels of planning and capacity management are shown in Figure 3-1.

Note that Figure 3-1 shows the most common usage, though there is an increasing tendency, because of the availability of computers, to use each level of capacity to evaluate a higher level plan. For example, rough-cut capacity planning might be used to evaluate an operations plan, particularly in situations with shorter time frames or more dynamism. Under all circumstances, however, capacity strategy must be driven from the top down; that is, long-range planning must precede mid-range efforts, and mid-range efforts must precede those in the short range (Correll, 1991).

The capacity evaluation process integrates operations and capacity plans from the long range to the short range and to execution. Resource planning has strategic implications because it defines the long-term capabilities of the firm. Rough-cut capacity planning (RCCP) and capacity requirements planning (CRP) delimit operations plans in the mid-run and short run. Finally, shop floor control (SFC) or activity control defines the limits of operations capabilities in the execution stage. This capacity strategy process both influences and is influenced by operations strategy (Melnyk and Narasimhan, 1991).

FIGURE 3-1 Levels of Planning and Capacity Management

Time Frame	Level of Operations Planning	Level of Capacity Management
Long- to Mid-range	Operations Plan	Resource Planning
Mid- to Short-range	Master Production Schedule	Rough-cut Capacity Planning
Short-range	Material Requirements Plan	Capacity Requirements Planning
Execution	Priority (Sequence) Control	Shop Floor (Activity) Control

Reprinted by permission, APICS, *Master Planning Certification Review Course*, 1991, Transparency 4-3.

Capacity Activities

At each level, the capacity activities are similar, but there are some distinctions in terms of time periods, inputs, and outputs, and in the detail of the resource management method. At the highest level, resource planning evaluates an operations plan, usually on a monthly or quarterly basis. Such evaluations deal in product families or groups and in monthly or quarterly time periods. Because of these long time periods, it is not necessary to offset the operations requirements for lead times. At this high level of aggregation, resource planning provides a general check of all resources and identifies those which may, when scheduled in greater disaggregation, cause problems of availability, either of quantity or timing.

In the mid-term, the RCCP is used to assess the viability of the master production schedule (MPS), which is defined in daily or weekly time periods and in product items. Lead-time effects are computed and a process load profile, if not a bill of materials, defines product structure information. The RCCP assesses capacity needs for all key resources, including components and raw materials, finance, labor, machine time, storage, and others. The rough-cut process is the highest level of planning at which management can affirm that the schedule is feasible.

CRP is used to evaluate the materials requirement plan (MRP) in the short term. MRP defines the orders, both internally to the shop and externally to suppliers, that are necessary to meet the MPS. CRP translates these orders into work center commitments (defined either as labor or machine hours) per time period (days or sometimes weeks). Other capacities are also checked, including available warehouse space, adjustments for scrap, and materials or components availability. Similarly, techniques such as priority and capacity control address the same requirements as operations systems are executed. The planning activities are summarized in Table 3-1.

At each level of capacity, management must answer four key questions. Those questions are considered by various types of planning activities and are:

How much volume is needed?

Where will the volume be needed?

When will the volume be needed?

How (or with what technology) will the product or service be produced?

TABLE 3-1 Capacity Activities

	Resource Planning	Rough-cut Capacity Planning	Capacity Requirements Planning
Period	quarterly/ monthly	weekly/ daily	daily/ "bucketless"
Time Offset	no offset	lead-time offset	lead-time scheduled
Inputs	operations plan	master production schedule	materials requirement plan
Detail	family/group to items	items to components	components raw materials
Outputs	resource requirements	rough-cut capacity requirements	dispatch list purchase orders
Method	general resource profile	detailed process load profile	bill of materials

These questions are considered by the appropriate long-range, mid-range, and short-range plans, each of which states the volume of production required per facility or work center per time period, and by process technology. Additionally, the planning process should identify communication channels, process flows, and other relationships to ensure that operations are fully integrated. This process of capacity design, scheduling, schedule adjustment, and continuous capacity improvement is called *total capacity management* (Wortman, 1992).

Measurement of Capacity

Capacity strategy is generally defined as the process of identifying, adjusting, or measuring the limits of the transformation process toward competitive priorities. More specific statements of this definition, however, increase its usefulness to operations managers. Three different ways of defining capacity have emerged in the body of knowledge: design capacity, effective capacity, and actual capacity.

Design capacity is the output per time period under ideal or design conditions.

Effective capacity is the output per time period that can be realistically achieved, given various constraints, such as product/service mix, maintenance, quality, setups, and other known or anticipatable scheduling realities.

Effective capacity is less than design capacity due to known or anticipatable inefficiencies.

Actual capacity is the output of a process; it is usually less than effective capacity due to unanticipated processing inefficiencies.

These capacity distinctions permit the definition of the efficiency and utilization of a facility or a process, the key measures of capacity.

$$\text{Efficiency} = \frac{\text{actual capacity}}{\text{effective capacity}}$$

$$\text{Total utilization} = \frac{\text{actual capacity}}{\text{design capacity}}$$

Thus, efficiency is a measure of "how closely predetermined standards are achieved," while total utilization is a measure of "how intensely fixed resources are being used." These measures are exemplified by Decision Model Box 3-1.

Though the T&G example shows only one work center these measures can also be applied to multiple processes or to facilities. In fact, a process usually involves a flow through several work centers, not just the load behind one machine or work center. Thus, the measurement of capacity and load must be considered in a system of several sequential or concurrent processes.

Capacity, the rate of flow, is also differentiated from load, which is the amount of planed, scheduled, and actual work in the system, measured either in total or at a particular point. The importance of the distinction between load and capacity is most apparent in just-in-time operations. Though other elements (such as human resource management and training) contribute to effective just-in-time operations, capacity considerations, including small loads or work-in-process, rapid setups and changeovers, low breakdown rates, ongoing preventive maintenance schedules, and high quality all are critical to the continuous improvement of just-in-time operations. Specifically, JIT reduces setups and changeovers and improves scrap rates and unexpected mechanical down time. JIT thus increases actual capacity and reduces the load behind each operation, thus decreasing inventory and storage requirements and lessening confusion. JIT operations often permit the processing of a greater variety of products/services through less costly setups.

The flow through the process is only as rapid as the flow through the slowest, or "bottleneck" work center. Process efficiency thus requires a reasonably smooth and continuous flow through required work centers or, in an integrated processing system, facilities or modules. A key consideration of the capacity of sequential activities is the fact that losses of efficiency in earlier processes in the sequence cannot be recovered in later sequences (Goldratt, 1986). Consider the effect of inefficiencies or lost utilization suggested by Decision Model Box 3-2.

Types of Operations Capacity

Capacity can also be defined in more general product/service, market, and distribution system terms. A classic study by Hayes and Schmenner (1978) on the growth of capacity identifies four ways that management can strategically define and modify capacity to fit the goals of the organization.

Adapted from Orlicky, 1975, p. 265, and Williams, 1991.

1. Increase or decrease volume within a given market area.
2. Broaden or contract product/service lines.
3. Increase or decrease span of process (vertical integration).
4. Expand or contract geographic market areas.

The traditional approach to capacity strategy suggests an hydraulic analogy, with product sequentially flowing from work center to work center as inputs, loads, and outputs, and with process capacity adjusted to provide for smoothing of the flow. These four components are shown in Figure 3-2. Note that the classic hydraulic analogy has been supplemented with a process variability "valve." Process variability exists, to some degree, in all processes. However, it only becomes visible when, as in the case of Work Center 3 and part YB 142 (Decision Model Box 3-2), it reduces system throughput. As variability of the process increases, either capacity or throughput, or both, are reduced. Similarly, as transfer batch or lot size increases, either capacity or throughput, or both, are lost. If, in the T&G example, part YB 142 was transferred from WC3 to WC4 in containers that required exactly 30 units, transfers would occur during periods 2–3, 4–5, and 6–7, resulting in an additional loss of 15 units (from 95 to 80 because the first transfer would occur at 2 hours and 40 minutes, leaving only 5 hours and 20 minutes for production in WC4. At 15 units per hour, 80 units would be produced). High process variability and large lot sizes both impede smooth production flows and reduce capacity (Williams, 1991).

A closely related concept is process flexibility, which permits the process to be rapidly changed so that different parts may be produced by the same work center. With process flexibility, both throughput and capacity are likely to be increased, because the flow of the processing system is smoothed. Flexible capacity permits the same facility to process a wide variety of products/services. Examples include automobile assembly lines that can produce a mix of products/services, including sedans, hatchbacks, convertibles, and station wagons, or a photo processing center that uses a specific mix to process one type of film, and sequentially adds several chemicals changing the concentration or mix for other types and speeds of film.

Vertical integration would be represented by increasing the number of sequential troughs (see Figure 3-2). An oil producer might have many sequential troughs, from exploration to retail, while a soap producer might only have one trough producing bulk soap powder from purchased ingredients that are packaged in bulk and sold to distributors. The fourth dimension of capacity, the development of several geographic markets, could be represented by the modification of the "buckets" to include additional output valves.

To summarize, capacity is measured as design, effective, and actual capacity. These measures are used for planning, whereas load is both planned and released work in the system. Capacity measures are used to calculate efficiency and utilization. In addition to

DECISION MODEL BOX 3-2 The Capacity of Sequential Operations at T&G Manufacturing Company

The T&G Manufacturing Company processes parts YB 141 and YB 142 through two sequential work stations. The first work station of each process is human paced and the second is machine paced. The work stations have been extensively studied to determine the amount of time that each process takes. The following table shows the production of the two parts with a schedule based on those studies. Note that for simplicity, this example considers only daily production, with hourly transfers and no carry-overs. Production in work centers 1 and 3 is not considered for hour 7–8 because that production would not be finished during the particular day and production in work centers 2 and 4 is not considered in hour 0–1 because no work is available.

Parts YB 141 and 142—Capacity Planning						Hour of the day					
Work Center	Human/ Machine Paced	Units/ Hour	0–1	1–2	2–3	3–4	4–5	5–6	6–7	7–8	Total Units
Part YB 141—Planned Run											
1	Human	15	15	15	15	15	15	15	15		105
2	Machine	15		15	15	15	15	15	15	15	105
Part YB 142—Planned Run											
3	Human	15	15	15	15	15	15	15	15		105
4	Machine	15		15	15	15	15	15	15	15	105

According to the plan, T&G expects to be able to produce 105 units by the end of the day. However, T&G supervisors report that variances occur in both of the human-paced operations. They are concerned that, if the output of the human-paced operations varies, the lower volumes in one time period will not be absorbed by higher volumes in later time periods. They argue that, when lower capacities occur in a sequential operation, lower capacity continues throughout the process. These effects usually result from either worker slowness or poor-quality production. One supervisor provides the actual schedule from a similar job completed several weeks ago.

Parts YB 141 and 142—Actual Run—February 14						Hour of the day					
Work Center	Human/ Machine Paced	Units/ Hour	0–1	1–2	2–3	3–4	4–5	5–6	6–7	7–8	Total Units
Part YB 141—Actual Run											
1	Human	15	20	15	10	15	20	15	10		105
2	Machine	15		15	15	15	15	15	15	15	105
Part YB 142—Planned Run											
3	Human	15	10	10	15	20	15	15	20		105
4	Machine	15		10	10	15	15	15	15	15	95

The initial run in work center 1 is over capacity; thus there is an excess during the entire day at work center 2. However, the initial runs by work center 3 are under capacity; thus work center 4 cannot make up the lost capacity during the day. This example shows the logic of the theory of constraints. The operations manager should define capacity in terms of the bottleneck work center and should fix the bottleneck to attempt to smooth production. In this case, the bottleneck at work center 3 should be addressed to ensure that its output is never so low that it affects work center 4.

FIGURE 3-2 The Hydraulic Analogy

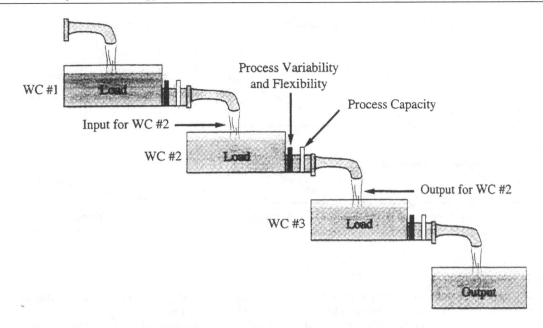

those computational assessments of capacity, the dimensions of capacity change include volume, range of products/services, extent of vertical integration, and number of markets. The hydraulic analogy is useful to depict the capacity strategies of the organization.

MANAGEMENT OF CAPACITY

The preceding definitional and conceptual constructs are used by the operations manager to evaluate capacity. Operations management should regularly review key capacity concerns such as the cost of production, the related best operating level, economies of scale and scope, and the required versus the available capacity. These variables, taken together, form the foundation for periodic capacity decisions.

Cost Analysis

The selection of process technology directly affects capacity. Because each process alternative requires a sunk or fixed cost investment in technology and constrains the further per-unit variable cost, the selection of the process technology significantly delimits the unit cost of the item. Consider, for example, the description in the introductory case of the Volvo Kalmar or Uddevalla facilities, compared with the General Motors Lordstown facility and its logical successor, the Saturn plant. Each facility uses a different proportion of fixed and variable cost contributions to production. The Kalmar facility, though viewed by some as a "step forward" at the time, was never able to demonstrate the competitiveness of a relatively labor-intense, job-shop-like process to build standardized automobiles. Alternatively, General Motors' experience in building for a different segment of the market emphasizes the use of minimal labor (or variable cost) contributions and high fixed-cost contributions. Thus, both Lordstown and Saturn have relatively high fixed costs, and lower per-unit variable costs, compared to Kalmar or Uddevalla. Of course,

FIGURE 3-3 Relative Fixed and Variable Costs of Automobile Facilities

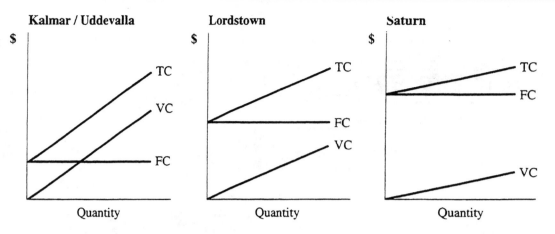

the number of units of production is a key planning variable in determining the total cost. These different cost proportions are shown in Figure 3-3.

The break-even point (BEP) for any production process is defined by the volume, where total cost equals total revenue, or where fixed costs plus variable costs equal the price per unit times the number of units produced. These formulas are:

$$TC = TR$$

or

$$FC + VC \times U = P \times U$$

where

TC = total costs of production of U units
TR = total revenues from the sale of U units
FC = fixed costs
VC = variable costs per unit
P = price per unit

A mathematical adjustment of the above formula gives the volume at the break-even point (V_{BEP}), which is more useful.

$$V_{BEP} = \frac{FC}{P - VC}$$

These relationships are shown graphically in Figure 3-4. Note that the variable cost has the same slope as the total cost.

Several different technology alternatives can be viewed together, as shown in Figure 3-5, suggesting a volume range over which a particular process technology should be selected. For example, for volumes in the range from the origin to Q_1, the lowest total cost alternative is technology 1. Technologies 2 and 3 are respectively best for the volume ranges Q_1 to Q_2 and above Q_2. These technology alternatives might roughly correspond to the Kalmar, Lordstown, and Saturn facilities. This lowest total cost at a particular volume is shown by the heavy solid line.

FIGURE 3-4 Break-even Point

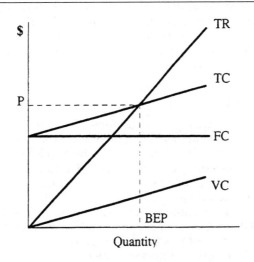

The point at which a decision maker is indifferent between process alternatives is identified by equating the total cost of one method to that of the second method, or

$$TC_1 = TC_2$$

or

$$FC_1 + VC_1 = FC_2 + VC_2$$

Though it is often assumed that questions of fixed facility costs and the corresponding variable labor costs are the realm of corporate financial analyses, the preceding discussion shows that these costs are directly related to capacity and to the performance of the operations function. Note that Figure 3-5 shows several total cost alternatives, which form a broken total cost line, not a continuous curve, which would be suggested if there were many technology alternatives. Schmenner (1976) uses the term "indivisibilities" to

FIGURE 3-5 Multiple Total Cost

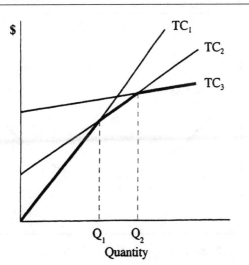

suggest that only a small number of technology and process alternatives are available. In most environments, it is not possible to add small increments of capacity. Of course, the break-even point can also be identified on the multiple technology line at the point where total revenue intersects the composite total cost line. Clearly, capacity decisions are a major contributor to the efficiency and effectiveness of the operation—the operations manager must be directly involved.

Best Operating Level

After a volume decision has been made and the appropriate production method or process technology has been selected and installed, the operations manager must manage the facility at the volume of greatest efficiency for the given technology. This most efficient volume is called the best operating level (BOL). The BOL addresses the economies of the process and considers the cost per unit over a range of units produced. For example, if a particular process were selected with a $1000 fixed cost, a $10 per-unit variable cost, and a price of $12, the break-even volume and total cost, calculated by the previously defined formulas, would be $1000/($12–$10) or 500 units and $1000 + 500($10), or $6000 in total costs. This gives a cost per unit of $6000/500 or $12, which, as would be expected at the break-even point, equals the price. However, if the demand had not been forecast accurately, and only 250 units were required, the total cost would be $1000 + 250($10) or $3500 and the cost per unit would be $3500/250 or $14 per unit, a diseconomy of $2 per unit. The diseconomy results because there was insufficient volume over which to efficiently prorate the fixed cost investment.

Similarly, if the number of units required increases notably above the projected 500 volume, for which the technology was chosen, diseconomies would also occur. Faster machine speeds may require greater maintenance and result in more breakdowns, and a second shift would likely cost more than the regular shift, both in pay and in greater confusion and training requirements. Due to these diseconomies associated with significant variance from the selected process, volume, the cost per unit will rise, creating a U-shaped BOL curve, as shown in Figure 3-6.

Though the BOL curve is inelastic in the vicinity of the minimum point, the BOL point, there are clear cost penalties if a particular process deviates significantly from the BOL. If the volume is notably less than the BOL (insufficient units over which to prorate the fixed costs), or if the volume is notably above the BOL (the inability of the process to effi-

FIGURE 3-6 The Best Operating Level Curve

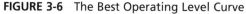
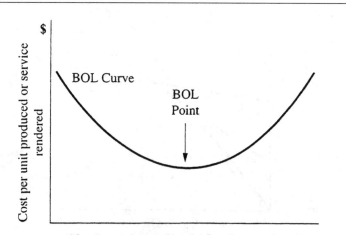

ciently handle volumes for which it was not designed), diseconomies of scale occur. The diseconomies of scale were initially identified by C. Northcote Parkinson in what is called Parkinson's law (Parkinson, 1957).

More recently, these diseconomies of scale have been defined by Hayes and Wheelwright (1984) in four categories: distribution, bureaucracy, confusion, and vulnerability to risk. In each situation, an "overhead" increases disproportionately with greater unit volumes, resulting in a less cost-effective process. For example, in a distribution diseconomy of scale, a large factory must distribute higher volumes over a greater distance to a less densely populated area. Similarly, larger organizations often have greater bureaucracies and thus more confusing management processes. Additionally, a single facility is potentially more vulnerable to natural, as well as human, disasters such as earthquakes or strikes.

One BOL curve defines the cost of a specified technology. Movement along the BOL curve away from the BOL point, and the associated cost-per-unit and volume changes, results from inefficiencies or misutilization of the process. For example, all else being equal, if the number of employees in a one-shift, five-machine/five-employee work center were decreased, the number of units produced per period would decrease and the cost per unit would increase as the number of units produced moved left along the BOL curve. Similarly, if the number of employees increased above the required five persons, diseconomies of scale would gradually result as the greater number of employees got in each other's way. Thus, if the technology of the process is constant, a single BOL curve is defined and notable variation from the BOL volume will result in diseconomies of scale.

FIGURE 3-7 The BOL and Multiple Process Technologies

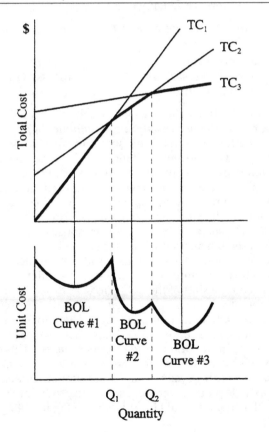

The BOL curve is derived from the total cost structure of a product or service. The BOL represents per-unit cost at various production volumes, whereas the total cost structure identifies the total fixed and variable costs for a specified volume of production. Thus, if there are multiple process technology alternatives, several total cost structures and the corresponding BOL curves would result, as shown in Figure 3-7. Note that each BOL curve is applicable to the range of production quantities from the associated total cost line. For each technology, as the production quantity increases, the cost per unit decreases to the BOL point. Then, as volume increases, diseconomies set in and the BOL curve increases.

Based on the description of multiple process technologies in Figure 3-5, the change of technology from a low-volume process (low fixed costs, high variable costs) to a high-volume process (higher fixed costs, lower variable costs) will usually result in a downward and outward shift of the BOL curve. However, the exact shift of the curve depends upon the change in the fixed cost, the variable cost, and the diseconomies per unit associated with the specified technology. Figure 3-7 depicts the usual situation. When the process changes to a higher technology, greater unit volumes are produced, and thus the outward movement of the BOL curve. Additionally, because the incremental TC curve is increasing, but at a decreasing rate, the per-unit cost is decreasing at a decreasing rate and the BOL curve shifts in a downward as well as an outward direction. Note that the BOL, which is defined by the costs of the technology choice, does not necessarily correspond to the break-even point, which is defined by both costs and revenue.

Economies of Scale and Economies of Scope

The economies and diseconomies of the BOL curve can result in either changes of scale or changes of scope. The traditional BOL rationale related to economies of scale, but recently developed operations practices have broadened the application to include economies of scope. These terms are defined as:

Economies of scale: the efficiencies of prorating processing costs over greater volumes of a single product/service.

Economies of scope: the efficiencies of prorating processing costs over a greater number of different products/services, which are processed in smaller item volumes but at greater total volumes.

Schmenner (1976) identifies three ways to achieve economies of scale, called *economies of volume, economies of capacity,* and *economies of process technology.* Economy of volume is the traditional approach of "spreading fixed costs" over a greater number of units. This corresponds to movement along the BOL curve from the upper left toward the BOL and the resulting lower per-unit costs. Economy of capacity, the second type of economy of scale, results because larger operations can function using proportionately fewer resources. Schmenner uses the example of inventory. Because the economic order quantities increase only as the square root of volume, not in direct proportion to volume, the per-unit costs of larger facilities, such as warehouses, are less. Similarly, the incremental cost of adding a second and a third shift is generally less than the costs of setting up a new first shift, because much of the overhead is already in place. Economies of process technology, the third type of economy of scale, result in a different contribution of fixed and variable costs and cause a shift of the BOL curve, as described in Figure 3-7.

In recent years, operations have increasingly used more flexible equipment to produce different, but functionally similar, products or services (for example, a product group or service line). Thus, though the volume of each product/service, considered separately, is lower, the volume of the group or line is the same or higher. This concept is the foundation for economies of scope, as exemplified by recent innovations of variable production lines, flexible manufacturing systems, and computer integrated manufacturing. If a single technology or a single process were redesigned to produce two items instead of one item, the resulting BOL situation would be as shown in Figure 3-8.

FIGURE 3-8 The BOL with Economies of Scope

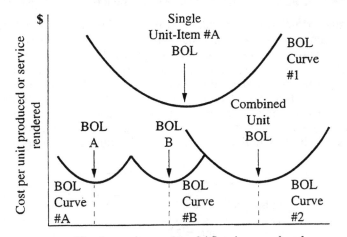

BOL curve 1 represents one inflexible process technology and various operating volumes with the corresponding cost per item. BOL curve 2 represents the use of that same equipment, but with a minor variation to produce two different products, represented by BOL curves A and B. Note that the BOL volumes of products A and B sum to the BOL of curve 2. BOL curve 2 is often located downward and to the right of BOL curve 1 because the potentially greater markets for differentiated products would permit greater production volumes and lower per-unit costs. However, lower volume and higher costs could result from poorly managed or marketed situations. The efficiencies of economies of scope are particularly important for applications like laser-cutting machines, which can be programmed to do multiple operations, such as cutting, etching, drilling, or finishing metal or other materials. An application of the BOL is described in Decision Model Box 3-3.

The discussion of the BOL has assumed, so far, a static decision environment. That is, one process technology alternative is selected; then the operations manager implements the changeover to the selected process and operates the process at or near the BOL. However, there are a number of economies of either scale or scope that can result from unexpected or dynamic factors. For example, changes in the process to produce a second model may have varying effects on the demand for the first model. Product differentiation often results in greater total markets for both products; however, the second model may reduce the market for the first, resulting in only marginally greater total sales. Similarly, output productivity improvements would also likely occur due to learning curves, particularly in the long run. However, movement of the learning curve may be spiked due to numerous effects on the learning process (Hirschmann, 1964). Additionally, the integration of labor and equipment may result in some greater or lesser amount of synergy, or the enhanced productivity or effectiveness due to joint or combined effects. These dynamic effects would likely move the BOL curve downward and outward, adding to the effect of the static process economies described above.

Required Capacity versus Available Capacity

Capacity strategy considers two distinct, yet closely related quantities: required capacity and available capacity (Blackstone, 1989). Required capacity identifies the amount of resource that will be required for each product, job, or family of products. This information is used to evaluate the plan (operations plan, master production schedule,

DECISION MODEL BOX 3-3   The Best Operating Level for The 'Copyrite' Print Shop

The 'Copyrite' Printe Shop is a small job printer located in a university town. Their color printing equipment is five years old and, though dependable, is relatively labor intense. Management is considering purchasing new, less labor-intense equipment. Their initial step is to review only the fixed and variable costs of equipment options; subsequently, they expect to evaluate a range of financial, maintenance, and other support system costs as part of an overall decision. The current equipment is compared with two alternative upgrades. For each, the fixed cost, the variable cost, and a cost associated with incremental loss of efficiency is given in current dollars. Data are given in hundreds of dollars and for hundred-thousands of units of production (color copies).

Current Equipment	Improvement Option 1	Improvement Option 2
Fixed cost (current $) = $100	Fixed cost = $200	Fixed cost = $200
Variable cost = 10	Variable cost = 5	Variable cost = 2
Diseconomy/unit = 5	Diseconomy/unit = 2.5	Diseconomy/unit = 1

Note that the loss of efficiency sets in after the second hundred-thousand units of production, and the diseconomy/unit occurs with every additional hundred-thousand units.

	Unit Cost				Unit Cost				Unit Cost		
Number of Units	Total Cost	Cost/ Unit	With Inefficiency	Number of Units	Total Cost	Cost/ Unit	With Inefficiency	Number of Units	Total Cost	Cost/ Unit	With Inefficiency
1	$110	$110	$110	1	$205	$ 205	$205	1	$202	$202	$202
2	120	60	60	2	210	105	105	2	204	102	102
3	130	43.3	48.3	3	215	71.7	74.2	3	206	68.7	69.7
4*	140	35	45	4	220	55	60	4	208	52	54
5*	150	30	45	5	225	45	52.5	5	210	42	45
6	160	26.7	46.7	6	230	38.3	48.3	6	212	35.3	39.3
				7	235	33.6	46.1	7	214	30.6	35.6
				8	240	30	45	8	216	27	33
				9*	245	27.2	44.7	9	218	24.2	31.2
				10	250	25	45	10	220	22	30
				11	255	23.2	45.7	11	222	20.2	29.2
								12	224	18.7	28.7
								13	226	17.4	28.4
								14*	228	16.3	28.3
								15*	230	15.3	28.3
								16	232	14.5	28.5

*Asterisks show the best operating level.

The BOL for the current equipment is between four and five hundred-thousands of units and the unit cost, including inefficiencies, is just below 4.5¢. For option 1, the BOL is at 9 ten-thousands of units, and the unit cost including inefficiencies is 4.47¢ for option 2, the BOL is between 14 and 15 hundred-thousands of units and the unit cost, including inefficiencies, is just less than 2.83¢. In the above data sets,

the cost per unit represents the economies of volume, and the unit costs with inefficiency represent the progressively increasing effects of inefficiency on the costs of
volume. This is the diseconomy of volume. The fixed cost of option 1 is double that
of the current equipment, while the variable cost is one-half that of the current
equipment and the inefficiencies of option 1 are half those of the current equipment.
These effects counteract each other, resulting in a best operating level which, though
at a higher volume, is at the same cost/unit. The fixed cost of the second option is
double that of the current equipment, but the variable costs and the inefficiencies
are both one-fifth those of the current equipment. The lower variable costs and inefficiencies result in a lower unit cost and a higher volume of the BOL.

or material requirements plan) and to determine the amount of capacity necessary
to process the required number of products/services. Alternatively, the available
capacity evaluation starts from the resources available, then adjusts the resources to
reflect the realities of labor, materials, or machine unavailability. Capacity evaluation is
the analytic process that identifies and measures processing production requirements
and resource availability and then makes adjustments in one or both so that resources
meet requirements.

Available Capacity.   The critical or constraining resource in a factory is often machine
or materials availability and in a service business, it is often labor hours. This concept is
generally introduced in Decision Model Box 3-1. If labor were required to feed, set up, or
maintain the machine, and were not available for a second or third shift, the process would
be called *labor constrained*. Alternatively, if the machine could be operated without significant human involvement, it could be used for a second and third shift (maintenance
would be performed only during the day shift), and the process would be called machine-
constrained. In a three-shift environment, the available capacity in Decision Model Box
3-1 would be 396 units × 3 shifts, or roughly 1188 units per 20-day working month.
     Labor-constrained capacity is computed by determining the total number of labor
hours available, and then adjusting that value for various factors, including direct labor
rates, efficiency, and absenteeism. Alternatively, materials/machine-constrained capacity is computed by identifying the total amount of machine time or materials possible and
factoring the amount of actual availability. Resource availability factors for machines,
materials, or labor are often stated in terms of resource efficiency and resource utilization
rates. A commonly used formula for computing available capacity is

$$\frac{\text{Available}}{\text{capacity}} = \frac{\text{time}}{\text{available}} \times \frac{\text{resource}}{\text{efficiency}} \times \frac{\text{resource}}{\text{utilization}}$$

Decision Model Box 3-4 gives an example of the available capacity computation.

Required Capacity.   Once the available capacity of the process is determined, the process
is loaded with job requirements. Required capacity is computed for each job, or, in the
long range, capacity evaluations are developed for expected product family volumes in
each time period. Decision Model Box 3-5 shows a simple, though classic, representation of required capacity in a work center.
     However, as shown in Decision Model Box 3-2, the flow of jobs through a process is
not necessarily stable. Jobs moving through a process, particularly if the process involves

DECISION MODEL BOX 3-4   Available Capacity at T&G Manufacturing

The T&G Manufacturing Company has organized a final assembly inspection operation in work center F. That operation employs five workers, including a group supervisor. Thus, work center F has a total of 5 workers × 8 hours per day × 20 days or 800 labor hours available in a 20-day month. However, the supervisor must spend two hours per day coordinating the work of the others. This 40 hours (2 hours × 20 days) of supervisory time is often expressed as a direct labor inefficiency. In this case, the available direct labor divided by total labor equals 760/800, or 95% labor utilization.

Efficiency is computed from resource availability. Records show that one-half hour per worker per day is wasted due to labor unavailability. This would be 4.75 workers × .5 hours × 20 days or 47.5 total hours lost per month. Note that four workers produce 20 days per month, but the supervisor produces product only 75% of the time, thus the 4.75 (rather than 5) workers. Machine/materials unavailability results in an additional 40 hours per month being lost. Thus, the efficiency would be reduced by 87.5 hours per month, which is 672.5/760 or 88.5%. The traditional computation of available capacity uses these efficiency and utilization calculations; the formula is

$$
\begin{aligned}
\text{Available capacity} &= \text{time available} \times \text{resource efficiency} \times \text{resource utilization} \\
&= 800 \qquad\qquad \times 0.885 \qquad\qquad\quad \times 0.95 \approx 672.5 \text{ hr}
\end{aligned}
$$

These computations are detailed as follows.

Design capacity or
time available $\quad= 8 \text{ hr/day} \times 5 \text{ workers} \times 20 \text{ days} = 800 \text{ labor hr}$

Effective capacity $\quad= \text{design capacity} - \text{supervisory time} = 800 - (2 \times 20)$
$\qquad\qquad\qquad = 760 \text{ hr}$

Actual capacity $\quad= \text{effective capacity} - \text{labor unavailability} - \text{machine/materials}$
$\qquad\qquad\qquad \text{unavailability}$

Labor unavailability $= 4.75 \times 0.5 \text{ hr} \times 20 = 47.5 \text{ hr lost}$

and

Machine/materials
unavailability $\qquad= 40 \text{ hr/month} \quad = \dfrac{40}{87.5} \dfrac{\text{hr lost}}{\text{hr lost}}$

thus

Actual capacity $\qquad= 760 - 87.5 \qquad = 672.5$

Resource efficiency $= \dfrac{672.5}{760} \approx 88.5\%$

Resource utilization $= \dfrac{760}{800} = 95\%$

Total utilization $\qquad= 800 \times 0.95 \times 0.885 \approx \dfrac{672.5}{800} = 0.841$

DECISION MODEL BOX 3-5 Required Capacity at T&G Manufacturing

The capacity requirements of six jobs at T&G are calculated based on the number of items required and the standard hours per item, and then adjusted for efficiency. These computations are shown. For example, the computation of job A, 200 units, is due in month 1 and would take 200×0.2 or 40 total standard hours. Dividing 40 by the efficiency of 0.95 gives a required capacity of 42.105 hours. The requirements are represented, often by a histogram, for each time period. With the present data, if a cap of 672.5 hours of available capacity per month were placed on the process (calculated in Decision Model Box 3-4), it would cause the process to be overloaded in month 2 and underloaded in months 1, 3, and 4. Though additional future requirements may be defined for months 3 and 4, this comparison of required and available capacity suggests that the plan currently should be adjusted by rescheduling or expediting roughly 200 hours of either job C or D to month 1.

This example shows the identification, measurement, and adjustment of a plan. Of course, more extensive capacity shortages would be resolved with overtime, additional shifts, machine speeds, outsourcing, or using flexible equipment, among other approaches. This application could be similarly, and in much more detail, applied to a plant or an industry.

Job	Due Month	Number of Units	Std Hr/Unit*	Total Std Hr	Efficiency*	Capacity Required (hr)
A	1	200	0.2	40	0.95	42.105
B	1	500	0.75	375	0.90	416.667
C	2	1000	0.4	400	0.85	470.588
D	2	600	0.6	360	0.90	400.000
E	3	2000	0.3	600	0.95	631.579
F	4	150	2.5	375	0.90	416.667

*Data based on historical records.

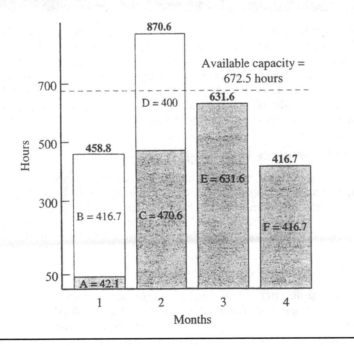

many steps, may be viewed as a series of random inputs and outputs, rather like the logic of queuing theory. The jobs may show extensive variance, or, in fact, randomness of arrival time due to the situation at upstream work centers. For this reason, Blackstone (1989) convincingly argues that the definition of available capacity should be restated to categorize utilization into factors of resource availability and facility activation, or:

$$\frac{\text{Available}}{\text{capacity}} = \frac{\text{time}}{\text{available}} \times \frac{\text{resource}}{\text{efficiency}} \times \frac{\text{resource}}{\text{availability}} \times \frac{\text{facility}}{\text{activation}}$$

where   resource = standard hours of output divided by hours worked
           efficiency   (the classic efficiency computation)

           resource   = 1 − the fraction of time down due to machine
           availability   breakdown or labor unavailability

           facility   = 1 − the fraction of time down due to lack of work
           activation

The use of a facility activation factor to adjust capacity, based on the availability of work, is the foundation of the theory of constraints. If capacity is not activated at a particular work center in a particular time period, that represents a constraint on the throughput or flow of the process. The term *bottleneck* is traditionally used to describe the buildup of load behind activated work centers; however, the term *constraint* more precisely describes the capacity evaluation of multiple system processes, because it includes the notion of both load and inactivity. When multiple products, multiple work centers, or multiple flows are involved, the resolution of constraints requires extensive interaction and evaluation of the process.

RESOURCE PLANNING

Resource planning is the process of establishing, measuring, and adjusting levels of mid- and long-range capacity, both required capacity and available capacity. It is often driven by the operations plan, but may be based on higher-level business plans. It is distinct from the rough-cut capacity plan, which operates in the mid- and short range, and from capacity requirements planning, which operates in the short range. The techniques of rough-cut capacity planning and capacity requirements planning correspond, albeit in much greater detail, to those of resource planning.

Concepts of Resource Planning

Resource planning evaluates available and required capacity in the mid- and long run. Initially, the operations manager must identify the key resources. Though the evaluation will usually involve either machine or labor hours, or possibly both, it may also involve components or processes for which there is a long lead time, raw materials or components with uncertain availability, constrained warehouse or storage facilities, or financial assets.

Four-Step Resource Evaluation Process

There are several different procedures that may be used in developing the capacity plan. These procedures are generally identified in Table 3-2. and further described in Orlicky (1975) and Fogarty et al. (1991). As shown in Table 3-2, the amount of information and complexity differ rather significantly among procedures. Using a simulation to evaluate different capacity planning approaches and considering the criteria of missed due

TABLE 3-2 Information Used by Capacity Planning Procedures

Capacity Planning Procedure	MPS	Accounting Direct Labor Summary	Routing & Time Standards	Bill of Materials	Manufacturing Lead Times	On-hand, In-Process Inventory, Lot Size, Safety Stock
CPOF	X	X				
CB	X		X	X		
RP	X		X	X	X	
CRP	X		X	X	X	X

Note: MPS—master production schedule; CPOF—capacity planning using overall factors; CB—capacity bill (which is the materials profile as used here); RP—resource profile, uses lead time associated with rough-cut planning; CRP—capacity requirements planning, which assesses all of the preceding and inventory status and is used with materials requirement planning.

dates, capacity deviations, and time fence requirements, Schmitt et al. (1984) conclude that the simple capacity planning method using overall factors (CPOF) worked as well as the capacity bill (CB) or resource profile (RP) methods. Capacity requirements planning (CRP) worked better than the other methods, but required a computer-based system. These findings are consistent with the intuitive conclusion that, for long-range resource planning efforts, the simpler CPOF method is sufficient, but for mid- and short-range capacity management, the more detailed, computer-based system is appropriate. It also suggests the benefits of using capacity planning methods to evaluate longer-range plans.

Regardless of the level at which it is conducted, the resource evaluation process involves four general steps. These steps are

1. Obtain the planned production for each product family or group by period (day, week, month, quarter).
2. Determine the product structure (resource profile or bill of materials) for each product family or group.
3. Determine the bill of resources (resources per unit) for each product, family, or group.
4. Calculate the total resource requirements.

The first step of resource planning involves obtaining the planned production for each product group or family by time period. This information comes from the operations plan, the master production schedule, or the material requirements plan. The second step is determining the product structure, defined as a listing of the amounts of key resources necessary to produce an item or family. The product structure describes a product group in terms of the mix of specific product items, major work processes, and components of the product mix. More detailed capacity evaluation methods substitute the resources profile or the bill of materials (bill of labor) and approximate lead times for this purpose.

The third step, determining the bill of resources for each product family or group, identifies the per-unit time (machine or labor time, or lead time), cost (financial cost or planning time), or risk (uncertainty of success or probabilities of greater costs) or each key resource. For machine or labor times, the following formula is often used:

$$\text{Average assembly time} = \text{product mix proportion} \times \Sigma \left(\text{standard assembly hours/unit} \right)$$

The formulas for cost- or risk-measured resources would be similar, though the cost factor might be stated in dollars per unit.

The final step, calculating the resource requirements, multiplies the number of units required by the per-unit resource measure and determines the total resource requirement, broken down by work center or process. This total required capacity is compared to the measure of available capacity, however developed, and permits the computation of the capacity overage or shortage. An example of this process is shown in Decision Model Box 3-6.

In summary, capacity strategy involves two general computations, capacity requirements and resource availability. These decisions should be sequentially considered at the long-, mid-, and short-range time periods. To use rough-cut capacity planning, or capacity requirements planning, which are mid- and short-range techniques, to evaluate longer-range planning processes, such as operations planning, or long-range business planning is certainly possible, but may be overkill. Capacity processes are designed to provide the appropriate level of specificity for the operations planning method.

IMPLEMENTATION OF CAPACITY DECISIONS

Implementing capacity decisions involves three issues: the amount of the capacity cushion, the timing of the capacity change, and the size of the capacity increment. In most situations, such decisions are considered on a quarterly basis, and major decisions are rarely made at less than one-year intervals. Thus, the decisions, when made, are very important.

Capacity as a Cushion

Initially, capacity must be considered to be a cushion, much as inventory safety stock is used. Capacity is particularly important as a cushion in make-to-order and assemble-to-order environments as well as in many services. Available capacity permits the operations manager to "gear up" for an unexpected short lead-time requirement. Depending upon the key resource, the operations manager may schedule at only 90% of actual capacity or may have several units of long lead-time components set aside against such an unexpected requirement.

Capacity Time Changes

A capacity change decision can occur before the need for a changed capacity, can be concurrent with that need, or can be lagged behind the need. There are numerous ways to popularly describe these capacity timing strategies. For example, the lagging strategy is described as a "don't build it until you need it" approach, and the concurrent strategy might be called a "build for current demand" approach. The leading strategy might be labeled "build because it is the right thing to do" or "build because the market is going to turn." Figure 3-9 shows a stable increase in demand pattern over time, with the leading strategy creating capacity in anticipation of the increased demand, and the concurrent and lagging strategies respectively positioned with and behind the movement of demand. A more realistic representation of requirements would likely involve some amount of cyclical variation. If demand fluctuates extensively on an annual or other cycle, anticipating those swings to bring new capacity on line may be very difficult. For this reason, some companies may select to build capacity during the down-cycle, which is called a "contracyclical" capacity expansion.

The timing of capacity changes is related to the BOL because the leading, concurrent, and lagging strategies suggest that the firm will be operating at different positions on the BOL. Firms using a leading strategy will shift to a greater capacity approximately when they

DECISION MODEL BOX 3-6   Resource Evaluation at T&G Manufacturing

The T&G Manufacturing Company uses a variety of titanium and alloy materials to build joints and other parts for airframe manufacture. Because of the cost of the metals involved, and the labor hours required to build them, these parts are considered to be key resources. Thus, T&G uses the four-step resource planning process to evaluate the milling operations of those resources. Given the following values:

Product mix for product group A of products 1, 2, and 3:	0.50, 0.30, 0.20
Standard assembly hours of products 1, 2, and 3 of Product Groups A, B, and C:	0.342, 0.294, 0.210
Efficiencies for surface A, surface B, and final milling:	0.95, 0.95, 0.95
Available capacity for surface A, surface B, and final milling:	320, 280, 300

Step 1. Obtain the planned production for each product family or group by period.

The planned production for product group A in the specific month is 720, for product group B is 240, and for product group C is 160. This information would be obtained from the production plan.

Step 2. Determine the product structure for each product family or group.

The product structure for a particular family of airframe parts would be given in process documents and is

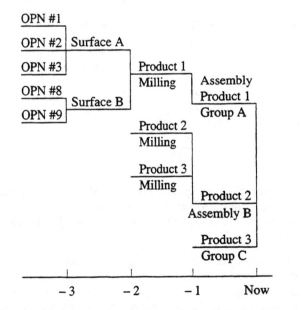

Step 3. Determine the bill of resources for each product family or group.

The bill of resources is computed with the formula:

Product mix proportion × standard assembly hr/unit = average milling time

DECISION MODEL BOX 3-6 *Continued*

Product	Product Mix (given)	Standard Assembly Hr/Unit (given)	Average Assembly Time
1	0.5	0.342	0.171
2	0.3	0.294	0.088
3	0.2	0.210	0.042
			0.301

Bill of Resources Analysis[1]

	Surface A	Surface B	Final Milling
Product Group A	0.274	0.250	0.301
Product Group B	0.222	0.185	0.285
Product Group C	0.241	0.241	0.256

Step 4. Calculate the resource and materials requirements.

Thus, to build 720 of product group A in one month, the following capacity is required.

Bill of resources analysis	0.274	0.250	0.301
Number of units	720	720	720
Total capacity required	197.28	180.00	216.72

Similar computations would result in the data for each product group.

Product group A	197.28	180.00	216.72
Product group B[2]	53.28	44.40	68.40
Product group C[2]	38.56	38.56	40.96
Total hours	289.12	262.96	326.08
Efficiency (given)	0.95	0.95	0.95
Plan[3]	304.34	276.80	343.24
Available capacity[4]	320	280	300
Shortfall			43.24

Thus, there is a shortfall of capacity for final milling. The production plan must be adjusted, or supplemental resources planned for.

Reprinted by permission, APICS, *Master Planning Certification Review Course*, 1991, Transparencies 7-14, 7-15, and 7-16

---

[1]The computations for product groups B and C correspond to those for product group A, though the necessary input data is not provided.

[2]Though not explicitly shown here, the total capacity required for product groups B and C would be found by multiplying the production plan requirement (step 1—240, 160) times the bill of resources (step 3) for surface A, surface B, and final milling.

[3]The resource requirements of the plan are calculated as total hours divided by efficiency.

[4]The available capacity would be calculated as in Decision Model Box 3-4; but for this problem, it is given.

reach the BOL, and will generally operate on the left side of the BOL curve. Firms with concurrent strategies will operate at the center of the BOL curve, incrementing capacity at some point of increasing inefficiency. Finally, the lagging strategy changes its process technology and capacity by moving directly to the BOL of the lower curve and operating to overcome the inefficiencies of scale or scope. These strategies are depicted in Figure 3-10.

Of course, there are a variety of risks and advantages associated with each strategy. The leading capacity strategy is analogous to safety stock inventory in that it permits the manufacturing or service company to immediately or rapidly respond to changing market demands or to a growing market. These advantages, however, are counterbalanced by the associated risks that the up-front investment is higher and that a change may occur in the environment that reduces per-period revenues and slows the return on investment. Alternatively, a firm that decides on a lagging strategy reduces the risks of investment in potentially unused capacity or products that don't sell, but bears the risk of not being able to respond to customer demand—and the ensuing potential of back-order costs or lost sales (Leone and Meyer, 1980). The strategic capacity decisions of leading and lagging firms are shown in Table 3-3.

Leone and Meyer (1980) further suggest that, in addition to its representation of the economics of one or several processes, the BOL curve can be applied to the economic costs and risks in a multibusiness environment. During the 1950s and 1960s, productivity improvements associated with increasing volume, new technologies, learning curves, and general factors commonly outpaced inflation and other cost increases. Computers, communications, chemicals, and metals, among other industries, are examples of such "declining cost" industries. However, by the late 1960s and 1970s, the economic environment of many businesses began to change. Productivity improvements no longer could be counted on to offset cost increases due to inflation, capital costs, energy, or government regulation, and firms were not able to easily recover investments in capacity.

Size Increment of Capacity Changes

Similarly, the size of the capacity increment also can be controlled by management, though within some limits. Capacity increments cannot be managed as a continuous function; they must be added in discrete chunks. The questions that arise are "how often?" and "what increments?" Figure 3-11 depicts that issue.

For various reasons, including organization structure, facilities availability, or process technology, it may not be possible to increment capacity in small amounts. However, the greater the capacity increment, the greater the risk of process or product obsolescence. Correspondingly, the longer the wait, the greater the risk that firm may not be able to get

FIGURE 3-9 Timing of Capacity Changes

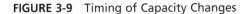

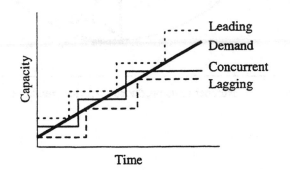

FIGURE 3-10 Capacity Change Timing and the BOL

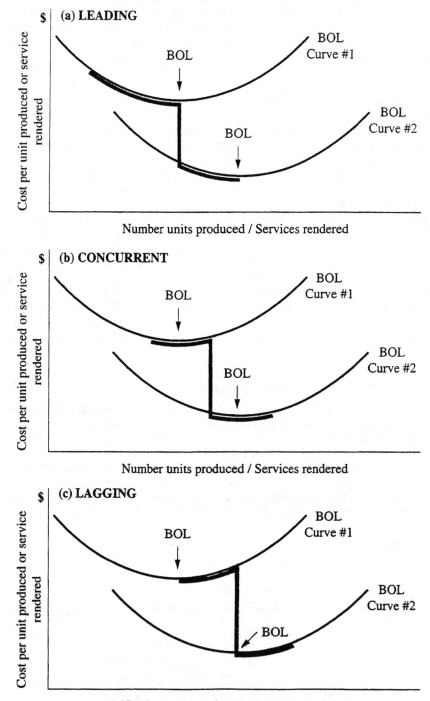

FIGURE 3-11 The Increment and Periodicity of Capacity Change

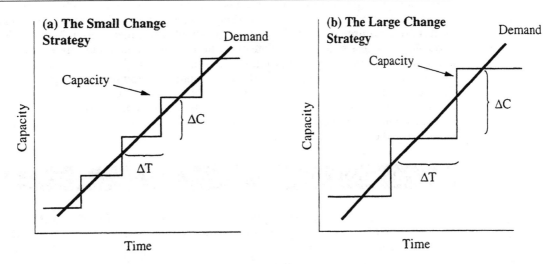

TABLE 3-3 Capacity Decisions of Leading and Lagging Firms

Leading	Lagging
Build large-scale facilities	Build small-scale facilities
Build new facilities	Renovate or acquire existing facilities
Compete on basis of price	Compete on the basis of quality, delivery, or other criteria
Locate in developing areas	Locate in existing markets
Choose capital-intense technologies	Choose variable-cost or labor-intense technologies
Forecast demand using simple, less accurate methods	Forecast demand using sophisticated and likely more accurate methods

Adapted from Leone and Meyer, 1980.

to the market first with a sufficient concentration of products and may have to overcome a competitor's advantage of an early-established and well-entrenched product. The costs of larger increments in longer time frames, and the associated risks (and costs) of catching up to and overcoming a competitor's strategic advantage are traded off against the costs of continually directing assets to a capacity decision and the risks associated with building capacity too far ahead of demand.

SUMMARY

In summary, the capacity strategy must be evaluated for each business environment. It is clearly one of the most important decisions that a firm makes and must involve top management, because they involve the long-range direction and financial viability of the firm. Unfortunately, operations involvement in capacity decisions has traditionally been limited, even though the decision is central to the performance of the operations function. The selection of a capacity alternative is directly related to efficiency and facility utilization. It is founded in the analysis of fixed-cost and variable-cost process alternatives and the associated BOL curves of the selected process technology.

The capacity strategy must also address the advantages of static economies of scale and of scope and the potential dynamic economies of scale and scope that may ensue.

Recent emphases on flexibility and innovation are explicitly based on the concept of economies of scope. Resource planning is one of the essential methods of capacity evaluation; it identifies and measures required and available capacity and adjusts either or both so that requirements can be met with available resources. This adjustment involves a four-step process that disaggregates production requirements into resource needs. At a minimum, the capacity evaluation process must assess the general question of leading, concurrent, and lagging demand requirements and the resulting capacity cushions that are created. Though risks of incorrectly diagnosing the environment are costly, the costs of not addressing capacity questions are greater. Few operations managers can successfully manage an operations process if they have not actively participated in the decisions that led to the selection of the process.

DISCUSSION QUESTIONS

1. Capacity has been called a costly necessity. Give several examples of capacity (both in services and in manufacturing operations) from your own experience and state the costs of that capacity and why they are necessary.

2. What basic questions do capacity strategies answer?

3. Identify several levels at which capacity activities occur and describe an example from your readings or experience which shows what these capacity activities do at each level.

4. Identify three specific definitions of capacity and show how they are helpful to the operations manager.

5. What are the four ways that operations capacity may be dimensionalized? Give an example from your experience of each of these dimensions.

6. Why are the fixed and variable costs of a particular operations process important to the operations manager?

7. Considering Figures 3-6, 3-7, and 3-8, define and give an example of economies of scale, multiple process technologies, and economies of scope.

8. Differentiate required capacity and available capacity. Give an example of each.

9. List the four steps of resource evaluation. From your experience, give an example of each step. (*Note*: Resource evaluation can be applied to as simple and widespread an example as preparing for a backyard barbecue, managing a charity carwash, or scheduling classes or social activities.)

10. Relate the best operating level to the timing of capacity change decisions. Describe operations that would tend to lead demand, those that would tend to be concurrent with demand, and those that might lag demand.

11. Using the concept of best operating level, graphically relate total costs to produce a quantity of units with per-unit costs to produce that number of units.

12. Discuss the circumstances under which a lower-level capacity evaluation process would be used to evaluate a longer-term (higher-level) operations planning process. Are there advantages of using rough-cut capacity planning to evaluate an operations plan and capacity requirements planning to evaluate a master production schedule? What are the disadvantages?

STRATEGIC DECISION SITUATIONS

1. The North LaSalle Bank and Trust Company suggests guidance for its suburban branch banks on how many tellers should be scheduled for drive-through lane operations at different times of the day. The local suburban branch has four drive-through lanes; how-

ever, those lanes are staffed at different levels during the day because, during low-volume periods, bank personnel can be better used at other duties. Typically, an open lane can service one customer every five minutes. The drive-through windows are open from seven o'clock in the morning until seven o'clock in the evening, Monday through Friday, and staff are scheduled for three-hour shifts in the drive-through. Bank policy permits employees to take one 20-minute break during the three-hour period, and, because employees bring their cash trays to the drive-through window area, shift changeover time is nominal. The bank has found that some customers bring multiple transactions or transactions that require greater processing times; these "high-density" transactions require an average of seven and one-half minutes each, and are estimated to occur at the indicated rate per line per hour. Evaluate the daily design capacity, effective capacity, actual capacity, efficiency, and utilization of the local suburban branch. Be prepared to advise management on their current use of resources.

	Time			
	7:00–10:00	10:00–1:00	1:00–4:00	4:00–7:00
Number of employees	2	3	2	4
High density transactions per line per hour	1	3	4	2

2. The downtown library is anticipating the installation of a new computerized book checkout system, which will replace their currently used manual system. The new system may be used to "wand" bar code identification panels on the inside covers of books. Given a normal manual operation with three librarians at three checkout counters, represent the following situations, using a BOL diagram.

    a. The scheduling of five librarians to manually check out books at the checkout counter.

    b. One of the three librarians calls in sick with the result that only two librarians are available to staff the three-position checkout operation.

    c. The installation of the new computer system at the three stations and the gradual implementation of the system as the staff is trained to use it.

    d. A power surge requires that manual operations procedures be used while the computer is reinitialized and the software is reloaded, a process that takes two to three hours.

    e. The installation of software and bar code panels so that records, videos, and CDs can also be checked out with the computer system.

3. The Windy City Pump Company makes three sizes of valve in three different machine centers. With customizations, however, process standard hours and efficiency of specific jobs vary. The valve halves are initially cast and welded together, then machined in separate operations, each of which is done in a different machine center. The company operates one eight-hour shift per day on a 20-day monthly calendar, and has three employees in the casting area, four employees in the welding center, and five employees in the machine center. The senior employee in each area/center spends four hours per week on administration, and unplanned-for employee absenteeism results in one day per month lost per production center, while unavailable materials result in the loss of one labor day per month per employee in each center.

    a. Find the available capacity of each center.

    b. The following jobs are planned for the centers. Note that a job must be first cast, then welded, then machined. Determine the resource requirements and, considering available capacity (part 1), advise management. The current backlog in the welding center uses all available capacity in week 1, and the backlog in the machine center uses all available capacity in weeks 1 and 2. The jobs may be broken in any volume, but only at the end of the week, and they may be moved from work center to work center as "broken" jobs.

Job	Due Week	Units	Cast Std hr/unit	Cast Efficiency	Weld Std hr/unit	Weld Efficiency	Machine Std hr/unit	Machine Efficiency
A	3	200	0.3	0.95	0.15	0.85	0.30	0.95
B	3	400	0.2	0.90	0.50	0.80	0.70	0.90
C	4	100	0.4	0.85	0.30	0.90	0.80	0.90
D	5	300	0.3	0.90	0.25	0.80	0.60	0.85
E	6	250	0.5	0.90	0.55	0.85	0.50	0.90
F	7	330	0.3	0.95	0.30	0.90	0.30	0.95

4. The South Lake Steel Company manufactures three product groups of metal kitchen cabinets, which require rolled steel inputs and milling, mechanical assembly, and final assembly. The production plan data is provided below, as is a bill of resources. If the total capacity of the final assembly operation is 2.6 units/day, the mechanical assembly is 4.3 units/day, the milling operation is 2.5 units/day, and the steel is 4 tons/day, advise the South Lake management on the feasibility of the production plan.

Production Plan of Family

Product Group	Jul.	Aug.	Sep.	Oct.	Nov.	Dec.
Number of days/mo	17	23	19	22	20	16
X	85	115	95	110	100	80
Y	170	230	190	220	200	160
Z	85	115	95	110	100	80

Bill of Resources

Product Group	Work Center	Description	Unit of Measure	Quantity/Unit	Months Lead Times
X	001	final assembly	hours	0.2	0
	002	mechanical assembly	hours	0.2	1
	003	milling	hours	0.1	1
	004	steel	tons	0.1	2
Y	001	final assembly	hours	0.1	0
	002	mechanical assembly	hours	0.2	1
	003	milling	hours	0.1	1
	004	steel	tons	0.2	2
Z	001	final assembly	hours	0.1	0
	002	mechanical assembly	hours	0.2	1
	003	milling	hours	0.1	1
	004	steel	tons	0.3	2

REFERENCES

Blackstone, John H., Jr. *Capacity Management.* Cincinnati, Ohio: South-Western Publishing Co., 1989.

Casella, Bill, and Todd Barnes. "Finite Capacity Scheduling Is also a Forecasting Tool for Beth Forge," *APICS, The Performance Advantage.* January 1992, pp. 20–23.

Correll, James G. "Capacity Management: The Answer to 'Do the Best You Can,'" *APICS, The Performance Advantage.* September 1991, p. 50–54.

Fogarty, Donald W., John H. Blackstone, and Thomas R. Hoffmann. *Production & Inventory Management.* Cincinnati, Ohio: South-Western Publishing Co., 1991.

Fogarty, Donald W., Thomas R. Hoffmann, and Peter W. Stonebraker. *Production and Operations Management,* Cincinnati, Ohio: South-Western Publishing Co., 1989.

Goldratt, Eliyahu M., and Jeff Cox. *The Goal.* Crotonon-Hudson, N.Y.: North River Press, 1986.

Greene, James H. *Production and Inventory Control Handbook.* New York: McGraw-Hill, 1987.

Grover, Ronald, Sandra D. Achison, and Gail De-George. "Heartbreak Hotel for Tourism," *Business Week.* January 20, 1992, p. 36.

Hayes, Robert H., and Roger W. Schmenner. "How Should You Organize Manufacturing?" *Harvard Business Review.* January–February 1978.

Hayes, Robert H., and Steven C. Wheelwright. *Restoring Our Competitive Edge: Competing through Manufacturing.* New York: John Wiley and Sons, 1984.

Hirschmann, Winfred B. "Profit from the Learning Curve," *Harvard Business Review.* January–February 1964.

"How GM's Saturn Could Run Rings Around Old-Style Carmakers," *Business Week.* January 28, 1985.

Lee, Hak-Chong. "Lordstown Plant of General Motors (A) and (B)." State University of New York at Albany, 1974.

Leone, Robert A., and John R. Meyer. "Capacity Strategies for the 1980s," *Harvard Business Review.* November–December, 1980, pp. 133–140.

Levenbach, Hans, and James G. Thompson. "Tying the Forecasting Process into Finite Scheduling," *Production & Inventory Management.* January 1992, pp. 17–20.

Melnyk, Steven A., and Ram Narasimhan. "Uniting Capacity, Shop Floor Control and Strategy," *APICS: The Performance Advantage.* November 1991, pp. 33–45.

Orlicky, Joseph. *Materials Requirement Planning.* New York: McGraw-Hill, 1975.

Parkinson, C. Northcote. *Parkinson's Law.* Boston, Mass.: Houghton-Mifflin, 1957.

Plossl, George W. *Production and Inventory Control: Principles and Techniques.* Englewood Cliffs, N.J.: Prentice Hall, 1985.

Plossl, George W. *Managing in the New World of Manufacturing.* Englewood Cliffs, N.J.: Prentice Hall, 1991.

Schmenner, Roger W. "Before You Build a Big Factory," *Harvard Business Review.* July–August 1976.

Schmitt, Thomas G., William L. Berry, and Thomas E. Vollmann. "An Analysis of Capacity Planning Procedures for a Materials Requirement Planning System," *Decision Sciences.* Vol. 15, 1984, pp. 522–541.

Vollmann, Thomas E., William L. Berry, and D. Clay Whybark. *Manufacturing Planning and Control Systems.* Homewood, Ill.: Irwin, 1992.

Wight, Oliver W. *Production and Inventory Management in the Computer Age.* New York: Van Nostrand Reinhold Company, 1984.

Williams, Blaire R. "Understanding Available Resource Capacity in the Manufacturing Sector," *APICS: The Performance Advantage.* November 1991, pp. 39–41.

Wortman, David B. "Managing Capacity: Getting the Most from Your Company's Assets," *Industrial Engineering.* February 1992, pp. 47–49.

CHAPTER 4

FACILITIES STRATEGY

*Taking advantage of the speed and flexibility offered by modern
air cargo carriers, manufacturers are no longer limited by
distance. They can gather materials from all over the globe; . . .
parts, components, subsystems, products, services, and
information are continuously intermingled, . . . bypassing
traditional warehousing facilities.*
—Fred Smith, President and CEO, Federal Express

*And Japanese multinationals . . . are pouring staggering
amounts of money into manufacturing plants in developing
countries. They are in Tijuana on the U.S.-Mexican border,
throughout South America, in Southern Europe, and in
Southeast Asia. The standard explanations for moving
manufacturing out of Japan are "foreign protectionism" and
"Japan's growing labor shortage." Both explanations are
legitimate, but they are also smoke screens. The real reason is
the growing conviction among Japan's business leaders and
influential bureaucrats that manufacturing work does not
belong in a developed country such as Japan.*
—Peter F. Drucker

Objectives

After completing this chapter you should be able to:

- Explain the contribution of facilities strategy to operations strategy.
- List the four components of facilities strategy.
- Discuss the major factors that influence facilities location decisions.

- Link facilities layout with performance and analyze the different types of facilities layout.
- Describe the benefits of focused facilities.
- Describe the contribution of handling systems to improved productivity.

INTRODUCTORY CASE: THE GENERAL MOTORS SATURN PLANT*

When General Motors announced plans in January 1985 for its $5 billion Saturn small car project, Tennessee played it cool. GM was trying to pull together the most advanced technology possible in a bid to revolutionize automobile manufacturing, and gain a competitive advantage. Where the plant was to be located remained a question. Unlike other states, Tennessee officials did not dispatch caravans of politicians and state officials to Detroit to tantalize GM with concessions. Tennessee state officials coveted the Saturn plant, but they believed that temporary incentives would not change the decision. Rather, GM's location decisions would be based on more fundamental factors.

As it turned out, Tennessee was correct. The lack of tax breaks or free giveaways had little to do with the location decision. GM never asked for any incentives. The decision to

---

*Materials drawn from: David Whiteside, Richard Brandt, Zachary Schiller, and Andrea Gabor, "How GM's Saturn Could Run Rings Around Old-Style Carmakers," *Business Week*, January 28, 1985, pp. 27–28; Pete Engardio and Maralyn Edid, "Why a 'Little Detroit' Could Rise in Tennessee," *Business Week*, August 12, 1985, p. 21; Alex Taylor III, "Back to the Future at Saturn," *Fortune*, August 1, 1988, pp. 67–72; Majorie A. Sorge and Stephene E. Plumb, "Can Saturn Keep the Revival Meeting Going?" *Ward's Auto World,* Vol. 5, 1990, pp. 43–49.

locate the Saturn facility and its 6000 workers on some 2400 acres of rolling countryside south of Nashville, near the one-stoplight town of Spring Hill, apparently had little to do with the state's promotion efforts and a lot to do with fundamentals.

Spring Hill, Tennessee, was selected by a process that evaluated various factors. GM and state officials said Spring Hill was chosen because of central Tennessee's strategic location, climate, ample supplies of water and electricity, and its eager work force. A University of Tennessee study showed that state manufacturers rated their employees as having "good worker attitude" and high productivity. The president of Nissan USA, Marvin T. Runyon, said, "The people here are just very good, loyal workers." Saturn president William E. Hoglund called Tennessee "absolutely perfect for the type of people we want to hire."

Low property taxes is another reason Tennessee was chosen. But the primary factor may have been simple geography. According to state figures, central Tennessee is close to GM's suppliers and within 500 miles of 76% of the U.S. population. Three interstate highways crisscross nearby Nashville, and there is a rail link to the 234-mile-long Tennessee-Tombigbee Waterway, a new $2 billion barge canal to the Gulf of Mexico. That means low freight costs, which Hoglund cited as the most important economic factor in the selection. Another factor was the infrastructure. Nissan USA makes light trucks and the Sentra car in nearby Smyrna, Tennessee. The proximity of Nissan, say state officials, also may have weighed heavily in the decision. Since the Japanese company's arrival, dozens of parts suppliers have sprung up, making everything from car seats to catalytic converters.

The Saturn plant represents the largest single construction project in GM history and covers an area of 4.4 million square feet, roughly the size of 100 football fields. The mile-long installation combines all essential operations on one site, similar to what the Japanese do in many facilities. The Spring Hill site houses sheet-metal stamping and body assembly, a foundry for casting engine blocks, a power-train assembly line, a plastics-molding unit, and an interior trim shop. Each operation is surrounded by dozens of loading docks so that material and parts can be delivered just in time close to the assembly lines. A unique feature of the plant is the ergonomically designed skillet conveyor, which moves the auto spaceframes along the assembly line. Employees work on the spaceframes while riding along with the moving line at speeds of 14-18 feet per minute. There are four skillet lines and 17 transfer points. Two of the lines use "scissor" skillets, which can be raised or lowered to the height that is best for the assembly team. The auto spaceframes are placed "door to door" instead of "bumper to bumper" to maximize use of space. Moving the partially assembled vehicles from one line to another involves lifting the skillets off the floor and moving them overhead to the next line to keep aisles clear for delivery of materials, for easy movement of plant personnel, and for safety reasons. Overall, 350 robots are used for welding, painting, and material-handling applications. Artificial vision is used in the paint shop and body-system areas, but there are no automated-guided vehicles.

Though the Saturn plant has had some quality problems, management has moved quickly to minimize the inconvenience of recalls. The Saturn project has shown that a quality car can be designed and built in America at a competitive cost.

FACILITIES STRATEGY

Total business expenditures for new plant and equipment in the United States accounted for 11% of national output, compared with 14% in Germany and 21% in Japan. Investment by U.S. firms in new plant and equipment now trails Japan by $60 billion a year, and the U.S. advantage over Europe in new plant and equipment is decreasing steadily. This low investment in new plant and equipment is one of the primary reasons for the lack of competitiveness of U.S. manufacturers. Most experts attribute this low investment rate to a focus on short-term financial goals. Hugh L. McColl, Jr., National Bank Corporation chairman and CEO, says, "We need to find a way to make it more attractive for companies to get back in the business of doing the things they did historically to build their companies. If we want to be successful as a country, we need to be encouraging investment" (Mandel and Farell, 1992).

A facilities strategy will fall short if it fails to identify innovative opportunities for improving the operating efficiency of a new facility and also to consider that facility's potential effects on competitiveness. For example, it is estimated that between 20 and 50% of total operating expenses are attributed to materials handling. An effective facilities strategy can decrease these costs by 10 to 30% (Tompkins and White, 1984). A manufacturing facility often represents a company's largest and most expensive asset and, therefore, must be planned carefully. Firms often make facilities decisions in response to changing conditions, a reaction that could result in facilities decisions that are inconsistent with the manufacturing tasks and which could lead ultimately to the facilities' demise. Hayes and Wheelwright (1984, p. 109) suggest that "rather than waiting until the growth in one's own market makes it imperative to add additional capacity, or increasing unprofitability of an existing facility requires a major change in technology or organization, firms should think of their facilities decisions as some of their most powerful levers for achieving their long-term objectives." Facilities strategy must be regarded as a *proactive* component of the overall operations strategy. By any measure, facilities strategy has major cost, productivity, and competitive implications for an organization.

The term *facility* is often taken to mean "factory"; however, facilities equally apply to distribution warehouses and retail or service locations. Facilities strategy and decisions must include all real properties of the firm and must integrate operations, distribution, and service delivery activities.

An Overview of Facilities Strategy

There are four components of facilities strategy: size and structural design, location, layout, and materials handling systems. These are the four primary topics of this chapter. Facilities strategy must be integrated with operations strategy as well as with other elements of the business strategy. Figure 4-1 shows the major inputs to the facilities strategy. For example, investment decisions regarding the facility are directly dependent on both the financial and marketing strategies. Product and packaging decisions have an impact on processing, material, and information needs, which in turn influence layout and material handling decisions. In service organizations the facility must be designed to facilitate customer interaction and to present a positive impression of service activities. Vertical integration affects the make-buy decisions and thus the size and layout of the facility. Production scheduling and control decisions determine the lot sizing and timing of production, which affects the layout and handling system. We have seen how the capacity decision affects the size of a facility. The organization design determines overhead and support staff, and work force size, which impacts the structural design, size, number, and location of the facilities. A facilities strategy must support operations and purchasing in the way materials are received, stored, and moved through the production system, and in the way finished goods are shipped through the distribution systems. An information system is required to keep track of materials as they flow through the system and must be integrated with accounting and operations planning systems.

Facilities Life Cycle

A facility, much like a product, goes through a life cycle. The facilities life cycle consists of four stages: design and start-up, progressive expansion, maturation and reinvestment, and renewal or shutdown (Hayes and Wheelwright, 1984). These stages roughly correspond to stages 4 through 7 of the product-process life cycle explained in Chapter 1. As Schmenner (1983, p. 129) states, the life cycle's "usefulness comes from recognizing that plants are subject to all kinds of changing forces, many of which are related to age but all

FIGURE 4-1 Inputs to Facilities Strategy

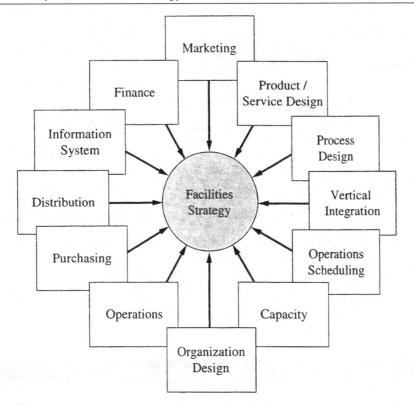

of which must be carefully considered and coped with. Anticipating a plant's needs in this way is sound preventive medicine."

Stage one involves planning and designing a new facility. There are several reasons why a new facility may be needed: competitive pressures, shifting markets, expected increase in demand, inability of the present facility to be cost competitive, obsolescence, steadily increasing transportation costs, and inability to service customers properly. We should note that the majority of these factors are related to changes in the market for products or services. This is an important stage since it affects future efforts to improve the facility and operations. Facilities typically represent the largest and most costly assets of a company, which once constructed represent a long-term commitment. Therefore, the facilities strategy must be integrated with operations, marketing, human resources, and financial strategies and must be consistent with the overall business strategy.

After the initial start-up, the utilization of a facility is expected to increase with an increase in market share of the product. This growth stage is the most profitable stage of a facility's life cycle and is marked by investment and incremental expansion of the facility to cope with increasing demand. There are three possible pitfalls at this stage. The first is that management may be too preoccupied with incremental expansion and fail to recognize the need for renewing the facility, improving worker skills, and upgrading operating systems. The second is that the addition of new products/services may be inconsistent with the long-run capabilities of the facility. This is the stage where a facility can become unfocused and lose its competitiveness. To cope with this type of situation, Skinner (1974) proposes the concept of "focused facilities," which will be discussed later in this chapter. The final pitfall is that the facility may be overexpanded to the point where it exceeds its optimal size.

Gradually, expansion of the facility slows down and the facility moves into the third stage, maturation and reinvestment. At this stage, not only is the facility maturing, but so are the work force and production/service delivery processes, especially if management has focused on incremental investment in new products/services and process technologies instead of maintaining existing products/services and processes. An important consideration at this stage is whether some of the products or services can be transferred to other facilities. Ultimately, the facility will be at the stage where management must decide whether to continue to renew, to overhaul, or to shut down the facility. The continued renewal of the facility is largely dependent on whether management has laid the groundwork for ongoing, incremental expansion. Failure to plan for this eventuality would mean that an overhaul is necessary, involving major changes in products/services and markets and investments in new process technologies at the facility. Such changes usually take several years to accomplish and are seldom successful. Schmenner (1983) reports that 46% of the respondents in his survey of plant closings cited inefficient or outdated process technology, layout, or materials handling as the primary reasons. Other reasons for plant closings are significant increases in labor cost, transportation cost, raw material cost, and union- or labor-related problems.

For example, Kmart realized that sales were stagnating in the 1980s and profits were down. Customers perceived the stores' appearance to be dull and antiquated. Kmart's stores were thought to be in the mature and declining stages of their life cycles. Competitors such as Wal-Mart and Sears were using larger spaces to display more merchandise. In response, Kmart formulated a facilities strategy that included modernizing its more than 2000 discount stores and experimenting with a new layout with better signs and lighting and bar-code scanning technology.

FACILITY SIZE AND STRUCTURAL DESIGN

The size of a facility is largely dependent on the capacity strategy because the size of capacity expansion, whether incrementally or in large chunks, impacts the facilities decision. Similarly, the decision on the number of locations is interrelated with the size of a facility. If multiple facilities are to be built, should each facility be identically sized? The solutions to these problems are industry and company specific. For example, Hewlett-Packard's strategy is to build identical facilities around the world such that "if you've seen one, you've seen them all." McDonald's, Hertz, and Marriott Hotels all have similar strategies.

A question that is often raised concerns the optimal size of a facility. Although the optimal size is difficult to identify exactly, an understanding of the factors that affect it is useful. External factors that have an impact on size include government regulations, market conditions, and the competitive environment, whereas internal factors include workforce size, process technology, and organization structure. The well-established trend is toward smaller and more focused facilities (Skinner, 1974; Schmenner, 1976). Lieberman (1989) finds that 96% of U.S. manufacturing plants are small in size, each with less than 500 workers, but collectively these plants account for 61% of total manufacturing employment.

Lieberman (1989) suggests that the optimal size of a facility depends on the trade-offs among the three dimensions of *volume:* (1) scope—the number of items, (2) scale—the total annual volume, and (3) vertical integration—the average number of processing steps that is carried out in the facility. Differences in facility size are motivated primarily by vertical integration economies rather than economies of scale or scope. Businesses with heavy or complex products or services typically pursue vertical integration economies and have the largest facilities, both in number and size. However, it is often necessary to subdivide a large facility into smaller focused units.

Hayes and Wheelwright (1984) observe that the optimal size of a facility lies somewhere between the *minimum* and *maximum* size of a facility. At the facility start-up stage, management is concerned with the *minimum* size that allows the facility to be operationally viable and competitive. As demand increases, the facility moves into the growth stage, characterized by incremental expansion to take advantage of economies of scale. Management must be careful not to expand beyond the threshold, or *maximum* size of a facility, where significant diseconomies of scale set in. Chapter 3 shows the best operating level approach to size.

FACILITY LOCATION

Facility location is the determination of the best possible placement of a facility relative to its customers, suppliers, and other related facilities. The decision to locate a facility should be consistent with the long-term strategic direction of the company and not focused strictly on operating cost and/or marketing issues. The objective is to provide a firm with a competitive advantage obtained by virtue of its location.

Location is strategically more important in industries such as retailing, lodging, and distribution than in others, such as the consulting industry. Ghosh and McLafferty (1984, p. 5) note that "a well-designed location strategy is an integral and important part of corporate strategy for retail firms. Whether selling goods or services, the choice of outlet location is perhaps the most important decision a retailer has to make. . . . Even slight differences in location can have a significant impact on market share and profitability." For example, Wal-Mart's strategy to locate in small communities and avoid direct competition with major discount stores in large metropolitan areas has been very successful. By providing better service and quality products at reasonable prices to its customers, Wal-Mart has a competitive advantage over the small independents and less efficient discounters found in small towns.

Levels of the Location Decision

There are three levels of decisions to be addressed in the plant location problem: (1) selection of the global region or country, (2) selection of the subregion or state, and (3) selection of the community and site. This sequential process is intuitively clear. The "big picture" location factors at the country selection phase are examined first, followed by the more detailed aspects of state and community and site selection. Various location factors are associated with each level; these can be overlapping, with differences in the level of detail. A list of the location factors is provided in Table 4-1. Typically, a company will generate a list of factors that can be further subdivided into: (1) critical factors that must be present for a location even to be considered, and (2) desirable factors that are nice to have but not absolutely essential and can be traded off against one another. The list of factors that are considered critical is both industry and company specific.

Selection of Global Region or Country

The first phase involves deciding whether to locate a facility in the home country or abroad. The global market can be broken up into three key geographic regions: North America, western Europe [European Community (EC) and European Free Trade Association (EFTA) countries], and Pacific Rim. The trend is toward greater global integration; U.S. firms are buying European companies, European companies are investing in the United States, and the Japanese are very active on both sides of the Atlantic. A *Wall Street Journal* survey on the appeal of globalization shows that 20% of CEOs from U.S. companies said they would open a new plant abroad compared to 42% of CEOs in Japan, 36% of CEOs in Europe, and 25% of CEOs in the Pacific Rim countries (Anders, 1989). This indicates that foreign firms appear to place a higher emphasis on a global facility strategy than U.S. companies.

In Harris Bank's series of *Conversations for the 90s: Simple Truths About International Competition*, several experts suggest that in going into a foreign market a corporation should not only look at return on capital but also look at the reasons for the investment— "What are the opportunities?" and "What are the threats if the company does not do it?"

TABLE 4-1   Location Factors and Importance at Different Levels of Decision Making

Location Factor	Global Region or Country Selection	Sub-Region or State Selection	Community and Site Selection
Stability of government	*		
Political structure	*		
Economic growth	*		
Trade barriers—tariff protection, import duties	*		
Federal government policies and regulations	*		
Federal government incentives	*		
Currency exchange rates	*		
Cultural issues	*		
Access to markets	*	*	*
Availability and cost of transportation system	*	*	*
Availability and cost of materials	*	*	*
Availability and cost of labor	*	*	*
Climatic influences	*	*	*
Availability and cost of utilities	*	*	*
Proximity to company's facilities	*	*	*
Environmental regulations	*	*	*
Construction cost		*	*
Community attitude			*
Labor union setup			*
Labor productivity			*
Labor turnover			*
State/local government incentives			*
Availability and cost of land			*
Services—health, fire, and police			*
Educational, recreational, and civic facilities			*
Residential housing			*
Banking services			*

Companies are now finding it necessary to invest in offshore facilities to get better access to markets because of tariff restrictions and other trade barriers imposed by countries or regional blocs to protect their own industries. Some manufacturers have taken advantage of foreign tariffs that enable them to set up facilities while excluding competition from local foreign markets. Before making such a commitment, firms should consider the stability of the government and political system, general attitude, incentives, and policies of the host country toward foreign investors. Other factors to be considered are competitor strategies, major supplier locations, distribution costs, and major customer locations (see Table 4-1).

Many services, unless embodied in goods, are intangible and not storable. As a result, services require simultaneous processing and consumption at the same place and time. Thus, foreign direct investment (FDI) is the predominant mode of delivery in foreign markets. Physical proximity to customers is essential. Thus, if McDonald's wants to sell hamburgers in a particular market, they must set up facilities at the places of demand for its service or engage in franchising. This explains why McDonald's restaurants are found around the world, in far-flung cities such as London, Hong Kong, Kuala Lumpur, Tokyo, and Moscow. Leasing, advertising, investment banking/brokerage, accounting, insurance, and retail trading are examples of services that predominantly use FDI. The information, communication, construction, consulting, software, and transportation industries use a combination of exports and FDI. Table 4-2 provides the competitive advantages of various service industries, important country advantages, and an explanation of the organization form used to penetrate foreign markets.

TABLE 4-2 Competitive Advantages and Country Advantages in Selected Service Industries

Industry	Competitive Advantages	Country Advantages	Organizational Form
Accounting, auditing	• Access to transnational clients • Experience of standards required • Professional expertise • Branded image of leading accounting firms	• On-the-spot contact with clients • Accounting tends to be culture sensitive • Adaptation to local reporting standards • Oligopolistic interaction	• Mostly partnerships or individual proprietorships • Overseas subsidiaries loosely organized, little centralized control
Hotels	• Experience in home countries of supplying up-market services • Experience with training key personnel • Quality control • Referral systems • Economies of geographical specialization, access to inputs	• Location bound when selling a "foreign" service	• Vary, but mainly through minority ventures or contractual relationships
Insurance	• Reputation of insurer, image (e.g., Lloyds of London) • Economies of scale and scope; sometimes specialized expertise (e.g., marine insurance) • Access to transnational clients	• Need to be in close touch with insured (e.g., life insurance, shipping, and finance) • Oligopolistic strategies among large insurers • Government prohibits direct imports; regulatory provisions • Economies of concentration (in reinsurance)	• Mixture; strongly influenced by governments, types of insurance, and strategy of insurance companies
Investment banking	• Reputation of insurer; professional skills • Substantial capital base • Knowledge of and interaction with international capital markets • Finance innovations	• Need to be close to clients • Need to be close to international capital/finance markets, and also main competitors • Availability of skilled labor	• Mainly via 100 percent subsidiaries
Restaurant	• Brand name, service image, quality control • Reputation and experience • Referral systems • Economies of scale and scope • Tie up deals with airlines and hotels	• Location bound	• As with hotels
Software, data processing	• Linked to computer hardware • Highly technology/ information intensive • Economies of scope • Government support	• Location of high skills agglomerative economies often favor home country • Government incentives encourage offshore data entry	• Often part of computer companies

Continued

TABLE 4-2 *Continued*

Industry	Competitive Advantages	Country Advantages	Organizational Form
Transportation, shipping, airlines	• Highly capital intensive • Government support measures, and/or control over routes of foreign carriers • Economies of scope and coordination • Linkages with producing goods firm (in shipping)	• Essentially location linking • Need for local sales office, terminal maintenance, and support facilities (at airports and docks)	• Mostly 100 percent subsidiaries • Some consortia of transnational corporations

Adapted from *Foreign Direct Investment and Transnational Corporations in Services*. United Nations Center on Transnational Corporations, United Nations, New York. 1989.

Setting up facilities in foreign countries requires that management be sensitive to local traditions and customs. For example, when Motorola was close to finishing its $400 million Silicon Harbor complex in Hong Kong, a soothsayer was summoned by the Chinese president of Motorola's Asia-Pacific semiconductor division to check the facility's *feng shui*, (Chinese for wind and water) for good luck. The prognosis was good—the facility was built on reclaimed land, so the project had water, which is a symbol for wealth. Another good omen was the mountains that surround the facility—a source of power to the Chinese. The soothsayer did find that the layout of the executive suite was inappropriate. This required a major renovation to give the president a direct view of the bay with the Horse Shadow Mountain in the background. By going to such lengths to honor local traditions, Motorola has shown its determination to succeed in Japan's backyard. The Hong Kong division is currently one of Motorola's most profitable and fastest-growing semiconductor units (Engardio et al., 1991).

Foreign Investment in the United States.   The United States has been able to attract FDI because of the size of its market. Foreign investment in the United States has been increasing steadily and is predicted to exceed $400 billion per year for the remainder of the decade. The countries with the greatest amount of FDI are the United Kingdom with approximately 30% of the total, Japan with 16%, and the Netherlands with nearly 15%. Although Japan is not the largest foreign investor in the United States, it is worth noting that as much as 50% of corporate Japan's foreign investment ends up in this country. The manufacturing sector accounts for the largest share, with more than 35% of total FDI.

In the early 1980s, Japan was not a major investor in the United States. However, the investment scenario changed dramatically when the U.S. and Japanese governments set up a voluntary restraint agreement to limit the shipment of vehicles into the United States. Japanese firms realized that they have to locate manufacturing facilities in the United States if they wish to continue to increase their share of the U.S. auto market. Honda led the way by building an auto assembly plant in Marysville, Ohio, in 1982. Today, there are eight Japanese transplant facilities assembling automobiles in the United States. Each transplant has a long-term global strategy of locating manufacturing facilities in the markets they serve. For example, Subaru-Isuzu Automotive Inc., which is the smallest and least productive of the transplants, is willing to wait seven years to recover their investment of $550 million (Miller, 1990). According to the Japan External Trade Organization, Japanese corporations have a 10% ownership in more than 1500 U.S. factories. California has the most Japanese companies with 287, followed by Ohio with 121, and Illinois with 112 (Kinni, 1992).

Western Europe.   The Single European Act, ratified July 1, 1987, has established the guidelines for creating a single market "without internal frontiers in which the free movement of goods, persons, services, and capital is ensured" in the 12-nation European Community (EC). In addition, an agreement has been reached between the EC and the European Free Trade Association (EFTA) to create a free trade zone of 19 nations. A unified Europe will have a population of over 355 million and a combined GNP of $5 trillion compared to the U.S. GNP of $4 trillion, potentially making it the world's largest market. A unified Europe presents new opportunities as well as challenges for both European and non-European companies. It has tremendous implications for a firm's location strategy. Increased protectionism is expected to result in more non-European companies setting up manufacturing facilities within the 19-nation customs area.

An established multinational corporation would now need to reconsider the opportunities for greater efficiencies of production and transportation, and more integrated marketing efforts in the EC. Specifically, firms would be encouraged to locate within the area to bring access to the market or to consolidate in one regional facility. In the past, the fragmented markets required local strategies, but a unified Europe calls for a European strategy. For example, Bayer, the German chemical company, is currently producing chemicals in several EC countries but intends to merge production for some of its product lines. Bayer plans to expand its production in Spain for export to other EC countries instead of making products solely for the Spanish market. There is a gradual shift of labor-intensive industries toward southern Europe to take advantage of lower labor costs, with services and high-value-added specialties concentrated in northern Europe. The trend is similar to the migration of industries to the Sunbelt in the United States in the 1950s to 1970s (Magee, 1989).

Pacific Rim.   Whereas a unified Europe may emerge as the world's largest integrated market, the Pacific Rim is the world's fastest-growing economy. Japan is the largest market in the Pacific Rim region; however, its protective policies have limited the opportunity for U.S. firms to penetrate the Japanese market. Yet, companies such as IBM, Motorola, Schick, Coca-Cola, Toys-"Я"-Us, and Amway have shown that it is possible to succeed in Japan.

Many other Pacific Rim countries have probusiness policies, which include offering investors highly attractive incentives, grants, and loan programs to set up manufacturing facilities in the region. For example, Singapore offers investors tax holidays, investment credits, and reimbursement of a substantial portion of employee training costs. The newly industrialized countries of South Korea, Taiwan, Singapore, and Hong Kong, often referred to as the "four tigers," have been the focus of U.S. investments. However, as labor costs rise in the increasingly prosperous economies of the four tigers, manufacturers have in recent years opted for other Asian offshore manufacturing sites such as Malaysia, Thailand, and Indonesia, where wages are relatively lower.

It has been projected by trade experts that U.S. investment in east Asia will exceed $4.4 billion annually. According to Hubbard, Texas Instruments's (TI) president for Asia, "unless you invest in manufacturing capacity, you cannot gain market share" in this region (Kraar, 1991). TI's strategy is to locate design centers and factories close to prime customers in South Korea, Singapore, and Taiwan. Colgate-Palmolive's investments in manufacturing facilities in Thailand have enabled the company to garner 40% of the shampoo market, formerly dominated by the Japanese. Investments in service industries in this region have also taken off. Today, McDonald's sees sales growth coming from overseas markets, especially the Asia-Pacific region. The number of McDonald's restaurants in the region is impressive: 809 in Japan, 277 in Australia, 58 in Hong Kong, 49 in Taiwan, 37 in Singapore, 23 in Malaysia, 6 each in South Korea and Thailand, 1 each in China and Indonesia. Citibank has expanded banking facilities throughout the region, offering a variety of services such as automated teller machines, credit cards, and home equity loans.

North America.   North America (United States, Canada, and Mexico) is one of the world's largest markets. To increase bilateral trade and economic activity, the United States and Canada signed a free trade agreement that took effect in 1989. Shortly thereafter, the United States, Canada, and Mexico began negotiations on the North American Free Trade Agreement (NAFTA) to eliminate a broad range of tariffs and trade barriers. This agreement has been approved by the United States Congress in November, 1993. North American unity has been pursued for more than a quarter century.

Mexico initiated the maquiladora industrial plan in 1965 to encourage foreign investments and to provide more jobs for its people. A maquiladora is a manufacturing facility in Mexico that produces goods from predominantly imported materials, which are then reexported. These manufacturing facilities can have 100% foreign ownership. As noted by Groff and McCray (1991), the major advantages of the maquiladora program are

- *Low labor cost.* A recent U.S. Labor Department study indicates that the hourly wage rate including benefits in Mexico is $1.85 compared with $14.77 in the United States, $21.53 in Germany, $12.64 in Japan, $3.82 in South Korea, and $2.64 in Brazil.

- *Preferential tariff treatment.* Raw materials imported into Mexico are not subject to tariff or duty; only the value added in Mexico is liable. Goods returned to the United States are entirely or partially exempt from tariff, provided that certain conditions are met.

- *Easy transportation and communications links.* Maquiladoras are located near the Mexican–U.S. border and are close to U.S. interstate highway systems. Communication with U.S. companies is generally by phone, although satellite links are becoming popular.

The United States owns nearly 70 percent of the maquiladoras, although European and Japanese firms have invested in similar operations. Ford, General Motors, Chrysler, IBM, Hewlett-Packard, Thomson, Nissan, Matsushita, Sony, Volkswagen, and Samsung are examples of companies that operate maquiladoras in Mexico. Growth in the number of maquiladoras has been phenomenal, with more than 1500 plants operating today. Recently, Zenith announced plans to shift its TV-assembly operations from Taiwan to Mexico, possibly marking the beginning of a trend for U.S. manufacturers with offshore plants in Asia to locate operations "closer" to home.

The North American Free Trade Agreement is expected to continue the growth of this regional market. However, there are concerns in the United States whether NAFTA will create more high-paying jobs to offset displaced workers. In addition, many Americans are concerned with the environmental impact of the agreement.

Selection of Subregion or State

Once the global region or country has been determined, the facility location decision considers a subregion or state inside the country. Markets for most industries tend to be focused on a subregion or state rather than on specific localities. For example, the location of a major hub for an airline company determines how well it is able to serve the needs of customers in that region, increase its customer base, and improve profits. Factors in analyzing the attractiveness of a subregion or state are proximity to market, labor availability and cost, materials availability and cost, transportation system availability and cost, and so on (see Table 4-1).

Changing demographics have dramatically altered the market potential for most businesses. Over the last two decades, the United States has seen a net migration to the South which can be attributed to changes in the economy and life-style. Numerous industries have shifted from the "Rustbelt" to the "Sunbelt" to take advantage of tax incentives and cheaper, nonunionized labor. The South has also seen growth in the electronics industry, which does not rely heavily on rail transportation but rather on trucking and air freight. Other contributing factors are improved communications, climatic influences, widespread use of air conditioning, improved cultural amenities, increased educational opportunities, narrowing of regional differences in standards of living, and lower costs of living.

Selection of Community and Site

After the desired subregion or state has been determined, the community and site must be selected. The community and site selection are grouped in one level because the factors influencing these decisions interact to a large extent. Note that a bad subregion or state choice cannot be remedied by the site selection decisions since the *best* site will not be achieved; instead only the best site within the designated subregion or state is chosen. The objective of site selection is to determine the best possible site over the useful life of a facility. A number of tangible and nontangible factors shown in Table 4-1 must be evaluated before the final choice is made. The challenge is in merging tangible and intangible factors in the decision process.

The selection of a facility site has tremendous long-term social and economic consequences not only for the organization but for the community as well. For example, Kentucky gave Toyota incentives totaling $140 million for worker training, purchase of the 1600-acre plant site, and site improvements. Toyota's investment in the auto plant amounted to nearly $2 billion. Benefits to the community include payroll and other taxes of $1.5 million annually, and payment to the Scott County school system of $15 million over 20 years (O'Boyle, 1991).

Three significant site selection trends are described below:

- *Movement to the suburbs.* Traffic congestion, higher city taxes, and a rise in crime rates, especially in the inner city areas, combined with improved transportation and communication systems, have resulted in a migration of organizations to the suburbs. The advantages are a lower cost of living for employees, better quality of life, and easier plant expansion.

- *Industrial parks.* Industrial parks are large plots of land which are planned and maintained for use by several industries. These parks are usually located next to a major highway or close to a major airport, are industrially zoned with an established infrastructure and utilities, and provide the community with greater employment.

- *Movement to locate close to user.* The Just-in-Time philosophy, which requires suppliers to make more frequent and reliable deliveries to the customers, has greatly influenced the facility location decision. For example, when Honda located its manufacturing plants in the midwestern United States, other Japanese suppliers quickly set up shop nearby.

Evaluation of Alternate Locations

Solving the location problem is a complex process requiring good business judgment and experience, because it involves examining a large number of factors, evaluating data that are often contradictory and conflicting, and reconciling tangible and intangible factors. The tangible factors include those for which estimated costs can be made, such as labor, taxes, utilities, transportation, insurance, pollution control, and sewerage. Although it is important to assess the costs involved, that should not be the only criterion. A recent survey of 600 executives concerning America's best cities for business identified the following attributes as most demanded for a city: (1) a flexible, high-quality work force, (2) proximity to markets, (3) a strong local probusiness attitude, (4) a good public education system, (5) convenient air service to key cities, (6) low costs—housing, labor, facilities, and taxes, (7) an efficient highway system, and (8) "quality of life" (Huey, 1991). Thus, other noneconomic factors must be considered in the evaluation of location alternatives.

When United Parcel Service (UPS), which specializes in package delivery, wanted to move from its home in Connecticut, the final choices were Atlanta, Baltimore, and Dallas. One of the quantifiable factors that led to basing in Atlanta over Dallas/Fort Worth was the travel time and cost involved. The choice of Atlanta would save UPS over two person-years of travel time annually, based on 18,000 commercial air trips per year out of its headquarters. UPS's planned expansion into the European market would also make Atlanta, which is closer to Europe, a better choice than Dallas. Nelson, CEO for UPS, had this to say about the final selection of Atlanta, "I think it was the trees and the rolling hills. They reminded everybody of Connecticut" (Huey, 1991).

Single Facility Location

This section involves the location of a single facility relative to a number of existing facilities. Examples are the location of: new equipment in a machine shop, a copying machine in an office building, a new storage area within an existing plant, a new ware-house to service production facilities and customers, a new plant relative to suppliers and customers, or a hospital, police station, library, or fire station in a city. The objective is to minimize the travel distance, time, or cost. In this case, travel distance is a surrogate for transportation or material handling costs.

Travel distances can be measured in two different ways: rectilinear and euclidean. Eculidean distance is the straight-line measure between two points. Air travel, pipeline design, and conveyor systems are examples of euclidean distances. Another measure is rectilinear distance, which is also referred to as rectangular, metropolitan, or Manhattan distance. It is applicable to machine location problems, where travel in a factory is limited to aisles arranged in rectangular patterns parallel to building walls. Downtown streets in most cities are orthogonally arranged. Hallways and aisles in most offices are arranged similarly.

Techniques abound for solving the single facilities location problem. A solution method using subjective judgment of the location factors is presented in Decision Model Box 4-1. The weighted factor technique permits the simultaneous evaluation of both qualitative (access to market and community attitude) and quantitative (taxes and land costs) factors in one integrated model. A quantitative solution technique, the center of gravity method, is given in Decision Model Box 4-2. The center of gravity method may be used to minimize transportation costs incurred between the proposed facility and the existing facilities. Although the least transportation cost approach ignores other nontangible factors, nonetheless it provides the basis for judgmental modifications when other considerations are included.

Multifacility Location

When an organization has several facilities, management must decide on the effective allocation of particular products/services, processes, customers, and markets to specific facilities. Geographical network analysis can be used by firms in the basic materials or heavy commodity industries, where transportation costs dominate the total delivered cost of a product, or by companies customizing products or in service industries, where proximity to markets and customers is a prerequisite.

Schmenner (1982) suggests four types of multiplant manufacturing strategies: product plant, market area plant, process plant, and general purpose plant. In the product plant strategy, each plant focuses on manufacturing a distinct set of products or product lines to serve a well-defined market niche. This strategy allows process technology, equipment, and organization to be consistent with the appropriate competitive priorities, such as cost, quality, product flexibility, and delivery performance, that are associated with the plant's products. When a company has several product lines, each with high demand, it makes sense to use this strategy. By focusing on only a limited set of manufacturing tasks, the plant can benefit from economies of scale or scope. Typically, these plants are located in one or two regions around the country. Examples of companies using the product plant strategy are Colt Industries, Fairchild Industries, and Insilco.

A market area plant strategy calls for a plant to manufacture a majority or all of the company's products to serve a particular market. This strategy is applicable when transportation costs are high relative to the product's cost, demands are spread over a large geographic area, or customers require fast delivery. Companies that manufacture food, glass, can, and building products are likely to use the market area plant strategy. For example, Anheuser Busch has breweries located at several geographic locations to cater to regional market needs.

DECISION MODEL BOX 4-1 Weighted Factor Technique

The Buckeye Supply Company has identified five cities within Franklin County as possible locations for its new facility. Four factors have been identified by management as important to the location decision. Weights are given to each location factor to reflect its relative importance. The weights that are solicited from management must sum to 100%. A score (1 = poor to 10 = best) is given to each location based on how well the site is rated on each factor. What is the best location?

Scores of the five locations are shown below.

Location Factor	Weight	Columbus	Upper Arlington	Worthington	Bexley	Gahanna
Access to market	40	9	10	8	7	6
Community attitude	30	5	7	10	8	9
Taxes	20	6	9	9	9	10
Land	10	10	6	8	5	7

The operations manager computed the following weighted score (weight $\times$ factor score) for each location.

Location Factor	Weight	Columbus	Upper Arlington	Worthington	Bexley	Gahanna
Access to market	40	360	400	320	280	240
Community attitude	30	150	210	300	240	270
Taxes	20	120	180	180	180	200
Land	10	100	60	80	50	70
Total weighted score	100	730	850	880	750	780

Worthington has the highest total weighted score and is therefore selected. If the two best sites have identical total weighted scores or the difference in scores is minimal, further investigation might be warranted. For example, additional location factors could be included for further evaluation of these two sites.

Process plants can be viewed as a series of feeder plants that manufacture the components to be sent to one or more final assembly plants. This approach allows a plant to take advantage of economies of scale by scheduling high-volume production of the products on specialized equipment. The strategy is applicable to the auto, computer, and machine tools industry, where the products are complex, and to industries such as shoes, apparel, and chemicals, where significant economies of scale can be realized. This strategy is also appropriate for vertically integrated industries such as aluminum and forest products which are linked closely to sources of energy or natural resources.

The general-purpose plant strategy involves responsibility for a variety of products, market areas, process segments, or some combination of these responsibilities. The

DECISION MODEL BOX 4-2 Center of Gravity Method

The McCreery Company is investigating where to locate a new plant relative to two warehouses (A and B) and two suppliers (C and D). The following information has been obtained.

Location	Coordinates in miles (x_i, y_i)	Weight of Goods in tons (W_i)
Warehouse A	(50, 120)	1000
Warehouse B	(80, 50)	1500
Supplier C	(110, 90)	3000
Supplier D	(120, 70)	2500
Total		$\sum_i W_i = 8000$

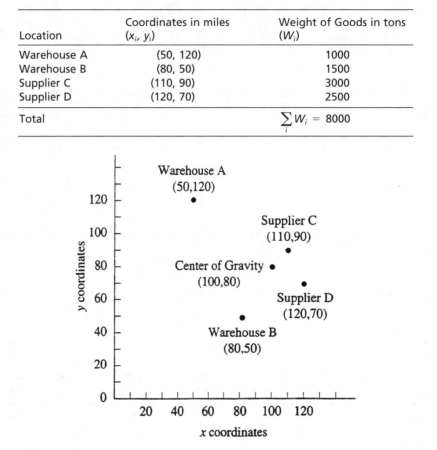

Management decided to use the center of gravity approach to locate the new facility. The center of gravity approach determines the location that minimizes the euclidean squared distance. The coordinates of the center of gravity are computed as:

$$X^* = \frac{\sum_i W_i x_i}{\sum_i W_i} = \frac{50(1000) + 80(1500) + 110(3000) + 120(2500)}{(1000 + 1500 + 3000 + 2500)}$$

$$= \frac{800,000}{8000} = \underline{\underline{100}}$$

$$Y^* = \frac{\sum_i W_i y_i}{\sum_i W_i} = \frac{120(1000) + 50(1500) + 90(3000) + 70(2500)}{(1000 + 1500 + 3000 + 2500)}$$

$$= \frac{640,000}{8000} = \underline{\underline{80}}$$

where X^* = x-coordinate of the center of gravity
Y^* = y-coordinate of the center of gravity
x_i = x-coordinate of the location i
y_i = y-coordinate of the location i
W_i = load (e.g., number of trips, volume of goods) traveling between the new facility and location i

The "best" location for the new facility is (100, 80). If, however, subjective factors required that the facility be located near a major population center, judgmental adjustment of the site by, possibly, five miles in any direction should be considered.

concern here is with flexibility of the facility and the ability to adapt to frequently changing product needs. Government defense contractors in the aerospace and shipbuilding industries use this strategy.

Network Approaches

Trus Joist Corporation (Wheelwright, 1975), a manufacturer of customized roof and floor support systems, was under tremendous competitive pressures from two fronts—small as well as large firms in the construction industry. The smaller firms had numerous local sales and distribution outlets and thus were able to provide faster delivery service to customers. The larger firms took advantage of economies of scale and were very cost competitive. Trus Joist realized that to compete in this market against both the large and the smaller firms it would have to develop cost effective, low-volume production processes and then set up a network of small production facilities all over the United States to improve customer service delivery. The "spider web" facilities strategy permitted Trus Joist to improve its market position. Improved sales in a particular region enabled them to expand the facility to take advantage of economies of scale.

The "hub-and-spoke" network strategy has been particularly popular in the airline industry. Airlines identify major hubs to serve a region. Major airline hubs in New York and Washington serve the northeastern United States; Chicago and Detroit serve the midwestern United States; Atlanta, Miami, and Dallas serve the southern United States; and Seattle, Los Angeles, and San Francisco serve the western United States. Federal Express uses a similar approach in the package delivery industry. Packages are collected nightly by Federal Express offices all over the United States, transported to the hub at Memphis and then rerouted to their final destinations. Although the hub-and-spoke strategy was extremely successful in the United States, it did not work particularly well in Europe, because regulations imposed by different countries made it difficult to centralize operations. This difficulty might ease when EC integration is realized.

FACILITY LAYOUT

Facility layout involves the optimum arrangement of a facility to obtain a smooth flow of goods, services, people, and information. A well-planned layout can lead to an increase in product and process flexibility, improvements in product/service quality, reductions in manufacturing/service delivery cost, good housekeeping and maintenance, effective use of space, improved safety and employee morale, better communication between workers and supervisors, and a reduction in material handling costs. Thus, layout of a facility can directly impact the performance areas of cost, quality, flexibility, and customer delivery. In addition, facility layout has long-lasting effects because product/service, process technology, operations, marketing, distribution, and human resource plans will be impacted by and will have an impact on the layout.

Although often neglected, safety is a very important consideration in designing the layout of a facility. For example, Du Pont estimates it saves between $150 to $200 million annually as a result of its stringent safety program (Calise, 1991). Du Pont's policy statement, established in 1911, states: "No employee may enter a new or rebuilt mill until a member of top management has personally operated it." The design of a layout must be closely integrated with product or service, process technology, schedule, and handling systems design. It should be evaluated for its impact on personnel requirements in terms of space, separation of workers, and special facility features. For example, the paint shop or sand-blasting facility should be located away from other work areas for environmental and safety reasons.

Types of Layout

There are three basic types of layout for a facility: fixed position, process, and product. Hybrid approaches such as the cellular and modular layouts are becoming increasingly popular and are also discussed. The three basic layouts and the cellular layout are shown in Figure 4-2. The selection of a particular layout is greatly influenced by the type of industry it supports. The physical organization of the layout of a facility is discussed next.

Fixed Position Layout

In this type of layout, the position of a product or customer is fixed and materials, equipment, workers, and the like are transported to and from the product or customer. Fixed position layouts favor industries where the products are very bulky, massive, or heavy, and movement of the product is problematic. Examples are shipbuilding, large aircraft assembly, oil drilling, and most construction projects. In construction projects, a portion of the fabrication work may be done in the factory before the fabricated pieces are transported to the customer's site for final assembly work.

In some service industries, it is often necessary to make repairs at the site of the problem. For example, stores offer in-house repair of large-screen TV sets, furnaces, or other large appliances. Convenience is another reason for using a fixed position layout. Recently, several auto-lube companies have begun experimenting with customer site routine maintenance service. The service crew drives to the customer's location, provides the necessary service, and leaves for the next assignment. The customer pays a premium for the service of not having to turn in and collect the car at the service facility.

Process Layout

In a process or functional layout, similar processes or functions are grouped together. This layout is often called a "job shop" layout. A process layout is used when the volume of parts to be produced does not warrant the use of a product or cellular layout. The flow of the products or customers through the departments does not follow any fixed pattern. Examples are machine shops, hospitals, universities, automobile repair shops, tailor shops, department stores, and supermarkets. In a machine shop, lathes, milling machines, drills, and so on are grouped together by function. The flow of jobs through the shop is best described as a jumbled flow. In a hospital, X-ray machines are located in one department, laboratories in another, and so on. Patients are moved from one area to another depending on the type of service required. A university is organized by colleges and departments. Students pursue different degrees and attend different classes, moving from one room or building to another. A process layout for Kmart's hypermarket is illustrated in Application Box 4-1.

The biggest advantage of a process layout is the flexibility that helps the facility to cater to the production of nonstandard items or provide customers with a variety of services in the same facility. The objective is to maximize the utilization of the equipment.

FIGURE 4-2 Four Types of Layout

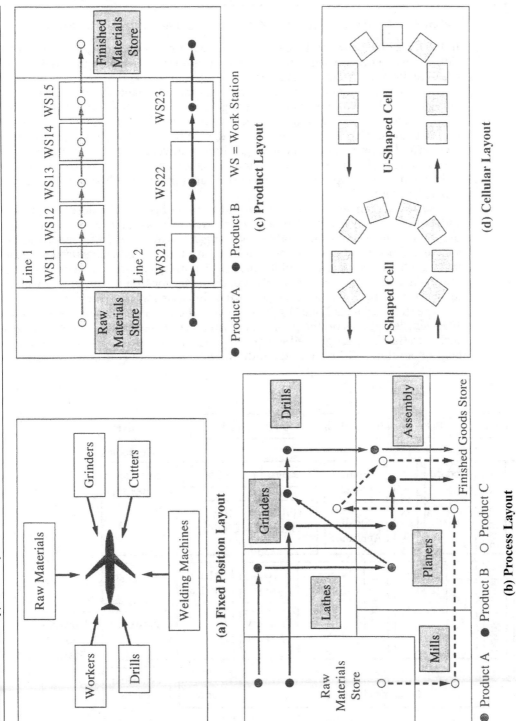

(a) Fixed Position Layout

(b) Process Layout

● Product A ● Product B ○ Product C

(c) Product Layout

● Product A ● Product B WS = Work Station

(d) Cellular Layout

APPLICATION BOX 4-1 Layout of Kmart's Hypermarket (American Fare)

In 1989, the first American Fare hypermarket was opened in Stone Mountain, outside Atlanta, Georgia. American Fare is a joint venture between Kmart and Bruno's, a leading food retailer in the Southeast. The hypermarket is simply a typical Kmart discount store integrated with a supermarket. American Fare operates in a trading area of over one million consumers living within a 30-minute drive of the store. According to Larry Parkin, Kmart's executive vice president of warehouse and grocery operations, "We will be known for food, children's clothing, toys, leisure adult apparel and footwear, home decorating, home improvement, horticulture, sporting goods, and health and beauty aids. Our perishables, apparel, horticulture, and toys will be particularly impressive and go beyond anything currently being offered in a super store format."

Customers can be assured of speed and accuracy because the store is equipped with 80 scanning checkouts. Reordering for inventory is done electronically through the point of sales system. The food section is organized to create a marketplace atmosphere as if people were shopping on a street in a little town. A large portion of the merchandise is featured on mobile modules, allowing changes to be made to the presentation quickly, and to replenish goods in the stockroom. The store is willing to invest extra money on lighting and fixtures but saves with concrete floors.

The store occupies 244,000 square feet and there is a parking lot that can hold 1800 vehicles. Spaces on the perimeter of American Fare are leased to companies such as: a Handleman operated store that carries CDs, movies, and tapes; a Waldenbooks bookstore; a Citizens and Southern Bank; a card and gift specialty shop; a

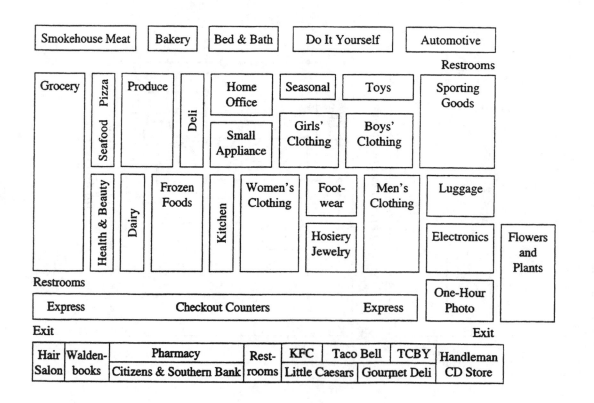

pharmacy; and a hair salon. There is a food court that includes Taco Bell, TCBY, Kentucky Fried Chicken, and food stands run by Little Caesars, Gourmet Pizza, and Gourmet Deli.

_____

Materials drawn from Jay L. Johnson. "American Fare Opens in Atlanta," *Discount Merchandiser,* February 1989, pp. 28–30, and from Jay L. Johnson, "Kmart's Hypermarket: American Fare," *Discount Merchandiser*, March 1989, pp. 32–40.

The disadvantages are greater handling of material/customers, more complex scheduling and control activities, problems in one department not readily visible in another department, higher work-in-process or the build-up of customers in front of departments.

Product Layout

The product layout arranges the processes or work stations in the sequence in which the product is manufactured or the service is rendered. This layout is also referred to as a production line or assembly line. Although a straight line appears to be the most logical for the shape of the layout, the Japanese have suggested using U- or C-shaped lines, which provide for closer communications. In a manufacturing environment, the raw materials enter at one end of the line and exit at the other end as finished products. In a service environment, customers are serviced in an orderly sequence as they move from one station to the next before exiting the facility. This type of layout is suitable for high-volume production with standardized products or services. Work-in-process and handling of materials/customers are minimized. The equipment is highly specialized and capital intensive. Manufacturing examples are automobile assembly and small appliances assembly. Service examples are: processing of mail by the U.S. Postal Service, check processing by a bank, and preparation of hamburgers in a fast-food restaurant.

The output of a production line is dependent on the slowest work station. To maximize the line output, the line must be balanced, that is, activities are assigned to each work station to obtain similar work cycle times at all work stations. An unbalanced line means that there are resources that are not fully utilized, representing waste that should be eliminated. Because of the large number of ways that tasks and operations can be assigned to several work stations, line balancing is a challenging and complicated problem. Although numerous techniques such as linear programming and dynamic programming are available, less complicated heuristic and trial-and-error methods are commonly used. An example of a heuristic procedure for balancing an assembly line is presented in Decision Model Box 4-3.

Cellular Layout

The cellular layout involves grouping a number of machines in a cell to produce a family of parts that require similar processing (see Figure 4-2). This layout is a hybrid layout representing a cross between the product and process layout. Cellular layout often uses group technology (GT), which groups parts according to similarities in processing requirements. Part grouping criteria include size, shape, and routing sequence. The machines are arranged for line flows in a U- or C-shaped layout to minimize the workers' walking distance and to improve communication flows for quicker identification of manufacturing inefficiencies. With this layout, one or more workers can operate several machines in a cell. A major advantage of the U-shaped layout is that it provides flexibility in moving workers within the cell to balance operations. Other advantages include reductions in space requirements, material handling, setups, lead time, and work-in-process inventories.

Modular Layout

When a layout has to be reconfigured frequently to accommodate changes in requirements for space, equipment, and people arising from a redesign of existing products/services,

DECISION MODEL BOX 4-3 Assembly Line Balancing

The Lewis Company plans to produce whistling tea kettles on its assembly line at its Nittany Lion manufacturing facility. Management has identified the following operations required to produce the kettle.

Operation	Description	Time (minutes)	Immediate Predecessor(s)
A	Fabricate body	1.13	—
B	Fabricate base	0.51	—
C	Weld body to base	2.55	A, B
D	Fabricate spout	0.21	—
E	Weld spout to body	2.55	C, D
F	Grind off excess weld	1.75	E
G	Buff	2.45	F
H	Construct handle	4.58	—
I	Construct lid lever	2.96	—
J	Construct lid	3.65	—
K	Assemble handle, lid, and lid lever	1.25	H, I, J
L	Screw handle to body	1.52	G, K
M	Inspection	2.65	L
	Total	27.76	

The assembly line must be able to handle an output rate of 60 tea kettles per day. Although the factory works an eight-hour day, the actual productive time is only seven hours after deducting time for lunch and coffee breaks. Holly, a graduate operations management major, balanced the line using a six-step process with a primary rule of "largest number of following operations" and a secondary rule of "longest operating time." What is the performance of the line?

Step 1. Diagram the sequential relationships. Nodes represent operations and arcs denote the sequence.

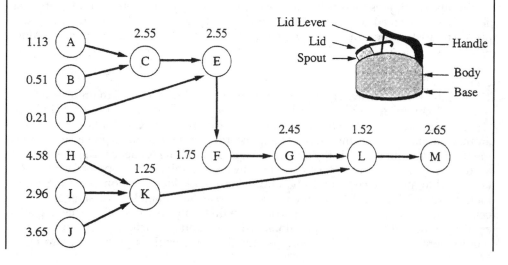

Step 2. Calculate the cycle time (C) based on the desired output rate and the theoretical minimum number of work stations (N^*) (round fractional values up).

$$C = \frac{\text{total operation time per day}}{\text{units of output per day}} = \frac{\text{7 hours (60 minutes per hour)}}{\text{60 units}}$$
$$= 7.00 \text{ minute/unit}$$

$$N^* = \frac{\text{sum of all operation times } (T)}{\text{cycle time } (C)} = \frac{27.76}{7} = 3.97 = \underline{\underline{4}}$$

Step 3. The primary decision rule to assign operations to a work station is the "largest number of following operations." Ties are broken with the secondary rule of "longest processing time."

Ranking of Operation	Primary Rule Largest Number of Following Operations	Secondary Rule (Tie Breaker) Longest Processing Time
A	6	1.13
B	6	0.51
C	5	2.55
D	5	0.21
E	4	
H	3	4.58
J	3	3.65
I	3	2.96
F	3	1.75
G	2	2.45
K	2	1.25
L	1	
M	0	

Step 4. Assign each operation to a work station, starting with the first station, based on the specified decision rules so that the sum of all operation times in the station does not exceed the cycle time and precedence relationships are satisfied. Proceed to the second station when no more operations can be added because of time or sequence requirements. Stop when all operations are accounted for.

Work Station	Time Remaining	Feasible Operations	Selection (Time)	Cumulative Time	Idle Time
1	7.00	A, B, D, H, J, I	A (1.13)	1.13	5.87
	5.87	B, D, H, J, I	B (0.51)	1.64	5.36
	5.36	C, D, H, J, I	C (2.55)	4.19	2.81
	2.81	D, H, J, I	D (0.21)	4.40	2.60
	2.60	E	E (2.55)	6.95	0.05
2	7.00	H, J, I, F	H (4.58)	4.58	2.42
	2.42	F	F (1.75)	6.33	0.67
3	7.00	J, I, G	J (3.65)	3.65	3.35
	3.35	I, G	I (2.96)	6.61	0.39
4	7.00	G, K	G (2.45)	2.45	4.55
	4.55	K	K (1.25)	3.70	3.30
	3.30	L	L (1.52)	5.22	1.78
5	7.00	M	M (2.65)	2.65	4.35

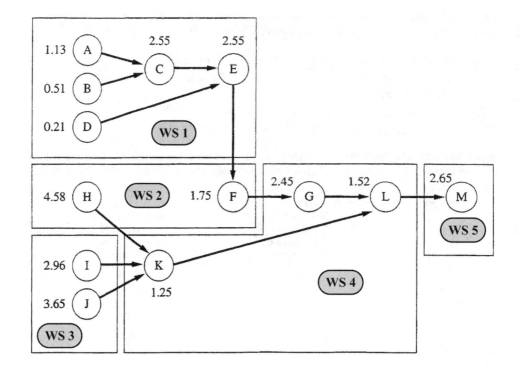

DECISION MODEL BOX 4-3   *Continued*

Step 5. Compute the performance of the line as:

$$\text{Life efficiency}(E) = \frac{\text{sum of all operation times } (T)}{\text{number of work stations } (N) * \text{cycle time } (C)}$$

$$= \frac{27.76}{5(7)} = \underline{\underline{0.793}}$$

Line imbalance $= 1 - E = 1 - 0.793 = \underline{\underline{0.207}}$
Idle time $= N*C - T = 5(7) - 27.76 = \underline{\underline{7.24}}$

Step 6. The line can be rebalanced by using some other rules, such as select operation with the shortest time first, and select operation with the highest positional weight first. The positional weight is the sum of the operation's time and all following operation times. General Electric's Assembly-Line Configuration (ASYBL$) program uses this decision rule. Determine if the line balancing result is sensitive to changes in operation times. Note that this solution used five stations, while the theoretical minimum number of stations is four. There is not always a solution that uses only the theoretical minimum. In this case $N* = 3.97 = 4$. Since $N*$ is so close to a whole number, it is unlikely that there is a solution that uses only four stations. However, if we can reduce the inspection time for operation *M* to less than 1.78 minutes, the fifth station can be eliminated.

elimination of existing products/services, or introduction of new products/services, it is advantageous to plan for change and develop a flexible layout. A flexible layout is one that can be changed, expanded, or reduced without much difficulty. The modular design concept is one approach to achieving layout flexibility. Modular designs are applicable to offices, industrial plants, and service facilities. Texas Instruments has designed several manufacturing facilities by applying the modular design concept to its production/service areas, offices, and warehouses. TI's objective is to "achieve a system effect—a facility in which all functions are served by a system of components using the fewest parts to satisfy the most demand. This modular system is composed of small elements that allow us [TI] to meet custom requirements with off-the-shelf components, rather than creating equipment dedicated to a single function" (Tompkins and White, 1984, p. 248).

Focused Facilities

When a company is growing rapidly, a proliferation of products/services can occur over time. The facility could be saddled with an increasing number of products/services to meet diverse market needs. Firms try to expand on site to minimize capital investments

---

APPLICATION BOX 4-2 Focusing of Factory at Cummins Engine

The Cummins Engine Company, a manufacturer of diesel engines, had tremendous success and held a 50% market share through the mid-1970s. Until that time, Cummins enjoyed a stable product line which enabled high-volume production on dedicated machining lines with high efficiencies. The environment changed quickly when federal regulations and intense competition from Komatsu and Caterpillar necessitated faster product introductions. This meant shorter product life cycles. The factory had to contend not only with producing replacement parts for existing models but also with manufacturing new engine families and options in the same facility. For example, for just one engine family there are 86 different flywheels, 49 flywheel housings, 17 starter motors, and 12 possible mounts, which explains why there are more than 100,000 parts in the sales catalogue. Compounding the problem of parts proliferation was the mandate from management to the factory to reduce lead time and cost. The conflicting demands placed on the factory by the variety of products required a reexamination of the factory organization. To accomplish the goals set by management, Cummins realized that it had to "focus the factory not only by product but also by volume." Cummins reorganized its facilities, using a four-step procedure (Venkatesan, 1990):

1. Lay out the factory into product-focused cells, routing families or similar products across tightly clustered groups of machines.
2. Once production is running smoothly, reorganize again, dividing the factory conceptually into different classes of production on the basis of volume, design stability, and predictability of demand.
3. Map each product, depending on its production requirements, onto the appropriate class of production machinery. Making parts on the wrong class of equipment—low-volume parts on transfer lines, for example—leads to a loss of flexibility, inefficiencies, and eventually, uncompetitiveness.
4. Continuously manage the transition of parts from one class of production to another as product life cycles evolve.

Benefits from the reorganization include: materials handling reduced by 95%; floor space reduced by 30%; work-in-process decreased by 50%; and lead time reduced by 50%.

———
Material drawn from Ravi Venkatesan, "Cummins Engine Flexes Its Factory," *Harvard Business Review*, March-April 1990, pp. 120–127.

and spread overhead over a wider range and volume of products/services. The objective is to take advantage of "economies of scale," a concept that is often poorly understood and misapplied by managers. Schmenner (1976, p. 77) notes that the phrase "economies of scale" is "so vague that it can be used to justify any number of decisions, which all too often turn out to be wrong." The increased product mix results in increasing complexity and conflicting manufacturing tasks within one facility. Skinner (1974, p. 114) notes that:

> *A factory that focuses on a narrow product mix for a particular market niche will outperform the conventional plant, which attempts a broader mission. Because its equipment, supporting systems, and procedures can concentrate on a limited task for one set of customers, its costs and especially its overhead are likely to be lower than those of the conventional plant. But more importantly, such a plant can become a competitive weapon because its entire apparatus is focused to accomplish the particular manufacturing task demanded by the company's overall strategy and marketing objective.*

When a company is faced with multiple product/service lines, process technologies, markets, or volumes, Skinner (1974, p. 121) suggests using the plant-within-a-plant (PWP) concept to achieve focus: "Each PWP has its own facilities in which it can concentrate on its particular manufacturing task, using its own work-force management approaches, production control, organization structure, and so forth. Quality and volume levels are not mixed; worker training and incentives have a clear focus; and engineering of processes, equipment, and materials handling are specialized as needed." The PWP approach, or other techniques to focus a facility, allows management to easily realign operations and system elements as market needs change over time. Application Box 4-2 describes how Cummins Engine has refocused its factory.

Systematic Layout Planning

Systematic layout planning (SLP) is a qualitative approach to layout planning developed by Muther (1973). An analysis is performed initially to determine the process flow. The analysis of material flows is especially important when large and bulky materials are handled, when handling costs are high compared with cost of operations, or when a large number of moves is required. Next the intensity of the flows between departments is established. The resulting flows are converted into traditional A-E-I-O-U-X closeness relationships and placed into an activity relationship chart. Basically, a relationship chart shows each of the activity's relationship with other activities, the importance of the closeness between these activities, and reasons for the proximity requirements. For example, in a manufacturing plant, the finished goods storage and shipping should be close together because of the flow of materials. The activity relationship chart is then converted into a space relationship diagram, which shows the size of the department and the magnitude of movement between departments. Based on practicality and feasibility considerations, several alternative layouts are developed using space templates representing each department. Often experience, judgment, and intuition are important elements in the generation of good layout alternatives. After careful evaluation, the preferred layout is then recommended. An example illustrating the SLP procedure is provided in Decision Model Box 4-4. For more complex layouts, computerized procedures, discussed in the next section, may be necessary to generate layouts based on the activity relationship chart.

Computerized Layout Planning

Instead of using manual, analytical, or subjective procedures for solving the layout problem, computers can be used to generate a number of solutions quickly. In addition, a computer has the capability to solve much larger problems involving huge amounts of data. It should, however, be pointed out that the computer is an aid, not a substitute for human involvement in the decision process. In the final analysis, managers must make the critical

DECISION MODEL BOX 4-4 Systematic Layout Planning

Berardi Custom Decor Corp. designs and manufactures a wide range of interior furnishings for many nationwide fast-food restaurants such as McDonald's and Hardees. Berardi used the systematic layout planning technique to develop the layout for its manufacturing facility, which has nine departments. Initially, a process flow analysis is used to define relationships among the activities. Then, an activity relationship chart for the nine departments is constructed. Next, a space relationship diagram is drawn. Based on this information, a layout is recommended.

Activity Relationship Chart

The activity relationship chart identifies the work areas that should be located in close proximity and those that should not. The space relationship diagram then identifies the amount of space required and shows the closeness requirement by the number of lines (A = four lines, E = three lines, etc.) When the relationships of the space layout diagram are established, the proposed layout is much more easily visualized.

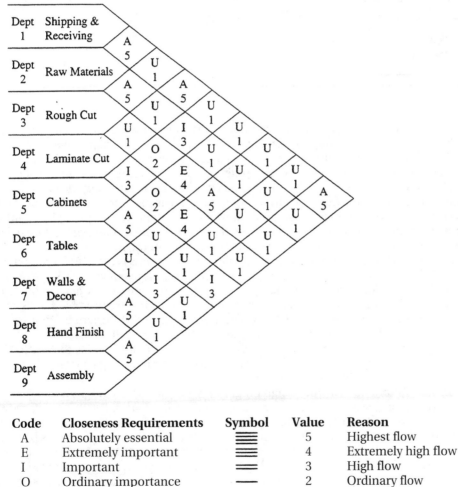

Code	Closeness Requirements	Symbol	Value	Reason
A	Absolutely essential	≡≡≡	5	Highest flow
E	Extremely important	≡	4	Extremely high flow
I	Important	=	3	High flow
O	Ordinary importance	—	2	Ordinary flow
U	Unimportant		1	Low flow
X	Not desirable	〜〜〜		

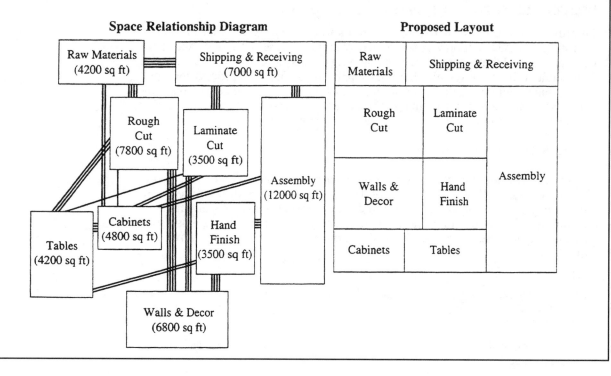

Space Relationship Diagram

Raw Materials (4200 sq ft)
Shipping & Receiving (7000 sq ft)
Rough Cut (7800 sq ft)
Laminate Cut (3500 sq ft)
Assembly (12000 sq ft)
Cabinets (4800 sq ft)
Hand Finish (3500 sq ft)
Tables (4200 sq ft)
Walls & Decor (6800 sq ft)

Proposed Layout

Raw Materials
Shipping & Receiving
Rough Cut
Laminate Cut
Walls & Decor
Hand Finish
Assembly
Cabinets
Tables

decision on which layout best meets their objectives. The solutions from these computerized layout programs are only approximate, with the work centers or departments arranged in blocks. These outputs must be modified to guarantee a practical and useful design.

The solution procedures for the computerized layout planning use either construction of improvement methods. Construction techniques are normally used when a layout is being designed for the first time; they "construct" a feasible first layout. Improvement procedures require an initial design as input which they iteratively improved. The initial layout could be the existing layout or one generated by a construction procedure. However, none of these procedures can guarantee optimality of the solutions.

One of the earliest computerized layout planning programs is **CRAFT** (Computerized Relative Allocation of Facilities Technique), which is an improvement technique (Armor and Buffa, 1963). A pairwise interchange of departments is iteratively carried out until no further reduction in the total cost is possible. The cost is measured by the distance moved between departments. **COFAD** (Computerized Facilities Design) is an improvement procedure that jointly develops a layout and material handling system that tries to minimize both movement and handling costs (Tompkins and Reed, 1973). **SPACECRAFT,** which is an extension of **CRAFT,** allows large-scale layout planning problems in multistory buildings to be addressed (Johnson, 1982).

ALDEP (Automated Layout Design Program) is a construction program that seeks to maximize the closeness between departments (Seehof and Evans, 1967). The procedure uses a relationship chart to provide the subjective input to develop a layout plan. As shown in Decision Model Box 4-4, an activity relationship chart shows the interactions between departments and the reasons for the proximity of departments. **CORELAP** (Computerized Relationship Layout Planning) is another construction program that develops layouts based on subjective inputs provided by a relationship chart (Lee and Moore, 1967). The objective is to maximize the closeness between desired departments. **PLANET** (Plant Layout Analysis and Evaluation Technique) is a versatile construction program that allows

TABLE 4-3   Principles of Materials Handling

1. Minimize the number of material moves.
2. Maximize the unit load handled, that is, move full as opposed to partial unit load.
3. Maximize safety of materials handling equipment.
4. Simplify the materials handling process.
5. Design materials handling equipment that will maximize space utilization.
6. Integrate storage and handling systems.
7. Integrate materials and information flows.
8. Minimize human effort in materials handling.
9. Design for improved operability, reliability, and maintainability.
10. Design materials handling equipment to be sufficiently flexible to operate under various conditions.

three alternative methods of specifying material flow data and three algorithms for constructing layouts (see Deisenroth and Apple, 1972 for more details).

MATERIALS HANDLING SYSTEMS

Materials handling is an integral part of a facilities strategy. The term *material* is used broadly to refer to finished goods, work-in-process, raw materials, purchased parts, packaging materials, maintenance and repair supplies, scrap, and rework in a manufacturing plant; to products in a warehouse or distribution center; to checks, money, and customers in a service business; to mail in a post office; and to airline passengers in a transportation system. Tompkins and White (1984, p. 116) define materials handling as using "the right method to provide the right amount of the right material at the right place, at the right time, in the right sequence, in the right position, in the right condition, and at the right cost."

Materials handling involves more than just handling; it includes storage and control of materials. Therefore, materials handling must be integrated with facilities layout as well as with manufacturing/service, distribution, and information systems. For example, sufficient space must be provided for a conveyor system. Similarly, the structure and foundation of a facility must be strong enough to support an electric overhead crane running along gantry rails. Designing a facility without considering the storage and retrieval system seriously limits the amount of useful storage space. Fitting a materials handling system to a layout after construction is completed could present serious problems and involve considerable time and effort to remedy the situation.

It has often been stated that materials handling "adds cost but not value" to a product or service. The axiom is "Never move anything that does not need to be moved." With that in mind, there is a need to simplify handling by eliminating, reducing, or combining unnecessary movements. It is estimated that materials handling represents 10 to 80% of the product/service cost depending on the type of facility. Miller and Vollmann (1985) note that transaction costs represent 10 to 20% of total manufacturing overhead costs. Transaction costs include costs of ordering, execution, confirmation of materials movement from one area to another, costs of personnel in receiving, shipping, expediting, data entry, and processing, and so on. These costs are directly related to the materials handling system. Thus an improved handling system can have a major impact on the company's total operating system and presents significant potential for cost saving and improved productivity.

There are several objectives in choosing a materials handling system:

1. Increasing the speed and precision with which materials (customers) are moved through the facility, that is, removing any bottlenecks in the system.

TABLE 4-4   Materials Handling Equipment

1. **Automated Guided Vehicle (AGV)**
   Driverless vehicle that transports materials, guided by magnetic, chemical, or optical devices along defined routes on the floor. AGVs are used in assembly-line operations, flexible manufacturing systems, storage/distribution systems, etc.

2. **Automated Identification Systems**
   Automatic identification systems use various technologies to automatically collect product data for entry into a computer. The computer processes the data, which can be used to track, account for, and control movement of materials speedily and accurately. Examples are bar codes, machine vision, magnetic strips, optical character recognition, and radio frequency identification.

3. **Automated Storage/Retrieval System (AS/RS)**
   AS/RS is defined as "a combination of equipment and controls which handles, stores, and retrieves materials with precision, accuracy, and speed under a defined degree of automation" (The Material Handling Institute, 1977). The components of an AS/RS are the storage structure, the crane that stores and retrieves the materials, unit load containers such as pallets and bins, pickup and deposit stations, and computerized control system.

4. **Conveyors**
   Conveyors are best suited to move large volumes of material repetitively between fixed points in a facility and are used to transport bulk as well as discrete materials. Conveyors can be installed on the floor or overhead, depending on operating needs or space limitations. Typically, the flow of materials is in one direction only.

5. **Hoists and Cranes**
   Hoists are manually, electrically, or pneumatically driven devices that are used to lift and lower large and heavy materials. Cranes have hoists mounted on steel structures that run on rails installed on the floor or on gantries. Typically cranes are used to move and position materials in a limited area within the facility.

6. **Elevators**
   A cage or car attached to a hoist through cables to raise or lower people or materials in a building or mine. In high-rise buildings, hotels, and apartments, elevators are absolutely necessary to transport people between floors.

7. **Escalators**
   A moving stairway comprised of steps linked in a continuous belt used in buildings, department stores, subway stations, and the like to move people from one floor to another. Horizontal escalators are used in large airports to transport people quickly from one area to another on the same floor.

8. **Pipelines**
   Pipelines are used to transport fluids such as petroleum and natural gas over long distances using either electric pumps or gravity flows.

9. **Trucks**
   Trucks are termed *variable path equipment* and allow much greater flexibility in moving materials than conveyors in a facility. Trucks can be diesel, electric, gasoline, or manually powered.

---

2. Maximizing the use of space and equipment.
3. Increasing safety and working conditions to allow employees to work more efficiently.
4. Reducing damage.
5. Increasing the amount of control that managers have over the handling process by improving data gathering and processing.

The principles of materials handling are presented in Table 4-3.

There are many reasons why an organization considers improvement of its present materials handling operations. Problems can arise that are not immediately perceived to be associated with materials handling. They often represent symptoms of inefficient materials handling such as excess idle time, crowded receiving areas, delays in shipping orders to customers, and high error rates. The more common materials handling devices are described in Table 4-4.

FINANCIAL ANALYSIS OF FACILITIES INVESTMENTS

DECISION MODEL BOX 4-5 Financial Analysis of Investment in a New Plant

The Minor Paper Company (MPC) is analyzing a proposal to build a pulp mill in Virginia. The initial cost of investment is incurred at the start of year 1. The plant is depreciated over an eight-year period using the straight line method. The plant is assumed to have no salvage value at the end of eight years. Estimated annual sales and variable operating costs are shown in the table below. Currently, the marginal income tax rate is 40%. MPC's cost of capital is 10%. Management would like to compute the following: payback period, ROI, NPV, PI, and IRR. There is some concern that the cost of capital could go as high as 12%.

Proposal to Invest in a New Pulp Plant (in Thousands of Dollars)

End of Year	Investment	Sales	Costs	Before-Tax Cash Flow[1]	Depreciation[2]	Profits[3]	Tax on Profits[4]	After-Tax Profits[5]	After-Tax Cash Flow[6]
0	$1600								
1		$ 800	$ 710	$ 90	$200	$(110)	$(44)	$(66)	$134
2		900	450	450	200	250	100	150	350
3		950	500	450	200	250	100	150	350
4		1000	500	500	200	300	120	180	380
5		1100	500	600	200	400	160	240	440
6		1100	500	600	200	400	160	240	440
7		1100	600	500	200	300	120	180	380
8		1200	800	400	200	200	80	120	320
Total	$1600	8150	4560	3590	1600	1990	796	1194	2794

[1]Before-tax cash flow = sales − costs.
[2]Depreciation = (1600/8) = 200 per year.
[3]Profits = before-tax cash flow − depreciation.
[4]Taxes = (tax rate)(profits) = 0.40 (profits). A loss is indicated by a number in parentheses.
[5]After-tax profits = before-tax profits − taxes.
[6]After-tax cash flow = before-tax cash flow − taxes.

The operations officer assisted in calculating the following financial measures.

a. $\text{Payback} = \dfrac{\text{initial investment}}{\text{average after-tax cash flow}} = \dfrac{1600}{(2794/8)} = \underline{4.6 \text{ years}}$

b. $\text{ROI} = \dfrac{\text{average annual after tax profits}}{\text{average beginning-of-year investment (book value)}} = \dfrac{(1,194/8)}{900} = 0.166 = \underline{16.6\%}$

[*Note:* Average beginning-of-year investment

$= \dfrac{(1600 + 1400 + 1200 + 1000 + 800 + 600 + 400 + 200)}{8} = 900$]

DECISION MODEL BOX 4-5 *Continued*

c. $\text{NPV} = \left[\dfrac{CF_1}{(1+i)^1} + \dfrac{CF_2}{(1+i)^2} + \cdots + \dfrac{CF_n}{(1+i)^n} \right] - \text{initial investment}$

$= \left[\dfrac{134}{1.10^1} + \dfrac{350}{1.10^2} + \dfrac{350}{1.10^3} + \dfrac{380}{1.10^4} + \dfrac{440}{1.10^5} + \dfrac{440}{1.10^6} + \dfrac{380}{1.10^7} + \dfrac{320}{1.10^8} \right] - 1600$

$= 199.4 \Rightarrow \underline{\$199,400}$

where CF_n = cash flow for year n
i = cost of capital

d. Profitability index (PI) $= \dfrac{\text{NPV}}{\text{initial investment}} = \dfrac{199.4}{1600} = \underline{0.125}$

e. IRR = discount rate for which NPV is equal to zero. For the new pulp mill, IRR = 13%.

f. If the cost of capital is 12%, the only changes are to NPV and PI. Payback, ROI, and IRR remain the same.

$\text{NPV} = \left[\dfrac{134}{1.12^1} + \dfrac{350}{1.12^2} + \dfrac{350}{1.12^3} + \dfrac{380}{1.12^4} + \dfrac{440}{1.12^5} + \dfrac{440}{1.12^6} + \dfrac{380}{1.12^7} + \dfrac{320}{1.12^8} \right] - 1600$

$= 63.0 \Rightarrow \underline{\$63,000}$

$\text{PI} = \underline{0.039}$

Hayes and Wheelwright (1984) use a framework for evaluating the financial attractiveness of a proposed investment that comprises the following:

1. *Security—How quickly will the investment be recovered?*
    A common measure of security is payback, the number of years required to return the initial investment. For example, in the semiconductor industry it is common for companies to require paybacks on new investments to be less than two years. The volatile environment characterized by shorter product cycles, obsolescence of process technology, and shortage of capital due to rapid industry growth explains why a short payback is deemed necessary.

2. *Recompense—What is the return on investment?*
    After a company has decided that the payback period is acceptable, it is necessary to measure the expected earnings that will be generated from the project. Financial measures of recompense are return on investment (ROI), internal rate of return (IRR), net present value (NPV), and profitability index (PI).

3. *Predictability—What is the level of confidence regarding the anticipated returns from this investment?*
    Sensitivity analysis is carried out to deal with the impact of uncertainty on a proposed investment. For example, what is the impact on payback if the cash inflows are 10% lower than estimated, or what happens to the internal rate of return if the initial investment is 5% higher than predicted?
    An example of financial analysis of facilities investment is provided in Decision Model Box 4-5. It must be pointed out that financial analysis is not the only approach to support an investment. It is increasingly necessary to justify an investment based on strategic considerations where long-term market positioning is more important than short-term performance.

SUMMARY

This chapter has discussed the four components of facilities strategy: size and structural design, location, layout, and materials handling system. It has been emphasized that facilities strategy has major implications for the competitiveness of an operation, and thus for the firm. A facility typically represents a company's largest investment and therefore a company is committed to the facility for a long time once it is built. Facilities strategy must be integrated with operations strategy and other components of the business strategy. Inputs must be obtained from marketing, distribution, purchasing, product/service design, process design, production/staff scheduling and control, and so on. In addition, facilities strategy should be proactive instead of a piecemeal reaction to changing conditions.

In making location decisions, it is necessary to first identify the global region or country. The globalization of markets requires a rethinking of the way companies view their facilities strategies. Western Europe and the Pacific Rim represent tremendous growth markets for businesses, and failing to recognize these opportunities can be potentially disastrous. The formation of a free trade zone comprising Mexico, Canada, and the United States also has tremendous ramifications for a company's facilities strategy and profitability. In entering a foreign market a corporation should not only consider return on capital but also examine the consequences of not entering and the opportunities for entering the market. After a country has been selected a subregion or state is identified. This is followed by the selection of a suitable community and site.

Layout decisions are an important part of facilities strategy. This chapter has identified three basic layouts: fixed position, process, and product. The modular design concept (hybrid layout) provides for maximum flexibility to respond to change. The hybrid cellular layout has been shown to be efficient and to improve communications. Layout decisions must be integrated with materials handling decisions. Since materials handling adds cost but not value to a product or service, it is best not to move anything that does not need to be moved.

DISCUSSION QUESTIONS

1. What are the four components of facilities strategy?
2. What are the stages of a facilities life cycle?
3. Describe Kmart's approach to facilities strategy in its overhaul of more than 2000 discount stores. Is this strategy proactive or reactive?
4. What are the major advantages of building maquiladora plants in Mexico?
5. Discuss three trends that must be considered in determining community and site location.
6. What is the objective in single facility location? Also discuss the two types of measures used.
7. List five types of facility layout and provide an example of a situation in which each layout might be used.
8. How did Cummins Engine take advantage of the plant-within-a-plant (PWP) approach to develop a focused facility? Give the four steps that Cummins followed and the benefits realized.
9. Define the three phases of decision making in determining a plant location. In what way(s) can the list of location factors be subdivided into smaller groups?
10. Discuss some of the new opportunities and challenges offered by a unified European community.
11. What are some of the objectives in choosing a materials handling system?
12. Describe the factors that led General Motors to choose Spring Hill, Tennessee, as the location for its Saturn automobile plant.
13. What are the principles underlying the concept of the focused facility?

1. The Speedy Distribution Company is considering four midwestern cities as possible locations for its warehouse and distribution facility. Five factors have been identified by management as key variables in the location decision. Weights (which sum to 100) have been assigned by management to each factor according to its relative importance. A score from 1 to 10 is given to each location based on its rating for each factor. A score of 1 signifies a poor rating, and a score of 10 is the best possible rating. Which location is most appealing to management?

Location Factor	Weight	Chicago	Cincinnati	Detroit	Green Bay
Access to market	30	6	5	4	3
Access to suppliers	30	7	5	6	3
Community attitude	10	3	7	4	9
Taxes	10	3	6	6	7
Land	20	2	3	2	8

2. The Hilo Company currently has four warehouses A, B, C, and D and is considering building a new plant to service these warehouses. The locations of the warehouses and the expected volume of goods transported between the new plant and the four warehouses are shown in the table below. Use the center of gravity approach to determine the location of the new plant.

Location (W_i)	Coordinates (x_i, y_i)	Volume of Goods in Tons
Warehouse A	(6, 11)	200
Warehouse B	(11, 3)	250
Warehouse C	(12, 7)	175
Warehouse D	(10, 8)	225

3. The SolarCalc Company is setting up an assembly line in its Indiana manufacturing facility for its solar calculators. Management has identified the following operations required to produce the calculators.

Operation	Description	Time (seconds)	Immediate Predecessor(s)
A	Mount frame on jig	10	—
B	Insert solar-powered batteries	15	A
C	Insert power circuit	20	B
D	Insert chip into frame	26	A
E	Insert display into frame	24	A
F	Solder circuit connections	45	C, D, E
G	Insert keyboard	20	F
H	Install top body	16	G
I	Install bottom body	16	G
J	Test calculator	30	H, I
K	Packaging	20	J
	Total	242	

The assembly line must be able to produce 1728 calculators per day. The factory runs on three shifts of 8 hours per day. Balance the line, using a primary decision rule of selecting the operation with the shortest processing time first and a secondary rule of selecting the operation with the largest number of following operations. What is the line efficiency? What steps can management take to try to improve the solution?

4. The ElbowGrease Company, makers of fine car wax, are considering investing in a new canning machine that would increase capacity. The following estimates have been made. The initial cost of the machine is $120,000; this investment is incurred at the beginning of year 1. Depreciation of the machine is over a 10-year period using straight line depreciation. It is assumed that the machine will have no salvage value at the end of 10 years. The increases in annual sales and operating costs are given in the table below.

End of Year	Sales	Operating Costs	End of Year	Sales	Operating Costs
1	60,000	36,000	6	80,000	48,000
2	70,000	42,000	7	80,000	48,000
3	80,000	48,000	8	80,000	48,000
4	80,000	48,000	9	80,000	48,000
5	80,000	48,000	10	60,000	36,000

The marginal income rate is 35%, and the cost of capital is estimated at 12%. ElbowGrease is looking for a payback period of 6 years. Should the project be authorized? What other financial measures should be computed? What would be the decision if the cost of capital is 15% instead of 12%?

REFERENCES

Anders, George. "Going Global: Vision vs. Reality," *Wall Street Journal.* September 22, 1989.

Armour, G. C., and Elwood S. Buffa. "A Heuristic Algorithm and Simulation Approach to Relative Location of Facilities," *Management Science.* Vol. 9, No. 2, 1963, pp. 294–309.

Calise, Angela K. "Du Pont Workers 'Shocked' by Co.'s Tough Safety Plan," *National Underwriter.* August 12, 1991, pp. 8, 46.

Deisenroth, M. P., and J. M. Apple. "A Computerized Plant Layout Analysis and Evaluation Technique (PLANET)," *AIIE Technical Papers*, Twenty-Third Conference of the American Institute of Industrial Engineers, Anaheim, Calif., 1972.

Drucker, Peter F. "New Strategies for a New Reality," *Wall Street Journal.* October 2, 1991, p. A12.

Engardio, Pete, and Maralyn Edid. "Why a 'Little Detroit' Could Rise in Tennessee," *Business Week.* August 12, 1985, p. 21.

Engardio, Pete, Lois Therrien, Neil Gross, and Larry Armstrong. "How Motorola Took Asia by the Tail," *Business Week.* November 11, 1991, p. 68.

Foreign Direct Investment and Transnational Corporations in Services. United Nations Center on Transnational Corporations, United Nations, New York, 1989.

Ghosh, Avijit, and Sara L. McLafferty. *Location Strategies for Retail and Service Firms.* Lexington, Mass.: Lexington Books, 1987.

Groff, James E., and John P. McGray. "Maquiladoras: The Mexican Option Can Reduce Your Manufacturing Cost," *Management Accounting.* January 1991, pp. 43–46.

Hayes, Robert H., and Steven C. Wheelwright. *Restoring Our Competitive Edge.* New York: John Wiley & Sons, 1984.

Huey, John. "The Best Cities for Business," *Fortune.* November 4, 1991, pp. 52–70.

Johnson, Jay L. "American Fare Opens in Atlanta," *Discount Merchandiser.* February 1989, pp. 28–30.

Johnson, Jay L. "Kmart's Hypermarket: American Fare," *Discount Merchandiser.* March 1989, pp. 32–40.

Johnson, Roger V. "SPACECRAFT for Multi-Floor Layout Planning," *Management Science*. April 1982.

Kinni, Theodore B. "Keiretsu in America," *Quality Design*. December 1992, pp. 24–31.

Kraar, Louis. "How Americans Win in Asia," *Fortune*. October 7, 1991, pp. 133–140.

Lee, R. C., and J. M. Moore. "CORELAP—Computerized Relationship Layout Planning," *Journal of Industrial Engineering*. March 1967, pp. 194–200.

Lieberman, Marvin B. "Optimal Plant Size," Research Paper #1058, Graduate School of Business, Stanford University, August 1989.

Mandel, Michael J., and Christopher Farell. "How to Get America Growing Again," *Business Week*. 1992 special/bonus issue, pp. 22–24.

Miller, Edward K. "The Transplants: State of the Industry 1990," *Ward's Auto World*. January 1990, p. 23.

Miller, Jeffrey G., and Thomas E. Vollmann. "The Hidden Factory," *Harvard Business Review*. September–October 1985, pp. 141–150.

Muther, Richard. *Systematic Layout Planning* 2nd ed. Boston, Mass.: Cahner Books, 1973.

O'Boyle. Thomas F. "To Georgetown, Ky., Toyota Plant Seems a Blessing and a Curse," *Wall Street Journal*. November 26, 1991.

Schmenner, Roger W. "Before You Build a Big Factory," *Harvard Business Review*. July–August 1976, pp. 77–81.

Schmenner, Roger W. *Making Business Location Decisions*. Englewood Cliffs, N.J.: Prentice Hall, 1982.

Schmenner, Roger W. "Every Factory Has a Life Cycle," *Harvard Business Review*. March–April 1983, pp. 121–129.

Seehof, J. M., and W. O. Evans. "Automated Layout Design Program," *Journal of Industrial Engineering*. December 1967, pp. 690–695.

Skinner, W. "The Focused Factory," *Harvard Business Review*. May–June 1974, pp. 112–121.

Sorge, Majorie A., and Stephene E. Plumb. "Can Saturn Keep the Revival Meeting Going?" *Ward's Auto World*. Vol. 5, 1990, pp. 43–49.

Taylor III, Alex. "Back to the Future," *Fortune*. August 1, 1988, pp. 67–72.

Tompkins, James A., and John A. White. *Facilities Planning*. New York: John Wiley and Sons, 1984.

Tompkins, James A., and R. Reed, Jr. "Computerized Facilities Planning," *AIIE Technical Papers 1973*, Twenty-Fifth conference of the American Institute of Industrial Engineers, Chicago, Ill., 1973.

Venkatesan, Ravi. "Cummins Engine Flexes Its Factory," *Harvard Business Review*. March–April 1990, pp. 120–127.

Wheelwright, Steven C. Trus Joist Corporation (Case 9-675-207), Boston: Harvard Business School, 1975.

Whiteside, David, Richard Brandt, Zachary Schiller, and Andrea Gabor. "How GM's Saturn Could Run Rings Around Old-Style Carmakers," *Business Week*. January 28, 1985, pp. 27–28.

CHAPTER 5

OPERATIONS SYSTEM DESIGN

It is no trick to formulate strategy—the trick is to make it work.

Objectives

After completing this chapter you should be able to:

- Identify the stages of the operations system life cycle and show how those stages affect product/service, process technology, and facility decisions.
- List and describe the classical operations system alternatives.
- State the key variables of the product/service–process continuum and show the costs of operating "off the diagonal."
- Describe product/service and process focus and diffusion and note how emerging process technologies and business practices facilitate the diffusion of operations.
- Identify the levels of the operations system design hierarchy and how management decisions are integrated among the levels.

Outline

INTRODUCTORY CASE: HOW APPLE GREW

In early 1976, two computer engineers pieced together parts of a television screen, a circuit board, a cassette tape recorder, and a typewriter keyboard to create a prototype personal computer. Steve Jobs and Steve Wozniak later presented the model at a computer hobbyist club. Jobs convinced this group of the value and potential market for his product. The first order was for 100 fully assembled and tested personal computers. Each circuit board was hand-assembled and then placed in a case. The first fifty machines were produced in Jobs' home, after which the work areas were moved to the garage. The product was simply named "Apple."

In the early years, Apple struggled to maintain its competitive edge in the new market. The primary focus was on the unique and innovative technology, evident in the second model, which offered an expandable memory from 4 thousand to 48 thousand bytes. As demand for the product increased, Apple and its approximately 25 employees moved to a nearby office building, where the small management team stringently curtailed operating costs and pursued their technological advantage. Apple's focus was on designing, educating, and marketing. Outside manufacturers were used to produce anything that Apple could not internally produce more cheaply. The business was growing rapidly, and neither time nor expense could be spent to master the rudimentary skills necessary to produce reliable components. Large quantities of printed circuit boards were purchased externally and tested by outsiders in order to insure quality in the least costly and most time-efficient way.

In early 1979, operations were relocated to a new facility, 15 times the size of the prior space. The manufacturing department now consisted of one supervisor and 28 employees, who manually built approximately 30 computers per day at various work stations. Another group built and shipped 15 disk drives per week. New employees were being added each week to keep up with rapidly growing demand. However, flexibility of the production

---

Materials drawn from Lee Butcher, *Accidental Millionaire*, 1988; and Regis McKenna, *Who's Afraid of Big Blue?* 1989; and John Markoff, *Beyond the PC: Apple's Promised Land*, 1992.

process decreased as management emphasized high volume at low cost and greater customer delivery responsiveness through efficient planning and scheduling.

By September 1980, 130,000 Apple IIs had been sold and the payroll topped 1000 employees. The company occupied 15 buildings in Silicon Valley, California; large-scale assembly-line manufacturing was accomplished in Texas. Warehouses existed throughout the United States and the Netherlands, and production plants had opened in Ireland and Singapore. Components were increasingly mass produced at company plants. In order to manage the business more effectively and pinpoint profit and loss areas, divisions were formed to produce disk drives, personal computer systems, and office systems.

Apple maintained its leading edge position through the 1980s with such innovations as the touch screen, laser disk storage, desk-top publishing, and graphics. What began as a project to build several prototypes has expanded through numerous stages of development, including job-shop and line assembly processes, to become a publicly held, divisionalized, multinational company—all in less than 10 years. Apple is expected to continue to grow through the 1990s with innovations in lap-top and miniature computers, including the powerbook portable computer and portable personal organizers like the Newton, and with programming and interface functions that make the products more friendly, versatile, and easy to use.

Design of an Operations System

While capacity and location decisions involve the inputs and interactivity of most staff activities, as well as of top management, the design of the operations system, which includes manufacturing, distribution, and service delivery, more directly involves the operations function. In fact, the design of the operations system is likely the most important planning and control decision made primarily by the operations manager and operations staff. In addition, the system design is strategically important, because it is directly related to productivity and to the four competitive priorities, cost, quality, delivery, and flexibility. Typically, all director staffs will be involved in the higher levels of operations system design decisions, such as capacity and facilities location, but once those decisions are made, other decisions are usually made by the operations manager.

As the introductory quotation suggests, it is easy to formulate strategy for capacity and facilities strategy; the tough part is implementation of the operations system. The difficulty occurs because even the best capacity and location strategies provide only a rough framework; operations system design decisions establish the mechanisms of production or service delivery.

This chapter defines operations system design, describes the classic operations processes, and then introduces the product-process continuum, a matrix for strategic positioning of corporate resources. The conflicting requirements for flexibility and focus are discussed, and several emerging operations and system management methods and business practices are considered. Finally, the process technology selection hierarchy is introduced as a means of integrating long- and mid-range operations system decisions with short-range and scheduling procedures.

Operations System Life Cycle

Like people and facilities (Chapter 4), operations systems, including products, services, and process technologies, have lives. Like the lives of people, these lives may be stable and successful, or turbulent and unsuccessful, depending upon how well they are managed. As Derks (1993) notes, the focus of the operations manager is to satisfy the customer and thereby the company stakeholders. The product/service–process technology life cycle, with seven identifiable stages, is the conceptual foundation for the classification and management of the operations system as it is conceived, grows, matures, then declines and is renewed. The seven stages of the life cycle, first introduced in Chapter 1, with their primary activities, are

1.	Birth of the operations system	Identification of the need for the product or service, description of how the product or service works, and the conceptualization of process technology to produce or deliver it
2.	Product/service design and process technology selection	Definition of the form and appearance of the product or added value of the service and specification of the process technology
3.	Design of the operations system	Creation of the operations system and the system management facilities
4.	Start-up of the operations system	Building of the initial product on the production system or delivering the initial service
5.	Growth of volume	Modification of the product/service and expanding production and distribution systems to meet customer demand
6.	Stable state	Production in consistent volumes with carefully planned resources
7.	Decline and renewal of the system	Cessation of production or delivery, shut-down of the facility, and return of the resources to an acceptable state for subsequent reuse

The classification of these seven stages is important because different decisions are made and different management capabilities are required at each stage. The first stage is a conceptualizing and planning stage, which involves extensive use of analytic and evaluative models to assess the feasibility of the product or service. In the second stage, prototype products, sample services, and scale models of the process technology are prepared to show product or service and process technology viability. Stage 3 involves a major funding commitment to build the facility. Chapter 1, Dimensions of Operations Strategy, describes the decisions of the first two stages and Chapter 4, Facilities Strategy, primarily describes the closely related third stage. This chapter makes some general comments about the third stage, and then concentrates on the final four stages of the life cycle.

Product/service and process technology each change in corresponding ways as the system grows through the last four stages of the life cycle. As the product or service evolves from initial production through growth and stable state to decline of the model and renewal by either redesign or a follow-on line, the process also may evolve from a fixed project to small batch mode, to a line flow, and then to continuous production. the correspondence of the final four stages of the product/service and the process technology life cycles and related industry characteristics is shown in Figure 5-1.

Note that, as the product/service and process technology are evolving, so too are the structure and competitive criteria of the industry. Initially, the industry consists of very small shops or offices that are competing on the basis of flexibility. As the market grows, demand tends to become more specific in product/service definition, and there is a consolidation as successful firms adopt standardized technologies and a fallout (or failure) of other firms. With mature markets, the competition among the few (not more than 10 or 15) major firms in the global marketplace is based on consistent delivery, as well as price (cost). In declining markets, price (cost) becomes the key competitive variable among the survivors. The management of the developing product/service and process technology interrelationship over the life cycle of the system is called *operations system design*— it is a very complex task, requiring both focus on system objectives and flexibility to adjust to changing environmental and technology conditions.

FIGURE 5-1 Product/Service and Process Technology Life Cycles

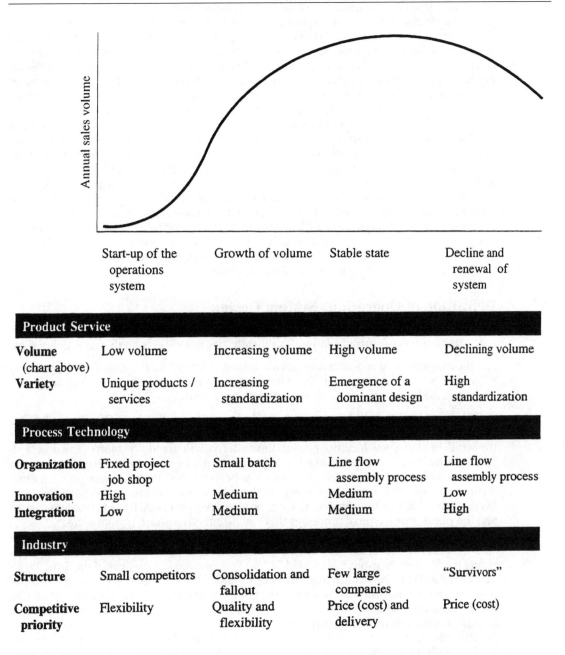

	Start-up of the operations system	Growth of volume	Stable state	Decline and renewal of system
Product Service				
Volume (chart above)	Low volume	Increasing volume	High volume	Declining volume
Variety	Unique products / services	Increasing standardization	Emergence of a dominant design	High standardization
Process Technology				
Organization	Fixed project job shop	Small batch	Line flow assembly process	Line flow assembly process
Innovation	High	Medium	Medium	Low
Integration	Low	Medium	Medium	High
Industry				
Structure	Small competitors	Consolidation and fallout	Few large companies	"Survivors"
Competitive priority	Flexibility	Quality and flexibility	Price (cost) and delivery	Price (cost)

The introductory case describes the phenomenal growth of Apple Computers and the corresponding changes in production methods. Note that Apple Computers has sequentially gone through several life-cycle stages; however, if an organization has system design experience, it may move quite rapidly to the stable state. For example, despite the extensive product and process innovations, Saturn moved quickly through the start-up and growth stages. Yet examples of declining operations are also just as relevant. Though some firms are able to be successful by doing things in the traditional way, such tradition-oriented processes often become uncompetitive. For example, the Baxter Health Care Corporation Surgical Instrument manufacturing facility in Skokie, Illinois, was scheduled to close because the line manufacturing process was not cost competitive. At the last minute, a management team argued for a process redesign from the assembly line to a work cell. The change, initially implemented as a test on one line, resulted in labor reductions of roughly 50% and productivity improvement of about 400%. Though the final decisions have not been made, the redesign of other lines is proceeding and the reorganization will likely save the facility.

The facility life cycle (Chapter 4) corresponds very closely to the final four stages of the product/service and process technology life cycle, and facilities decisions are closely involved with stage 3, start-up of the operations system. Effective management of products/services and process technologies can prevent the early failure of a facility, enhance facility growth, and prolong the stable state stage, thus avoiding a gradual and insidious slide into mediocrity and decline. According to Schmenner (1983), the key symptoms of sliding into mediocrity are the proliferation of product variations, the ignoring of process technology advances, the repeated use of small expansions, and labor problems. One of the most important ways these difficulties can be controlled is by focusing the facility on one process technology. Thus, products/services and process technologies, and often the facility, are managed over several stages of the operations system life cycle with attention to the requirements of both focus and flexibility.

Definition of Operations System Design

The design of an operations system involves products/services and process technologies, and often extends to entire facilities. Specifically, operations system design is defined as

the integration of products and service delivery with the facilities and process technologies over the life cycle of the operations system, which permits production of goods and services at desired quality, volumes, and costs.

Operations system design is constrained by several considerations. Of course, there are the obvious issues of feasibility and acceptability. The availability of funding might preclude the acquisition of a new facility, and thus limit alternatives to modification of existing facilities. Alternatively, some process technologies might not be acceptable. The use of nuclear reactors for power generation, for example, has been unacceptable in some political jurisdictions. Within those limitations, however, there are further constraints on both the number and type of products or services that can be effectively produced by an operations system and the number and type of processes that can be effectively used by that system.

Though the operations system may not be limited to one technology, there is a constraint on the number or range of different process technologies that can be efficiently used in one facility. For example, Sasser et al. (1982) describe the experiences of the Time Products Division (TPD) of Texas Instruments Company. TPD separated the final assembly of watches and the assembly of the electronic components of those watches into two facilities because the technologies of those two processes were sufficiently different that they could not efficiently use one operations system or be managed by one management group. Additionally, as the TPD final assembly line was balanced, there were several "nonstandard operations" which, because of length or variability of task time, were done "off line." Further, the specifications of several parts could not be changed to facilitate assembly by TPD, even though those parts were produced by another division of Texas Instruments.

This example identifies the necessity to separate different process technologies, the importance of smooth and consistent production flows, and the requirement to integrate product/service design between two or more vertically integrated facilities. Operations system design thus involves the integration of product/service specification and process selection procedures over the life cycle of the operations system, though primarily starting with stage 3 and continuing to stage 7. The management of this process is constrained by the requirement to focus the facility, to control the production flow, and to be flexible in an often rapidly evolving environment.

Classical Operations System Alternatives

Process technologies are classically defined as fixed position projects, process (or job shop) flows, and product (or line) flows. This distinction of classical process alternatives was described in Chapter 4 and is based on differences in equipment and materials movement, the nature and variety of labor skills required, and the information and process management characteristics. The typical physical layout pattern of these process technology alternatives is shown in Figure 4-2. The three classical process technology alternatives are supplemented by several more specific classifications, including small batch, large batch, continuous flow, intermittent lines, and repetitive flow. Though these elaborations add specificity and applicability, the three classical terms define the conceptual dimensions of process alternatives. The characteristics of classical process technology alternatives are listed in Table 5-1.

The project is exemplified by construction of a bridge, a highway, a large ship, an airplane or a building, a consulting project, property remodeling, an in-house maintenance program, custom-tailored clothing, or an entertainment production. The project is characterized by disposition of materials around a fixed production site and the flow of materials toward the site. High labor training and skill are required, and each hour of labor adds high value to the process. Projects usually have a large work in process and uncertain scheduling, which necessitate estimating, sequencing, and work-pacing evaluation methods.

The process, or job shop, flow is exemplified by printing or machine tools companies and some photographic processing. Service applications include most automobile maintenance and repair, fitting and tailoring of off-the-rack clothing, standardized consulting services, and restaurant food preparation and service. Job shops typically have numerous patterns of material flow, depending upon the requirements of the job, and require high skills and training with broad job content and high labor value added. Setups are frequent and the process is slow. Schedules are changed as jobs are expedited, delayed, or resequenced to make more efficient use of equipment or available materials or to respond to changing customer requirements. The challenge of the job shop operation is to minimize the effects of bottlenecks and to maximize the utilization of critical resources, often human skills, to deliver quality goods and services on schedule.

Finally, the line (product) flow is represented by a variety of different processes. Hydroelectric power generation or petroleum and sugar refinery operations represent a continuous flow of indistinguishable individual products. Alternatively, the assembly of most large durable goods uses a discrete line flow that may be broken at one or several points, like the Texas Instrument TPD line, to accommodate activities that are highly variable or take long periods of time. An intermittent line may be used when a flow is periodically broken, as with the printing of a newspaper. The line is set up for each edition by redefining the size of the paper and the content of the pages. Service examples of a line process include mail sorting operations and cafeteria-style meal selection. The classic product flow operation has a clear and rigid flow of materials with each product following in exactly the same sequence. The labor contribution is relatively low, particularly in highly automated operations, and material requirements and inventories vary predictably. Numerous tools are used to optimize resources in often inflexible and costly processes.

There are many different classifications of the operations processes, but all classifications assist in characterizing manufacturing, distribution, and service operations. With allowances for more specific process technology alternatives, the continuum from projects to process flow and to product/service flow operations is a useful way to structure process concepts. Thus, the potential flexibility of an operation is extremely important.

TABLE 5-1 Classical Process Technology Alternatives

Characteristic	Project	Job Shop	Line Flow
Equipment and Physical Layout Characteristics			
Size of facility	varies	small	large
Process flow	from circumference	numerous patterns	rigid flow
Type of equipment	general purpose	general purpose	highly specialized
Capital intensity	varies	low	very high
Capacity addition	incremental	small changes	large chunks
Bottlenecks	constant shift	shifting	predictable, stationary
Speed of process	varies	slow	fast
Control of pace	worker	worker and supervisor	process design
Set-ups	each job	frequent, inexpensive	infrequent, expensive
Technology change rate	slow	average speed	fast
Direct Labor and Work Force Characteristics			
Labor value added	high	average	very low
Job content scope	large	average	small
Skill level	high	average	low
Wage rates	high	average	low
Worker training	very high	high	low
Material and Information Control Characteristics			
Material requirements	varies	unpredictable	very predictable
Vertical integration	none	limited	backward and forward
Inventories			
Raw materials	none	small	large
Work in process	large	large	very small
Finished goods	none	small	very high
QC responsibility	direct labor	direct labor	QC specialists
Product/service information	very high	high	low
Scheduling	uncertain	many changes	inflexible
Process Management Characteristics			
Challenges	estimating	labor utilization	avoid downtime
	sequencing	debottlenecking	time expansions
	pacing	learning curves	cost minimizing
Tools	PERT/CPM	load charts	line balancing
			linear programming

REQUIREMENT FOR PROCESS FLEXIBILITY

There are three ways in which a production process can be flexible: changeover flexibility, scheduling flexibility, and innovation flexibility. These sources of flexibility were suggested as an increasingly important basis for the definition of competitive priorities, particularly as industry approaches the twenty-first century. Even today, in many industries, flexibility has become the key criterion, due to the costs and risks of the dynamic and global environment.

Process Flexibility

Numerous definitions and categorizations of the term "flexibility" have been offered (Gerwin, 1982; Brown, 1984; and Leong et al., 1990). Simply stated, flexibility allows the

TABLE 5-2 Categories of Process Flexibility

Type of Flexibility	Responds To	Subcategories of Flexibility
Changeover flexibility	product/service variations (market driven)	product/service volume product/service range product/service mix product/service modification
Scheduling flexibility	availability of resources (resource driven)	materials equipment labor
Innovation flexibility	product/service, process technology, or information (technology driven)	process technology process control technology

operations manager to deploy or redeploy resources in response to variations in products/ services, availability of resources, or process technology.

Each of the three types of process flexibility corresponds to a type of operation system variation. That is, changeover flexibility redeploys resources to different products or services, scheduling flexibility redeploys available resources in response to shortages or unavailability of other resources, and innovation flexibility redeploys resources to changed products/services or processes. These types of flexibility are further elaborated in Table 5-2.

Changeover flexibility allows greater response to product/service variations, either of product/service family volume, range, item mix, or product/service modification needs. Changeover flexibility can accommodate minor modifications of product specifications, but major modifications of product specifications would likely require resource (scheduling) and process (innovation) modifications as well. The different categories of process flexibility thus are highly interrelated. The requirement for changeover flexibility often occurs as a result of changes in the marketplace and thus is considered to be market driven. For example, manufacturers of durable goods, such as automobiles, diesel engines, appliances, and CRT tubes find that mixing different models of product in the production process sequence reduces inventory and improves productivity.

Scheduling flexibility is driven by the requirement to adjust for availability of resources, primarily materials, equipment, or labor skills. Examples of scheduling flexibility include the use of buffer stock, alternative routings, substitute components, labor cross-training, overtime, on-line equipment maintenance, and variable shift operations. The purpose of scheduling flexibility is to anticipate and minimize the effect of resource unavailability; thus it is resource driven.

Innovation flexibility is driven by changes in products/services, process technology, or the method of managing processes. For example, a laser may be used instead of cutting, drilling, and milling machines, in which case a programmable tool replaces three less automated machines. At the same time, a computer program may be used to control the laser, thus reducing the setup time and enhancing the flexibility of the equipment. Innovation flexibility is driven by process technology and the management information technology used to control the process. Technology innovation may be either within the firm or external to the firm; if it is external, it is less controllable. In general, each type of flexibility is sufficiently important that few firms can ignore for long their effects and stay in business. Changeover, scheduling, and innovation flexibility are each essential for operations in a dynamic and global environment.

Classical Product/Service–Process Technology Continuum

The classic way to simultaneously represent flexibility of products/services and process technologies was proposed by Hayes and Wheelwright (1979). The stages of the product/service life cycle, as adapted from Hayes and Wheelwright, are linked to the corresponding process technology life cycle stages. The normal growth pattern was labeled as the diagonal. Thus, as a product or service evolved, a corresponding shift in process technology was expected. The product/service–process technology continuum is shown in Figure 5-2, which gives examples of different industry types along the diagonal.

For example, Apple Computers, noted in the introductory case, started in the upper left corner of the continuum with low volume fabrication of computers and with little process flow. As volume grew and as the product and process developed, Apple moved downward and to the right on the continuum. At some times, Apple moved very rapidly, while at other times the movement was not as dynamic. The key management tasks required by the project and batch environments are high flexibility and quality; those of continuous process industries are delivery and low cost. Similarly, the dominant competitive criteria of the industry differ among low-volume processes and high-volume processes. Though the Hayes and Wheelwright "dominant competitive criteria" are more elaborate than the business strategy distinctive competencies defined by Porter, the left side of the matrix generally is market focused, the center of the matrix is concerned with product/service differentiation, and the right side concentrates on cost-leadership-related factors. Because of differences in competitive priorities and management (and ultimately labor) tasks, it is difficult for an organization to rapidly change the product/service or the process technology. This is why the "focus" of an operation is important. Management and labor have difficulty adjusting from one environment to another. Similarly, it is difficult for most managers, particularly those at lower levels and in introductory positions, to move from one industry type to another.

The positioning of the firm on this matrix, and the corresponding fit of the management tasks and competitive criteria are an extremely important part of strategic assessment. Movement to the left and below the diagonal suggests greater product diversity and more standardized production methods, such as might be achieved through economies of scope (Noori and Radford, 1990). Alternatively, movement to the right and above the diagonal suggests greater product standardization, using a jumbled process. Once the current position of the firm or facility is defined, a further strategic step is to direct the firm or facility as it moves to dynamically reposition itself toward a better competitive niche.

Off-Diagonal Operations

The product/service–process technology continuum emphasizes the difficulties of managing the repositioning of the operations system of a company or a facility. Despite management efforts to coordinate a change, it is not easy to change the position of a system on the product/service dimension and simultaneously on the process technology dimension. Movements tend to be linked to either the product/service dimension or the process technology dimension. An operation can rarely handle movement on both dimensions at the same time. Particularly with major projects, it may be easier to build an entirely new facility. General Motors made such a decision with the Saturn project (see Introductory Case, Chapter 4).

The classic product/service–process technology continuum suggests that there are cost penalties for moving an operation away from the diagonal. Below and to the left of the diagonal, there are the costs of unrecoverable investments in high-volume processes that produce products or services for which there is not sufficient total demand. A different interpretation of this situation is that the high-volume production process may be used for several different products, perhaps a product line, which would result in economies of scope. Alternatively, it is possible to use a fixed site or job shop to produce a highly standardized item, but because of the very flexible process, volumes would be lower and there is a cost of the volume lost, called the opportunity cost. These sunk and opportunity costs require, according to traditional operations management thought, that an operation to produce goods or services stay relatively close to the diagonal.

FIGURE 5-2 The Product/Service–Process Technology Continuum

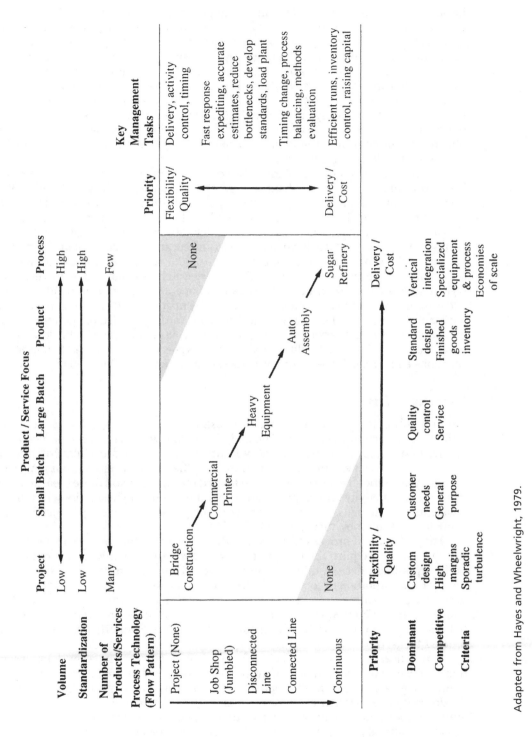

Adapted from Hayes and Wheelwright, 1979.

REQUIREMENT FOR FOCUS

Realistically the repositioning of a firm may require the use of existing facilities. For example, the firm's financial situation may preclude construction of a new facility, yet the growth required by corporate goals may necessitate strategic repositioning despite the difficulties and risk exposure. The most obvious danger of repositioning is that the shift on one dimension will not be accompanied by a corresponding shift on the other dimension, resulting in a lack of focus. Often, through several successive shifts in one dimension, a company may be drawn significantly off the diagonal and incur substantial unforeseen costs. Typically, a company will automate a process in several increments, but retain the product or service variety that the previous nonautomated process permitted. Such piecemeal repositioning can have serious effects, though they may be insidious and difficult to identify.

The second danger of lack of focus is even more consequential. If a firm repositions itself on one dimension and simultaneously expands its range of activity on the other dimension, the result is an increased range over which the firm attempts to focus its operation. For example, the retail merchandise business has changed dramatically in the past 10 to 15 years with the advent of specialty stores and "factory warehouse" retail operations. Specialty stores are positioned in low-volume, customized, and high-cost situations within very narrowly defined areas of business. Examples would include specialty bicycle shops and jeans stores. However, simultaneously, the factory warehouse retail outlet has entered the high-volume, standardized, and low-cost range of operation. Examples include Office Max and Fedders or Silo appliance outlets. Several of the major retail distribution firms (including Sears, Roebuck, J. C. Penney, and Montgomery Ward) have tried to operate simultaneously with the product variety and image of the specialty stores yet with the low costs of a warehouse operation. The resulting loss of focus has cost those major merchandisers. Such situations emphasize the need for both process and products/services focus.

Process Focus

The necessity of focus was introduced by Wickham Skinner (1974), who stated that each facility should focus on a few tasks. The underlying concept is to identify a particular competitive priority (cost, quality, delivery, or flexibility) and a measure of that criterion (such as percent rejects or percent on-time delivery), and then to create an environment wherein simplicity and repetitive tasks are focused toward the criterion and those measures. Focus increases productivity and empowers the operation to be the best in its selected niche. Finally, to ensure focus, the characteristics of the products/services produced, in terms of quality and volumes, must be similar.

The rationale of process focus is that the diffusion of any resource beyond a narrow limit would require the facility to operate over an inefficient range of employee skills, equipment design, or even competitive priorities, resulting in loss of control. Another interpretation of focus is that the focused facility makes many different products/services through the use of a variety of process technologies. For example, the manufacture of a Rolls Royce automobile involves many different production processes to build a small number of highly customized products. Similarly, most job shops are process focused.

In practice, however, every facility faces some variability. However, there is a clear trade-off between high variability of the process and ease of control. Finch and Cox (1988) found that greater variability of process resulted in more frequently updated master production schedules, greater need for material requirements planning, greater need for a formal and detailed capacity planning function, and more frequent priority control reporting. More diffused processes are feasible, but require greater individual skill and effort to control. Simply, diffuse processes violate the rule of simplicity of operations; yet, with greater control efforts, they are possible, and in some situations, necessary.

Product/Service Focus

The product/service, including product/service lines, can be focused in terms of the volumes, range, mix, and the rate of modifications. For example, a firm may choose to manufacture and market one type of automobile, a four-door sedan. Alternatively, the firm may select a product line of three or four different types of vehicles, including two-door models, hatchbacks, and station wagons, as well as the four-door sedan. The product mix of, for example, 30% four-door models, 20% hatchbacks, 10% station wagons, and 40% two-door models could be regularly adjusted, and the rate of product modification could also be varied. Some manufacturers modify the product/service line every several months, while others make changes every year or two. Of course, these ranges, volumes, mixes, and modifications affect the focus of the manufacturing or service delivery effort. Most line operations are product/service focused.

Just as diffusion of the process focus causes increased confusion and overload of people and equipment, so does product/service diffusion. Repeated but minor adjustments of product/service volumes or mix or excessive range can diffuse the product/service focus. Broad product/service range may be a matter of corporate pride or reputation, and likely will involve some strong stakeholder positions. However, excessive product/service range results in diffusion and higher operations and support costs. A criterion such as contribution to profit of each product may be an appropriate basis to evaluate product ranges and thereby assess product/service focus.

The rationale of greater product/service range is that, like economies of scope, it permits the spreading of fixed costs across a larger number and thus greater total volume of products or services. Though it may be difficult to measure exactly the proportion of overhead that should be costed against particular models, this sort of analysis may have a further shortfall because it fails to consider the marginal contribution to profit and the different transaction costs of each item within a product line. Considering the marginal contribution to profit, those products or services that provide the highest total revenue are generally high-volume items. Though some high-volume items may be temporarily sold as loss leaders, over time most make a relatively high marginal contribution to profits and require less overhead per unit. Thus, the contribution to profit of the product/service with the highest total revenue is likely larger than for products or services with lower total revenues.

Alternatively, low-volume products, unless sold with a hefty price mark-up, generally contribute only marginally to total revenue because per unit overhead costs are higher. Such products may be a drain on profits. This analysis suggests that there is a range beyond which the loss of focus results in decreasing marginal contribution to total revenue and increasing support costs. Though diffusion of product/service range may be undertaken for marketing or line image reasons, the costs of such diffusion should be recognized. Figure 5-3 presents a Pareto (sequenced by item from largest to smallest total revenue) analysis of this situation and shows the cumulative total revenue, the unit support costs, and the cumulative profits.

This type of analysis suggests that, as a product or service line grows, despite the continued increase of cumulative total revenue and because of increasing item support costs, cumulative profits may peak and decrease. Of course, this analysis is highly dependent upon an accurate statement of per unit overhead, yet it does suggest that there are limits of product/service diffusion.

Product/Service Versus Process Focus

Over the life cycle of a production/service system, the emphasis toward a product/service or process focus will likely shift. As an operation starts up and moves toward the growth of volume stage, the emphasis is on the process. Modifications and volume, range, or mix changes are likely. However, as the product or service enters the stable state stage, increasing concern is directed toward efficient process technology or product focus. The sales

FIGURE 5-3   Item Contribution to Product/Service Line Profitability

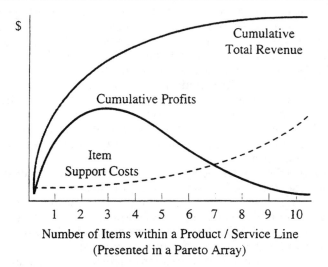

volumes are higher and the process becomes more stable, both in volume and product mix and in quality and dependability. But, as the product further continues in the stable state and starts toward decline and renewal, a renewed emphasis on process becomes apparent. Schmenner's (1983) description of the "failing" stage of a facility life cycle has already been noted (Chapter 4). Often, however, it is easier to stop production abruptly than to try to reverse the movement on the product/service–process technology continuum and adjust the product/service and process technology back toward lower-volume positions.

In the case of several automobile manufacturers, the decision was made to close the facility, rather than to try to redirect the production system. The turnaround of a "declining system" requires the reintroduction of job-shop-like processes, with the labor skill, methods, equipment, and management style changes. Some companies are able, in special circumstances, to make the transition back up the product/service–process technology continuum. Studebaker, for example, closed its South Bend, Indiana, assembly line in the 1960s, but continues to build automobiles in small volumes using a job shop in Canada. And the Baxter Health Care Skokie (Illinois) plant reorganized from a line flow to work cells, adjusting back up the product/service–process technology continuum. This relationship of the process technology and product/service volume and mix over the life cycle is shown in Figure 5-1.

One important aspect of Figure 5-1 is that it identifies the focus of an operations system for a particular stage of its life cycle. That is, at the start-up and early growth stages, and in the decline and renewal stage, the system should focus on the product or service and then fit the necessary process technology. Alternatively, in the stable state stage, the system should focus on the process technology and fit the appropriate product or service characteristics. The exact mix of product/service and process technology focus will vary by industry, by stage of the operations system life cycle, and by the commitment of management. The product/service–process technology continuum dimensionalizes the options and alternatives for management to use in planning the development of the operations system life cycle.

Movement off the Diagonal

The focused facility concept suggests that the specific product/service or process technology focus must be defined for each facility; then, using the product/service–process technology continuum, the corresponding point on, or off, the diagonal must be identified. Repositioning the operations system should be carefully planned, according to conventional operations management thought, to avoid movement off the diagonal or too much diffusion. However, the realities of operating in a dynamic environment may not permit the luxuries of this approach. Particularly where competition is intense and global, a firm may be required to position itself off the diagonal or to accept a certain amount of diffusion, particularly in the short run. In fact, off-diagonal and diffuse operations systems may be the basis for competitive advantage.

Movement downward along the diagonal of the product/service–process technology continuum enhances the economies of scale; however, positioning to the left and below the diagonal enhances economies of scope. This is one example of how operations managers may define an operations system off the diagonal as a way of seeking competitive advantage. Several techniques to position an operations system off the diagonal are described in the following paragraphs.

Modular Structures and Variable Production Lines.   Both modular product or service structures and variable production lines will permit increased variation and customization of products or services from a continuous or connected line process. Modular structures use a few high-volume component modules produced with line processes. Final assembly, packaging, or customer selection integrates different groupings of those modules, giving the appearance of a small-batch, or even customized, product. Various electronic products, from radios to sound systems to televisions and computers, have used product modules for years. Additionally, modular production is used for many furniture items, including bookshelves, chairs, suite units, and modular office furniture. In services, modular options are commonly offered with credit cards, life and health insurance policies, and consulting packages. Modular components permit the appearance of a greater product range; however, the components are produced with standardized high-volume production processes.

Variable production lines use a single line, with minor process variations, to build different products. For example, Toyota uses the same "mixed model" assembly line to sequentially build a sedan, then a hardtop, then a sedan, then a station wagon (Wantuch, 1983). However, Ford's Wixom plant is a true mixed model plant, assembling Lincolns, Continentals, Town Cars, and Mark VIII automobiles on the same assembly line. Additionally, newspaper presses are used to publish many different editions and sizes of newspaper. Most major publications now print many highly customized products, defined by geographic area (often local government or zip code) and by the timing of the publication, on the same continuous production line. Some publications change and update headlines and articles over the three- or four-hour life of an edition. Other publications, including *The New York Times* and *USA Today*, disseminate copy electronically for local printing and distribution. Newspaper inserts, printed and assembled on a variable production line, may be defined for specific subscriber groups. Thus, they resemble product modules, their counterparts in manufacturing.

One of the more elaborate applications of variable production lines is the Allen-Bradley computer integrated contactor (industrial switches) facility in Milwaukee, Wisconsin. Though each job follows the same production line flow, different machine settings, controlled by a computer, are used at each step of the process to build different models. The same production line may be used for lot sizes as small as one and for a wide variety of products. Flexibility of the production facility and modular structure design directly contribute to economies of scope and are called *left lateral movement*. These methods are shown in Figure 5-4.

Flexible Processes.   Numerous companies have found that they are able to improve productivity by designing more variation in the process technology. This may appear to be a "deautomation" of the system, in the sense that the process is being redesigned from a

FIGURE 5-4 Product/Service and Process Technology Diffusion

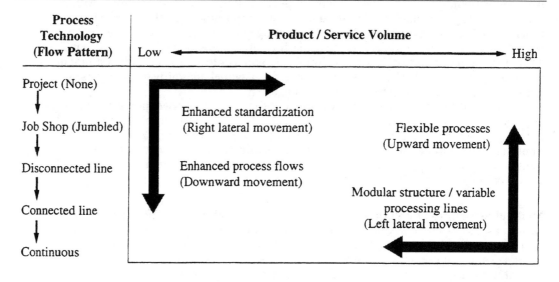

continuous process or line flow to a batch or even a project method. However, in converting to manufacturing cells or service teams, companies often include more extensive computer or human control systems and a higher level of process automation. An example is the Baxter Health Care Skokie Surgical Instruments plant, described previously. There an assembly line has been replaced with a manufacturing cell. The automation of the production controls, as well as of the production process, permits what would normally be a line process to function more like a batch or project operation. This is called *upward movement*.

Enhanced Process Flows. The third type of movement off the diagonal enables a project or job shop flow to acquire equipment or services and operate more like a line or continuous flow, but without the heavy front-end investment in facilities or equipment. For example, many agribusinesses find it less expensive to subcontract the services of harvesting companies than to own and maintain their own equipment. These subcontractors provide state-of-the-art equipment and trained operators to enable the farmer to rapidly harvest at the best possible moment, considering weather, market, price, and the state of the crop. Without such harvesting teams, farmers would have to use their own equipment, which likely would be older and less efficient. More importantly, however, the harvesting subcontractor, moving from farm to farm, uses a more continuous type of process than a single farmer could.

Similarly, many small businesses purchase telephone services (such as call waiting and call forwarding) and lease computers or information processing services, such as inventory management, payroll, or tax preparation. These methods permit a small proprietor to use expensive capital equipment and costly or diverse labor skills without the risk of capital commitment. For example, a university printer, anticipating higher demand for multi-color individualized instructor and student course packets, might contract to lease a high-speed four-color copy machine for a trial period of one year. The purchase of such equipment would be both costly and risky; however, leasing the equipment would permit a small entrepreneur to test the market for the product without extensive risk. This *downward movement* off the diagonal permits acquiring equipment or services to facilitate a smoother, faster flow of single and low-volume jobs, but with less risk.

Enhanced Product Standardization. The corresponding right lateral movement permits fixed or jumbled job shops to competitively offer a few high-volume, highly standardized products or services. Group technologies, such as the use of common parts, mounting bosses, or handling lugs, permit a firm to produce higher volumes at competitive costs in a manufacturing cell. In service operations, these facilitators of standardization are exemplified by a variety of franchise or cooperative agreements, such as motels, fast-food restaurants, chain stores, and real estate agencies. All are essentially fixed-site businesses; however, the franchise defines standardized products, permits bulk purchasing, centralizes many services, and establishes customer expectancies. This encourages, at a cost, a wider population of customers.

Similarly, various techniques permit entrepreneurs or job shop operators to provide a standardized product or service in direct competition with larger, more product-focused operations (Noori and Radford, 1990). For example, spreadsheet or data base management software programs, such as accounting packages, have enabled many individual tax preparers and consultants to provide quite standardized and higher-volume services. Desk-top publishing software, for example, permits an individual entrepreneur with a laser printer to compete in a higher-volume production market that previously was restricted to larger job shops. These *right lateral movements* permit a fixed-site small business to increase its volume.

In each case, these technologies and methods permit the operations manager to move the production system away from the traditional diagonal with less cost or risk. Thus, opportunities for a specified market niche or focus (either in cost, based on above-the-diagonal higher volumes, or in product differentiation, based on below-the-diagonal lower volumes) are increasingly available. Additionally, a wide range of emerging process technologies are facilitated.

EMERGING PROCESS TECHNOLOGIES

Recent advances in information processing, and materials and data handling technologies permit redefinition, and allow greater diffusion, of traditional production systems. Four generalized manufacturing approaches have emerged, which deserve further emphasis. They are called *variable production lines, manufacturing cells, flexible manufacturing systems,* and *computer integrated manufacturing.* These process technologies are generally sequential and apply primarily to manufacturing operations, though service applications are rapidly developing. For example, the operations of consulting teams correspond to manufacturing cells or flexible manufacturing systems.

Variable Production Lines

Variable production lines are dedicated high-volume lines that are reconfigured to permit some process variation and thus several different products or services. They usually incorporate a simple information system that gives the necessary process variability information to employees in sufficient time for them to make appropriate adjustments. For example, the Cummins diesel engine plant custom builds several different types of diesel engine, ranging from small automobile and light truck engines to large emergency power generators, on one assembly line. The line uses a product carrier frame and an information panel that is visible to downstream assembly employees. The panel, with color blocks at particular positions, indicates which components should be prepared for assembly to the particular unit. This information system, combined with accurate component usage factors, permits product variability on a continuous production line.

Manufacturing Cells

Manufacturing cells are dedicated subsets of the manufacturing system designed to process part families or product groups. For this reason, they are sometimes called a plant-within-a-plant. Cells usually involve the designation of a small group of workers and machines to be responsible for one subset of the business and may be based on several high-volume and standard products or on one or several high-priority customers. Typically, a cell is responsible for all aspects of the particular category of business from order taking to scheduling, production, and shipping. Cells have a limited product flow and are often U- or C- (or horseshoe-) -shaped, to permit better employee communication and movement in the cell area. (See Chapter 4.)

Cells are able to achieve economies of setup, employee learning, reduced work in process, shorter throughput times, and notably improved responsiveness to customers. They are particularly useful to reduce inventory costs or where short delivery times or high quality standards are required by customers. Manufacturing cells were initially designed to reduce manufacturing throughput time (New, 1977) and to minimize inventory. The John Deere Waterloo, Iowa, diesel engine plant (Spencer, 1980) is an often noted example. More recent examples have been designed to provide flexibility of response to customer needs and to reduce operating costs.

Flexible Manufacturing Systems

A flexible manufacturing system (FMS) integrates and enhances the flexibility of manufacturing cells through the use of centralized control systems. Often a standard mounting boss or lug is used to simplify materials handling and permit computer-controlled machines to rapidly change setups for the specific job. Seventy-five percent of machine parts produced in the United States are produced in lot sizes of 50 or less (Jaikumar, 1986; Buffa, 1985). For cost efficiency, these jobs must be produced by using line flow techniques; however, each job requires a different setup. FMS is ideal for such situations. FMS is often called an "island of automation" because it involves activities that are fed by and feed to nonautomated systems. The premise of FMS is to provide flexibility approaching that of a job shop, but with the materials handling capabilities of a line flow (Jaikumar, 1986). A computer manages variable setups as well as the routing of those parts through the process.

The Quill Corporation, applying a similar concept to distribution systems, packages customer orders for national distribution from its warehouse in Lincolnshire, Illinois. A two-mile-long conveyor system moves presized boxes to some 30 stations, where items are either automatically or manually picked, based on a bar-coded order number. Orders are shipped within 36 hours of receipt, and the accuracy of the semiautomated pick system is almost 100%. In fact, most returns result because of customer error.

Computer Integrated Manufacturing

Computer integrated manufacturing (CIM) is the application of a computer system to link several separate information systems and technologies at different functional levels. Though the technology is very complex, the purpose of CIM is to simplify, automate, and integrate. The CIM system connects several components of a production system into an integrated whole, as shown in Figure 5-5.

Computer integrated manufacturing draws information from several levels of the business and from various functional areas. Figure 5-5 describes the more common types of information that are used by a CIM system; however, other types of information may be useful in various specific applications. Few organizations could claim to have a fully integrated CIM system, because moving toward CIM involves simultaneous automation of process technologies (work station tasking and execution and performance measurement) and process control systems (facility level and process planning). This requires simultaneous growth of the process technology and the process control system, as shown in Figure 5-6.

As suggested by Figure 5-6, the growth from traditional manufacturing toward CIM is usually achieved in several stages, each of which permits the traditional line flow manufacturer to enhance the production variety. The information system gives greater process flexibility and greater control. In fact, a well-developed CIM system permits an operation to function efficiently at almost any position on the product/service–process technology

FIGURE 5-5 Computer Integrated Manufacturing Systems

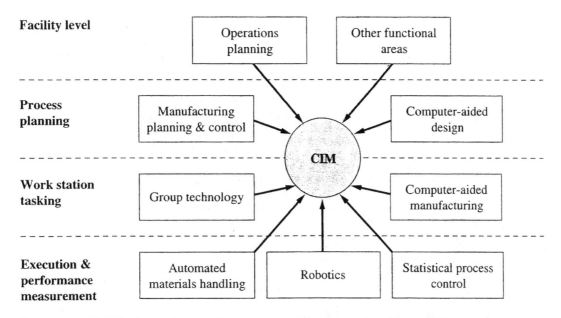

Computer-aided Design: the use of computers to draw and store engineering designs.

Computer-aided Manufacturing: the use of computers to program and control production equipment, often based on computer-aided designs.

Statistical Process Control: a system to monitor numerous process technology performance indicators and identify potential out-of-tolerance conditions.

Robotics: the use of programmable machines to handle materials or tools in the performance of manufacturing tasks.

Automated Materials Handling: equipment which permits the storage, retrieval, and movement of materials and parts.

Group Technology: an engineering method which identifies sameness of parts, equipment, or processes and uses that sameness in subsequent design of parts, equipment, or processes.

Manufacturing Planning & Control: the interface of the master production schedule with the production system to execute the production plan.

Operations Planning: evaluation of long- and mid-range information in terms of capacity and requirements.

Other Functional Areas: integration of various human resource, marketing, and cost measures with the operations function.

continuum. Firms usually start movement toward a CIM system by increasing the variability of the traditional production process, then sequentially developing manufacturing cells, linking those cells with a flexible manufacturing system, and finally automating all parts of the system with a CIM system.

The use of CIM logic is becoming increasingly widespread in distribution and service systems. The automated storage and retrieval systems (AS/RS) which are used by

FIGURE 5-6 Toward a CIM System

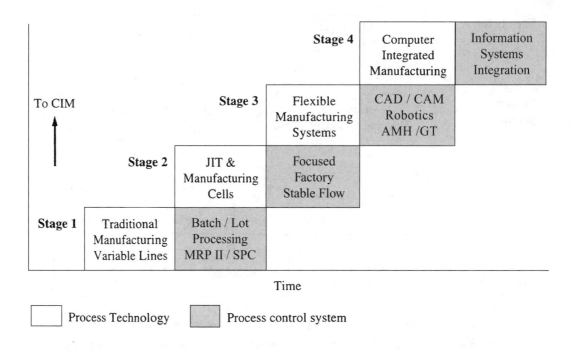

Time

☐ Process Technology ▨ Process control system

major distributors, such as W. W. Grainger and Sears, Roebuck, are examples. Additionally, the use of bar codes for product identification, combined with automated credit validation, is a way that CIM concepts significantly speed customer order processing in most retail environments.

The type of information and control system will depend upon whether the objective is materials planning or process control and upon the amount of lead-time variability or the flexibility required of the production system. Manufacturing cells and just-in-time systems work well in stable, continuous-flow, pull materials planning situations. Alternatively, if the system is push-oriented, or involves custom product design, then lead-time variability is likely to be higher and material requirements planning is more appropriate. At the shop-floor level, continuous and stable flow situations are best managed by Kanban or other visible mechanisms to pull materials, but if flexibility is high, then the shop floor should be managed by traditional operations scheduling. These dimensions of information system flexibility, adopted from Karmarkar (1989), are shown in Table 5-3.

TABLE 5-3 Process Information Systems

	Materials Planning	Process Control
Inventory pull systems Continuous flow Low lead-time variability	Just-in-time	Kanban
↕		
Inventory push systems Custom engineering High lead-time variability	Material requirements planning	Traditional scheduling

EMERGING BUSINESS PRACTICES

Though many large firms in traditional business environments require the efficiencies of purchasing and owning their own facilities and equipment, there is increasing support, even among large firms, for the use of leased or contracted facilities, equipment, and services. The advantages of leasing are most apparent in new and untested market areas or technologies, or with items that experience rapid technological changes or require frequent servicing. Of course, leasing is a common practice in situations where there is only a short-term need for the equipment or service, such as in the construction industry. In the 1960s and 1970s, computers were often leased because the costs were quite high, the technology changed rapidly, and the first applications were risky. More recently, as costs have decreased and applications have become accepted and proven, a greater proportion of computers is being purchased.

Of course, there are costs associated with leasing, yet surprisingly, the total cost of leasing may be well below the cost of purchasing a piece of equipment. A notable portion of the cost advantage of leasing is explained by the tax advantages of not owning the equipment and depreciation losses of ownership. Decision Model Box 5-1 shows the costs of leasing compared with the costs of purchasing computer equipment.

Firms may also lease services, such as payroll, security, and janitorial services. Information and education services are also widely demanded, as the plethora of consultants in almost every field and academic discipline attests. Firms find that, because of specialization, they can obtain such services at lower costs and greater quality with less risk and commitment than if they hire their own staff.

Each of these methods increases the process flexibility of the facility and decreases the potential risks of long-term resource commitments. These, combined with increased product/service flexibility, suggest that it is possible to operate on a greater range of the product/service–process technology continuum than in immediate proximity to the diagonal. Additionally, though there are still costs of operating off the diagonal, the costs and risks are both different and much reduced from the classical model. The key requirements for a firm to operate away from the diagonal are a highly educated and trained work force and a responsive information system. Though there are limits of movement off the diagonal, there are also opportunities and conditions that facilitate effective off-diagonal operations for those who have the work force and information systems. Figure 5-7 reflects the positioning of various example situations used in this chapter on the product/service–process technology continuum.

Though these technologies permit the operations function to operate away from the traditional diagonal, there may be some hidden costs. Such costs are often rather insidious in that they may be difficult to measure and aggregate. For example, software automation costs, such as training and implementation time, are usually not considered to be sunk capital investments and thus might not be measured or monitored as closely by management.

Ultimately, the greater flexibility of the system must be costed against the sometimes very high total system (including system development) costs. Additionally, the likelihood and costs of failure to implement a system (an MRP system, for example) can be rather high. An early study by Anderson et al. (1982) found that 60% of firms that implemented MRP systems classified themselves as class C or class D users (suggesting limited functioning of the system and numerous data errors) with average costs of more than one-half million dollars. However, if the effort is not made, there are long-range risks that a competitor may successfully implement a system and experience significant cost, flexibility, delivery, or quality improvements.

These emerging process technologies, information control systems, and business practices permit increased flexibility of process technology. The traditionally defined risks of lost opportunity costs or unrecoverable sunk investments are dramatically reduced; yet other risks appear to be taking their place, including the difficulty of cost measurement, the risk of information system failure, and the risk that a business will be strategically and competitively outflanked.

DECISION MODEL BOX 5-1 The Lease-Purchase Decision at True Value Retail

The management of the True Value Retail Store wants to acquire a small computer system to manage sales and inventory records, with future applications in tax accounting and purchasing. The store expects to use the computer system for five years. Application Table 5-1-1 shows the computation of total costs to lease the computer, which is compared with the data in Application Table 5-1-2, the cost of owning the system. The lease cost, including maintenance, is $1200 per year, and the purchase price of the equipment is $10,000 with a salvage value of $6250 in five years. The maintenance contract is $300 per year. The value of tax write-offs is 40%, and the annuity factor is 20% (which may be somewhat higher than bank interest rates, but represents the opportunity costs-or rate of return of money invested in other ways-of the store). A fixed depreciation scale of 25%, 20%, 15%, 10%, and 5% is used; all costs incurred at end of year.

APPLICATION TABLE 5-1-1 Cost of Leasing

(1) Year	(2) Lease Cost	(3) Tax Advantage (40%) [0.4 × (2)]	(4) Lease Cost after Taxes [(2) − (3)]	(5) Net Present Value Factor* (20%)	(6) Adjusted Lease Cost [(4) × (5)]
0	$1200	$480	$720	1.0	$720
1	1200	480	720	0.83	598
2	1200	480	720	0.69	497
3	1200	480	720	0.58	418
4	1200	480	720	0.48	346
				Total cost of leasing	$2579

*Calculated as $1/(1 + i)^t$.

APPLICATION TABLE 5-1-2 Cost of Owning

(1) Year	(2) Maintenance Cost	(3) Depreciation	(4) Business Cost [(2) + (3)]	(5) Tax Advantage [0.4 × (4)]	(6) Net Cost After Taxes [(2) − (5)]	(7) Net Present Value Factor (20%)	(8) Present Value of Money After Taxes [(6) × (7)]
1	$300	$2500	$2800	$1120	−$820	0.83	−$681
2	300	2000	2300	920	−620	0.69	−428
3	300	1500	1800	720	−420	0.58	−244
4	300	1000	1300	520	−220	0.48	−106
5	300	500	800	320	−20	0.40	−8
					Net cost of owning computer		−$1467

Summarization

Purchase price	$10,000
Cost of owning computer	−1467
Subtotal	8533
Salvage recovery ($6250 × 0.40)	2500
Total cost of ownership	$ 6033

tage and for the net present value of money. Alternatively, the cost of ownership in Application Table 5-1-2 is based on the annual maintenance and depreciation costs, which sum to the business costs, and are the basis for the 40% tax advantage. The present value factor is applied to the maintenance cost minus the tax write-off, or net cost after taxes. The present value of these costs is summed over the five-year period and deducted from the purchase price, as is the salvage value of the equipment.

Very obviously, the cost of the computer equipment for five years is more than two times the cost to lease the equipment. The majority of the difference occurs because the value of the computer depreciates, and the owner bears that depreciation. However, these computations are dependent upon the cost of the item, the lease cost, maintenance and depreciation costs, the net present value factor, and other values of the store.

OPERATIONS SYSTEM DECISION-MAKING HIERARCHY

After the position or range on the product/service–process technology continuum and the direction and momentum of movement on the continuum have been identified, the operations manager must make some more specific decisions, among them, the major technological choice, the equipment and layout selection, and activity scheduling. These specific decisions, though time consuming, involve extensive computational algorithms and more direct management control. Thus, starting with the positioning of the operations system, these decisions are best accomplished sequentially as a hierarchy of operations system decision-making, as shown in Table 5-4.

FIGURE 5-7 The Product/Service–Process Technology Continuum with Diffusion

Process Technology (Flow Pattern)	Product / Service Volume Low ←——————————————————→ High				
Project (None)		University Printers	Franchises & Cooperatives	Software Company	
↓					
Job Shop (Jumbled)	Avanti		Desktop Publishing	Volvo Kalmar	
↓					
Disconnected line		Modular Office Furniture			Baxter Health Care
↓					
Connected line	Allen-Bradley	Quill Distribution System	Cummins Diesel		
↓					
Continuous			News Publishing		

TABLE 5-4 Operations System Decision-Making Hierarchy

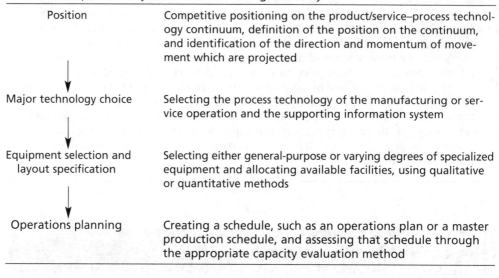

Position	Competitive positioning on the product/service–process technology continuum, definition of the position on the continuum, and identification of the direction and momentum of movement which are projected
Major technology choice	Selecting the process technology of the manufacturing or service operation and the supporting information system
Equipment selection and layout specification	Selecting either general-purpose or varying degrees of specialized equipment and allocating available facilities, using qualitative or quantitative methods
Operations planning	Creating a schedule, such as an operations plan or a master production schedule, and assessing that schedule through the appropriate capacity evaluation method

Major Technology Choice

As might be expected, long-range and strategic perspectives drive the operations system design effort. Once the focus or diffusion of the operations system is defined, then the process technology is selected. Table 5-5 classifies various alternative manufacturing and service processes. The manufacturing processes change the physical properties, shapes, dimensions, and surfaces of materials or join parts. The corresponding classification of service operations involves location, storage, exchange and physical, physiological, or information transformations. This list is not inclusive; it is offered only to suggest the range of different manufacturing and service processes.

Equipment Selection and Layout Specification

The equipment selection and facility layout specification is an important, though particularly detailed and mechanical type of evaluation. As one operations manager stated, "Equipment selection is like buying the right tire, and facility layout is where the rubber meets the road." For example, a general service garage might use general-purpose equipment to change a car's oil, whereas a company which did only oil changes would use more specialized equipment.

The nature of the equipment selected can have a significant effect on the capacity, efficiency, and utilization of the operation. Similarly, the location of that equipment can have significant effects on organization productivity. From the process perspective, the alternatives apply to both manufacturing and service environments and span a range from general-purpose to specialized machines. Table 5-6 gives the general characteristics of those two "pure" alternatives. It is no surprise that Table 5-6 corresponds rather closely to parts of Table 5-1. General-purpose equipment is often used in a job shop, while more specialized equipment is commonly associated with a continuous process. Thus, general-purpose equipment would be preferred in the start-up and growth stages, and more specialized equipment would be selected during the stable state stage.

The second equipment and layout selection decision is the method of deciding upon the location of the equipment. This two-step procedure involves identifying the amount of space or capacity of each center and, second, the configuration of the centers. None

TABLE 5-5 Classification of Manufacturing and Service Processes

Manufacturing	Service

Manufacturing

1. Processes for changing physical properties

a. Chemical reactions	d. Hot working
b. Refining/extraction	e. Cold working
c. Heat treatment	f. Shot peening

2. Processes for changing the shape of materials

a. Casting	l. Spinning
b. Forging	m. Stretch forming
c. Extruding	n. Roll forming
d. Rolling	o. Torch cutting
e. Drawing	p. Explosive forming
f. Squeezing	q. Electrohydraulic forming
g. Crushing	
h. Piercing	r. Magnetic forming
i. Swaging	s. Electroforming
j. Bending	t. Powder metal forming
k. Shearing	u. Plastics molding

3. Processes for machining parts to a fixed dimension

   Traditional chip removal processes

a. Turning	e. Boring	i. Milling
b. Planing	f. Reaming	j. Grinding
c. Shaping	g. Sawing	k. Hobbing
d. Drilling	h. Broaching	l. Routing

   Nontraditional machining processes

a. Ultrasonic	f. Chem-milling
b. Electro-arc	g. Abrasive jet cutting
c. Electrochemical	h. Electrical discharge
d. Optical lasers	i. Plasma-arc machining
e. Electron beam machining	

4. Processes for obtaining a surface finish

a. Polishing	g. Superfinishing
b. Abrasive belt grinding	h. Metal spraying
c. Barrel tumbling	i. Inorganic coatings
d. Electroplating	j. Parkerizing
e. Honing	k. Anodizing
f. Lapping	l. Sheradizing

5. Processes for joining parts or materials

a. Welding	f. Pressing
b. Soldering	g. Riveting
c. Brazing	h. Screw fastening
d. Sintering	i. Adhesive joining
e. Plugging	

Service

1. Processes for relocating goods

a. Messenger	f. Delivery service
b. Airline	g. Ship or boat
c. Auto or taxi	h. Railroad
d. Bus or subway	i. Mail
e. Truck	j. Canal/river barge

2. Processes for storing goods

a. Bank account/vault	e. Warehouse
b. Storage rental unit	f. Pipeline
c. Freezer	g. Padlock
d. Public lockers	h. Data storage

3. Processes for exchanging items

a. Retail sales units	e. Barter/swapping
b. Banks	f. Retail/leasing
c. Credit card sales	g. Contracts
d. Catalog sales	h. Informal sales

4. Processes for physical transformation

a. Cleaning	e. Lighting
b. Eating/drinking	f. Noise abatement
c. Motel and hotel	g. Item modification
d. Heating/cooling	h. Item maintenance or repair

5. Processes for physiological transformation

a. Entertainment	e. Appreciation (art)
b. Exercise	f. Religious
c. Medical	g. Personal and vanity
d. Dental	h. Other clinical

6. Processes for information transformation

a. Telephone	g. Conferences
b. Mail	h. Face-to-face
c. Radio and television	i. Beeper
d. Newspapers	j. Education/training
e. Magazines/journals	k. Consulting
f. Data links	l. Fax

Note: Manufacturing classifications are adapted from Amstead et al., 1977.

of the numerous methods is inherently optimizing, and the methods are measurement bound, particularly if the facility is large, or with multiple floors, and with many separate activities. Additionally, there are questions of variable routings, one-way and return trips, and multidestination trips. For these reasons, layout algorithms are appropriate as mechanical tools, but they must be supplemented by human evaluation.

TABLE 5-6 Equipment Selection Alternatives

Cost	General Purpose Low	Specialized High
Operator skill and control	high skill, more control	low skill, less control
Output rate	low—human paced	high—system or machine paced
Setup time	lower—problems predictable and controllable	high—problems random and highly technical
Maintenance cost	low—lower skill required/ greater parts availability	high
Product/service quality	based on human control	high—based on machine accuracy
In-process inventory	high	low—fewer "run-ins"
Obsolescence	slower-easier updating/modification	high

Operations Planning

Table 5-1 noted several of the process management characteristics and challenges for each of the classic process alternatives. A fixed process might use the program evaluation review technique/critical path method (PERT/CPM) to manage the flow of materials, while a job shop might use a variety of debottlenecking and scheduling algorithms, and line flow operations would use line balancing or linear programming. Though some of these decision methods are "optimal," they are dependent upon uncertain or variable input information. However, these approaches are very useful as estimation and evaluative tools. They offer an initial mechanical assessment that can be subsequently adjusted through judgmental processes or by trial and error.

The topics of layout specification and activity scheduling are dependent upon the higher decisions of the operations system planning hierarchy. Additionally, they are computationally bound. Dependence upon higher-level decisions is exemplified by the scheduling changes that would be required by a decision to replace assembly line processes with manufacturing cells or just-in-time systems.

SUMMARY

This chapter has addressed the need for focus and simultaneously the positioning of product/service and process capabilities. The hierarchy of operations system design provides a long-range to short-range integrating framework of manufacturing and service operations systems. This chapter has emphasized the positioning and focus of the operations system with brief discussions of the other three levels of the operations system design hierarchy. The technological choice is not further discussed here because it is highly industry specific. The strategic considerations of equipment selection are very closely related, as noted, to process selection.

The product/service–process technology system life cycle provides a central starting point for product/service, process technology, and often facility analysis. The operations manager must define the position of a particular situation on the product/service–process technology continuum, then consider the amount of focus or diffusion and the direction and momentum of movement desired for the operations system. The risks and opportunities associated with each situation must then be gauged. The classical approach is that the facility or process must be focused for productivity and efficiency; yet emerging process technologies and practices may permit more diffused positioning. These emerging positioning approaches involve greater complexity and information flows, but possibly less cost and risk. Certainly, the costs and risks are of a different nature. There are very clear reasons for some diffusion, but the exact definition of focus or diffusion for a situation is a difficult and continual process, particularly in dynamic environments. Reassessment and repositioning must be considered regularly.

Once the position of the firm is determined, the remaining decisions are much more highly constrained and mechanical. The hierarchy of operations system planning identifies the three additional stages of that process. Clearly, any changes at the position/focus level will have major impacts at the lower levels of the hierarchy; yet simultaneously, lower levels of the hierarchy represent measures of efficiency and effectiveness by which the effectiveness of the operations system is evaluated.

DISCUSSION QUESTIONS

1. Identify the final four stages of the product/service–process technology life cycle. Give an example of a company that has dynamically adjusted the position of its operations system on the life cycle.

2. From your personal experience or readings, identify and briefly describe one company in each of the last four stages of the product/service–process technology life cycle.

3. Describe the corresponding changes that occur in the product/service and process technology life cycles along with the related industry characteristics. Give an example of a company that has experienced these changes.

4. Briefly note some possible constraints on operations system design.

5. What does an operations system design involve?

6. Name and describe the characteristics of the three classical process alternatives.

7. From your personal experience or readings, identify and briefly describe several products and several services that are built or delivered by using the classical processes.

8. List the three types of process flexibility and the driving factors associated with each. Give an example of each type.

9. Identify and support the key variables of the product/service–process technology continuum.

10. Describe briefly the cost penalties of operating off the diagonal.

11. Identify and describe from your experience or readings, a cost penalty that resulted from operating off the diagonal.

12. Briefly describe product/service and process focus.

13. Identify the relationship of product/service versus process emphasis with that of the product/service and process technology life cycle. Give an example of a company and explain how the company has positioned itself.

14. Why is a manufacturing cell sometimes called a "plant within a plant"?

15. Two advantages of leasing are the increases in process flexibility of a facility and the decreases in potential risks. These advantages, combined with the product/service flexibilities, suggest the possibility of operating on a greater range of the product/service–process technology continuum (that is, off the diagonal). What are the key requirements for a firm to operate away from the diagonal? Give an example of a successful application and an unsuccessful application.

16. Identify the levels of the process planning hierarchy and briefly describe the management decisions required at each level. Give an application of how a decision was made through the four levels. (*Note:* The primary discussion of the final two levels is in other chapters.)

STRATEGIC DECISION SITUATIONS

1. The president of Xenon Industries is concerned about the focus of the company and has asked for a three-to-five-page summarization considering three topics: the focus, the major technology, and the type of equipment used by the company. Select a specific company that you are familiar with, or research a company in business publications and, using those details, respond to the president's concerns. Your comments should be directed toward the current situation of the company, and where you think the company should be in three to five years.

   a. Identify the product line of the company; then specify the position of the product/service line on the product/service–process technology continuum and state the degree of focusing or diffusion and the direction of movement on the continuum.

   b. Identify the major technology of the manufacturing or service process and the information system which supports that process.

   c. Identify the general-purpose or specialized equipment that is appropriate for the process and identify the allocation of facilities to be used.

   Note: Appropriate appendices may be included to support your report with substantive capacity evaluation and layout information (see Chapters 3 and 4).

2. The Speedy Delivery Pizza Company plans to acquire company vehicles, which will replace personal vehicles that are used for home delivery of their products. The lease cost is $1000 per year and the purchase price per vehicle is $7000 with a salvage value of $2000 in five years. A maintenance contract for leasing is required, costing $300 per year, and insurance costs are considered to be equal under either option. The tax advantage is 30% and the annuity factor is 15%. A fixed depreciation scale of 25%, 20%, 15%, 10%, and 5% is used. Advise the company on the best option.

3. The West Side Publishing Company wants to upgrade its printing equipment with an integrated high speed printing unit that costs $60,000. The unit could be purchased and then sold to and leased back from an equipment holding company, which would cost $8000 per year for a five-year contract or $6000 per year for a ten-year term, with a required maintenance cost of $500 per year. For a five-year fixed contract, the company could get 10% on its money, while for a ten-year fixed contract, 12.5% would be the annuity factor. Using a tax advantage of 30%, a fixed depreciation rate of 14%, 13%, 12%, 11%, 10%, 9%, 8%, 7%, 6%, and 5%, which contract would be preferred? After five years, the unit is expected to have a value of $48,000 and after 10 years, the unit will have a value of $35,000.

REFERENCES

Amstead, B. J., P. F. Ostwald, and M. L. Begeman. *Manufacturing Processes*. New York: John Wiley and Sons, 1979.

Anderson, John C., Roger G. Schroeder, Sharon E. Tupy, and Edna M. White. "Material Requirements Planning Systems: The State of the Art," *Production and Inventory Management*. October–December 1982.

Brown, J. "Classification of Flexible Manufacturing Systems," *The FMS Magazine*. April 1984, pp. 114–117.

Buffa, Elwood S. "Meeting the Competitive Challenge with Manufacturing Strategy," *National Productivity Review*. Spring 1985, pp. 155–169.

Butcher, Lee. *Accidental Millionaire*. New York: Paragon House Publishers, 1988.

Dean, James W., Jr., and Gerald I. Susman. "Organizing for Manufacturable Design," *Harvard Business Review*. January–February 1989, pp. 28–37.

Derks, Richard P. "Purpose-Driven Product and Process Design," *Industrial Engineering*. January 1993, Vol. 25, No. 1, pp. 38–42.

Finch, Byron J., and James F. Cox. "Process-Oriented Production Planning and Control: Factors That Influence System Design," *Academy of Management Journal.* Vol. 31, No. 1, 1988, pp. 123–153.

Gerwin, Donald. "The Do's and Don'ts of Computerized Manufacturing," *Harvard Business Review.* March–April 1982, pp. 107–116.

Gerwin, Donald. "Manufacturing Flexibility in the CAM Era," *Business Horizons.* January–February 1989, pp. 78–84.

Goldhar, Joel D., and Mariann Jelinek. "Computer Integrated Flexible Manufacturing: Organizational, Economic, and Strategic Implications," *Interfaces.* May–June 1985, pp. 94–105.

Greene, James H. *Production and Inventory Control Handbook.* New York: McGraw-Hill, 1987.

Hayes, Robert H., and Steven C. Wheelwright. "Link Manufacturing Process and Product Life Cycles," *Harvard Business Review.* January–February 1979.

Hayes, Robert H., and Steven C. Wheelwright. "The Dynamics of Process-Product Life Cycles," *Harvard Business Review.* March–April 1979.

Hayes, Robert H., and Steven C. Wheelwright. *Restoring Our Competitive Edge: Competing through Manufacturing.* New York: John Wiley and Sons, 1984.

Hill, Terrence J., and R. M. G. Duke-Woolley. "Progression or Regression in Facilities Focus," *Strategic Management Journal.* Vol. 4, 1983, pp. 109–121.

Jackson, Richard H. F., and Albert W. T. Jones. "An Architecture for Decision Making in the Factory of the Future," *Interfaces.* November–December 1987, pp. 15–28.

Jaikumar, Ramchandran. "Postindustrial Manufacturing," *Harvard Business Review.* November–December 1986, pp. 69–76.

Karmarkar, Uday. "Getting Control of Just-in-Time," *Harvard Business Review.* September–October 1989, pp. 122–131.

Kotha, Suresh, and Daniel Orne. "Generic Manufacturing Strategies: A Conceptual Synthesis," *Strategic Management Journal.* Vol. 10, 1989, pp. 211–231.

Leong, G. Keong, and Peter T. Ward. "Multifaceted View of Manufacturing Strategy." Working Paper Series, WPS 90–50, Ohio State University, June 1990.

Leong, G. K., D. L. Snyder, and P. T. Ward. "Research in the Process and Content of Manufacturing Strategy," *Omega International Journal of Management Science.* Vol. 18, No. 2, 1990, pp. 109–122.

Markoff, John. "Beyond the PC: Apple's Promised Land," *New York Times.* November 15, 1992, Section 3, p. 1.

McKenna, Regis. *Who's Afraid of Big Blue?* Reading, Mass.: Addison-Wesley Publishing Co., 1989.

Moody, Patricia E. *Strategic Manufacturing: Dynamic New Directions for the 1990s.* Homewood, Ill.: Dow Jones Irwin, 1990.

New, C. Colin. "MRP and GT: A New Strategy for Component Production," *Production and Inventory Management.* Vol. 18, No. 3, 1977, pp. 50–62.

Noori, Hamid, and Russell W. Radford. *Readings and Cases in the Management of New Technology: An Operations Perspective.* Englewood Cliffs, N.J.: Prentice Hall, 1990.

Sasser, W. Earl, Kim B. Clark, David A. Garvin, Margaret B. W. Graham, Ramchandran Jaikumar, and David H. Maister. *Cases in Operations Management: Analysis and Action.* Homewood, Ill.: Irwin, 1982.

Schmenner, Roger W. "Every Factory Has a Cycle," *Harvard Business Review.* March–April 1983, pp. 121–129.

Skinner, Wickham. "The Focused Factory," *Harvard Business Review.* May–June 1974.

Spencer, Michael S. "Scheduling Components for Group Technology Lines," *Production and Inventory Management.* October–December 1980, pp. 43–49.

Wantuck, Kenneth A. "The Japanese Approach to Productivity," *Proceedings of the American Production and Inventory Control Society Annual Conference,* 1983.

Whitney, Daniel E. "Manufacturing by Design," *Harvard Business Review.* July–August 1988, pp. 83–91.

CHAPTER 6

OPERATIONS PLANNING

Decisions exist only in the present. The question that faces the long-range planner is not what we should do tomorrow. It is what we have to do today to be ready for an uncertain tomorrow. The question is not what will happen in the future. It is: what futurity do we have to factor into our present thinking and doing, what time span do we have to consider, and how do we converge them to a simultaneous decision in the present?
—Peter Drucker

The production plan is the "regulator." It regulates the amount of inventory or backlog that will exist by controlling the production rate. It regulates the amount of material that will be made and purchased because the master schedules, the material requirements plans, and the capacity plans are all derived from it. It regulates the level of work-in-process because it drives the master schedules and material requirements plans that release work into the factory. Because it is the regulator for all these activities, it regulates cash flow and is the foundation for the business plan.
—Oliver Wight

Objectives

After completing this chapter you should be able to:

- Understand the importance of effective operations planning.
- Describe the interactions of operations planning with other plans.
- Identify the inputs to operations planning.
- List the options available to manage supply and demand.

- Discuss various operations planning strategies.
- Explain the concept of hierarchical planning systems.

Outline

INTRODUCTORY CASE: OPERATIONS PLANNING AT OWENS-CORNING FIBERGLAS

Owens-Corning Fiberglas (OCF) is the world's leading producer of glass fiber products. The Anderson plant in South Carolina, one of OCF's largest manufacturing facilities, produces a large number of fiberglass mat products. The mat product line consists of over 200 distinct items sold in a variety of widths, weights, binder treatments, and edge trimmings. Mat products are used primarily in the construction of boat hulls, as a reinforcement in pipeline construction, and in bathroom fixtures such as bathtubs and showers.

In 1982, OCF implemented a computer-based model to address production planning and scheduling decisions at its Anderson plant. Since the initial development of this model, major advances in manufacturing and information systems and a drastic corporate reorganization have occurred. In 1986, OCF reorganized management and decentralized both customer service and information management functions. These forces have individually contributed to a dramatic change in production planning within OCF.

Owens-Corning Fiberglas uses the production switching rule (PSR), a heuristic procedure to develop production plans, because mathematical models tend to be too complex. The PSR has five shift settings from which production for a planning period can be selected. Management's preference to reduce the effects of work-force changes explains why the number of shift settings allowed over the entire planning horizon is limited to five. The fiberglass mat is manufactured on two production lines, each with different capacities and capabilities. Each line can be scheduled to run on four shifts. Three normal shifts are provided by working three eight-hour periods from Monday to Friday. A "fourth" shift represents the weekend shift, and 0 represents shutdown.

The fiberglass mat products can be aggregated easily into pounds. The time period is one month and the planning horizon is twelve months. Forecasted demand is provided by the marketing department. A production plan is generated every month when new information becomes available. In developing production plans, the PSR attempts to minimize the total of payroll costs, overtime costs, hiring and firing costs, and inventory costs in satisfying forecasted demand. An example of OCF's production plan showing the shift settings for the two production lines, the projected monthly aggregate ending inventories, and various cost elements is provided in the table.

Production Plan at OCF

Period	Demand (lb)[1]	Production (lb)[1]	Inventory (lb)[1]	Shift Setting[2]	Regular Wages ($)	Hiring Cost ($)	Layoff Cost ($)	Inventory Cost ($)	Total Cost ($)
Jan.	132	100	152	(3, 0)	90,000	0	0	20,400	110,400
Feb.	124	140	168	(4, 0)	120,000	12,000	0	23,600	155,600
Mar.	155	140	153	(4, 0)	120,000	0	0	20,600	140,600
Apr.	187	155	121	(4, 1)	130,000	7,000	0	14,200	151,200
May	174	170	117	(4, 2)	140,000	7,000	0	13,400	160,400
Jun.	194	170	93	(4, 2)	140,000	0	0	9,300	149,300
Jul.	169	170	94	(4, 2)	140,000	0	0	9,400	149,400
Aug.	132	155	117	(4, 1)	130,000	0	3,000	13,400	146,400
Sep.	151	155	121	(4, 1)	130,000	0	0	14,200	144,200
Oct.	167	155	109	(4, 1)	130,000	0	0	11,800	141,800
Nov.	97	140	152	(4, 0)	120,000	0	3,000	20,400	143,400
Dec.	140	140	152	(4, 0)	120,000	0	0	20,400	140,400
Total					1,510,000	26,000	6,000	191,000	1,733,100

Materials drawn from: Oliff and Burch (1985); Oliff and Leong (1987); and Leong, Oliff, and Markland (1989).
[1]Beginning inventory in January = 184. Beginning shift setting = (3, 0).
[2]$(i, j) = i$ is the number of shifts on line 1, and j is the number of shifts on line 2.
Values for inventory, production, and demand are in 10,000 pounds.
A minimum aggregate inventory level of 900,000 pounds must be held in stock.

OPERATIONS PLANNING

Operations planning links top management's strategic plans with manufacturing or service operations. We use operations planning to refer generically to production planning in manufacturing firms and staff planning in service organizations. A production plan attempts to set production, work-force, and inventory levels to meet sales objectives while minimizing manufacturing costs and effectively utilizing limited organizational resources over a specified planning horizon. A staff plan determines the work-force level and labor-related capacities that can satisfy customer demand by utilizing limited organizational resources over a specified planning horizon. Effective operations planning allows an organization to balance the sometimes conflicting objectives of maximizing customer service,

FIGURE 6-1   Operations Planning Framework

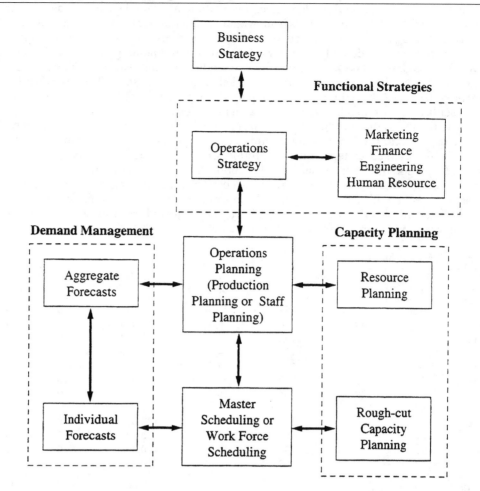

maintaining a stable production or work-force level, minimizing inventory investment, and maximizing profits.

In today's highly competitive environment, delivering the right goods or services at the right time and in the right quantities to the customer at minimum cost requires a smooth flow of operations and information. The development of an effective operations planning and control system to support this flow can enhance customer service and provide a firm with a competitive advantage. An operations planning framework is presented in Figure 6-1. The objectives of operations planning are derived from the operations strategy interacting with the key functional areas of marketing, finance, and human resources. The overall objective for the company is to combine the inputs from all functional areas in order to maximize profits. Plant and equipment are considered fixed in the time period for operations planning. In the long run, operations planning provides the input for resource planning, involving the acquisition of new equipment, expansion of the existing facility, or construction of a new facility (see Chapter 4). Therefore, operations planning has strategic implications for allocating corporate resources such as materials, equipment, facilities, personnel, and money. The operations plan presents a broad framework for performing specific activities. For manufacturing, a master production schedule is developed which is consistent with the operations plan. In the case of service organizations, the operations plan is disaggregated into a master schedule or work-force schedule. Exact specification of time and work activity in which the operation is to be performed are not the concern of the operations plan. Such details are left to operations sequencing and dispatching, which are performed when more accurate and reliable data are available.

Drucker (1959, p. 239) explains that planning allows us to do things today "to be ready for an uncertain tomorrow." The operations plan helps management to focus attention on potential problems in advance. Discovering a problem after it has occurred is too late and is worrisome to management. Many manufacturing problems can be traced to operating in a "reactionary" or "fire-fighting" mode. For example, in response to delays in delivery, many companies hire expeditors to draw up shortage lists and focus on "hot jobs." Expediting seldom works because by pulling these "hot jobs" through the plant, other jobs are neglected. Additional setups are incurred, which compound the capacity and scheduling problem in the shop. Soon more jobs are added to the shortage list and more expeditors are needed to handle the increased number of "hot jobs." Work-in-process inventories are piled up all over the floor waiting for processing, and customer service suffers. By focusing only on expeditors to get jobs out through the door, companies can get trapped in a vicious cycle. An effective operations plan that attempts to match supply with demand will help management avoid these pitfalls.

Although operations planning is used in a majority of businesses, it is often an informal and incomplete process. As Oliver Wight (1974) notes, "Whether they explicitly recognize it or not, most companies establish some kind of production plan." While this is commendable, it is not enough in today's competitive environment. Without a formal system in place, an informal system will evolve to overcome inconsistencies and eventually get the job done. However, the operations plan is achieved at a price: increased organizational slack. Organizational slack is defined as anything that is in excess of what is effectively needed to get the job completed. Symptoms of organizational slack are excess inventories, excess workers, excess overtime costs, excess capacity, long lead times, and long new-product-introduction cycles. Examples of early warning signs of poor operations planning include:

- Marketing is complaining that the right quantities of the right products are not being produced at the right time, and wants an increase in inventories to prevent lost sales.
- Finance is unhappy about the high inventory levels and wants them reduced because of the high cost incurred.
- Purchasing is frustrated that numerous production schedule changes require frequent rescheduling of vendor shipments.
- Marketing cannot comprehend why manufacturing is not producing items in closer alignment with the sales forecast.
- Manufacturing is unhappy with the short, inefficient production runs necessitated by the product mix and quantities specified in the production schedule. Numerous additional machine setups are made, which are time consuming and costly.
- Manufacturing is asking for more expeditors to go after the "hot jobs," which are fast becoming "superhot jobs."
- Quality is being sacrificed to get jobs out to meet delivery dates.
- Evidence of a highly charged emotional environment includes severe tension and pressure in the last week of the month and numerous incidences of finger-pointing.
- Unplanned overtime costs are high.

Operations planning, if implemented successfully, can lead to numerous benefits, such as improved productivity and customer service levels, decreased expediting, and reduced setup and inventory costs. For example, in the early 1980s, Bendix Corporation implemented operations planning at all its manufacturing facilities. Benefits reported were the following: productivity at a European subsidiary improved by 9% and inventory turnover increased by 30% in three years; favorable investment ratios were maintained at a domestic subsidiary, even though customer orders decreased by 30%; customer service was improved at a Canadian subsidiary with a reduction of inventories of $4 million within the first year of implementation (Wantuck, 1989).

FUNCTIONAL INTERFACE

The operations plan provides a direct channel for consistent discussion and communication between manufacturing and top management as well as with other functions. An integrated approach to operations planning is the only way to ensure that all parties agree to one plan and that the operations manager can be held responsible for meeting the plan. A well-documented operations plan can help alleviate fear of the future and resistance to change. Using a comprehensive approach to operations planning can lead to the discovery of previously unknown inefficiencies. In the quest to achieve overall strategic goals, the collaborative approach with its "no stones left unturned" philosophy can spawn new ideas that could be used to improve the system's operations. In addition, a realistic and achievable operations plan discourages informal systems and suboptimal minimeetings from developing, and consequently, less time is spent in hand-wringing and second-guessing the plan. While it is desirable to have stability so that operations can justly be held responsible for meeting plans, there should be sufficient flexibility for the company to respond to actual customer requirements. What is needed is an overall, dynamic plan for the company which changes according to market conditions and at the same time allows each function to adapt accordingly.

An integrated approach is needed because functional conflicts often arise in meeting overall business strategic goals. The operations plan must be supportive of the operations and business strategies as well as the bottom line. For example, a company's objective is to produce "high-quality, customized products, with dependable delivery performance." Customization requires producing goods or services to customers' specifications, which in turn necessitates that operating processes be sufficiently flexible to accommodate the diversity of these requirements. The operations plan must be designed to consider all these factors to enable deliveries to be met and permit the company to be profitable. Several important areas of potential disagreements among different functions within an organization and their impact on the operations plan are discussed below. Shapiro (1977) provides a good discussion on potential conflicts between marketing and manufacturing.

Capacity
Capacity is at the heart of the operations plan (see also Chapter 3). The classic trade-off is between having too much capacity and too little capacity. Either way, management is not going to be happy, and for different reasons. Insufficient capacity can lead to lost sales, and excess capacity can be costly. The issue of capacity is very important to operations planning. Given a choice, operations would prefer to work with excess capacity, since it is easier to schedule jobs and meet promised deliveries. Making significant changes to a plant's capacity is a long-term proposition involving capital investments. Therefore, marketing must provide accurate demand forecasts to ensure that capacity and facilities plans can be made effectively.

On-time Delivery
On-time delivery is a major bone of contention between marketing and operations. The operations plan provides the basis for trade-offs and dialogue between marketing and operations. For example, if marketing requests to have some products or services delivered earlier than planned, operations would in turn require marketing to take delivery of some other products or services at a later time. This is the only possible outcome if capacity is constrained and cannot be increased easily. Without a new, revised operations plan,

marketing and operations must work closely together to maximize the utilization of scarce resources to meet competing needs. Some companies resort to expediting to resolve delivery problems. Expediting basically implies that one customer is more important than another. Such a near-sighted policy seldom works in the long run. When sales are booming, the loss of sales from small customers is not considered critical by management. However, in periods of economic downturn, every customer, small or big, becomes extremely important as the company tries to maintain sales. The industry is marked by excess capacity as demand falls. Customers previously "spurned" in terms of delivery may be lost forever because they can shop elsewhere for better service. On-time delivery requires objectives regarding lead times to be defined clearly and understood by all parties involved. Reductions in setup time allow more productive utilization of equipment and can help simplify operations scheduling and reduce lead times. Setup reduction is an important element of just-in-time systems.

Inventory Levels

Marketing may want to hold inventories at various distribution centers to provide fast delivery time, especially for make-to-stock products. Customers expect a high probability that their orders will be filled immediately from inventory for make-to-stock products. Management must decide the level of inventory needed and the financial budget that can support this investment. The operations plan is designed to reflect these objectives. Several operations plans with varying levels of inventory can be generated so that management can examine the cost trade-offs among the alternatives before deciding on the appropriate plan to achieve the strategic goals.

Breadth of Product/Service Line

Marketing strategies regarding the breadth of a product/service line, the number of product or service variations, and the product or service mix have major implications for operations planning. A change in product or service mix could result in different processing requirements and cause capacity and scheduling problems, even though the total number of units produced or customers served could be the same. Purchasing would have to adjust orders for raw materials and parts. Trying to produce too many products or services in one facility could lead to a loss of focus. (A detailed discussion of "focused facilities" is provided in Chapter 4.) Operations planning allows problems associated with these strategies to be openly discussed so that attention can be focused on what needs to be done. For example, in 1986 Cummins Engine's sales catalog offered more than 100,000 parts (Venkatesan, 1990). In addition, in one engine family, there were 86 different flywheels, 49 flywheel options, and 17 types of starter motors with 12 possible mountings. Based on these options, there were approximately 1200 assembly combinations. Federal emissions regulations and intense competition from companies such as Komatsu and Caterpillar forced Cummins to introduce new products and be more responsive to the customers' needs. At the same time Cummins had to manufacture parts for discontinued products for existing customers. The result is a proliferation of parts and products. Cummins had to cut prices 20–40% in order to retain its market share. Senior management asked the factory to reduce costs and lead time, which meant that work in process had to be reduced at the time the factory was trying to cope with an increase in the number of parts produced.

New Product/Service Introductions

New product/service introductions have major implications for operations and purchasing and should be included in the operations plan. While demand for new products/services should be a part of the marketing forecast, there may be marketing objectives regarding design changes on existing products/services. There is also the timing of new product/service introduction and the impact on existing capacity. Problems inherently present in new product/service introductions take more time to iron out, which can have

FIGURE 6-2 Operations Planning Inputs

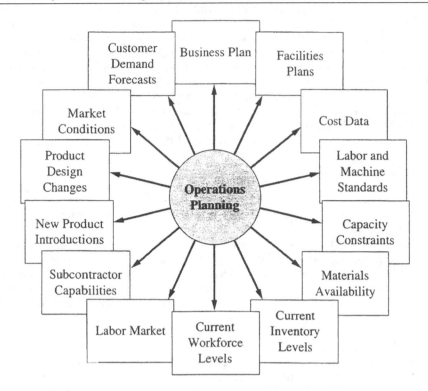

an impact on process utilization. Engineering should interact with operations regarding processing requirements, time standards, quality levels, and the like. Purchasing input is required as to the availability of materials. An important question is whether the production of low-volume new products should be mixed in with the production of mature products that require high-volume production runs.

The interface with other plans allows potential problem areas to be identified and discussed so that operations can play a more *proactive* role instead of reacting to problems as they occur. Inputs from various functional areas to the operations planning process are summarized in Figure 6-2.

INFLUENCING SUPPLY AND DEMAND

If demand is constant, solving the operations planning problem is an easy task. However, companies are often faced with turbulent and seasonal demand. To deal with seasonal demand, companies may initially attempt to stabilize aggregate demand. After all efforts to stabilize demand have been made, various techniques to affect the supply through short-term adjustments to capacity can be used to meet demand.

Controlling Demand

There are several ways to control or influence demand, such as the use of complementary products/services, flexible pricing, promotions and advertising, reservations, and flexible delivery dates. Although managing demand is important to manufacturing, it is even more critical in service organizations, especially those offering a service bundle with a low percentage of facilitating goods.* The reason is that the build up of inventory in slack periods may not be a viable option.

Complementary Products and Services

By providing complementary products or services, companies can even out the seasonal impact on existing capacities. Usually, manufacturers consider adding products that require similar processes. A manufacturer of snow blowers may want to build lawn mowers to balance aggregate demand. Manufacturers of air conditioners have developed heat pumps, which function as heaters in winter and provide air conditioning in summer. Demand for heat pumps should be less cyclical than demand for air conditioners only. However, companies must be cautious as they expand their market activities lest their facilities become unfocused, an issue discussed in Chapter 4.

Many busy restaurants now provide lounges with television sets where customers can sit and have a drink while waiting their turns at the dining tables. In addition to fewer complaints from customers about waiting in line, restaurants derive additional profits from the lounge. Fast-food restaurants are offering breakfast to complement lunch and dinner, and to increase the use of cooking facilities. After McDonald's introduced its breakfast services, Burger King was slow to respond, because the broilers used for meat patties were not suitable for preparing eggs. Burger King eventually overcame this problem and expanded into the breakfast market.

Flexible Pricing

The objective of flexible pricing is to even out demand by reducing peak demand or to increase demand during "down" periods. Prices are raised during peak periods to discourage heavy demand and lowered to increase sales during off-peak periods. Examples include higher rates charged by electrical power utilities in summer to lower the use of air conditioning; heavily discounted tickets requiring a Saturday night stayover offered by airlines to attract nonbusiness travelers; discount prices for matinee shows; "happy hours" at bars; and differential rates offered by telephone companies which favor calling during evenings, weekends, and holidays. Golf courses often charge lower "winter" greens fees to prolong the golf season. Manufacturers facing seasonal demand generally give discounts for early season delivery of goods.

Promotions and Advertising

The use of flexible pricing is closely coordinated with promotions and advertising. Advertising can be used to stimulate sales by offering discounted prices during nonpeak or low-demand periods. Airlines heavily advertise their cheap winter fares to encourage nonbusiness travelers to fly instead of driving to their final destinations or to make additional trips because of affordable ticket prices. Sales promotions are advertised so that customers are made aware of the upcoming event. Ski resorts publicize the availability of snow machines to generate artificial snow on the ski slopes. This lets customers know in advance that their ski vacation is less dependent on nature to provide the snow needed for skiing. Thus snow machines allow demand to be spread over a longer season instead of concentrating demand on heavy snowfall days.

Reservations and Flexible Delivery Dates

Customers are often asked to make appointments in advance to reserve capacity. This option allows the organization to match supply and demand as closely as possible. Appointments are common in service organizations such as medical practitioners, auto

---

*The service bundle consists of supporting facility, facilitating goods, explicit services, and implicit services. Facilitating goods are defined as "material purchased or consumed by the buyer" (Fitzsimmons and Sullivan, 1982, p. 17). The term "facilitating goods" was suggested by John Rathmell in *Marketing in the Service Sector* (Cambridge, Mass.: Winthrop Publishers, 1974).

repair shops, law firms, airlines, and hotels. Although the reservation system has its merits, "no-shows" by customers not financially responsible for such actions have resulted in inefficient use of capacity and lost profits. Airlines have been known to over-book their capacities to compensate for no-shows and run the risk of alienating their customers. A customer who is "bumped" from a reserved seat is typically compen-sated by the airline with a free ticket to any destination in the continental United States. Airlines have also introduced nonrefundable, advanced purchase supersaver tickets tar-geted at nonbusiness travelers with inflexible departure and return flight dates and times. Customers are penalized for any changes made to confirmed flight schedules. Most hotels now require a one-night prepaid room charge for reservations made by the customers, but the down payment is refundable if cancellation is made at least one day in advance.

Sometimes customers are asked to wait for products that are not immediately avail-able, which results in a back-order situation. When back orders occur, two things can hap-pen. One scenario is the customer is mildly annoyed at the poor service but is willing to wait and there is an additional cost involved for the company to keep track of the order. This scenario, although costing the company a little, is much better than the second sce-nario in which the customer is lost. The cost of lost sales is much harder to assess but gen-erally involves loss of goodwill and future sales and, therefore, future profits. Back orders allow production to be postponed to a period where slack capacity is available.

Controlling Supply

In addition to the previous short-term techniques to affect demand, there are several short-term alternatives for affecting supply. These are hiring and layoffs, undertime and over-time, temporary and part-time workers, inventory, subcontracting, cooperative arrangements, and consumer participation.

Hiring and Layoffs

When operations are labor intensive, changes in the work-force level can have an impact on the capacity. The ability to hire more workers is sometimes limited by other resources such as the availability of equipment that supports the workers. Also, some equipment requires a minimum number of workers to operate, thus placing a lower limit on the work-force level needed to maintain operations. Sometimes a second shift can be added. The disadvantages of a second shift are the difficulties associated with finding workers will-ing to work shifts and the generally lower productivity during the second or third shifts. In addition, union agreements may have an impact on hiring and layoff policies. Work-ers with more years of service may not be laid off ahead of newer employees; that is, lay-offs follow the "last in first out" policy.

There are costs associated with hiring and layoff of workers. The costs of hiring new employees are costs of advertising, screening, interviewing, medical examinations, employ-ment agency fees, company visitations, and training. Some localities have a severe short-age of skilled workers. This situation requires newly hired workers to go through an expensive training program. Newly trained workers may take several months to get up to speed and be fully productive. Frequent turnover of personnel can have a negative influ-ence on the work force in terms of morale and negative feelings, which could result in a loss of productivity. Workers who are laid off are compensated on the basis of seniority and years of service with the company. Intangible effects such as poor public relations and image of the company in the community are more difficult to estimate. Instead of using layoffs, some companies offer attractive early retirement packages to trim the work-force size. In the auto industry, job security is now becoming an important issue because of the high level of layoffs arising from excess auto plant capacities. In 1990, the UAW negotiated an agreement that pays hefty compensations for workers laid off as a result of plants that are permanently closed.

Companies must be careful not to have highly erratic employment levels. In general, employees are more willing and feel more secure working for companies that maintain stable employment levels. The benefits of a stable work force include higher employee morale and increased company loyalty, both of which can have a significant impact on productivity and quality levels. The Japanese believe in a system of lifetime employment, where employees are retrained for new jobs if no longer needed in their current jobs. This system encourages worker loyalty; it is discussed in greater depth in Chapter 8.

Undertime and Overtime

This alternative is one of the most common approaches to altering capacity. This approach can be easily and quickly implemented when compared to the hiring/layoff decision. Workers find overtime especially attractive, since they have an opportunity to earn more money. Manufacturers frequently use overtime to make up shortfalls in capacity. The company can maintain a stable work force and develop long-term relationships with its employees, which can lead to a loyal and productive work force.

On the down side, excessive overtime can cause worker fatigue, which can lead to poor performance, poor quality, and increased accidents. In addition, higher payroll costs are incurred, since a premium (50% to 100% of regular wages) is paid for overtime work. Union rules may permit workers to reject overtime work, making it difficult for a company to pull together a crew to work a production line after regular hours.

Undertime means that workers and equipment are not fully utilized; this situation is expensive to maintain for long periods of time. During periods of slow demand, workers may be asked to do housekeeping around their work area and routine maintenance. Workers can also be provided with additional training to acquire new skills or improve current ones. The assumption is that workers are being paid their regular wages during undertime. Increasingly, we are seeing companies temporarily idling facilities in periods of low demand. Workers get little or no compensation during the time off but retain benefits such as health insurance, a situation that is better than being laid off permanently. This happens more frequently in industries where there is excess capacity and production is carried out in shifts. Chrysler, Ford, and General Motors have temporarily closed plants in an effort to match supply with demand. Government and state employees have been forced to stay home without pay for short periods of time, lasting from several days to a couple of weeks, to balance the budget.

Temporary and Part-Time Workers

Depending on the level of training and skill needed, the use of temporary or part-time workers is an attractive and practical option. Temporary workers are often paid less and receive few or no benefits. The use of temporary workers is applicable to industries with highly seasonal demand and especially to service-related industries, such as department stores, fast-food restaurants, supermarkets, farms, recreational parks, and hotels. Post offices rely heavily on temporary workers during the Christmas season. Most worker unions are opposed to the hiring of temporary workers and typically build this provision into the collective agreements with their companies. The reason is that temporary workers do not pay any union dues and may actually diminish the influence of the union. The success of this option is dependent on the availability of a steady pool of temporary workers from which a company can hire at short notice. Students looking for part-time or summer work are a primary source of temporary workers.

There are several trends regarding the use of temporary and part-time workers worth noting here (Pollock and Bernstein, 1986):

1. The percentage of part-time workers in the airline industry has more than doubled since 1983, to 12% of employees.
2. "Contingent" workers account for 25% of the total work force.
3. Over 40% of jobs in the retail industry are filled by part-time workers.

4. The number of "telecommuters" who use technologies such as telephones, fax machines, and computers to stay in touch with the office while working at home has increased 400% since 1980.

5. A 10% to 15% annual growth in the number of temporary workers is anticipated to continue through the mid-1990s.

In addition to the above observations, the federal government has been allowed to hire temporary workers since 1989.

An example of a company that relies heavily on part-time workers is Tuesday Morning Inc., a retailing chain that specializes in upscale, limited quantity, closeout merchandise such as gifts and household items. The stores are open only four times a year for several months, yet the business is profitable. In 1990, annual sales totaled $107 million with net income of $4.7 million. Currently, there are 150 stores located in 22 states (mostly in the South), but plans are underway to expand throughout the United States to reach a target of 250 stores by 1995. Because the stores are open less than half a year, Tuesday Morning hires entirely part-time workers to staff the stores, except for store managers (Helliker, 1991).

The use of part-time workers is not without its drawbacks. Sears, in an effort to keep labor costs as low as possible, shifted its sales-force composition from 70% full-time employees to 70% part-timers. In the short term, this strategy led to aggregate wages and benefits being reduced significantly. The long-term effects are an increasing rate of employee turnover and a drastic drop in customer satisfaction (Schlesinger and Heskett, 1991).

Inventory

A company can use inventories to buffer production from seasonal demand. Inventories include raw materials, work in process, finished parts, assemblies, and finished goods. Because demand in peak periods exceeds the available capacity of a plant, inventories are built up in earlier periods when capacity exceeds demand to enable high demands in later periods to be met. Reasons for not holding excess inventories are discussed in more detail in Chapter 7. Obviously, the use of inventories is more applicable to manufacturing organizations, where goods can be stored, than to service organizations, where services (excluding facilitating goods) are not storable.

Subcontracting

Subcontracting is an effective method for a company to acquire temporary capacity. Problems associated with subcontracting are higher costs and less control over delivery and quality. The expertise of the subcontractor is an important consideration. If the facility's capacity cannot be increased without substantial investment and demand is not stable, subcontracting may be a viable approach. In manufacturing, a gear box producer may subcontract gears during peak demand periods. Many small and mid-size companies find it cost effective to subcontract janitorial services. The health-care industry makes extensive use of outside contract services such as food catering, laundry, and housekeeping. The contract management business in hospitals is expected to double to more than $8 billion a year by the mid-1990s. Hospitals are even subcontracting specialized services. For example, Psicor contracts with hospitals to provide equipment and supplies for open-heart surgery.

Cooperative Arrangements

This option is similar to subcontracting except that business could go either way. Hotels have been known to make arrangements where "overbooked" customers during peak holiday seasons are transferred to another hotel in the cooperating group. Power utility companies "buy" electricity from each other, depending on their ability to meet demand fluctuations. Aluminum manufacturers commonly "swap" customer contracts with each other to balance supply and demand. Customers receive their orders directly from the company to which their contracts have been swapped and not from the company where the original order was placed. This arrangement saves double handling and transportation costs, which could be passed on to the customers. Cooperative arrangements are more likely in industries where capacities have to be added in big chunks and which involve high capital investments.

Consumer Participation

This option is particularly applicable to the service industries. By transferring a portion of the service to the customer, the labor requirements for the delivery of services are reduced. Examples include self-service salad bars, self-service gas pumps, and self-bagging of groceries. Manufacturers are also taking advantage of increased customer participation by transferring parts of the assembly process to the customers. For example, bicycles, knock-down furniture, and gas grills are sold unassembled in cartons. By requiring customers to assemble the product, manufacturers can use their existing labor for other critical activities. Companies also benefit from lower packaging and transportation costs, because the unassembled products are less bulky. The use of this approach assumes that the assembly required is not complicated and customers can put the pieces together correctly by following the enclosed instructions. The downside risk is that customers are not adept at handling the assembly tasks and could be sufficiently frustrated to return the product for a full refund or exchange the product for another because they damaged the product during assembly.

OPERATIONS PLANNING STRATEGIES

The two basic strategies are level strategy and chase strategy. A comparison of these two strategies in terms of various characteristics is summarized in Table 6-1. In addition, an infinite range of compromise strategies may be selected from different combinations of the pure chase and level alternatives.

Level Strategy

A level strategy involves setting a constant output rate or maintaining a stable work force. In manufacturing companies, a constant output is achieved by using a steady work force and by allowing inventories to absorb fluctuations in demand. An example of a level strategy for a manufacturing firm is presented in Decision Model Box 6-1. Because services cannot be inventoried, a level strategy in a service organization involves keeping a steady work force and using overtime and undertime to buffer fluctuations in demand. An example of a level strategy for a service firm is provided in Decision Model box 6-2.

TABLE 6-1 Comparison of Chase and Level Strategies

	Chase Strategy	Level Strategy
Inventory costs	negligible (safety stock only)	high
Labor skill level	low	high
Job discretion	low	high
Quality of life	low	high
Worker compensation	low	high
Training per worker	low	high
Labor turnover rate	high	low
Hiring/layoff costs	high	negligible (attrition only)
Quality costs and problems	high	low
Supervision required	high	low
Capacity change costs	high	none
Forecasting requirements	short run	long run

DECISION MODEL BOX 6-1   Operations Planning at Lin Steel Company

The Lin Steel Company, a manufacturer of steel wires, is faced with cyclic demand for its products. The table below shows a monthly aggregate demand forecast for the next year. The following data have been collected. The production rate is 100 tons per worker per month. The average salary for a production worker is $2000 per month. Overtime is reimbursed at 150% of regular salary. Workers are limited to 25% overtime per month. The cost of hiring an additional worker is $800. Laying off a worker costs $1200. There is presently no inventory in stock. Inventory holding cost is $2 per ton per month. The inventory at the end of each month is calculated as: Ending inventory = beginning inventory + production − demand. All forecasted demand must be met; that is, no backorders are allowed.

Lin Steel wants to generate a production plan for the next 12 months to utilize its resources more effectively and to provide better customer service. Michelle, the materials manager, has been asked to prepare three alternatives for evaluation in an upcoming production planning meeting involving representatives from marketing, manufacturing, and finance. The production plans are generated by using: (a) a level strategy—maintain the current work-force level of 50 workers, using inventories to buffer demand, (b) a chase strategy—adjust the work force to meet demand exactly, (c) a mixed strategy—trim the work force to 48 workers, maintain this work-force level, and use overtime and inventory to buffer demand. Management would like the three plans to be presented in three formats: tabular, graphic, and cumulative. The costs of the three operations planning strategies should also be computed. If holding cost is 40% higher than estimated, what is the impact of this on the three plans?

Month	Forecasted Demand (Tons)	Month	Forecasted Demand (Tons)
Jan.	3000	July	6000
Feb.	4000	August	4000
Mar.	4000	September	4000
Apr.	4000	October	6000
May	7000	November	6000
Jun.	6000	December	6000

The materials manager computed the following plans:

(a)   Level Strategy—Tabular Representation

Period	Demand Forecast (tons)	Production (tons)	Inventory (tons)	Work-force Level	Regular Wages ($)	Overtime Cost ($)	Hiring Cost ($)	Layoff Cost ($)	Inventory Holding Cost ($)	Total Cost ($)
Jan.	3,000	5,000	2,000	50	100,000	0	0	0	4,000	104,000
Feb.	4,000	5,000	3,000	50	100,000	0	0	0	6,000	106,000
Mar.	4,000	5,000	4,000	50	100,000	0	0	0	8,000	108,000
Apr.	4,000	5,000	5,000	50	100,000	0	0	0	10,000	110,000
May	7,000	5,000	3,000	50	100,000	0	0	0	6,000	106,000
Jun.	6,000	5,000	2,000	50	100,000	0	0	0	4,000	104,000
Jul.	6,000	5,000	1,000	50	100,000	0	0	0	2,000	102,000
Aug.	4,000	5,000	2,000	50	100,000	0	0	0	4,000	104,000
Sep.	4,000	5,000	3,000	50	100,000	0	0	0	6,000	106,000
Oct.	6,000	5,000	2,000	50	100,000	0	0	0	4,000	104,000
Nov.	6,000	5,000	1,000	50	100,000	0	0	0	2,000	102,000
Dec.	6,000	5,000	0	50	100,000	0	0	0	0	100,000
Total	60,000	60,000			1,200,000	0	0	0	56,000	1,256,000

(b) Chase Strategy—Tabular Representation

Period	Demand Forecast (tons)	Production (tons)	Inventory (tons)	Work-force Level	Regular Wages ($)	Overtime Cost ($)	Hiring Cost ($)	Layoff Cost ($)	Inventory Holding Cost ($)	Total Cost ($)
Jan.	3,000	3,000	0	30	60,000	0	0	24,000	0	84,000
Feb.	4,000	4,000	0	40	80,000	0	8,000	0	0	88,000
Mar.	4,000	4,000	0	40	80,000	0	0	0	0	80,000
Apr.	4,000	4,000	0	40	80,000	0	0	0	0	80,000
May	7,000	7,000	0	70	140,000	0	24,000	0	0	164,000
Jun.	6,000	6,000	0	60	120,000	0	0	12,000	0	132,000
Jul.	6,000	6,000	0	60	120,000	0	0	0	0	120,000
Aug.	4,000	4,000	0	40	80,000	0	0	24,000	0	104,000
Sep.	4,000	4,000	0	40	80,000	0	0	0	0	80,000
Oct.	6,000	6,000	0	60	120,000	0	16,000	0	0	136,000
Nov.	6,000	6,000	0	60	120,000	0	0	0	0	120,000
Dec.	6,000	6,000	0	60	120,000	0	0	0	0	120,000
Total	60,000	60,000			1,200,000	0	48,000	60,000	0	1,308,000

(c) Mixed Strategy (Trial-and-Error Approach)— Tabular Representation

Period	Demand Forecast (tons)	Production (tons)	Inventory (tons)	Work-force Level	Regular Wages ($)	Overtime Cost ($)	Hiring Cost ($)	Layoff Cost ($)	Inventory Holding Cost ($)	Total Cost ($)
Jan.	3,000	4,800	1,800	48	96,000	0	0	2,400	3,600	102,000
Feb.	4,000	4,800	2,600	48	96,000	0	0	0	5,200	101,200
Mar.	4,000	4,800	3,400	48	96,000	0	0	0	6,800	102,800
Apr.	4,000	4,800	4,200	48	96,000	0	0	0	8,400	104,400
May	7,000	4,800	2,000	48	96,000	0	0	0	4,000	100,000
Jun.	6,000	4,800	800	48	96,000	0	0	0	1,600	97,600
Jul.	6,000	5,200	0	48	96,000	12,000	0	0	0	108,000
Aug.	4,000	4,800	800	48	96,000	0	0	0	1,600	97,600
Sep.	4,000	4,800	1,600	48	96,000	0	0	0	3,200	99,200
Oct.	6,000	4,800	400	48	96,000	0	0	0	800	96,800
Nov.	6,000	5,600	0	48	96,000	24,000	0	0	0	120,000
Dec.	6,000	6,000	0	48	96,000	36,000	0	0	0	132,000
Total	60,000	60,000			1,152,000	72,000	0	2,400	35,200	1,261,600

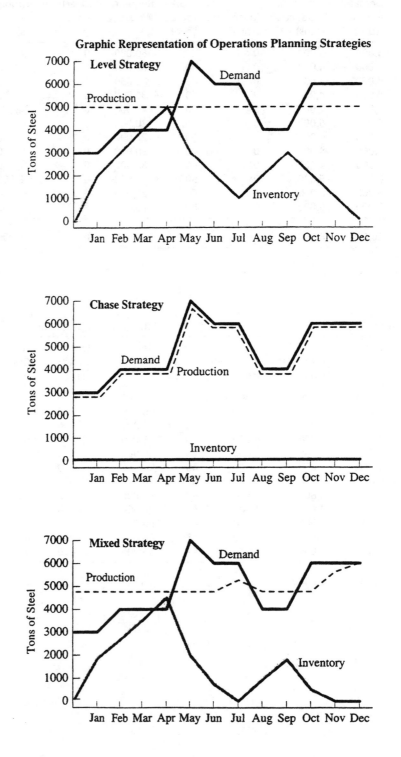

Graphic Representation of Operations Planning Strategies

Cumulative Production–Demand–Inventory Chart

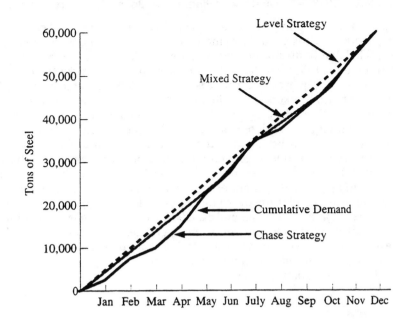

(d) Cost Comparison of the Three Operations Planning Strategies for Lin Steel

Strategy	Regular Wages ($)	Overtime Cost ($)	Hiring Cost ($)	Layoff Cost ($)	Inventory Holding Cost ($)	Total Cost ($)
Level strategy	1,200,000	0	0	0	56,000	1,256,000
Chase strategy	1,200,000	0	48,000	60,000	0	1,308,000
Mixed strategy	1,152,000	72,000	0	2,400	35,200	1,261,600

The least total cost incurred in this example is the level strategy. The reason is the high cost of hiring and laying off workers compared to the cost of holding inventory. Depending on the cost parameters such as holding cost, hiring/layoff cost, and the like, the outcome of the cost comparisons can vary widely. It should be pointed out that quantifiable costs are only one input used by management to decide on an acceptable production plan. The plan should be evaluated on how well it is able to meet the company's strategic goals.

(e) Costs of the Three Plans When Unit Inventory Holding Cost Is $2.80 per Month

Strategy	Inventory Holding Cost ($2 per month)			Inventory Holding Cost ($2.80 per month)		
	Level	Chase	Mixed	Level	Chase	Mixed
Regular wages	1,200,000	1,200,000	1,152,000	1,200,000	1,200,000	1,152,000
Overtime cost	0	0	72,000	0	0	72,000
Hiring cost	0	48,000	0	0	48,000	0
Layoff cost	0	60,000	2,400	0	60,000	2,400
Inventory holding cost	56,000	0	35,200	78,400	0	49,280
Total cost	1,256,000	1,308,000	1,261,600	1,278,400	1,308,000	1,275,680

Note that the least cost plan is provided by the mixed strategy when the unit inventory cost is increased by 40%.

DECISION MODEL BOX 6-2 Operations Planning at Boyer Construction Company

The Boyer Construction Company, which specializes in residential and commercial remodeling work, is facing seasonal demand for its services. The forecasted aggregate demand in labor hours for the next year are as follows: winter = 19,200, spring = 28,800, summer = 36,000, and fall = 24,000. Each employee works 480 hours per season. The average employee salary for a season is $5760. Overtime is reimbursed at $18 per labor hour. Workers are limited to 120 overtime hours per season. The cost of hiring an additional worker is $3000. Laying off a worker costs $2000. The company prides itself on completing all work within the season the service orders are due; that is, no back orders are allowed. The company currently has 50 workers. Boyer Construction wants to generate a staffing plan with a planning horizon of one year to utilize their resources more effectively and to provide better customer service. The staffing plans are generated using: (a) a level strategy—maintaining a stable work-force level and using overtime to buffer demand, (b) a chase strategy-adjusting the work force to meet demand exactly, (c) a mixed strategy—combination of hiring and laying off employees and using overtime. Which strategy would be the least expensive? If the costs of hiring and laying off a worker are $1500 and $1000, respectively, what are the effects on the three plans?

The following operations plans were computed.

(a) Level Strategy

Season	Demand Forecast (hours)	Work-force Level	Available Regular Hours	Overtime Hours	Regular Wages ($)	Overtime Cost ($)	Hiring Cost ($)	Layoff Cost ($)	Total Cost ($)
Winter	19,200	60	28,800	0	345,600	0	30,000	0	375,600
Spring	28,800	60	28,800	0	345,600	0	0	0	345,600
Summer	36,000	60	28,800	7,200	345,600	129,600	0	0	475,200
Fall	24,000	60	28,800	0	345,600	0	0	0	345,600
Total	108,000		115,200	7,200	1,382,400	129,600	30,000	0	1,542,000

To maintain a stable work force over the planning horizon, the focus is on the season with the peak demand. In this case, the summer season has maximum labor requirements of 36,000 hours. Each worker can work a total of 600 hours per season, made up of 480 regular hours and 120 overtime hours. Therefore, the total number of workers required is (36,000/600) = 60 workers. With this strategy there is undertime in the winter and fall seasons totaling 14,400 regular hours. This undertime is absorbed under regular wages.

(b) Chase Strategy

Season	Demand Forecast (hours)	Work-force Level	Available Regular Hours	Overtime Hours	Regular Wages ($)	Overtime Cost ($)	Hiring Cost ($)	Layoff Cost ($)	Total Cost ($)
Winter	19,200	40	19,200	0	230,400	0	0	20,000	250,400
Spring	28,800	60	28,800	0	345,600	0	60,000	0	405,600
Summer	36,000	75	36,000	0	432,000	0	45,000	0	477,000
Fall	24,000	50	24,000	0	288,000	0	0	50,000	338,000
Total	108,000		108,000	0	1,296,000	0	105,000	70,000	1,471,000

c) Mixed Strategy (Trial-and-Error Approach)

Season	Demand Forecast (hours)	Work-force Level	Available Regular Hours	Overtime Hours	Regular Wages ($)	Overtime Cost ($)	Hiring Cost ($)	Layoff Cost ($)	Total Cost ($)
Winter	19,200	40	19,200	0	230,400	0	0	20,000	250,400
Spring	28,800	60	28,800	0	345,600	129,600	60,000	0	405,600
Summer	36,000	60	28,800	7,200	345,600	0	0	0	475,200
Fall	24,000	50	24,000	0	288,000	0	0	20,000	308,000
Total	108,000		108,000	7,200	1,209,600	129,600	60,000	40,000	1,439,200

(d) Cost Comparison of the Three Operations Planning Strategies for Boyer Construction

Strategy	Regular Wages	Overtime Cost	Hiring Cost	Layoff Cost	Total Cost
Level strategy	1,382,400	129,600	30,000	0	1,542,000
Chase strategy	1,296,000	0	105,000	70,000	1,471,000
Mixed strategy	1,209,600	129,600	60,000	40,000	1,439,20

The total cost incurred in this example is the mixed strategy. The reason is the high cost of undertime incurred with the level strategy in response to highly seasonal demands. The chase strategy incurred a high cost associated with hiring and laying off workers. A different least-cost strategy will likely emerge with different costs associated with hiring, layoff, and overtime.

(e) Cost of the Three Plans When Hiring Cost Is $1500 and Layoff Cost Is $1000 Per Worker

Strategy	Hiring/Layoff Cost ($3,000/2,000)			Hiring/Layoff Cost ($1,500/$1,000)		
	Level	Chase	Mixed	Level	Chase	Mixed
Regular wages	1,382,400	1,296,000	1,209,000	1,382,400	1,296,000	1,209,600
Overtime cost	129,600	0	129,600	129,600	0	129,600
Hiring cost	30,000	105,000	60,000	15,000	52,500	30,000
Layoff cost	0	70,000	40,000	0	35,000	20,000
Total cost	1,542,000	1,471,000	1,439,200	1,527,000	1,383,500	1,389,200

Note that the least-cost plan is provided by the chase strategy because of the lower hiring and layoff costs.

The level strategy is appealing for several reasons. The costs associated with hiring and laying off workers are eliminated. The level strategy avoids ups and downs associated with frequent hiring and layoffs and low morale as a result of high worker turnover. With a steady work force, workers are better utilized if they are cross-trained in a variety of skills.

Chase Strategy

A chase strategy attempts to match supply with demand by varying the work-force size. Examples of a chase strategy in manufacturing and services are presented in Decision Model Boxes 6-1 and 6-2. In a manufacturing environment the use of this strategy avoids any inventory buildup and, therefore, saves on carrying cost. In a service environment the objective is not to have any undertime. A chase strategy is more applicable in an operating environment in which low-wage unskilled workers perform jobs with limited discretion. Training costs are much higher than for the level strategy because of the frequent turnover of employees. More supervision may be needed to ensure that the workers are carrying out their duties according to specifications, and chances for errors are usually much higher.

When the costs of hiring, layoff, overtime, and subcontracting are high relative to the costs of carrying inventory, the chase strategy becomes less attractive than the level strategy. The chase strategy is more prone to stockouts compared to the level strategy, because companies often experience difficulty in adjusting capacity fast enough to match sales exactly. Union agreements that heavily penalize employee layoffs also discourage companies from adopting a chase strategy.

Although there are obvious disadvantages associated with the chase strategy, several service industries such as fast-food industries, amusement parks, and resort hotels rely heavily on this strategy for their survival. An example is the Disney World theme park in Orlando, which has been particularly successful in using a large pool of temporary workers during the peak tourist season and yet maintains a high level of customer service. By utilizing students in the summer months, the company is able to tap into a huge and ready reserve of temporary workers, pay relatively low wages, and get a good-quality work force. Students are looking for part-time jobs in the summer, and this temporary arrangement works well for both employers and students.

Mixed Strategies

The basic level and chase strategies represent the two diametrical extremes of operations planning. Companies typically employ some combination of these two pure strategies. The level strategy with a steady work force in manufacturing can be modified to allow adjustments to the production rate, using overtime and undertime to respond to demand variations so that little or no inventory is maintained. Subcontracting can be used if overtime cannot solve the capacity problem. Another example of a mixed strategy is one that attempts to maintain a stable work force as long as possible, using overtime and undertime to meet demand, but recognizes that it is more realistic to keep some inventory and have some hiring and laying off of employees.

Whatever operations planning strategy is selected, it must be consistent with the operations and business strategies, and provide a firm with a competitive advantage. Japanese manufacturers are the biggest proponents of using smooth production techniques to apply the just-in-time (JIT) management philosophy to great competitive advantage. Many Japanese companies such as Toyota, Honda, and Sony have "lifetime employment" and no-layoff personnel policies. IBM is an example of a U.S. corporation which had a no-layoff policy for many years, though the recent downsizing has included layoffs. Japanese manufacturers prefer a level operations planning strategy that allows overtime and undertime to buffer against fluctuations in demand. Temporary workers are also used extensively. With smooth production and the kanban system, inventories are kept to a minimum. United States companies are now beginning to implement JIT (see Chapter 8), which favors leveling production as an operations planning approach. A discussion of operations planning in a JIT environment is provided in Application Box 6-1.

Operations Planning Decision Costs

There are three broad categories of quantifiable costs relevant to operations planning: regular production costs, inventory costs, and production rate change costs.

APPLICATION BOX 6-1   Operations Planning at Toyota

Toyota's production system calls for smoothing of production to minimize disruptions and inventory. A production plan showing the number of cars to be produced in the current year is prepared by Toyota. The yearly production plan is translated into the monthly and daily plans. For example, if the annual production plan calls for 168,000 units, then the production each month is 14,000 units. The monthly plans are then translated into daily requirements. For a 20-day month, the number of cars produced per day is 700. At the daily level, the different mix of the 700 autos must be considered: 400 sedans, 200 coupes, and 100 wagons. A daily schedule is then developed that shows the sequence of assembling the various types of cars: for example, sedan-coupe-sedan-coupe-sedan-wagon-sedan, and so on (see also Chapter 8, Table 8-1)

To adapt to changes in demand occurring within a year, temporary workers can be hired or laid off. Ordinarily, machines are loaded at only 50% of their full capacities. Toyota has multifunctional workers who can typically handle several machines, sometimes as many as a dozen machines. In periods of increasing demand, temporary workers can be hired so that each worker now works on half the number of machines he or she was responsible for previously. Toyota can double the machine capacity utilization with this approach. It is important to have equipment that newly hired, unskilled temporary workers can become fully competent on within a short period of time. An interesting policy is that although Toyota believes in minimizing the number of workers used, it is not deemed necessary to have a minimum number of machines to meet demand. It is not unusual to have excess machine capacity so that only temporary workers are needed to effectively expand production capacity in response to increases in demand. On assembly lines, temporary workers can be added to reduce the cycle time and increase the production rate.

Toyota uses a two-shift daily schedule with the first shift between 8 a.m.-5 p.m. and the second shift from 9 p.m.-6 a.m. Short-term increases in production output can be achieved by having employees work overtime to fill the time slots between shifts. During periods of weak demand, temporary workers will be laid off. Toyota's policy is to let redundant workers take a rest rather than to allow production of unnecessary inventory just to keep workers busy and utilization high. In slack periods, workers can work on process improvements that will become useful when demand increases. Other activities that can be organized during slow periods are quality control circle meetings, practicing and improving setups, and routine machine maintenance. Another option is to use excess workers and equipment to manufacture parts that have previously been purchased from suppliers.

Materials drawn from Y. Monden, "Smoothed Production Lets Toyota Adapt to Demand Changes and Reduce Inventory," *Industrial Engineering, August 1981,* pp. 42–51.

Regular Production Costs.   These costs apply to the production of one output unit during regular time. The applicable costs are the fixed and variable costs of production, direct and indirect material costs, and regular payroll costs. If all production is carried out during regular time, regular payroll cost is not a relevant cost and can be ignored in comparing various alternative strategies.

Inventory Costs.   Inventory costs include the cost of carrying inventory, back-order and stockout costs, and cost of adding storage facilities beyond those required for level production. The inventory carrying cost includes costs related to storage, opportunity cost, insurance, taxes, obsolescence, breakage, pilferage, and deterioration (see also Chapter 7). Back-order and stockout costs are harder to estimate and include expediting costs, loss of goodwill, and loss of sales income.

Production Rate Change Costs.   When production rates are changed there are costs involved in reorganizing and replanning for the new production level. For example, when a second shift is added, we may see an initial decline in labor productivity. A one-time cost of start-up and shutdown of a production facility may be incurred. Other items included in this category are costs associated with hiring and laying off of regular employees, overtime and undertime, temporary and part-time workers, subcontracting and outsourcing, cooperative arrangements, and customer participation.

Although we have looked at tangible costs, other intangible factors may need to be considered. An optimal solution that requires frequent hiring and firing of employees may not be acceptable to management either from a public image standpoint or because of restrictions imposed by the existing union agreement. The operations plan developed must be consistent with a firm's overall strategic goals.

Methods of Solving the Operations Planning Problem

Many techniques are available for solving the operations planning problem. These methods can be broadly categorized as either optimal or nonoptimal techniques.

Optimal Techniques

These techniques typically use mathematical programming to obtain optimal solutions to the operations planning problem. One of the earliest mathematical approaches is the linear decision rule (Holt, Modigliani, and Simon, 1955). The linear decision rule (LDR) assumes quadratic cost functions associated with hiring/layoff cost, inventory cost, and undertime/overtime cost and a linear regular payroll cost function. The optimum work force and production levels are obtained by differentiating the total cost function. Although the LDR was implemented at a paint factory, an evaluation of its performance several years later indicated that users overrode a large percentage of the plans generated because the logic of the LDR was not readily transparent. Linear programming, the transportation method, and goal programming are other optimal mathematical approaches that have seen limited applications. The limitations of these methods are the following: costs are not always linear, changes in the worker's productivity with time are not reflected in the formulation, and continuously changing the production rate may not always be possible.

Nonoptimal Techniques

Included in this category are the trial-and-error approaches, heuristics, and simulation. Most organizations develop an operations plan by using a trial-and-error approach. Experience plays an important part in the solution process. A trial-and-error method typically includes the following steps.

1. Develop an initial plan based on demand forecasts and agreed guidelines.
2. Check if the plan can be satisfied using available capacity. Otherwise, revise the plan accordingly.
3. Compute the cost of the plan.
4. Modify the plan to obtain a lower-cost solution.
5. Perform sensitivity analysis to determine the cost implications of parameter changes such as inventory holding cost rate, and hiring and firing costs.

This approach is simple to implement, but it depends greatly on the skill and experience of the planner. It can also be time consuming. Although a feasible and satisfactory solution is obtained, there is no guarantee that it is an optimum one. Decision Model Boxes 6-1 and 6-2 provide examples of using a trial-and-error approach to solve the operations planning problem in a manufacturing and service environment, respectively.

Heuristics are similar to trial-and-error methods, with the exception that a more formalized reasoning is adopted. Heuristics attempt to simplify the solution process but cannot guarantee optimal solutions. An example is the production switching rule used to develop production plans at Owens-Corning Fiberglas described in the Introductory Case. Heuristics are often more acceptable to management due to their simplicity, transparency, and efficiency.

Simulation approaches overcome the unrealistic assumptions of mathematical programming techniques. Although simulation does not guarantee an optimal solution, it allows the planner to formulate a model with nonlinear cost relationships, time-varying cost parameters, or costs that change with production quantities. Thus simulation provides a more realistic approximation of the operations planning problem than is possible with mathematical programming. The availability of commercial spreadsheets such as Lotus 123©, VisiCalc, and Multiplan has simplified the model-building process and allows many alternative plans to be evaluated easily.

Sensitivity Analysis

The operations plan is derived from demand forecasts and cost parameters, which are assumed to be deterministic. This situation is rarely true. Management's concerns are related to questions such as: If actual sales are higher or lower than forecasted demand, what is the cost impact of each on the operations plan? If costs associated with inventory or production rate changes differ from estimates used, will the operations plan be substantially different? The first question is related to the sensitivity of the operations plan to errors in demand forecasts; the second question addresses the robustness of the operations planning technique used. Management can use sensitivity analysis to focus attention on areas where forecast errors can be particularly problematic and to get a better handle on the operations planning problem. Examples of sensitivity analysis carried out in a manufacturing and service environment are provided in Decision Model Boxes 6-1 and 6-2.

ESSENTIALS OF EFFECTIVE OPERATIONS PLANNING

Effective operations planning requires the integration of the operations plan with the business plan and other functional plans as well as good communications among all functions. For the operations plan to be widely accepted, it must be realistic, consistent, and feasible. In addition, there are several critical issues that must be addressed to ensure the effective planning of operations:

1. Accurate demand forecasts
2. Aggregation

3. Time period and planning horizon
4. Frequency of replanning
5. Formalizing and controlling the operations planning process

Accurate Demand Forecasts

Demand forecasts are an important input to the operations planning process and are typically supplied by marketing. Without forecasts there can be no planning. The forecasting of aggregate demand is usually more accurate than forecasting for individual products or services. The further into the future forecasts are needed, the less they are likely to be accurate and reliable. The proportional decline in accuracy and reliability of individual forecasts is greater than for aggregate forecasts. It is precisely for these reasons that the use of aggregate forecasts is recommended for long-range planning.

Forecasts are expected to differ from actual demand. Minor variations from actual sales can often be absorbed by using overtime, inventory, or rescheduling orders. However, large mismatches can have a devastating effect on operations. If demand is over-forecasted, the firm may be left with a high level of inventory or forced to lay off employees to bring output in line with actual sales. Equally undesirable is demand forecasts that are consistently low. The likely outcomes are the following: the facility's capacity is severely strained; orders are lost as a result of stockouts; deliveries are delayed, which lead to a loss of goodwill; quality is sacrificed to get orders out quickly. Thus accurate demand forecasts are critical to the overall performance of the operations plan.

When actual sales have exceeded forecasts for the previous periods, management must decide if customers were making purchases early or if the increased demand will continue. If the increased demand is attributed to early purchases, then no drastic action is needed, since demand is expected to be less than planned in the immediate future. On the other hand, if the increased demand is due to a sudden upturn in the economy or a strike at a competitor, the forecasts should be revised accordingly and the operations plan should be adjusted. Few forecasting techniques are available that can effectively track turning points that represent periods of extraordinary opportunity or caution. Managers should "incorporate subjective judgments in dynamic situations when the quantitative forecasting models do not reflect internal or external changes" (Georgoff and Murdick, 1986).

Aggregation

In order to generate an operations plan, an aggregate unit of the various products or services must be developed. This can be a challenging problem, depending on the particular industry involved. The objective is to come up with a commonly understood aggregate unit that lies somewhere between the total dollars in the business plan and the individual products found in the master production schedule. Occasionally, dollars are used as an aggregating unit due to the type of products or services. The measure should be sufficiently broad that management does not get bogged down with too many details at this planning level. The units vary from company to company. Physical measures are appropriate when products are relatively homogenous. Examples are gallons of paint, tons of steel, cases of beer, square feet of tiles, and cubic feet of tiles, and cubic feet of concrete mix.

The aggregation of products becomes more challenging when there are multiple products involved. A thorough understanding of the products and their associated processing requirements is necessary to generate meaningful groups. A good approach is to develop product families based on commonality of processing requirements. Products using like quantities of similar resources should be grouped in the same family. Typically, five to 15 product families are considered manageable. Another approach is to use the input side of production, such as equivalent labor hours or machine hours. In service organizations, the different services offered are aggregated into equivalent labor hours. An important requirement of any aggregation process is the ability to translate the units in the operations plan to dollars in the business and marketing plans to ensure that these plans are consistent with each other. In addition, the aggregate units in the operations plan must be disaggregated to individual products in the master production schedule or to individual workers in a work-force schedule.

Time Period and Planning Horizon

A suitable time period is one month, although quarters have been used when longer planning horizons are desired. In some situations, such as the end of a peak sales season, companies may wish to use more precise time intervals, such as weeks, to enable inventories to be kept close to target. The planning horizon typically covers six to 18 months and is influenced by the time span of the business strategy. The availability and accuracy of demand forecasts is another factor impacting the planning horizon.

Frequency of Replanning

In executing the operations plan, there are several key issues that must be considered: when to change the plan, frequency of replanning, and what portion of the plan to stabilize. Obviously, we would like the plan to be sufficiently flexible to respond to market conditions. However, frequent changes to the operations plan are highly disruptive in managing operations. Without stable plans, workers and machine capacities cannot be effectively utilized, and customer service and profits may suffer as a result. Frequent changes can also lead to more execution problems. An adequate review period is one month, although the review could be carried out more frequently if sales are not up to the operations plan. Once the commitment to production is made, any drastic change will be very costly. There is a fine balance between trying to maintain stability in the operations system and the ability to respond to market conditions. Time fences are established to serve as guidelines in revising the operations plan and represent points in the production process where changes become expensive. The setting of time fences is dependent on capacity and lead times. The longer into the future the change is required, the easier it is to make adjustments to the plan. When changes to the operations plan become costly, they must be approved by top management.

The just-in-time (JIT) inventory management philosophy, increasingly popular in the United States, requires a smooth operations plan for the pull inventory management system (see Chapter 7) to work. The objective is to maintain a steady flow of production each day for long periods of time. Changes to the plan are made after careful analysis has been carried out. JIT manufacturers have greatly benefited from the smooth operations plans, as evidenced by the reduced inventory levels. Smoothed production will be discussed in more detail in Chapter 8.

Formalizing and Controlling the Operations Plan

For operations planning to work effectively, top management must play an active role in formalizing the planning process. The formal process enables top management decisions to be implemented on a focused, rigorous, and timely basis. Monthly operations planning meetings are held to discuss and review the operations plan, with the chief operating officer or general manager chairing these meetings. At these meetings, top and middle managers, including vice presidents from marketing, operations, finance, engineering, and other related areas, openly discuss problems, suggest alternative solutions, and make tough decisions. Inputs are sought from:

1. Marketing, regarding customer demands, significant changes in demand trends, upcoming promotions, new product or service introductions, competitors' activities, and market conditions.

2. Finance, regarding investment policy relating to inventory levels, new equipment, and facilities.

3. Operations, regarding actual production of goods or services, existing capacity, backlog of orders, frequency of equipment breakdowns, lead times, quality of manufactured items or services, work-force level, and inventory level.

4. Engineering, regarding new product/service introductions, engineering change orders, changes in process technology, routing changes, and new design changes.

5. Human resources, regarding labor problems and availability of a pool of skilled or temporary workers in the area.

6. Purchasing, regarding availability and delivery of materials, and the status of qualified subcontractors.

At the monthly operations planning meeting, several alternative plans are presented for discussion. The objective of this meeting is to resolve conflicts and build consensus in reaching an acceptable operations plan. When there is overall agreement, the chief operating officer or general manager signs off on the operations plan, indicating management's commitment. Copies of the signed operations plan are given to managers in charge of implementing the plan.

At the meeting, the past performance of the operations plan is evaluated, and the tentative operations plan, master schedule, resource plan, marketing, financial, and other associated plans are reviewed together. Monitoring the performance of the operations plan is vital to its acceptance and success. When a plan is frequently questioned with respect to its validity, managers lose faith in the formal process and resort to an informal system to overcome the deficiencies. Timely and accurate feedback of information regarding changes in demand, production rates, labor and material availability, and the like is necessary for monitoring the validity of the plan. Large variations in production rates, worker performance, frequency of equipment breakdowns, vendor lead times, and so on should be avoided, since they contribute to poor performance of an operations plan. To evaluate the performance of an operations plan, actual occurrences should be compared with planned outcomes.

Examples of performance categories are the following: forecasted sales against actual sales, planned production against actual production, planned work-force level against actual work-force level (or labor hours), and planned inventory against actual inventory, or planned backlogs against actual backlogs. Deviations from the plan should be analyzed and reasons provided to explain the source of the deviation to enable corrective actions to be taken. The results should be widely communicated to all relevant parties in the organization. The Tennant Company uses the following reports to control its operations plan: the conformity of the master production schedule to the operations plan (weekly), capacity utilization (weekly), delivery performance (daily), actual production to master production schedule performance (weekly), and inventory/backlog performance (weekly). Over the past few years, Tennant has met monthly operations plans in ten out of 12 months for each of these years and had not missed a quarterly operations plan (Vollmann, Berry, and Whybark, 1992).

DISAGGREGATING THE OPERATIONS PLAN

The operations plan uses aggregate units to examine general levels of work force, production, and inventory. Aggregate units are useful only at the higher planning level. The plan needs to be disaggregated to make it useful and meaningful for implementation by operations personnel. Disaggregation involves breaking down the aggregate units into individual items to be produced or services offered so that specific requirements for labor, materials, equipment, and inventory can be determined. To ensure feasibility, the total units in the disaggregated plan must sum to the total in the same time period in the operations plan. The outcome of disaggregating the operations plan is a master production schedule (in manufacturing), master schedule (in services), or a work-force schedule (in services).

A master production schedule (MPS) is a detailed plan of production that states the quantity and timing of individual end items over some specified time frame. The planning horizon for an MPS can vary from three months to one year, but normally covers a time frame much less than that for operations planning. The time periods are typically in weeks, although days, hours, or months can be used. As in operations planning, time fences play an important role in the master production scheduling process. Time fencing is often used to avoid inefficiencies and unnecessary disruptions on the shop floor. Many firms use three time fences: frozen, slushy, and free zones. The first few weeks of an MPS is typically frozen, meaning that no changes are allowed in this portion of the master production schedule except under exceptional circumstances. Any changes in the frozen period must be authorized by management because of the impact on other

---

APPLICATON BOX 6-2   Operations Planning at Texas Instruments

The Industrial Automation Division of Texas Instruments (TI) located in Johnson City, Tennessee, manufactures programmable logic controllers. In 1985, TI realized that a lack of functional linkage was preventing products and information from flowing smoothly through the system. To improve customer service, TI examined areas such as vendor deliveries, lead-time reduction, and the production planning process. An evaluation of TI's master production schedules (MPS) prior to 1985 showed a frozen interval of 16 weeks, which meant that changes could only be made beyond the 16-week window. The planning horizon of TI's MPS is six months. The frozen interval was needed to ensure that materials ordered could be delivered in time, labor could be made available, and machine schedules could be developed during that time. Supplier lead times were from 12–18 weeks, and manufacturing lead times ranged from four to eight weeks. TI realized that the long frozen interval was limiting the flexibility of the factory to respond to customer requirements. Combined with the volatile demand forecast and cyclical demand patterns, the problems that were created included expediting, high overtime costs in manufacturing, and poor customer service.

Over a five-year-period, TI improved the demand forecasting process, reduced the frozen interval, used a pull production system, and made more frequent adjustments to the plan. The frozen interval has been reduced to eight weeks for increases in demand and to three weeks for demand decreases. The disparity in the frozen intervals is because it is easier to decrease production than it is to increase capacity. The ability to reduce the frozen interval stems from a reduction in the vendor and manufacturing lead times. Long-term purchase orders were made with suppliers to provide better and more flexible deliveries. Manufacturing lead times were decreased by eliminating nonvalue-added processes, reducing lot sizes, using kanban, and so on. The benefits were the following: total inventory reduced by 45%; the number of orders completed within the standard lead time improved 26%; customer on-time deliveries improved 77%; past-due units decreased from an average of 2000 to 400; orders completed on time improved 50%.

———
Materials drawn from Mark Rose, "Production Planning at Texas Instruments Improves Service and Reduces Costs," *Industrial Engineering.* January 1991, pp. 33–34, 36.

customer-order commitments, purchasing requirements, equipment utilization, open shop orders, and profitability. Schedule stability in the short run is important. Beyond the frozen period is the "slushy" zone, where changes to the MPS are allowed provided that one order is traded with another equivalent order, and required materials and components are available. The "free" portion of the MPS allows more drastic changes as long as the operations plan is not violated. A description of how Texas Instruments improved customer service by reducing the frozen interval of the MPS is provided in Application Box 6-2.

Service organizations typically use work-force schedules, although some service organizations use master schedules. For example, universities and colleges publish and circulate a master schedule of course offerings two to three terms in advance. The schedule is used to arrange for classroom capacity requirements and faculty to teach these courses, as well as to allow students to make long-term plans for completing their degrees. These schedules are quite rigid, and only minor changes such as classroom reassignments are made. An exception is the cancellation of a course in which the specified minimum enrollment has not been met. A family doctor or a beautician uses a master schedule that includes customer appointments and time set aside for walk-in customers. Airlines, railways, and tour companies also generate a master schedule of services for the next six to 12 months. Work-force schedules are prepared to meet these schedules of services. Accounting, engineering, and management consulting firms translate contracts that show completion times of services to work-force schedules.

HIERARCHICAL PLANNING SYSTEMS

Hierarchical planning systems adopt an integrated approach to address the operations planning and scheduling problem. The operations planning and scheduling problem is partitioned into a series of subproblems that are solved sequentially, often iteratively, with constraints established by higher-level decisions imposed on lower-level subproblems. Meal (1984, p. 106) notes that hierarchical planning systems "fit the organizational structure and provide for ease of review at each managerial level. Higher-level decisions have longer lead times, longer planning horizons, and are concerned with aggregates such as total manpower requirements and total product-line demand. The lowest-level decisions have shorter lead times, shorter planning horizons, and are concerned with individual items, machines, and workers." The hierarchical planning structure allows a clear delegation of the detailed decision making to subordinates at lower levels of the organization and yet enables top management to retain overall control of the entire planning process. Senior managers contend with aggregate data in allocating valuable resources to achieve corporate objectives. The detailed responsibility of job and task assignments are successively delegated to superintendents, supervisors, production control assistants, and shop floor workers. A description of the hierarchical planning system employed at American Olean Tile Company is provided in Application Box 6-3.

SUMMARY

Ineffective or inadequate operation planning can lead to a "fire-fighting" mode of operating a business. The outcome is organizational slack, which translates to excess inventories, excess workers, excess overtime costs, excess capacity, long lead times, and long new-product-introduction cycles. For an operations plan to be effective it must be integrated with other plans and endorsed by top management. The operations planning process must be formalized to prevent suboptimal informal systems from evolving. An effective operations plan allows a company to better utilize its scarce resources to satisfy customer requirements. Operations planning, if implemented successfully, can lead to numerous benefits, such as improved productivity and customer-service levels, decreased expediting, reduced setup costs, and decreased inventory costs.

APPLICATION BOX 6-3 Hierarchical Planning System at American Olean Tile Company

The American Olean Tile Company (AOTC) manufactures a wide array of ceramic tile products. Their products include tile for floors and walls, indoor and outdoor use, residential and commercial customers, and elaborate mural designs. They are grouped into three basic product lines: quarry tiles, glazed tiles, and ceramic mosaics. The company operates eight factories in the United States, which supply approximately 120 sales distribution points (SDPs). The factories utilize many different production processes, but all begin with a crushing and milling procedure, and ultimately lead to the kiln firing of the tiles. AOTC's distribution network has expanded quite rapidly in recent years, prompting management to begin using a modeling program to supplement manual planning of production and distribution. To improve the integration of the annual plan, short-term scheduling, and inventory control the company developed a hierarchical production planning (HPP) system shown in the figure below.

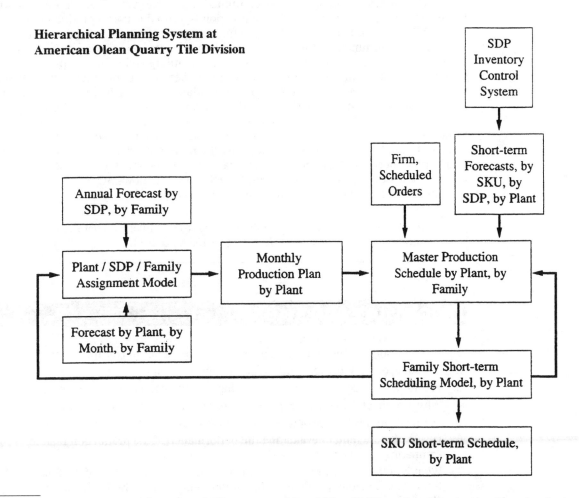

Hierarchical Planning System at American Olean Quarry Tile Division

Reprinted by permission of Matthew J. Liberatore and Tan Miller, "A Hierarchical Production Planning System," *Interfaces*, July–August 1985. Copyright (1985) the Operations Research Society of America and The Institute of Management Sciences, 290 westminster Street, Providence, Rhode Island 02903, USA.

APPLICATION BOX 6-3 *Continued*

AOTC's HPP system uses a simple aggregation–disaggregation scheme and a mixed-integer-programming model for short-term scheduling. The company first concentrated on the quarry tile division. Products that have similar seasonality patterns are grouped into a family. This aggregation procedure is appropriate for AOTC due to the nature of their products and its manufacturing process. The quarry tile line is grouped into ten product families, each consisting of several hundred stock-keeping units (SKUs), which accounted for over 98% of total quarry sales.

An annual subjective sales forecast for total quarry division sales in square feet of tiles provides the input necessary for production planning. The forecast is generated by the director of market planning and other top management on the basis of numerous inputs, including economic trends and market developments. The forecast is then applied to each of the ten product families on the basis of their percentage of total sales histories. From these forecasts, plus seasonal inventory targets and demand patterns, a monthly production plan is developed by the plant production personnel.

The monthly production plan, combined with large customer orders and short-range forecasts from the sales distribution points, form the master production schedule (MPS). The individual plant production assignments are then made to meet the MPS while minimizing the total of variable manufacturing, setup, and inventory costs. Using this hierarchical planning and scheduling system has improved coordination and communication between the marketing and manufacturing departments, enabled more consistent production planning and scheduling decisions to be made, reduced production and distribution costs, and saved the company between $400,000 and $750,000 annually. In addition, management can use the model to gauge the financial impact of various strategies such as capital investments in additional plant capacity and stopping the manufacturing of a specific product at a plant because the major raw material cost has become too high. Most importantly, the development of an integrated HPP system allows AOTC to significantly improve its capability to be more competitive in the market.

Material drawn from Matthew J. Liberatore and Tan Miller, "A Hierarchical Production Planning System," *Interfaces*, July–August 1985, pp. 1–11.

DISCUSSION QUESTIONS

1. What are some of the methods that are used to influence or control demand?
2. List some of the short-term alternative for affecting supply.
3. Provide a short definition for the following strategies: level, chase, and mixed.
4. Why is product demand aggregated for determining the operations plan?.
5. Define the terms time period and planning horizon.
6. Discuss the method of evaluating the performance of the production plan in terms of comparing actual occurrences with planned outcomes.
7. What inputs into the production plan are provided by managers of the following functional areas: marketing, finance, operations, engineering, human resources, and purchasing?
8. Discuss the interface between the production plan and the master production schedule (MPS).
9. What are some of the early warning signals of poor operations planning?

10. List some of the operations planning inputs.

11. State the individual objectives of manufacturing, marketing, and finance, as well as the overall company objective.

12. Discuss operations planning in a just-in-time (JIT) environment such as at Toyota.

13. Discuss some of the operations planning differences between a large manufacturer of ballpoint pens and a small neighborhood ice cream shop.

14. Compare a custom tailoring shop with a large chain of stores that offer mens' apparel in terms of aggregating product demand.

15. Explain why hospitals could be called the model of a chase strategy in action.

STRATEGIC DECISION SITUATIONS

1. Lawncare Inc. is a manufacturer of electric-powered lawn mowers. Demand for lawn mowers is very seasonal, with the highest demand occurring in the spring and summer quarters. The table below shows aggregate demand forecasts for the next four quarters.

Quarter	Forecasted Demand (Units)
Fall	3000
Winter	2000
Spring	6000
Summer	5000

   The following information has been collected. The production rate is 40 units per worker per quarter. The average salary for a production worker is $2200 per quarter. The overtime rate is 150% of the regular time rate, and workers are limited to a maximum of 25% overtime per quarter. The cost of hiring an additional worker is $1500, and the cost of laying a worker off is $1000. Currently there is no inventory in stock. Inventory is calculated at the end of the quarter as: Ending inventory = beginning inventory + production − demand. The holding cost is $20 per unit per quarter. All forecasted demand must be met and no back-orders are allowed.

   The management of Lawncare wants to generate an effective production plan for the next fiscal year, which starts in the fall quarter. Abe Favre, the materials manager, has been asked to prepare three alternative plans to be evaluated by managers from finance, marketing, and manufacturing in the next production planning meeting. The production plans to be generated are (a) a level strategy—maintain the current work-force level of 100 workers, using inventories to buffer demand, (b) a chase strategy—adjust the work-force level to meet demand exactly, and (c) a mixed strategy—trim the work force to 90 workers, maintain this work-force level, and use overtime and inventory to buffer demand. The cost of each strategy should also be computed. There is some concern that the cost of capital may increase in the near future, which will increase the original inventory carrying cost by 20%. What is the impact of this on the three plans?

2. The Funtime Amusement Park provides a range of rides, games, and shows throughout the year, but experiences highly seasonal demand, with peaks occurring in May–September and December. The forecasted aggregate demand in labor hours for the next year is provided in the table below. Funtime wants to develop a staffing plan with a one-year planning horizon in order to most efficiently meet customer needs. Each employee works 160 hours per month at an average rate of $8 per hour. Overtime pay is $12 per hour. The maximum amount of overtime per month per employee is 30 hours. The cost to hire an additional worker is $700, and it costs $400 to lay a worker off. All forecasted demand must be met, or revenues will fall. The company currently has 250 workers.

Three alternative staffing plans are being considered: (a) a level strategy—using overtime to buffer demand and maintain a stable work-force level, (b) a chase strategy—adjusting the work force to meet demand exactly, and (c) a mixed strategy-a combination of hiring/laying off employees and overtime. These strategies are to be compared on the basis of cost, with the least expensive being chosen. In addition, if the cost to hire a worker is $1400, what is the impact on the three plans?

Forecasted Demand

Month	Labor Hours	Month	Labor Hours
January	21,600	July	54,000
February	21,600	August	54,000
March	27,000	September	43,200
April	32,400	October	27,000
May	43,200	November	20,000
June	54,000	December	37,800

REFERENCES

Buffa, Elwood S. "Aggregate Planning for Production," *Business Horizons*. Fall 1967, pp. 87–97.

Buffa, Elwood S., and Jeffrey Miller. *Production-Inventory Systems: Planning and Control*. Homewood, Ill.: Irwin, 1979.

Drucker, Peter F. "Long-Range Planning," *Management Science*. Vol. 5, No. 3, 1959, pp. 238–249.

Everdell, Romeyn, and Judith A. Ryde. "The Production Plan—The Top Management Interface," *APICS Twenty-Fifth Annual Conference Proceedings*, 1982, pp. 231–238.

Georgoff, David M., and Robert G. Murdick. "Manager's Guide to Forecasting," *Harvard Business Review*. January–February 1986, pp. 110–186.

Helliker, Kevin. "If There's Hardly Anything Left to Buy, It's Tuesday Morning on Christmas Eve," *Wall Street Journal*. December 23, 1991.

Holt, Charles C., Franco Modigliani, and Herbert Simon. "A Linear Decision Rule for Production and Employment Scheduling," *Management Science*. October 1955, pp. 1–30.

Leong, G. Keong, Michael D. Oliff, and Robert E. Markland. "Improved Hierarchical Production Planning," *Journal of Operations Management*. Vol. 8, No. 3, 1989, pp. 90–114.

Liberatore, Matthew J., and Tan Miller. "A Hierarchical Production Planning System," *Interfaces*. July–August 1985, pp. 1–11.

Meal, Harlan C. "Putting Production Decisions Where They Belong," *Harvard Business Review*. March–April 1984, pp. 102–111.

Monden, Y. "Smoothed Production Lets Toyota Adapt to Demand Changes and Reduce Inventory," *Industrial Engineering*. August 1981, pp. 42–51.

Northcraft, Gregory B., and Richard B. Chase. "Managing Service Demand at the Point of Delivery," *Academy of Management Review*. January 1985, pp. 66–75.

Oliff, Michael D., and Earl Burch. "Multiproduct Production Scheduling at Owens-Corning Fiberglas," *Interfaces*. September–October 1985, pp. 25–34.

Oliff, Michael D., and G. Keong Leong. "A Discrete Production Switching Rule for Aggregate Planning," *Decision Sciences*. Fall 1987, pp. 582–597.

Pollock, Michael A., and Aaron Bernstein. "The Disposable Employee Is Becoming a Fact of Corporate Life," *Business Week*. December 15, 1986, pp. 52–53, 56.

Root, Cary M. "Production Planning: Past, Present and Potential," *Inventories and Production*. May–June 1983, pp. 6–10.

Rose, Mark. "Production Planning at Texas Instruments Improves Service and Reduces Costs," *Industrial Engineering*. January 1991, pp. 33–34, 36.

Sasser, W. Earl. "Match Supply and Demand in Services," *Harvard Business Review*. November–December 1976, pp. 133–140.

Schlesinger, Leonard A., and James L. Heskett. "The Service-Driven Service Company," *Harvard Business Review*. September–October 1991, pp. 71–81.

Shapiro, Benson. "Can Marketing and Manufacturing Coexist?" *Harvard Business Review*. September–October 1977, pp. 104–114.

Venkatesan, Ravi. "Cummins Engine Flexes Its Factory," *Harvard Business Review*. March–April 1990, pp. 120–127.

Vollmann, Thomas E., William L. Berry, and D. Clay Whybark. *Manufacturing Planning and Control Systems*. 3rd ed. Homewood, Ill.: Irwin, 1992.

Wantuck, Kenneth. *Just-In-Time for America*. Southfield, Minn: KWA Media, 1989.

Wight, Oliver W. *Production and Inventory Management in the Computer Age*. Boston, Mass.: Cahners Publishing Company, Inc., 1974.

CHAPTER 7

IMPROVING MATERIALS MANAGEMENT

The logic of MRP is universally applicable; the way it is applied depends upon the environment. —George W. Plossl, 1985

Parts is parts . . . is parts. —A Shop Floor Colloquialism

Objectives

After completing this chapter you should be able to

- Define materials management and describe four dimensions of materials management practices.
- Identify the four foundations of inventory decisions.
- Describe traditional inventory management methods and their shortfalls.
- Describe materials requirements planning and difficulties in implementing material requirements planning systems.
- Describe ways to continuously improve materials management practices.

Outline

INTRODUCTORY CASE: MRP IMPLEMENTATION AT HELENE CURTIS

Mike Garsombke looked around as he entered Room 2042C. He knew this would be a long meeting, yet there was no other way to ensure that every aspect of the program was coordinated. His implementation team, Don in scheduling, Laura in inventory, Roger in purchasing, Edna in automation, and Wayne on the shop floor, watched Mike enter. They also knew this would be a long meeting.

Helene Curtis*, a leading manufacturer and distributor of professional hair care products and beauty shop aids, had made the decision more than a decade ago to automate the punch card inventory control system. The first effort was a disaster. It seemed that the weekly printout was always late and inaccurate and never contained the needed information. Despite the difficulties of the first attempt, the nature of the product line almost required the use of an automated materials management system. Though its product would appear rather simple in structure (with components of base, soap, fragrance, colorizers, diffusers, softeners, and packaging), in fact, the company carries over 20,000 stock-keeping units.

Mike had joined Helene Curtis a bit more than seven years ago and since then, had spent what seemed to be more than one career in MRP. His first priority, as the assistant implementation team chief, had been to get the files in shape. Much of the early difficulties had been caused by inaccurate inventories of raw materials and schedule changes requiring supplier deliveries to be expedited. Mike remembered those early days. "Everyone had a small 'stash' of inventory; it was part of the company culture. The stash of inventory was like a bank account, you could draw on it to help a friend—or to get yourself through a squeeze. It was almost like job security. . . . And that system worked well when inventories didn't cost much and were less complex."

"We also had to replace the primary consultant and set up a schedule of training small groups for ten to 15 hours per week. And that was after you did your normal job. We didn't even touch a computer until the files were good and the people knew their jobs, and how the human system interfaced with the computer system. Then they understood how MRP could help them. It took about 18 months to get the first phase (bill of materials, sched-

---

*Materials drawn from conversations with "Mike."

ule, and inventory) on line. Despite the training and care in systems implementation, we had some glitches. We spent several months upgrading from a class C system to a class B; now we are close to an A system. It just has to be right, or it isn't worth doing." After his boss retired, Mike was promoted to the implementation team chief position and had directed the continuous improvement of the upgraded system.

Mike took a chair at the head of the table and leaned back. He looked thoughtfully at the flow charts on the wall and chuckled. They had come a long way. Inventory turns had tripled, costs had decreased, and stockouts, which used to constantly disrupt the manufacturing process, had been virtually eliminated. Reaching into his pocket, he pulled out a game spinner, the kind with a big arrow, and set it in the center of the table. "OK," he said. "Scheduling, who's up?" Don hit the spinner, and to the group's approval, it stopped at Laura. "You know," Mike said, as he nodded at Laura, "you just can't take this stuff too seriously."

MATERIALS MANAGEMENT SYSTEMS

The cost of materials has been estimated (Gunn, 1987) at roughly 50% of the total production cost with some variance depending upon the industry. The corresponding contribution of direct labor and overhead was estimated at 15% and 35%, respectively. However, by the year 2000, Gunn estimates that the cost of materials will increase to 75%, with labor and overhead shrinking to roughly 3% and 22%, respectively. Thus, the intensity with which materials resources are managed by operations managers can be expected to increase correspondingly.

Note that materials management is considered by some to be primarily a manufacturing concern; correspondingly, services are considered by those persons to be more concerned with the delivery of intangibles. This inaccurate stereotype seriously misrepresents the chain of transformations and the functions of an operations manager. Though service deliverables usually involve high proportions of intangibles, most services require some amount of inventory. For example, retail activities are at the end of a very long inventory distribution pipeline. A dentist cannot fill cavities without inventories of silver, replacement tools, and various drugs and liquids. Even telephone, electricity, gas, and other utility services require extensive inventories of spare parts and tools. The rapidly growing area of product distribution and service delivery involves extensive and often costly holdings of inventory.

Materials management systems are projected to become a more important and more visible operations resource in this decade because of increasing materials costs and the growing service economy. Materials management activities involve the flow of materials, including the volume and timing of materials transactions. As such, materials management incorporates purchasing, inventory control, and distribution systems. More formally, materials management is defined as:

> *Coordinated activities to* plan for and control *the* volume and timing *of materials flow through acquisition, transformation and movement (the* phases *of* materials management) *of raw materials, work-in-process, and finished goods (the* states *of materials).*

This definition emphasizes four dimensions of materials management. These are the primary topics of this chapter; other aspects of these topics are developed in the following chapter. Ed Heard (in Moody, 1990) describes the distinction between the materials and scheduling aspects of production as "visible" inventory (for example, units that are stored or awaiting use—or in inventory) and "invisible" inventory (for example, units that are currently being transformed—or scheduled for work). The significance of this distinction is that management usually counts only visible inventory. In fact, both visible and invisible inventory should be counted because visible inventory indicates the effectiveness of the forecasting–scheduling–distribution system, while invisible inventory is a measure of the effectiveness of the production process. The four dimensions of materials management are further defined as:

1. *Planning and Control.* Typically materials management planning activities extend a minimum of three months and often as much as two to three years into the future. Planning periods define the control mechanisms that are used in the execution of the plan.

2. *Volume and Timing.* Materials decisions involve both volume and timing, which, taken together, define the rate of flow. For example, if annual usage of a particular item is 500,000 units, then the movement of that item may be accomplished once yearly at volumes of 500,000, at quarterly volumes of 125,000, monthly volumes of 41,667, weekly volumes of 9615, or daily volumes, for 360 working days per year, of 1389.

3. *Phases of Materials Management.* The activities of materials management occur in various phases, which are functionally described as acquisition, transformation, and movement. These phases may also be categorized as purchasing, inventory management (storage, moving, queuing, setup, and transformation), and distribution.

4. *States of the Materials.* The states of the materials may be defined as raw materials, work-in-process, and finished goods.

Because of the differences in materials management situations and variations in the contribution of materials to the total production costs, numerous materials management techniques have emerged. This chapter initially describes materials management systems, and then notes the classic reasons for inventory and the categories of inventory management systems. Subsequently, various inventory management methods are discussed, including the traditional order quantity methods, automated materials planning techniques, and continuous improvement approaches. The central premise of the chapter, noted in the quotes on the chapter title page, is that the logic of materials management is universal, though applications vary extensively.

A Cushion against Uncertainty

As defined, the materials management system is one of three components that are central to the execution of operations strategy.

1. *Materials Decisions*—use prepositioned, internal and external (to the firm) inventories, defined as items and volumes, to reduce costs, processing, or delivery times.

2. *Scheduling Decisions*—use available capacity and, through flexibility and delivery, respond to customer orders.

3. *Customer Service Decisions*—design, create, and deliver the product/service as specified by the customer.

These components are traditionally regarded as often conflicting in terms of their cost. For example, a low-cost schedule traditionally involves longer production runs (with fewer change-overs or setups), but longer production runs often result in higher inventory costs and, in some environments, may cause poorer responsiveness to customer requirements or service. Alternatively, more varied, higher-cost scheduling results in lower material costs and better service performance. Similarly, high levels of customer service can be achieved through either large inventories or very flexible scheduling, or a compromise position. Conventional operations theory suggests that a strategy must be selected from these alternatives.

No one strategy is appropriate for all situations. For example, a stationery store would likely periodically order larger inventories of the ubiquitous throw-away pen, but more frequently order smaller quantities of a costly designer pen. Figure 7-1 shows the three "pure strategies" and suggests an area of compromise alternatives or niches.

Current operations strategy suggests that the operations manager competitively position the operations system in a strategically defined niche, considering materials, sched-

FIGURE 7-1 The Components in the Execution of Operations Strategy

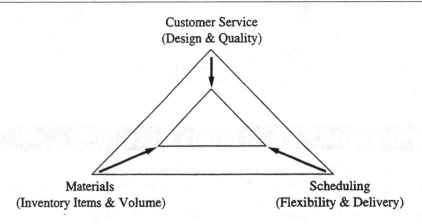

uling, and customer service requirements and costs. These three controllable components (materials management, operations scheduling, and customer service) must be mixed to achieve the best interests of the customer. Where the customer is involved, there can be no conflicts (Schaeffer, 1993). The materials management questions are closely related to the three components, as follows:

What product is needed?	Customer service—design and quality issues
How much is needed?	Materials management—inventory and volume issues
When is it needed?	Operations scheduling—flexibility and delivery issues

Many of the recent developments in materials management have emphasized continuous improvement of production systems to simultaneously reduce inventories, permit more flexible scheduling, and provide more responsive service to customer needs. Actions by a firm toward these goals can be shown as the smaller triangle in the center of Figure 7-1, which represents a smaller, yet more flexible and faster-moving pipeline.

The selected position of operations in Figure 7-1 also represents the type of cushion that will be used against the uncertainty of customer demand. Safety stock inventory and safety capacity are widely used by manufacturing managers; however, distribution managers regularly use no-cost trade-ups in the event of item stockouts. The ability of a firm to respond to customer demand uncertainty thus depends upon an aggregate of inventory, scheduling, and customer service decisions.

Inventory—Asset or Liability

Inventory, or items that are stocked against future expected use, represents both a potential asset and a potential liability to an operations manager. On the one hand, inventory represents stored production (capacity) or value added that, when the product is sold, will produce a profit for the firm. If the demand or the price for the product or service is expected to increase, a firm would be encouraged to stock additional inventories. Conversely, inventories usually involve a heavy capital investment in materials, labor, and overhead, which incur financial or opportunity costs. Additionally, building a larger inventory than is immediately necessary may be risky, particularly if the potential for shrinkage, including obsolescence, deterioration, or pilferage of the item is high.

More specifically, reasons to carry inventory or to increase inventory holdings are the need for improved customer service, efficiencies of transportation, reduced per-unit ordering or setup costs, and smoothed resource utilization. Alternatively, the reasons to reduce inventories are high interest rates or opportunity costs, unavailability of storage or excessive handling costs, undesirable insurance and tax costs, and shrinkage costs. Thus, to determine the "best" level of inventory for an item, the costs of carrying inventory must be compared with the corresponding costs of not carrying inventory. A number of methods are available to evaluate this decision, from the traditional order quantity methods, to more recent materials planning methods, and the now widely practiced continuous improvement approaches. Today, most materials managers agree with Beddingfield (1992) that reducing inventory increases cash flow and reduces carrying costs, thereby enhancing competitiveness.

FOUNDATIONS OF INVENTORY DECISIONS

Inventory is a fact of life. It is required for running water and is the reason for the use of refrigerators (to store food) and bank accounts (to store money). There are many situations that cause and require inventory, and thus there are many ways to classify inventory. Inventory results because of a need to smooth the flow of goods through the chain of transformations. Note that services are generally not storable and thus are usually not considered as an inventory item. Inventory can be classified as either dependent on or independent of other actions or decisions and may be categorized for varying amounts of management attention. This section describes the functions of inventory, differentiates dependent and independent demands, and evaluates inventory categories using ABC analysis.

Functions of Inventory

Inventory, whether considered as goods on hand or managed as a back-order or backlog capability, is required for four reasons: to *anticipate expected variances* in requirements, to *provide safety against unexpected variance* in requirements, to *permit efficient use of lot-sizing*, and to *smooth inventory flow in transportation*. There are two general cases for each of these functions, as shown in Table 7-1.

Anticipation inventory accounts for *expected* variations in the flow of inventory usage. For example, in most parts of the northern hemisphere, few snowblowers are sold in the months of June or July, and few lawn mowers are sold in the months of December or January. However, manufacturers of snowblowers and lawn mowers (this combination of products might be expected because of the common production technologies and processes), with a one-month delivery lead time, might build lawn mowers from February to June. After a one-month line changeover in July, they would build snowblowers in August through December, with a changeover back to lawn mowers in January. The lawn mowers

TABLE 7-1 Functions of Inventory or Backlogs

Anticipation Inventory
- Respond to expected cyclic demand for goods or materials
- Accommodate expected cyclic supply of goods or materials

Safety Stock
- Cover unexpected supplier shortfalls
- Absorb unexpected demand variation

Efficiencies of Lot-Sizing
- Prorate order costs of external purchases
- Prorate internal setup costs and permit partial deliveries

Transportation Inventory
- Allow for pipeline inventories
- Account for work-in-process

would be built and transported to retail outlets by March, in anticipation of the spring and summer sales period, and the snowblowers would be built starting in August in anticipation of sales in the fall and winter. Thus, an inventory buildup of lawn mowers would occur from February through April or May, when sales would increase; similarly, an inventory buildup of snowblowers would occur from August through October or November. This is anticipation inventory due to cyclical demand for the product. Similarly, because the supply of some goods, agricultural produce, for example, is cyclical, inventories are held until the item is demanded. In products that experience seasonal demand, anticipation inventories are established to smooth expected variations of demand or supply.

Safety stocks accommodate *unexpected* variations in supply or demand. Raw material safety stocks permit an operations manager to cover unexpected supplier shortfalls, for example, if a delivery truck is delayed by an accident or a supplier's equipment fails. Safety stock may also be used to protect against a stock-out due to an unexpected surge in demand, for example, after a major storm. Safety stock smooths inventory flow over random or uncontrolled events; it is a buffer which permits continued operation of a process.

Efficiencies of lot-sizing permit *prorating* of external purchase orders or internal machine setups over several or many units in an order or production lot. The more units that these one-time costs of purchasing or machine setup can be prorated over, the more efficient the processing, yielding economies of scale. However, with long runs and few setups, inventories increase. For example, it does not make sense for most businesses to order one box of business stationery. Given the costs of communicating the order, setting up a printing press, delivering the product, and setting up the payment, it is more efficient to purchase several boxes of stationery at one time. This example applies both to setting up an order for external purchase and to setting up a machine for internal production of a component.

Fourth, some transportation inventory will inevitably be required in the pipeline to *smooth* the materials flow. Perhaps the most apparent examples of pipeline inventory are the oil and gas stored in "pipelines," including rail and truck tankers and storage facilities. However, other less apparent pipeline inventories would include forestry and agricultural goods, foods such as milk or cheese, irrigation and commercial water supply systems, and many bulk raw materials. These materials may be held in external transportation or distribution systems or as internal work in process. Because of the bulk, weight, or perishability of an item, or to ensure a convenient flow of the product, the most efficient method of delivery or movement is by "pipeline."

Categories of Demand for Inventory

Demand for inventory or services can be categorized as either dependent or independent. Dependent demand is driven by a manufacturing schedule, by a required service, or by retail demand for a related product. Directly scheduled demands generally involve manufactured end items, such as furniture, automobiles, appliances, and the like. For example, most chairs require four legs, most automobiles require four tires (excluding the spare tire), and most stoves have four burners. Thus, once an end item is scheduled, the parts required to build that item are dependent on the schedule. Similarly, some styles of chair are sold with the corresponding foot rest, and stereo speakers are built and priced individually, but often sold in pairs. In services, examples of dependent demand include medical and dental facilities and inventories that are committed based on appointments or scheduled procedures.

Alternatively, demand for many services and end items is independent of a schedule or of demand for a related product. Demands for medical care, telephone service, repair parts for automobiles and after-market accessories, or entertainment services are not directly dependent upon a schedule or tie-in sale. Demand for these items must be forecast.

The importance of the distinction between dependent and independent demand is that each approach uses different inventory management methods. If demands are treated as independent, then those demands are forecast over time and the inventory decision is based on an inexact estimate of the period demand. Assumptions must be made about the regularity of the flow of demand and replenishment times. Thus, independent demand management methods are imprecise about how much is needed and when it is needed. However, if demands for inventory are dependent, say, on a production schedule, then inventory management decisions can be more exact—unless the schedule changes.

The preceding description emphasizes the dichotomy of dependent and independent demand management environments. In practice, the demand for most products and services is both dependent and independent. For example, demand for automobile tires by an automobile manufacturer is dependent upon the manufacturing schedule, but demand for replacement of those same tires is independent. Similarly, the use of communication lines by private individuals is likely to be independent, but usage of these same lines for transmission of business or financial data is dependent upon the updating process, which is planned.

Because of the increased exactness of dependent inventory management systems, businesses have been motivated to capture information about their demand and thus treat those demands as dependent or schedulable. For example, in many areas, requirements for gas and electric power are both commercial and residential. Those requirements are carefully planned in close coordination with major commercial users, and the remaining (often as little as 20%) demand is forecast for residential areas. By segregating dependent and independent demands, utility operations are able to manage capacity-bound resources more efficiently. The demands for natural gas and heating oil can be similarly managed. As demand dependencies for inventory are established, requirements planning and scheduling methods are increasingly feasible.

ABCs of Inventory Management

A nineteenth-century Italian economist, Wilfredo Pareto, found, in a study of the wealth distribution, that 20% of the population had 80% of the total wealth. The next 30% of the population had 15% of the wealth, and the final 50% of the population had 5% of the total wealth. Applied to inventory management, Pareto's "principle" suggests that there are the critical few high-cost items of inventory that should be carefully managed and the trivial many items, which are of less concern. So-called A items are the most costly, and should be carefully managed, while B and C items are less costly categories and receive less management attention. Note that in application, there may be more than three categories of items and that the proportion of items is set according to each situation.

Pareto analysis computes the total inventory value of the item, either in total dollars (the number of units times the item cost) or in item criticality (often measured by perishability, stockout penalty, the cost of closing a work center or facility, or the result of a quality defect) among several items; then the items are resequenced according to total cost. Applications of the Pareto principle include inventory management, quality control, forecasting accuracy, and other operations decisions. Simply stated, the operations manager should most carefully manage the categories that have the greatest cost or potential impact on the operation.

The highest-total-cost item would be given the most attention. The proportion of items defined in categories A, B, and C, and the proportional costs of those items, taken cumulatively, will vary among environments. For example, the inventory of a luxury jewelry store would likely be almost entirely A items, while most items of a feed and grain store would be managed as C items. Other operations might handle a wider range of items which, when categorized by cost, permit a more clear distinction of A, B, and C items. Decision Model Box 7-1 shows the computation and use of ABC analysis.

ABC analysis is widely used in support of cycle counting programs that are used in service distribution systems. The traditional physical inventory counting process is rarely used today because it requires the shutdown of major parts of an operation and because it may result in a greater number of counting errors.

DECISION MODEL BOX 7-1   The ABCs of Inventory at Compuserve Distributors

Compuserve Distributors stocks ten models of printer. Given the following data, determine which printers should be more intensely managed, using two ABC analysis approaches: one based on total inventory cost and the second based on the criticality of stocking out.

Stock Number	Volume/ Year	Cost/ Unit	Stockout Penalty/Unit
21	135	100	150
31	75	200	50
41	200	250	650
42	150	400	50
51	90	300	250

Stock Number	Volume/ Year	Cost/ Unit	Stockout Penalty/Unit
61	75	350	10
62	45	500	50
71	125	700	200
72	75	850	100
73	30	950	150

Total volume = 1000 Total cost: (volume × cost) = $394,000
Total cost: (volume × stockout penalty/unit) = $224,000

Generalized, the ABC procedure has three steps: (1) determine the input data values (annual volume, cost/unit, and, if needed, the stock-out penalty per unit) of each item. (2) Sum these values; then divide the unit cost or the unit penalty by the total value to find the percentage. (3) Resequence the values based on the percentages and categorize as A, B, or C.

ABC according to the percentage of total cost of inventory:

Stock Number	Volume/ Year	Cost/ Unit	Total Cost	Percent Total Cost
71	125	700	$87,500	22.21—A
72	75	850	63,750	16.18—B
42	150	400	60,000	15.23—B
41	200	250	50,000	12.69—B
73	30	950	28,500	7.23—C

Stock Number	Volume/ Year	Cost/ Unit	Total Cost	Percent Total Cost
51	90	300	$27,000	6.85—C
61	75	350	26,250	6.66—C
62	45	500	22,500	5.71—C
31	75	200	15,000	3.81—C
21	135	100	13,500	3.43—C

ABC according to the percentage of total cost of the stockout penalty:

Stock Number	Volume/ Year	Penalty/ Unit	Total Penalty	Percent Total Cost
41	200	650	$130,000	58.04—A
71	125	200	25,000	11.16—B
51	90	250	22,500	10.04—B
21	135	150	20,250	9.04—B
72	75	100	7,500	3.35—C

Stock Number	Volume/ Year	Penalty/ Unit	Total Penalty	Percent Total Cost
42	150	50	7,500	3.35—C
73	30	150	4,500	2.01—C
31	75	50	3,750	1.67—C
62	45	50	2,250	1.00—C
61	75	10	750	0.33—C

The ABC chart shows the *cumulative* percent of inventory items on the horizontal axis and the selected management criteria on the vertical axis. The left chart shows cumulative percent inventory cost, while the right chart shows cumulative percent stockout penalty. The determination of the number of percent of A, B, and C items is judgmental, but often approximates the 20%, 30%, 50% ratio found by Pareto. In this situation, ABC analysis would be particularly helpful in managing high-penalty items.

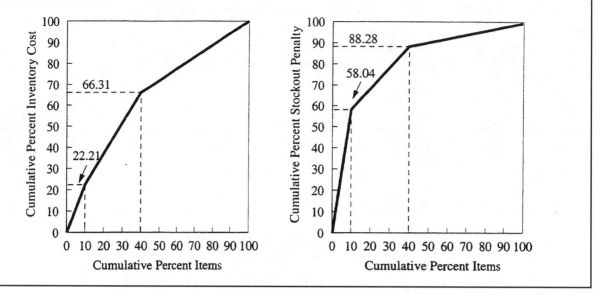

Alternatively, cycle counting may be used to count some proportion of the inventory items each day on a cyclic schedule. Typically, a cycle-counting team is required to verify the inventory items (including part numbers, number of items, and storage location) of a fixed number of records each day. Of course, the inventory status of A items would be more regularly checked than those for B or C items. However, as Greene (1987) notes, there are a number of other circumstances when a count many be warranted. "Opportunity" counts are scheduled when inventory quantities are low because, with low inventories, the counting effort and potential confusion are reduced. "Low-cost" counts are generated if a stock person is working with the item at the storage site. For example, in the process of picking an item for an order, a stock person could count the remaining items at the storage site with little extra effort. "Special" counts may be required by an unexpected outage or a major discrepancy—either of which indicates a system error or other significant problem (possibly pilferage or faulty stocking action).

TRADITIONAL INVENTORY MANAGEMENT

Traditional methods of inventory management involve inventory decisions directed toward reducing either the cost or the risk of holding inventory. Most traditional methods identify periodic demands (often annual) and calculate the minimum cost per unit based on the cost of ordering and a fixed per-unit carrying cost. Typically, such computations involve a trade-off between the cost of ordering (purchasing, delivery, inspection, and budget transactions) and the cost of carrying (interest, warehousing and security, and stock shrinkage, including pilferage, deterioration; and obsolescence). The traditional methods of inventory management classify inventory decisions in each of the three materials management questions (what product is needed, how much is needed, and when is it needed?). Unfortunately, traditional methods do not provide a complete analysis of these three questions.

Economic Order Quantity

The economic order quantity is commonly represented in two ways: (1) as the inventory level over time, and (2) as the total cost of inventory management (including item cost, setup cost, and carrying cost) for different amounts of products ordered. These relationships are shown in Figure 7-2. The Q^*, the economic order quantity, is the order amount

FIGURE 7-2   The Economic Order Quantity

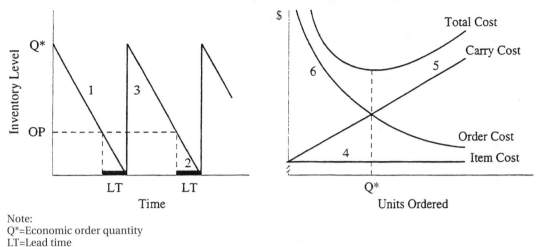

Note:
Q*=Economic order quantity
LT=Lead time
OP=Order point

at which total inventory costs are minimized. The basic EOQ model requires seven assumptions, which are (1) constant demand for inventory, (2) constant order lead times, (3) one-time receipt of the entire order, (4) constant item cost per unit—no quantity discounts, (5) constant per-unit carrying costs, (6) a one-time fixed order/setup cost that units are prorated over, and (7) single (not) transactions (Fogarty et al., 1991). These assumptions are represented in Figure 7-2.

These assumptions may appear to be rather constraining; however, the consequence of loosening some of these assumptions may not be severe. If the Q^* varies by, say 10%, there is very little change in the total cost of inventory. This is because the total cost curve is "inelastic" in the vicinity of the EOQ.

Additionally, a variety of models have been developed which permit the convenience of discrete period (for example, a week, a month, and so on) ordering. The more commonly used of these models include the lot-for-lot ordering (order the number of units required for each period), the period order quantity (order for the discrete period volume that is closest to the EOQ), the least unit cost, the least total cost, and the part period balancing. Most introductory operations management or management science texts review several of these models. Decision Model Box 7-2 shows the EOQ calculation.

Limitations of EOQ

Unfortunately, despite the extensive variations of the EOQ, this approach has several limitations. Even with the inelasticity of the total cost curve in the vicinity of the EOQ, the EOQ and the reorder point methods may be high-cost strategies. This is because they require the definition of a fixed annual demand (which would likely vary), they do not consider exactly when the demand occurs, and they overemphasize the minimum total inventory costs, rather than considering holding and order setup cost contributions to the total.

The total cost of inventory, given varying order sizes and different order quantity models, does not vary greatly because of the inelasticity of the total cost curve in the vicinity of the EOQ. This can be shown by calculating the total cost of an order policy of 10% or 25% greater or less than the EOQ, using the total cost formula in Decision Model Box 7-2, shown as follows:

DECISION MODEL BOX 7-2 Lot-sizing at the Mid-West Distributor

The Mid-West Distributor stocks and delivers Golden Eagle Beer in a three-state area. Demand is 200 cases/day, or, with 300 business days per year, 60,000 cases/year. The lead time for resupply from the brewery is one day, and the standard deviation of daily demand is 50 cases. If the annual interest rate is 15% and shrinkage is 5%, the cost is $10.00 per case, and the order cost is $20, calculate the economic order quantity, the interval between orders, the number of orders, and the safety stock (95% service level).

The formulas for the economic order quantity (Q^*) and reorder point with safety stock (r) are

$$Q^* = \sqrt{\frac{2DC_o}{C_h}}$$

$$r = \mu + z\sigma$$

where: Q^* = economic order quantity
D = demand rate in units *per period*
C_o = cost of ordering in dollars
C_h = period holding cost per unit [(interest rate (i) + shrinkage (s)) × item cost)]
r = reorder point
μ = demand over lead time
z = number of standard deviations for a specified service level
σ = standard deviation of lead time demand

Note: An annual period, as shown in this example, is commonly, though not mandatorily, used.

Solution, Q system:

$$Q = \sqrt{\frac{2(C_o = 20)\,(\text{days/yr} = 300)(\text{daily demand} = 200)}{(\text{Cost} = \$10)(i = 0.15 + s = 0.05)}} = 1095.445 = 1100 \text{ cases}$$

With a 95% service level, the z value is 1.65 (from a z table). Because the lead time is 1 day, demand during the lead time is 60,000/300, or 200 cases. The reorder point, with safety, is $r = \mu + z\sigma$, or $200 + 1.65(50) = 282.5$, or 285 cases. The number of orders is 60,000/1100, or 54.5, roughly one order every 5.5 days. The Q system places an order of 1100 cases when stock drops to 285 cases.

The period order quantity method adjusts the EOQ to a convenient discrete period. For example, if the order period were once per week (six-day business week), the POQ would be 1200 cases per order.

The relevant cost of inventory for one year would be the cost of holding plus the cost of ordering. Sometimes the annual item purchase cost is included in the formula. Including the annual item purchase cost, the total cost is:

Total cost = cost of holding + cost of ordering + annual item purchase cost
or

$$\text{TC} = QC_h/2 \quad + DC_o/Q \quad + DC$$
$$\text{or TC} = 1095 \quad + 1095 \quad + 600{,}000 = \$602{,}190$$

Variance	Q	Total Cost
−25%	≈ 820	820 + 1463.41 + 600,000 = $602,283.41
−10%	≈ 985	985 + 1218.27 + 600,000 = $602,203.27
EOQ	1095	1095 + 1095 + 600,000 = $602,190.00
+10%	≈ 1205	1205 + 995.85 + 600,000 = $602,200.85
+25%	≈ 1370	1370 + 875.91 + 600,000 = $602,245.91

Note that a 10% variance in the EOQ amounts to a roughly $12.00 variance in total inventory cost, which is about one-half of one percent of the inventory cost ($12/2190 = 0.00548). For a 25% variance of the EOQ, the cost increment is about 4%. When the annual unit purchase cost of $600,000 is included in the computation, the cost variance is trivial. Thus, it really does not make too much difference which order quantity or which models are used, particularly if the values used in the computation, such as the annual demand, the interest rate, or the cost (or procedures) for ordering, are subject to change.

The EOQ computation is dependent on stated values for annual demand, interest rates, costs of ordering, and of the item. Annual national economic projections, as aggregate forecasts, are often quite accurate; however, few operations managers would claim to forecast, with less than 25% error, disaggregate demand to item level or even regional sales level. Additionally, demand for most items is seasonal, which would require the computation of an EOQ for the higher season and another for the low season. The use of a quarterly or even a monthly period for EOQ computations is possible, but even this does not consider forecast errors.

Other areas of data inaccuracies are that the cost of the item may be stated as a standard cost, not the production cost, and shrinkage may be overstated or understated by the widely used 5% assumption. Further, several contributors to order setup costs, including ordering technologies, counting procedures, shipping methods, and internal machine setup technologies, have changed dramatically in the past few years, but may not be reflected in revised EOQ computations. In fact, it is very difficult to state several of the values used in the EOQ computation with accuracy (Rhodes, 1981). Thus, the EOQ is computed primarily from forecasts and estimates, which may be quite inaccurate. However, the inelasticity of the total cost curve in the vicinity of the EOQ makes it rather robust to changes or inaccuracies in the data. The square root radical in the formula gives a stabilizing effect. For example, a quadrupling or reduction of demand by three-fourths would respectively double or halve the EOQ. Similarly, reducing the holding costs or item costs by three-fourths or quadrupling the holding costs or item costs would only double or halve the EOQ.

Unfortunately, this stabilizing effect may tend to discourage efforts to operate on the contributing factors to inventory costs. By focusing management attention on the algebraic minimization of the total cost curve, the EOQ directs attention away from the contributors to total cost, the various carrying and ordering costs. Though the unit carrying

FIGURE 7-3 Total Inventory Costs as Setup Costs Decrease

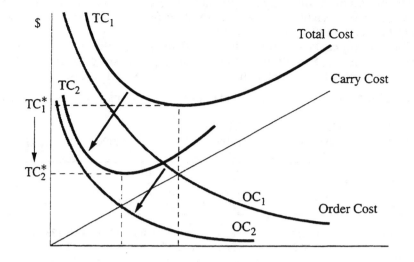

cost may be given (at least it is not directly controlled by the operations manager), efficiencies of ordering or internal setups are directly realizable by operations managers. Examples include the reduced costs and increased accuracy of cycle counting, long-term supplier contracts (for example, blanket contracts), telephone or fax ordering, computer-managed setups, external setups (for example, outside of the equipment, which can be prepared before the equipment is shut down), and shared deliveries. As order costs or setup costs are reduced, the total cost of inventory is reduced and the quantity of the Q^* decreases, as shown in Figure 7-3.

Probably the most significant deficiency of the EOQ is that is disregards the exact timing of the annual requirements. It defines an annual time period, which, as an aggregate, is likely quite accurate, but assumes constant demand for the items. It does not specify exactly when the units are needed. This is particularly important for high-valued items with bills of materials that have many levels. In such cases, the lead times may be constant, but of long duration, permitting efficiencies of timing (dependent demand). For example, if 100 units of an item are needed once per week on Friday, an EOQ model would likely hold some stock of the item all of the time. But, a timed lot-for-lot method would hold zero units from Monday through Thursday and schedule deliveries of 100 units on Friday morning, reducing the average annual holding time of the inventory. Thus, the EOQ is the method of choice when demands are independent. Alternatively, if the bill of materials structure and item lead times can be used to accurately schedule when the part is needed (dependent demand), then material requirements planning is the method of choice. Material requirements planning resolves the deficiencies of EOQ models, but requires that accurate demand information, product structures, and inventory status be available.

MATERIAL REQUIREMENTS PLANNING

Basic material requirements planning (MRP) systems use the bill of materials, the master production schedule, and inventory data to calculate time period requirements for materials. Though MRP was originally developed as a method of ordering inventory, it has been extended to accomplish scheduling and management control functions as well. There is a wide range of applications for MRP, including service and small business operations (Davis, 1983). For example, today some hospitals are using MRP, based on activity schedules, to manage inventories of irregularly used or expensive items, with a small amount of safety stock for emergencies. Additionally, many small retailers are realizing inventory reductions, and the associated savings, because they order additional units using distribution requirements planning (DRP) as those items are sold.

Though a few MRP systems cost more than $5 million installed, some systems are available for $100.00 (Grey, 1986, and Melnyk, 1992). Several small business systems are available for $3500, and some very complete academic and training systems (which limit the number of parts that can be managed or the capabilities) may be purchased for less than $1000. The key, however, to MRP is recognizing that, as a computer-driven automated system, it will reduce the visibility, tangibility, and understandability of materials decisions on the shop floor and require different skills to effectively manage inventories. These difficulties are highlighted by the introductory case.

Historical Development of MRP

The historical development of MRP has been associated with alternating periods of optimism and disillusionment, both among MRP consultants and technicians, and in the perception of the general public. These cycles of optimism and disillusionment are likely mirrored by companies as they go through an implementation process. Figure 7-4 represents the sequential developments of MRP and MRP II (manufacturing resource planning). Fully developed MRP II systems are a part of computer integrated manufacturing (CIM).

Though there were numerous early starts, according to Wight (1984) a key event in the development of MRP occurred in 1965, when IBM defined the production and inventory control system (PICS) approach, built around the bill of materials processor. Inventory and production schedule information were joined with the bill of materials and exploded. Those three key components, shown at the top of Figure 7-4, are driven by various manual or automated systems.

The basic parts explosion of MRP integrates the three key files in several logical processing steps. In a very simplified sense, those are

1. Identify the end item requirement in terms of units and due dates from the master production schedule.
2. Identify current and projected available inventory of the end item to meet that requirement.
3. If there is insufficient inventory of the end item:
   a. Use the bill of materials file to identify the availability of subcomponents of the end item (number required, lead time offset, safety stock and lot-sizing method).
   b. Use the inventory records to identify the current and projected available inventory of subcomponents of the item.
4. If there is insufficient inventory (excluding safety stock) of any subcomponent:
   a. Schedule the necessary production of that item, with appropriate lead-time offset and lot size.
   b. Identify the scheduled production (or parts of that job) with the job number of the higher-level component or end item so that the production can be "pegged" to the deliverable end item.
5. Repeat steps 3 and 4 for each lower level of the bill of materials and continue in this manner until sufficient units are available to produce (with lead time offsets) the requirements at all levels.

MRP II supplements the basic parts explosion by recommending purchasing and shop floor dispatch actions and by monitoring supplier deliveries and production management actions as the job moves from raw materials to finished goods and through the distribution network. Supplier management would include monitoring of procurement activities and supplier deliveries. Shop floor order management includes capacity adjustment and shop floor control, and then management of the production process. If exceptions

FIGURE 7-4 The Components and Relationships of MRP Systems

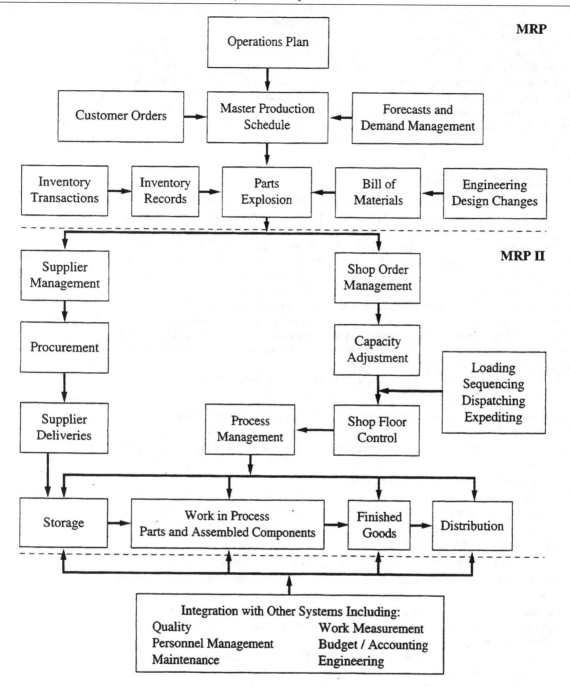

or variations occur, the MRP system identifies those exceptions, and depending upon the software, recommends a "fix." The master scheduler manages this process.

More specifically, the parts explosion involves gross-to-net and projected-available-balance computations. These computations are shown in detail in Decision Model Box 7-3.

The lot-sizing rules of MRP can include various order quantity methods and safety stocks. Thus, if the cost advantages of prorating setups are used and, if demand variances require safety stocks, then, as Sauers (1990) comments, the improvement of MRP over the EOQ is that it uses the actual schedule and the timed actions of a fully exploded bill of materials. This results because MRP uses dependent demands. In many businesses, however, this is an important improvement and can result in significant inventory cost reductions.

Early MRP systems were based on weekly time "buckets"; that is, the MRP schedule was exploded and published once per week. Information processing capabilities are now sufficiently fast to permit "bucketless" (based on transactions, not on time periods) MRP systems. With bucketless systems, MRP is updated with each transaction, and every schedule change is immediately calculated and evaluated. However, once the schedule is computed and dispatched and purchase orders are released, the schedule must be executed as planned—changes are very disruptive. Bucketless systems permit on-line assessment of changes and execution adjustments as desired, but discipline is required to minimize the number of changes.

Future Directions of MRP

Though the basic MRP processes are well established, much improvement can be achieved in implementation. The initial implementations of MRP systems were sometimes disappointing. An early study (Anderson et al., 1982) found that only 9.5% of respondents claimed to have Class A systems, a measure of system development and accuracy. Twenty-nine percent stated that they were Class B users, and fully 60% were Class C or D users. The Class A system, for example, is defined as "a closed loop system used by top management to participate in production planning, with deliveries on time, little or no expediting, and inventory under control" (Wight, 1981). The 9.5% of respondents who report Class A systems may be inflated because it does not include nonrespondents in a survey drawn from inventory managers and consultants.

A more recent and more optimistic report ("Computers . . . ," 1984) finds that in a survey of 3600 manufacturing and nonmanufacturing companies, 27% reported decreased materials costs and increased labor productivity, inventory turns, and customer service resulting from an MRP implementation. An even more recent study by Turnipseed et al. (1992) found significant relationships between worker involvement and control of the implementation, particularly during the early stages of implementation, and the outcome of the implementation. Participant involvement was shown as a determinant of satisfaction and of the quality of the implementation. Because more is known about MRP implementation, success rates are high, particularly where there is a strong commitment by top management.

The use of MRP systems is expected to grow dramatically for the foreseeable future (Baer, 1989). The greater cross-functional emphasis of MRP II is consistent with integrated operations management because it facilitates interaction with human resources, financial, and accounting planning and administration, as well as quality control and work measurement. Well-developed MRP systems can integrate ten to fifteen major information systems, as well as numerous subsystems, typically upwards of 150 to 200 different program files.

Where interactive files are used, however, there is little tolerance of data error, and several errors can be multiplicative in effect. For example, 90% accuracy in each of production schedule, inventory records, and bill of materials files would result in 73% ($0.9 \times 0.9 \times 0.9$) overall system accuracy. This assessment prompted Grey (1986) to recommend that prospective adopters consider the ease of implementation of a particular software as a primary decision factor. Cingari (1992) suggests that a continuous improvement program be applied to the MRP data and that communication is one of the habitual weak

DECISION MODEL BOX 7-3   MRP at the Schmidt Shovel Company

Over the next ten weeks, the Schmidt Shovel Company is scheduled to deliver 150 common shovels. The product structure and indented bill of materials are given:

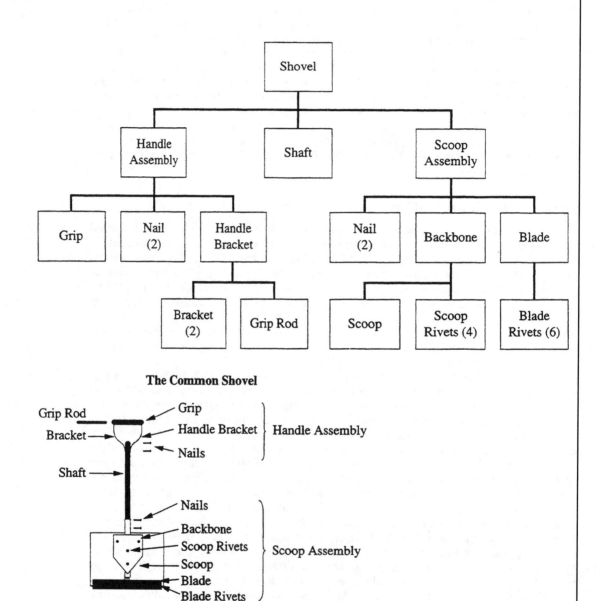

The Common Shovel

Indented Bill of Materials for a Common Shovel

Level	Nomenclature	Number Required
0	Shovel	
1	Handle assembly	1
2	Grip	1
2	Nail	2
2	Handle bracket	1
3	Bracket	2
3	Grip rod	1
1	Shaft	1
1	Scoop assembly	1
2	Nail	2
2	Backbone	1
3	Scoop	1
3	Scoop rivet	4
2	Blade	1
3	Blade rivet	6

Gross-to-Net Computations. Gross-to-net computations permit component parts in inventory or scheduled receipts to be included in the available inventory computation. the computation starts with the 0 (highest) level of the bill of materials and progresses to the bottom of the bill of materials. The gross requirement is computed for each part at each level, then current and projected inventory (on-hand inventory and scheduled receipts) are subtracted to get the net requirement of that part. The following table shows the gross-to-net computation for the handle assembly that would support an order for 150 shovels. The net requirement is the aggregate number of each part that will be required to build the 150 shovels during the ten-week period. For example, 150 shovels require a net of 110 handles, after subtracting the 40 units in inventory. This information is helpful for planning, but it does not indicate when the demands will occur.

Part Description	Number of Each	On-hand Inventory	Scheduled Receipts	Requirements Gross	Net
Handle assembly	1	40	—	150	110
Grip	1	32	35	110	43
Nail	2	70	50	220	100
Handle bracket	1	47	—	110	63
Bracket	2	15	40	126	71
Grip rod	1	39	30	63	—

Lead Time Offset Using Projected Available Balance. MRP records for the shovel show the exact timing of the demands. Gross requirements from the master production schedule and scheduled receipts are used to compute the projected available balance (PAB) and planned order release. The PAB is computed from period to period using the following formula and the handle assembly is calculated as an example for the second and fourth periods.

$$PAB_n = PAB_{n-1} - \text{gross requirements} + \text{scheduled receipts}$$

Handle assembly

$$PAB_2 = 40 - 35 + 0 = 5$$
$$PAB_4 = 5 - 35 + 30* = 0$$

---

*Note that the scheduled receipt of 30 in week 4 is carried as a planned order release until week 2, when it is ordered and becomes a scheduled receipt.

The use of varying lead times, different lot sizing and safety stock conventions, and a different number of components all cause variations in this basic calculation. The parts explosion uses the gross-to-net and lead-time-offset adjusted planned order releases of items at higher levels to compute the gross requirements for lower-level items.

Level 1

Handle assembly			Week									
			1	2	3	4	5	6	7	8	9	10
	Gross requirements (given)			35		35		30	5		35	10
	Scheduled receipts											
Lead time = 2	Projected available balance	40	40	5	5	0	0	0	0	0	0	0
Lot for lot	Planned order release			30		30	5		35	10		

Level 2

Grip			Week									
			1	2	3	4	5	6	7	8	9	10
	Gross requirements			30		30	5		35	10		
	Scheduled receipts			35								
Lead time = 2	Projected available balance	32	32	37	37	7	2	2	0	0	0	0
Lot for lot	Planned order release					33	10					

Level 2 ×2

Nail – 2 req			Week									
			1	2	3	4	5	6	7	8	9	10
	Gross requirements			60		60	10		70	20		
	Scheduled receipts		50									
Lead time = 1	Projected available balance	70	120	60	60	0	40	40	20	0	0	0
Lot size = 50	Planned order release				50		50					

			Week										Level 2
			1	2	3	4	5	6	7	8	9	10	
Handle bracket	Gross requirements			30		30	5		35	10			
	Scheduled receipts												
Lead time = 2	Projected available balance	47	47	17	17	0	0	0	0	0	0	0	
Lot for lot	Planned order release			13	5		35	10					

			Week										Level 3
			1	2	3	4	5	6	7	8	9	10	×2
Bracket – 2 req	Forecast			26	10		70	20					
	Scheduled receipts		40										
Lead time = 1	Projected available balance	15	55	29	19	19	0	0	0	0	0	0	
Lot for lot	Planned order release				51	20							

			Week										Level 3
			1	2	3	4	5	6	7	8	9	10	
Grip rod	Forecast			13	5		35	10					
Lead time = 3	Scheduled receipts			30									
*SS = 20	Projected available balance	39	39	56	51	51	20	20	20	20	20	20	
Lot for lot	Planned order release			4	10								

*SS = safety stock

links that management should address. Success of MRP implementation requires extensive employee training, the time and cost of which should not be underestimated.

One method of reducing errors in inventory counting is to relieve (or backflush) inventory records, which means to subtract out the parts and component inventories for each unit produced only after the unit has been shipped or placed in finished goods inventory. This technique reduces the errors in inventory, because it eliminates mistakes due to changed orders or volumes. However, with backflushing, inventories must be separately adjusted for scrap (Kutos, 1992). Additionally, Young and Nie (1992) identify an EOQ-like model that balances the costs incurred from cycle counting of inventory and those of stockout. They suggest that their model performs better than models that use traditional ABC logic. Under all circumstances both backflushing and effective cycle counting practices can reduce inventory counting errors significantly.

The complexity of MRP often takes inventory management functions away from the shop floor and places them in the purview of computer information systems. The understanding of the MRP system and the visibility of problems and solutions have been removed from the area where the solution must be implemented and from the people who must implement the solution. Typically, few people on the shop floor understand data processing, though most are very familiar with MRP. Increased use of PCs and local area networks, as well as employee training, resolves this question.

MRP system "nervousness" or instability results when seemingly minor changes of the master production schedule cause significant changes when they are exploded down through the bill of materials structure, sometimes affecting jobs or orders that have already been released and started. Bucketless systems are particularly prone to nervousness, because each transaction is considered as a time period, and subject to change. Schedule "freezing" and time fence management are used by the master scheduler to limit such adjustments. That is, within a designated time fence, say, one month, the production schedule is "frozen" and no further changes can be made, except within strict cost or approval constraints. "Necessary" changes often require approval by higher management.

Each of these directions relates to the quality of implementation. Poorly implemented systems with high levels of errors and limited capabilities (as defined in Figure 7-4) result in a variety of informal methods to bypass the system. The complexity and potential for problems with such methods are costly and just add to the errors of the formal system. Alternatively, well-implemented systems can result in tremendous cost reductions because of the ability to plan exact requirements (in terms of what product is needed, how much is needed, and when it is needed). Specifically, MRP corrects a key weakness in dependent demand methods by defining exactly when a requirement for specific volume occurs. For this reason, successful MRP implementation is a powerful source of strategic advantage for a firm. It is also a step in the direction of continuous improvement.

CONTINUOUS IMPROVEMENT OF MATERIALS MANAGEMENT

The materials management system can be improved by reducing the amount of inventory held, by stabilizing and smoothing the flow of inventory, and by reducing the loss of inventory (or value added) due to all causes (quality control, obsolescence, pilferage, and so on). Efforts toward these objectives generally have taken three forms—materials system integration, bill of materials restructuring, and just-in-time production.

Materials System Integration

Ideally, to ensure smoothness of materials flow, the materials management system should be integrated from the creation of raw materials to the delivery and servicing of the end item. One of the most effective techniques to increase the efficiency and reduce the cost of a logistics flow path is to synchronize lot size, load sizes, package sizes, and item quantities along the steps of the flow path (Nicholl, 1992). Though one corporation may not necessarily manage all of these activities, the materials information system should vertically integrate suppliers, manufacturers, and distributors. That is, the system should be viewed as links in a chain, each of which adds value through transformation, and each of which is both forward and backward linked. Suppliers should be given production scheduling information, and distribution centers should be linked to the production system through distribution requirements planning (DRP). This integration of supplier and distribution systems is shown in Figure 7-5.

Supplier Integration. Supplier integration can smooth and reduce the complexity of the purchasing function. To emphasize the importance of the purchasing function, consider the potential for savings. Purchased parts and materials constitute between 30% and 60% of the cost of goods sold in the United States, depending upon the industry. Thus, a small percentage decrease in the cost of purchased items can result in a much larger percentage increase in profits. For example, consider a purchasing operation where the cost

FIGURE 7-5 Supplier and Distribution System Integration

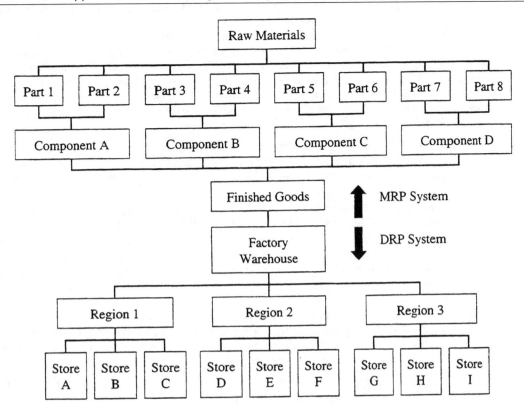

of purchased materials is 40% of the total sales, and profit is 10% of the total sales. If purchasing costs were reduced by 10% to 36% of total sales and other costs were constant, then profits would increase from 10% to 14%, or a 40% increase in profits. The significance of purchasing system savings is that such savings may be directly captured as profits.

Though the effects of improved product and process design, quality control, and inventory management process efficiencies would also be directly reflected in reduced costs and improved profits, the improvement of the purchasing function may be easier to achieve. Such cost savings in purchased materials are possible through a number of purchasing techniques. A starting point for purchasing system evaluation is to use ABC analysis to identify those purchased items that contribute the most to costs. The intense management of A items through such techniques as long-term contracts, integration of purchasing with design engineering to standardize and reduce the number of parts, improvement of purchasing lead times, and use of supplier evaluation methods (such as supplier certification) to reduce and manage the number of suppliers can yield notable cost reductions. Continuing reduction of purchasing costs is possible as analysis is applied to B and C items.

The purchasing process must be linked with the external environment, as well as with the operations system. Marketing likely will identify customer requirements and make the initial quality and quantity projection. If the product or process is complex, engineering will be required to write product specifications, including product configuration and quality requirements. Purchasing releases the contract, based on approval of the source's quality program, and delivery timing. Subsequently, based on production schedules, materials control releases specific orders, receives the order acknowledgment, receives and inspects the shipment, and places the item in stock or releases it for use. As the product is delivered, the distribution system will be involved with issues of product availability and quality. These linkages are shown in Figure 7-6.

Purchasing initiates order contracts through one of three types of systems: the cyclic order system, the fixed order quantity, and MRP. Cyclic orders are time-based, like the period order quantity; fixed order quantities are unit-size-based, using convenient lot sizes for transportation, or the EOQ, and MRP is requirements-based. Often purchasing contracts can be managed for longer periods (six months or a year) based on projected volumes. Subsequently, specific delivery schedules are defined on the basis of the requirement. There are four general types of purchasing contract arrangements.

1. *Blanker Order.* Minimum and sometimes maximum quantities are specified over a defined period (normally one year). Production then sends the requisitions directly to the supplier within the specified volumes and lead times. The blanket order reduces the administration required for separate orders.

2. *Standing Order.* The standing order is like a blanket order, except that it is defined for an indefinite period. Requisitions must be placed within specified lead times and volumes.

3. *Systems Contracts.* Suppliers maintain at buyer's facilities specified amounts of inventory and periodically refresh specified amounts of inventory. Contracts to stock vending machines are a simplified example of systems contracts. Often such approaches are used for consumables such as chemicals, glues, and small bulk parts such as nuts, bolts, expendable tools and instruments, and the like.

4. *Distribution Contracts.* Suppliers maintain specified amounts of inventory at their facilities, dedicated for your use. Delivery to buyer's facility is based on requisitions and must be within specified volumes and lead times. Distribution contracts define inventories offsite, but in sufficient volumes to ensure against stockout.

These different types of contract are particularly important as companies reduce inventory and smooth materials flow. They permit reduction of purchasing costs, more

FIGURE 7-6 Purchasing Integration

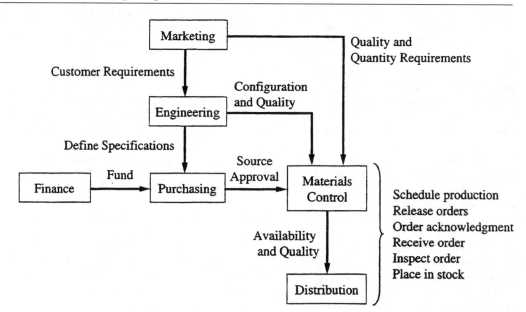

flexible response to changing demands, and reduced risk of stockout. However, care should be taken to avoid merely transferring the responsibilities and costs of inventories to "JIT warehouses," off-site, but closely located, storage operations whose only function is to hide large inventories of safety stock.

Supplier integration is achieved by extending the MRP schedule visibility to suppliers of components, parts, or raw materials. Similarly, distribution requirements planning extends the MRP logic through the distribution system, potentially to the retail level. This integration provides formal planning visibility throughout purchasing, operations, and distribution systems, with the associated benefits of inventory reduction, enhanced productivity, and improved customer service. The operations system becomes a fully integrated input-transformation-output structure throughout the length of the chain of transformations.

Distribution System Integration. According to industry estimates, distribution costs amount to more than 20% of the U.S. gross national product. The breakdown of the more than $400 billion per year of distribution costs is categorized as 47% in transportation costs, 21% in warehousing costs, and 21% in inventory carrying costs. An example of a DRP system is shown in Decision Model Box 7-4.

The significance of multilevel planning visibility is apparent as the "lumpy" demand from the warehouses is converted into reasonably stable and accurate planned requirements. Though the forecast for any aggregation of four weeks is rather accurate, the planned requirements project exactly when the demand will occur. Smaller lot sizes might reduce the lumpiness, but transportation costs would likely increase. The significance of DRP visibility is that it permits the distribution planner to look ahead at the regional demands and smooth them. Forward visibility permits the distribution manager to manage demand turbulence. Further, visibility in the distribution system, when linked to the master production schedule, gives manufacturing those same capabilities (Martin, 1990).

Additionally, the DRP system permits the operations manager to consider seasonality of demand, pipeline buildup and depletion, restructuring the distribution network to more accurately reflect demand flow, product phase-outs, and back-ordering requirements. Of course, the effectiveness of a DRP system depends upon information accuracy, education off users, management support, and communications among the participants.

Bill of Material Restructuring

The second dimension of continuous improvement is the restructuring of a product bill of material to permit increased plannability. The traditional bill of material is structured in the way that the product is manufactured. It includes a "list of all subassemblies, subordinates, parts, and raw materials that go into a parent assembly, showing the quantity of each required to make an assembly" (Cox et al., 1992). Traditional structuring activities involve product, parts and services definition, production instructions, engineering changes, service parts support, procurement planning, operations scheduling, and materials control.

However, recently developed methods of product structuring permit increased plannability. These methods, often involving modularization of the bill, permit optimal level scheduling, encourage more accurate product option forecasting, expedite order entry, allow more reliable product costing, and facilitate efficient data storage and system maintenance (Mather, 1989).

Simply, the traditional bill of material schedules at the highest, or end item, level of the product structure. Alternatively, modular bills schedule below that level, often at level 1 or 2, but potentially at the bottom level of the product structure. Product modules are defined for commonly purchased groupings of product options or alternatives. For example, an automobile air conditioning option module would include the compressor unit, tinted glass, dashboard switch options, different engine belts, and a supplement to the owner's manual. Other examples of modularly structured products are home entertainment

DECISION MODEL BOX 7-4 Distribution Requirements Planning at National Distribution

The National Distribution Company manages the distribution of durable appliances for a major retailer. National uses a central warehouse collocated with the factory and three regional warehouses. Demands are forecast at the regional level and are aggregated for long-range planning purposes at the central warehouse. However, a distribution requirements planning system is used to compute requirements for short-range demand at the central warehouse. Region safety stock, shipment size, and lead times are given. The central warehouse directly feeds the factory master production schedule.

			Week									
			1	2	3	4	5	6	7	8	9	10
Region 1	Forecast		15	15	15	15	15	15	15	15	15	15
Safety stock = 10	Planned receipts				25							
Lead time = 3	Inventory	40	25	10	20	30	15	25	10	20	30	15
Order size = 25	Planned order release		25		25		25	25				

			Week									
			1	2	3	4	5	6	7	8	9	10
Region 2	Forecast		50	50	50	50	30	30	30	30	60	60
	Planned receipts		75									
Lead time = 1	Inventory	25	50	0	25	50	20	65	35	5	20	35
Order size = 75	Planned order release			75	75		75			75	75	

			Week									
			1	2	3	4	5	6	7	8	9	10
Region 3	Forecast		35	35	35	35	35	35	35	35	35	35
	Planned receipts			50								
Lead time = 2	Inventory	40	5	20	35	0	15	30	45	10	25	40
Order size = 50	Planned order release		50		50	50	50		50	50		

		Week									
		1	2	3	4	5	6	7	8	9	10
Total region requirements	Region 1	25		25		25	25				
	Region 2		75	75		75			75	75	
	Region 3	50		50	50	50		50	50		
	Total of region requirements	75	75	150	50	150	25	50	125	75	

		Week									
		1	2	3	4	5	6	7	8	9	10
Central warehouse Safety stock = 100 Batch size = 200 Lead time = 2	Forecast needs	100	100	100	100	80	80	80	80	110	110
	Planned requirements	75	75	150	50	150	25	50	125	75	
	Planned receipts		200								
	Projected available inventory 180	105	230	280	230	280	255	205	280	205	205
	Master production schedule order 200	200		200			200				

Note that the use of planned requirements improves at the central warehouse based on the use of region planned orders, which give a more accurate projection than the aggregated region forecasted needs. Additionally, lot-sizing (lot for lot) methods at the central warehouse and reduced safety stock would improve this system even further, though possibly at greater risk of stockout.

and stereo racks and personal computers, which are sold with several sets of alternative component modules. These modules have standardized and pluggable interfaces with all other components. The definition of product modules permits item management at the module or component level and assembly of those modules with a much simpler final assembly schedule (FAS), or at the customer's site as part of the customer delivery process.

The value of modules is that they permit apparent product diversity based on the lower-level scheduling of a reduced number of items. Consider a grandfather clock. The traditional grandfather clock might have twelve different face plates, eight different pendulum and weight casing styles, four different cabinet styles or finishes, among other variations. Building and holding end item inventory of all possible product variations, or even a reasonably diversified product range, would be very costly. However, if these products were built and stored as modules, and then assembled or packed to customer specified options, the reduction of inventory and increased responsiveness to customer specifications would be tremendous. With traditional management techniques, each design variation requires a separate bill of material, and the total number of different bills and clocks is a *multiplicative* function of the number of component alternatives. But, if the product is managed at the module level, then the number of modules is *additive*. In the clock example, modularization reduces the number of bills and separate end items from as many as 7680 to 37. This reduction of bills and end items significantly reduces

FIGURE 7-7 Traditional and Modular Bills of Materials

Traditional BOM

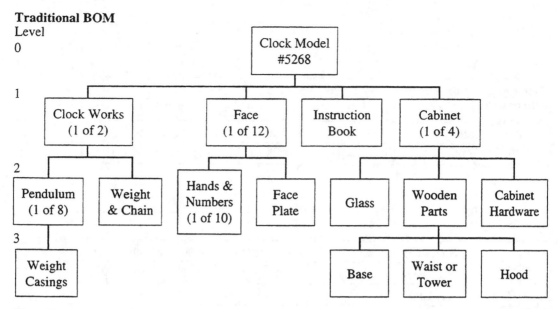

Note: Total number of products using traditional bills of material is potentially $1 \times 2 \times 12 \times 4 \times 8 \times 10 = 7680$. This is because products are managed at the end-item level of the bill of material.

Modular BOM

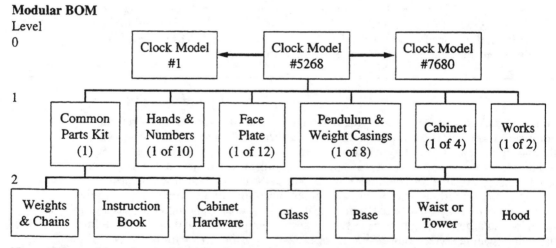

Note: At the end-item level of the bill of material there may potentially be 7680 different models; however, the total number of product modules managed using modular bills of material is equal to $1 + 10 + 12 + 8 + 4 + 2 = 37$. Products are managed at an intermediate level of the bill of material.

the time spent in inventory management—and cost of inventory. This comparison is shown in Figure 7-7.

Initial research (Stonebraker, 1991) tentatively suggests that modular bills can assist in improving inventory turns by a factor of five with a corresponding reduction of inventory costs. Additionally, modularized products show a twenty-fold reduction in product family size (and thus reduced product complexity). However, the complexity of the modular bill may result in a reduction of quality and delivery performance. Further research is necessary in this area.

An extension of the modular bill of material is the configurator. Instead of predefined modules (stated as part numbers, bills, and routings), as used by modular bills, the configurator bill uses algorithms, rule-based techniques, and conditional logic to define the product and manufacturing requirements. For example, a round table might be defined only as glass-topped or plastic, and, if plastic, then by color. The diameter of the table, along with these characteristics, would be used to specify all components. Iron legs, instead of wooden legs, would be required if the table were greater than three feet in diameter. The molding for the edge of the plastic table would be determined by πd, the formula for the circumference. If the top of the plastic table were white, the molding would be black; otherwise the molding would be white. The configurator bill logic replaces the modular bill with variable- or algorithm-based relationships (Lieberman, 1992). Configurator bills also have been shown to give a special advantage in make-to-order and assemble-to-order operations (Burke, 1991; Burke, 1992).

Just-In-Time Operations

Just-in-time (JIT) may be one of the most used—and misused—buzzwords of the 1980s and early 1990s. One somewhat ludicrouus application has extended JIT to the scheduling of learning activities just-in-time for an examination, otherwise called *cramming*. Other "fables" and misunderstandings about JIT include that it is entirely a Japanese idea, that it involves production only, and that it necessitates geographic collocation (nearness) of suppliers and users. As Ackerman (1988) clarifies, JIT was widely practiced in the United States well before World War II. JIT is a philosophy of management extending from suppliers through production to distribution systems. A carefully managed transportation system can reduce the need for proximity of supplier and user. This section will briefly introduce JIT as it relates to materials management; Chapter 8, Just-in-Time, will elaborate the JIT management philosophy.

As an inventory management technique (distinct from the broader definition of JIT as a philosophy of management), JIT reduces inventories by creating an unbuffered pull inventory management system. The pull system defines a linkage from retail distribution back to the raw material, or on a less global scale, among related production activities. As such, because it backward-links the production process, the pull system serves the function of a bill of materials. That is, as an end item is scheduled for assembly, production of components is required, which, in turn, drives demand for the subcomponents, and so on. For this reason, Goddard (1982) initially suggested that JIT would be applicable primarily in a repetitive environment. Zangwill (1992) found that the use of JIT in a highly dynamic environment may, in fact, result in an increase of inventory. JIT inventory management systems have been very effective in a variety of operations and distribution environments, though care must be taken with dynamic or nonrepetitive environments. These differences between traditional and JIT systems are shown in Table 7-2.

Though JIT production systems espouse a goal of zero inventories, most inventory management situations require some safety or buffer stocks at selected locations (Hall, 1983). The theory of constraints (Goldratt and Cox, 1986; Fogarty et. al., 1991) evaluates use of buffer inventories to smooth or protect constrained processes, shipping requirements, and assembly operations. Thus, though reducing inventories to zero may not be possible, JIT does increase the visibility of inventory decisions, particularly for shop floor personnel. In a repetitive and reasonably stable environment, the increased system visibility and simplicity permit control through problem identification and correction at a lower level of management.

As firms look to improvements in materials management processes, the efficiencies of demand chain integration, modular product structuring, and JIT production can poten-

TABLE 7-2 Comparison of Traditional and JIT Methods

Factor	Traditional Methods	JIT
Shop Floor		
Inventories	Large, asset, safety stock	Small, liability
Setups	Slow	Fast
Lot size	Balance setup vs. hold costs	Small, immediate needs
Queues	Preclude feeding problems	If problems, stop line
Quality	Statistics identify the problem for rework	Producing quality products the first time
Human Resources		
Management process	Management by edict	Management by consensus
Worker skill	Single function, routine	Multifunction
Communications	Complex, computer managed	Simple, visible
External		
Vendors	Adversaries (many sources)	Partners (few sources)
Deliveries	Few	Many
Distribution decisions	Push	Pull

Adapted from Goddard, 1982.

tially result in cost and flexibility improvements, but quality and delivery performance must be carefully monitored. With reference to Figure 7-1, improvements of the materials management system are likely to be accompanied by corresponding improvements of scheduling and customer service. In effect, the smoothed flow of inventory is moving more rapidly in a smaller pipeline, represented by the inner triangle of Figure 7-1. Continuous improvement methods reduce the costs associated with the traditional inventory questions: What product is needed, how much is needed, and when?

SUMMARY

Materials management practices affect both manufacturing costs and service delivery performance of a company; effective materials management directly contributes to a competitive edge. This chapter has initially defined several fundamental issues of materials management, including push and pull systems, dependent and independent demand, and evaluation of product lines for high-value items (ABC analysis). The historical development of materials management systems was traced by successively evaluating traditional lot-sizing methods, the development of automated material requirements planning models, and various continuous improvement approaches, including JIT. Each method was evaluated by the measure of how well it considers the key materials management questions: What is needed, how much is needed, and when is it needed? Each succeeding approach improves upon previous methods in some ways, but also has limitations, in terms of cost, appropriateness, accuracy, and employee skills and management effort. The decision of which system to implement is dependent upon the cost of implementation and the productivity criteria that the materials management system must meet.

Traditional lot-sizing methods are likely appropriate with product structures that have high volumes and stable requirements for a few low-cost end items. A plastic parts molder or a print shop might use traditional lot-sizing methods to order raw materials. Alternatively, if inventory costs are high and the production process is high volume and repetitive, then JIT would seem more appropriate. The manufacture of most durable goods, particularly high-cost durables, such as automobiles, has significantly profited from JIT. If the range of products and product options is wide and the market dynamic, as is the case with electronics and computer items, MRP may be the best method. The increasing complexity and dynamism of most production environments encourage materials managers to move toward inventory planning methods such as MRP and JIT and reduce the applicability of traditional methods, particularly if used alone. This variety of different methods to manage materials is supported in practice; Newman and Sridharan (1992) found that a wide range of materials management methods were used with varying performance, as evaluated by inventory turns, lead times, and other measures. To paraphrase the opening quotation from Plossl, though the logic of materials management is universal, the way that logic is applied varies depending upon the environment, or "parts is parts . . . is parts."

DISCUSSION QUESTIONS

1. Define four dimensions of materials management practices.
2. From your personal experience or readings, identify and give several examples of pressures to increase and decrease inventory holdings and the rationale for that action.
3. What is the difference between a push system and a pull system? Give an example of each.
4. List and describe four general reasons that require the maintenance of inventories or the maintenance of backlogs. Give an application of each.
5. From your personal experience or readings, list several examples of dependent and independent demands for inventory or services.
6. Why is the distinction between dependent and independent demand important?
7. Describe how ABC analysis focuses the inventory manger's attention to those items that are most costly, or most critical to the operation.
8. What is the most significant deficiency of the EOQ method of inventory management?
9. List the three essential components utilized to calculate requirements for materials in basic material requirements planning systems. Briefly describe the interaction of these components.
10. What do "bucketless" systems permit? How is MRP managed with such systems?
11. How can the typical material requirements planning system be improved? Select an example system from your experience or readings; describe the system and suggest improvements.
12. Distribution requirements planning (DRP) links the distribution center to the production system, thereby extending the MRP logic through the distribution system. What advantages are provided from such integration?
13. Briefly describe JIT's a contribution to the continuous improvement of materials management.
14. Explain, using as an example a product with which you are familiar, how a reduction in inventory is accomplished through the implementation of product modules.

1. Comdisc, Inc. has organized its CD players into ten product lines. The following table shows the stock number, the annual volume in units, the unit cost/item, the stockout costs, based on executive judgment, and order costs. The company is concerned about the dynamic market and that they are not managing the inventory effectively.

   a. Using inventory cost and stock-out penalty ABC methods, identify the product lines that should be the most carefully evaluated. Which technique would you recommend? Why?

   b. If the current interest rate is estimated at 20%, compute the economic order quantity for each product line.

   c. Make a recommendation to management of the best inventory management practices.

Line	Annual Volume (units)	Unit Cost	Stockout Cost	Order Cost
14	15,000	$39.00	$50.00	$679.00
21	800	52.00	75.00	462.00
35	5,500	132.00	300.00	396.00
42	12,000	145.00	300.00	428.00
56	2,100	160.00	75.00	285.00
69	650	240.00	250.00	484.00
73	8,000	280.00	500.00	524.00
87	250	420.00	600.00	124.00
90	1,200	670.00	1200.00	243.00
108	400	935.00	3000.00	324.00

2. The Round Lake Grocery Store stocks six-packs of canned beer from five distributors. Local ordinances permit the sale of alcohol on Sunday, and because tourism is a major industry in the three summer months, sales are relatively constant during the seven weekly sales days. The management uses a 10% quarterly cost of money and desires to maximize the use of its limited storage space and delivery capabilities through the use of economic lots. Given the data in the table,

   a. Calculate the economic order quantity.

   b. Calculate the safety order point (weekly orders, lead time = 2 days, the standard deviation of daily demand = 15 units, safety level = 95%).

   c. Calculate the total quarterly cost of inventory, including the cost of the item.

   d. Advise management on an ordering policy.

Beer	Quarterly Demand	Cost/Unit	Cost/Order
International Imports	1500	20	40
Golden Eagle	550	5	10
Western Water	950	12.5	20
Milwaukee's Finest	1300	7.5	5
Bush's Best	1200	9	6

3. The National Chain Distribution Company manufacturers and markets a line of bench saw. The company has three sales regions and the saw consists of two primary parts, a saw and a bench. Given the following region forecasts, plan demand for the product and make a recommendation.

		Week									
		1	2	3	4	5	6	7	8	9	10
Region 1	Forecast	30	30	30	30	30	30	30	30	30	30
Safety stock = 10	Planned receipts	50		50							
Lead time = 3	Inventory 40										
Order size = 50	Planned order release										

		Week									
		1	2	3	4	5	6	7	8	9	10
Region 2	Forecast	25	25	50	50	30	30	45	45	60	60
Safety stock = 20	Planned receipts	75									
Lead time = 1	Inventory 25										
Order size = 75	Planned order release										

			Week									
			1	2	3	4	5	6	7	8	9	10
Region 3	Forecast		35	35	55	55	35	35	25	25	45	45
Safety stock = 15	Planned receipts		70									
Lead time = 2	Inventory	40										
Order size = 70	Planned order release											

		Week									
		1	2	3	4	5	6	7	8	9	10
Total region requirements	Region 1										
	Region 2										
	Region 3										
	Total of region requirements										

			Week									
			1	2	3	4	5	6	7	8	9	10
Central warehouse	Forecast needs											
Safety stock = 100	Planned requirements		200	200								
Batch size = 200	Planned receipts											
	Projected available inventory	150										
Lead time = 2	Master production schedule order											

			Week									
			1	2	3	4	5	6	7	8	9	10
Saw assembly	Gross requirements											
Lead time = 2	Scheduled receipts											
Lot for lot	Projected available balance	250										
Safety stock = 50	Planned order release											

		Week									
		1	2	3	4	5	6	7	8	9	10
Bench assembly	Gross requirements										
Lead time = 2	Scheduled receipts										
EOQ = 300	Projected available balance	32									
Safety stock = 32	Planned order release										

REFERENCES

Ackerman, Ken. "Just-in-Time's American Practitioners," *Management Review.* June 1988, pp. 55–57.

Anderson, John C., Roger G. Schroeder, Sharon E. Tupy, and Edna M. White. "Materials Requirement Planning Systems: The State of the Art," *Production & Inventory Management.* October–December 1982.

Baer, Tony. "Closing the Loop: MRP II Takes the Next Step," *Managing Automation.* January 1989, pp. 60–62.

Beddingfield, Thomas W. "Reducing Inventory Enhances Competitiveness," *APICS—The Performance Advantage.* September 1992, pp. 28–31.

Black, J. T. *The Design of the Factory with a Future.* New York: McGraw-Hill, Inc., 1991.

Bourke, Richard W. "Configurators: Rule-based Product Definition," *APICS—The Performance Advantage.* December 1991, pp. 51–54.

Bourke, Richard W. "Configurators: An Update," *APICS—The Performance Advantage.* August 1992, pp. 38–39.

Cingari, John. "What Is the Role of MRP II in Quality?" *APICS: The Performance Advantage.* February 1992, pp. 24–26.

"Computers Take Control in Manufacturing and Warehousing," *Modern Materials Handling.* November 19, 1984, pp. 46–54.

Cox, James F., John H. Blackstone, and Michael S. Spencer. *APICS Dictionary.* Falls Church, Va.: American Production and Inventory Control Society, 1992.

Davis, Charles H. "Production and Inventory Processing: Material Requirements Planning," *Journal of Small Business Management.* July 1983, p. 25.

Fogarty, Donald W., Thomas R. Hoffman, and Peter W. Stonebraker. *Production and Operations Management.* Cincinnati, Ohio: South-Western Publishing Co., 1989.

Fogarty, Donald W., John H. Blackstone, Jr., and Thomas R. Hoffman. *Production & Inventory Management.* Cincinnati, Ohio: South-Western Publishing Co., 1991.

Goddard, Walter E. "Kanban vs. MRP II: Which is Best for You?" *Modern Materials Handling.* November 5, 1982.

Goldratt, Eliyahu, and Jeff Cox. *The Goal: A Process of On-going Improvement.* Croton-on-Hudson, N.Y.: North River Press, 1986.

Greene, James H. *Production and Inventory Control Handbook.* New York: McGraw-Hill, 1987.

Grey, Chris. "MRP II Software: Blueprint for Optimizing Manufacturing," *Computer World.* January 27, 1986.

Gunn, Thomas. *Manufacturing for Competitive Advantage: Becoming a World Class Manufacturer.* Cambridge, Mass.: Ballinger Publishing Company, 1987.

Hall, Robert. *Zero Inventories.* Homewood, Ill.: Dow Jones-Irwin, 1983.

Heard, Ed. "Competing in Good Times and Bad" in Patricia Moody, *Strategic Manufacturing.* Homewood, Ill.: Dow Jones-Irwin, 1990.

Hill, Terry. *Manufacturing Strategy, Text and Cases.* Homewood, Ill.: Irwin, 1989.

Karmarkar, Uday. "Getting Control of Just-in-Time," *Harvard Business Review.* September–October 1989, pp. 122–131.

Kutos, Scott. "Inventory Control in the 1990s," *Production & Inventory Management.* January 1992, pp. 23–26.

Lieberman, Mark. "Configuration Control: A New Way to Look at MRP II Manufacturing," *APICS: The Performance Advantage.* March 1992, pp. 35–38.

Martin, André. *DRP: Distribution Resource Planning: Distribution Management's Most Powerful Tool.* Essex Junction, Vt.: O. Wight Ltd. Publications, 1990.

Mather, Hal. *Bills of Materials.* Homewood, Ill.: Dow Jones-Irwin, 1987.

Melnyk, Steven A. "The State of MRP II Software," *APICS: The Performance Advantage.* February 1992, p. 33.

Moody, Patricia E. *Strategic Manufacturing: Dynamic New Directions for the 1990s.* Homewood, Ill.: Dow Jones-Irwin, 1990.

Newman, William, and V. Sridharan. "Manufacturing Planning and Control: Is There One Definitive Answer?" *Production and Inventory Management Journal.* Vol. 33, No. 1, 1992, pp. 50–54.

Nicholl, Andrew D. "Determining Optimum Logistics Costs," *APICS—The Performance Advantage.* February 1992, pp. 50–54.

Orlicky, Joseph. *Material Requirements Planning.* New York: McGraw-Hill, 1975.

Plossl, George W. *Production and Inventory Control: Principles and Techniques.* Englewood Cliffs, N.J.: Prentice Hall, 1985.

Rhodes, Philip. "Inventory Carrying Cost May Be Less Than You've Been Told," *Inventory Management Review.* October 1981.

Sauers, Dale. "Analyzing Inventory Systems" in Ahmad Ahmadian, Rasoul Afifi, and William D. Chandler, *Readings in Production and Operations Management.* Boston: Allyn and Bacon, 1990.

Schaeffer, Randall. "A New View of Inventory Management," *APICS—The Performance Advantage.*

Stonebraker, Peter W. "Configuring the Bill of Materials for Productivity," unpublished research papers, 1991.

Turnipseed, David L., O. Maxie Burns, and Walter E. Riggs. "An Implementation Analysis of MRP Systems: A Focus on the Human Variable," *Production and Inventory Management Journal.* January-March 1992, pp. 1–5.

Vollmann, Thomas E., William L. Perry, and D. Clay Whybark. *Manufacturing Planning and Control Systems.* Homewood, Ill.: Irwin, 1992.

Wight, Oliver W. *MRP II: Unlocking America's Productivity Potential.* Boston, Mass.: CBI Publishing Co., Inc., 1981.

Wight, Oliver W. *Production and Inventory Management in the Computer Age.* New York: Van Nostrand Reinhold Company, 1984.

Young, Scott T., and Winter D. Nie. "A Cycle Count Model Considering Inventory Policy and Record Variance," *Production and Inventory Management Journal.* Vol. 33, No. 1, 1992, pp. 11–16.

CHAPTER 8

JUST-IN-TIME

I have a friend who is responsible for two factories, one in Japan and one in the United States. He explained why the factory in Japan always outperforms the one in the United States: "They both set the same target, and they both may hit it. But when the Japanese hit it, they keep going, whereas the Americans tend to stop and rest on their laurels before pursuing the next goal. So in the end, the Japanese achieve more." They continuously strive for perfection with the goal of achieving excellence. —John E. Rehfeld,
President and Chief Operating Officer, Seiko Instruments USA, Inc.

Total Quality Control (TQC) is not a miracle drug; its properties are more like those of Chinese herb medicine.
—Kaoru Ishikawa

Objectives

After completing this chapter you should be able to:

- Discuss the JIT philosophy.
- Explain why JIT firms have a competitive advantage.
- Identify seven types of waste in an organization.
- List key JIT practices.
- Discuss the importance of continuous improvement.
- Describe the implementation process.
- Explain how JIT is applicable to services.

Outline

INTRODUCTORY CASE: TOYOTA DRILLS ILLINOIS FIRM TO BUILD BUMPERS FASTER AND CHEAPER*

Besides investing heavily in manufacturing and research and development facilities, Toyota also invests heavily in supplier firms to build a world-class network of quality suppliers. Toyota has a supplier development outreach program (SDOP) in the United States, which includes training on Just-in-Time (JIT), workshops, and seminars on total quality management. One U.S. company that has benefited from Toyota's SDOP is Bumper Works

---

*Materials drawn from Joseph B. White, "Japanese Auto Makers Help U.S. Suppliers Become More Efficient," *Wall Street Journal*, September 9, 1991; and Francis J. Gawronski, "Toyota Suppliers a Key Component of Long-Term Strategy," *Automotive News*, April 1, 1991, p. 16.

(BW), a small factory in Danville, Illinois, which employs about 100 workers producing lightweight pickup-truck bumpers. It took Shahid Khan, founder and owner of BW, five years of sales calls to Toyota before landing his first contract in 1985. Then, in 1987, Toyota informed Shahid and two other bumper makers to design new bumpers with specifications considerably more durable than those required by General Motors, Ford, or Chrysler. Such demands from Japanese companies are not uncommon. "We were the only ones who could demonstrate we could do that," Shahid says. In 1988, BW became the sole supplier of bumpers to Toyota's U.S. auto manufacturing facilities.

Bumper Works' relationship with Toyota seemed secure, but Toyota wanted more: annual price reductions despite rising costs for materials and labor, better bumpers, and more punctual deliveries. "We [had] benchmarked ourselves against the American industry," Shahid says. "I don't think we knew how bad we were." Toyota agreed to help BW and in September 1989, Shahid flew to Japan to get a first-hand look at the Toyota production system in operation. He discussed with Toyota management improvements that could be made at BW. "Their question," Shahid recalls, "was, 'Is there something inherently Japanese about the system? Or is it possible to export it?'"

In March 1990, Hiroshi Ginya, a manufacturing expert from Toyota headquarters, made the trip to Danville. Ginya pointed out that there was little Toyota could do for BW until it reduced the setup time for dies in the metal stamping presses to less than 22 minutes from 90 minutes or more. The reduced setup time would allow BW to be sufficiently flexible to make 20 different bumper models each day. BW could not afford new presses with quick-change features. However, with Toyota's help, the workers improvised by welding homemade metal tabs to their nine-ton dies. This made the job of aligning the dies on pins attached to the presses easier. Workers videotaped the die-change procedures and prepared an instruction manual so that other workers could learn from it. "We had no organization," recalls die coordinator David Harmon. "There were a lot of simple things we didn't think about until the Toyota team came in."

After BW achieved the die-change objective in July 1990, Toyota sent two more consultants from Japan to lead what Shahid calls a "boot camp." Shahid and his staff worked for about two weeks putting in 16-hour days to reconfigure the layout of the BW plant. This involved moving nearly every piece of equipment in the plant except the gigantic metal presses. The objective was to improve the process flow, with raw materials coming in at one end and leaving the other side of the plant as a finished bumper the same day. With the old layout, the bumpers were stamped, moved by forklifts to a holding area at the far end of the plant, and returned several days later for welding. With the new layout, bumpers go from presses to welding with only a brief stop in between. When a batch of bumpers is shipped, a card (kanban) is returned to the press operators to authorize more production. The operators now schedule their own work instead of waiting for instructions from a supervisor.

The next improvement program at BW involved operating with less inventory. BW encountered difficulties in implementing the program, and Toyota had to send another team to help iron out some of the problems. BW consults with Toyota whenever problems occur. "They call it open kimono discussions," Shahid says. The JIT system is paying off for BW with improved bumper quality and costs. For example, wasted material cost per bumper has been reduced from $1.28 to 73 cents, productivity has increased 60%, and the number of defects has gone down by 80%. These cost savings benefit both BW and Toyota. BW is able to keep Toyota's business and Toyota has a dependable, low-cost supplier and can pass the cost savings through to their customers.

JUST-IN-TIME—PATH TO WORLD-CLASS OPERATIONS

Just-in-Time (JIT) was developed in the early 1960s as the Toyota production system by Taiichi Ohno and his colleagues at Toyota, though it can be traced to American manufacturing practices in the 1930s. In Japan, it resulted from a need to improve quality and productivity after World War II and to catch up with more established automobile manufacturers in America and Europe. Japan is a land of limited natural resources and space. Constrained by this environment, the Japanese realized that there is no place for waste and inefficiency in their society. This philosophy has been extended to the workplace. Although the Toyota production system has been around for a long time, it was not until after the 1973 oil crisis that the system, now known as JIT, was adopted by other companies in Japan. JIT became more prominent after the second oil shock in 1978. Japan came out of that economic crisis in better shape than most other developed countries, and the world began to take notice of JIT.

In the face of increasing global competition, American firms have recently realized that traditional manufacturing philosophies are no longer meeting the needs of the marketplace. It is imperative that firms make dramatic changes in manufacturing philosophies and techniques. Companies must strive to be world-class manufacturers to gain a competitive edge. The path to world-class manufacturing requires firms to make fundamental changes in how they view elements of operations such as management—labor relations, job classification, training, quality, inventory management, maintenance, scheduling, automation, and supplier/customer relations. In addition, manufacturing must be sufficiently flexible to respond to changing customer needs. To achieve the status of world-class manufacturer requires "continual and rapid improvement" in quality, cost, lead time, and customer service (Schonberger, 1986). JIT is one way for firms to achieve excellence in manufacturing and to become world-class manufacturers by satisfying their customers.

Schonberger (1982) reported that JIT was reintroduced in the United States in the early 1980s. Today, JIT is used in various forms by both manufacturing and service companies. The success of Apple Computers, Black & Decker, Deere and Company, FMC Corporation, General Electric, Harley-Davidson, Hewlett-Packard, 3M, Omark Industries, and Xerox (Hall, 1983, 1987; Sepheri, 1986; Schonberger, 1983, 1986; Wantuck, 1989) has proved that the strategies of JIT are not culturally dependent, that in fact they work right here in America. Further, JIT is applicable to all parts of the chain of transformations from resource creation to service delivery. The following four specific examples show the benefits to manufacturing facilities that have implemented JIT (Sheridan, 1990).

1. Corning Inc., Corning, New York

   - Reduced defect rates from 1800 to 9 parts per million.
   - Reduced customer lead times from 5 weeks to several days.
   - Achieved customer delivery dates 98.5% of the time.
   - Reduced process losses 50%.

2. Dana's Valve Plant, Minneapolis, Minnesota

   - Reduced manufacturing throughput time 92%.
   - Increased productivity 32%.
   - Trimmed customer lead times from 6 months to 6 weeks.
   - Consolidated two plants into one, producing comparable output in half the manufacturing space.
   - Pared quality costs 47%.
   - Trimmed total inventory 50%; slashed inventory of subassemblies 94%.
   - Improved return on investment 470% and return on sales 320%.

3. Motorola, Boynton Beach, Florida

   - Reduced manufacturing cycle time 85%.
   - Improved "out-of-box" quality 250% and field reliability 350%.
   - Reduced 300 candidates to just 22 "best-in-class" sole-source suppliers, chosen for their willingness to commit to extremely high quality levels.
   - Achieved five sigma quality level (fewer than 200 defects per million).

4. Toledo Scale, Worthington, Ohio
   - Reduced manufacturing cycle time in its focused factory printed circuit board (PCB) area from 2 week to 3 days; reduced cycle time for the weight-indicator devices from 2 days to 30 minutes.
   - Reduced work-in-process inventory 67%.
   - Reduced defect rates in the PCB line 85%.
   - Achieved customer delivery dates 99% of the time.
   - Increased productivity 24% over a 2-year period, based on value of shipments per employee.

ELEMENTS OF JIT

As shown by the above examples, the essence of JIT is to improve productivity and quality, cut costs, and make money for a company. These ultimate objectives can only be achieved by focusing on four key and closely intertwined elements of JIT: elimination of waste, respect for people, continuous improvement, and focus on customer.

Elimination of Waste

Waste is defined by Fujio Cho of Toyota as "anything other than the minimum amount of equipment, materials, parts, space, and worker's time, which are absolutely essential to add value to the product" (Suzaki, 1987, p. 8). This definition implies that waste can be viewed as any "nonvalue-added activity." One reason why companies have difficulty making money is the failure to recognize wastes that are present in the work environment and the associated opportunities for improvement. In order to eliminate waste, a company should first establish what does and does not add value from the customer's perspective. Then it should eliminate activities that add cost but not value to the product and focus on activities that are directly related to things the customer sees and cares about. Toyota identified seven types of waste.

Waste from Overproduction
Overproduction is the biggest culprit in terms of waste in the factory. The reason is that overproduction hides other basic problems in the system. Overproduction is the result of producing goods before they are required or producing just to keep machine utilization high. Traditionally, American manufacturers have been guilty of allowing output to increase in order to create an illusion of improved efficiency, although production may be quite inefficient in reality. Toyota called this "an efficiency improvement for the sake of appearance." Resources are consumed that could be used more effectively elsewhere. Unnecessary inventories are created, which require additional paperwork, storage space, holding costs, and so on. Overproduction could lead to a situation where we have too much of something that is not needed, and not enough of something that is needed.

Waste from Waiting
Waiting is a common occurrence found in many workplaces. Numerous examples include: a worker waits at a work station when the preceding process is unable to deliver required parts to the present process; a part waits for machine availability to be processed; a machine operator waits for maintenance personnel to repair broken equipment. Wastes arising from waiting are clearly visible, and are therefore easy to identify and eliminate.

Waste from Transportation
Transportation wastes are caused by an item's having to be moved unnecessarily, stored temporarily, or rearranged. These wastes result mostly from poor layout design that requires goods to be transported over long distances. Often we are surprised to learn how far a prod-

uct must travel through a facility before it is completed. It is not uncommon for incoming shipments from the suppliers to be delivered to a warehouse and then transported to the work station where the parts are finally processed. This involves multiple handling and loading/unloading activities before the goods arrive at their final destination. Improvement in layout, transportation methods, workplace organization, coordination of activities, and the like can help eliminate this form of waste. For example, incoming parts could be transported several times a day directly to the line for processing.

Waste from Processing
Another source of waste may be the method of processing the product. Often the manufacturability of a product is not considered during the product design stage. Additional workers could be required to correct problems in the process itself. For example, plastic containers produced by an injection molding machine may require additional grinding to remove excessive flash. If the mold is of a better design and quality, the additional labor required for finishing could be minimized or eliminated. Tools, fixtures, or dies not properly installed could contribute to the expenditure of considerable time and energy in processing the materials. Certain defects in the product may arise from improper processing procedures.

Waste from Inventory
Carrying excessive inventory has tremendous impacts on cost and profitability, as discussed in Chapter 7. Figure 8-1 illustrates the "water and rocks" analogy; rocks represent problems and water represents inventories that have been traditionally used to protect and buffer these problems. Excess inventories hide problems such as poor quality, poor scheduling, line imbalances, vendor delinquencies, long setups, long transportation, and the like. Thus, excess inventory can be said to be the "root of all evil." Lowering the inventory level exposes problems in the shop. These problems need to be solved before further reductions in inventory can be made. The objective is to lower the inventory gradually so that problems can be uncovered, brought to the attention of the whole organization, and finally corrected.

The impact of inventories extends far beyond the walls of a manufacturing facility. In fact, most economists view excessive inventories as a major cause of the U.S. recession in the early 1980s. American firms have since learned from the inventory debacle of that recession and have improved their inventory turns. The objective for firms is to provide better service with less inventory.

FIGURE 8-1 Excess Inventories Hide Problems

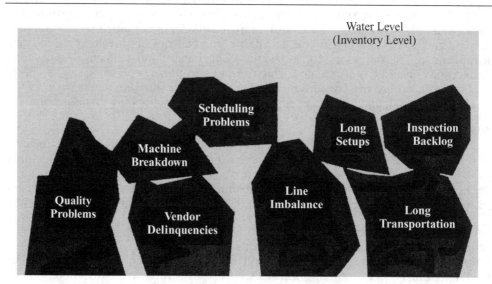

Waste from Motion

Unnecessary motion is time spent on movements that do not add value to the product/service. All work involves some motion. However, at Toyota, there is a clear distinction between "to work" and "to move." Ohno puts it this way: "Moving about quite a bit does not mean working. To work means to let the process move forward and to complete a job. In work there is little waste and only high efficiency" (Lu, 1986, p. 10). Therefore, in work there are two types of movement: one is necessary for making the product and the other is *wasted motion*, which does not move the manufacturing process forward or add any value to the product. For example, an operator can look busy searching for misplaced tools, dies, or fixtures without adding any value to the product. This wasted activity can lead to an increase in production cost and lead time.

Waste from Defective Parts

Failure to produce the product right the first time has serious consequences for the manufacturer. If the defects are discovered in the factory, then corrective action can be taken, but at a cost. Defective products found by the customer after delivery present the most serious problems. These include the possibility of lawsuits, warranty costs, and loss of future sales. The Japanese believe in "quality at the source." Any defective part should never be passed to the next process. The underlying philosophy is "The next process is your customer," a phrase first used by Ishikawa while attempting to solve quality problems at a steel mill in 1950. By treating the next process as your customer, all employees work with the same customer-driven quality goal. There is no ambiguity regarding how quality is viewed within an organization.

Respect for People

In addition to eliminating waste in the workplace, JIT is based on respect for people. Productivity improvements cannot be achieved without employee support (see Chapter 9). It is people who make things happen, people who are responsible for the success of an organization, and people who have ideas for quality improvements and waste elimination. Vern Pearson, Omark's production manager, says, "If we're talking about priorities in terms of Just-in-Time, I guess people would be number one. I'm only as good as the people in my organization. If we don't have people involvement we don't have anything. The people out in the plant make it happen" (Goddard, 1986, p. 15).

The question is "How do we get people to work to their fullest potential?" An important element is good people management, which starts with respect for the individual. Respect for the individual is demonstrated by eliminating wasteful operations, creating a safe and equitable work environment, and encouraging people to show their talents by giving them greater responsibility and authority. At Toyota, respect for people extends beyond the more tangible signs: all employees are referred to as associates; all associates wear the same uniform; there are no reserved parking spaces; all associates eat in the same cafeteria; there are no private offices; and desks are in one large room with no walls. In order for employees to be the best they can be, the fear of making and reporting mistakes must be eliminated. When things go wrong, the tendency is to find a scapegoat. This is a negative approach that should be avoided. Instead, management should focus on solving the problem instead of resorting to finger-pointing. This creates an atmosphere of respect for the individual's achievement, intelligence, hard work, and commitment.

Continuous Improvement (Kaizen)

The driving force behind continuous improvement or *kaizen* is that we should not rest on our laurels. No matter how good we think we are, there is always room to be better. If we stand still, the competition will pass us by. The goal is to set a benchmark and keep raising it. JIT is not a project with an end. Rather, it is an ongoing process, much like a life-long journey. The Japanese strongly believe that little things add up to big things, while

Americans have a tendency to go for the home run. As Shoichiro Irimajiri, president of Honda of America Manufacturing, said in his speech at Stanford University on April 7, 1987:

> *Mr. Honda used to say, "In a race competing for a split second, one tire length on the finish line will decide whether you are a winner or a loser. If you understand that, you cannot disregard even the smallest improvement." The same thing is true in the products we design and build for our customers. So many times the highest efficiency is achieved in design, in manufacturing, in service, by a series of improvements, each one of which seems small. We are now making major improvements in the efficiency of our automobile plant in Marysville, not from any single big change, but rather from thousands of improvements made by our associates. When added together, they will significantly increase our production efficiency and our competitiveness.*

Although continuous improvement involves making incremental changes that may not be highly visible in the short run, they can lead to significant contributions over the long run.

The achievement of continuous improvement requires a long-term outlook and the support of top management. It also requires the involvement of all employees in the organization. Firms adopting this approach must have the necessary support structures of training, management, resource allocation, measurement, and reward and incentive systems (Dingus and Golomski, 1988; Hayes and Wheelwright, 1984; Melcher et al., 1990). Employees must be motivated to accept continuous improvement as a means for the organization to achieve a competitive advantage in the marketplace. To increase performance, firms must "continuously push at the margins of their expertise, trying on every front to be better than before. Standards to them are ephemeral milestones on the road to perfection. They strive to be dynamic, learning companies" (Hayes, Wheelwright, and Clark, 1988, p. 25).

Motorola believes that the "company that is satisfied with its progress will soon find its customers are not." It is this belief that has resulted in a hundred-fold improvement in quality at Motorola since 1981. Motorola's formula consists of three steps: (1) banish complacency; (2) set heroic goals that compel new thinking; and (3) raise the bar as you near each goal, setting it out of reach all over again. The pursuit is total customer satisfaction.

Focus on Customer

Focus on the customer is the driving force behind quality, productivity improvements, and the success of the organization. Meeting the customer's need means delivering a high-quality product that will minimize the customer's overall cost of purchasing and using the product. The focus on the customer goes beyond just taking orders and being a good listener. Organizations must strive to be responsive to customer needs, which requires an understanding of the customer's internal operations and future requirements.

Many organizations see a need to be closer to their customers as a way of keeping customers happy. In traditional manufacturing organizations, employees are often not in touch with the customers and have little opportunity of seeing how the quality or a lack of quality of their work impacts the customer. Since employees work exclusively for specific departments such as fabrication, shipping, quality control, and the like, their main concern is to meet immediate goals of their department. By allowing factory workers the opportunity to have direct and continuous contact with the customers, employees can find out first-hand from them what their requirements and expectations are so that improvements can be made to address the customers' concerns. This employee–customer connection conveys the message that the company sincerely cares about their customers.

The "service factory" concept proposed by Chase and Garvin (1989) is one approach of offering better customer service and improving competitiveness. The factory personnel can work closely with the customer in areas such as manufacturability, troubleshooting quality problems, and solving production problems. For example, Tecktronix, an electronic equipment manufacturer, has a toll-free telephone number so that customers can call the factory and talk directly to shop floor personnel to get answers regarding quality problems, use of their oscilloscopes, and other Tecktronix products. Customers are invited to the factory to witness first-hand the superiority and quality of its manufacturing processes. Using the factory as a showroom serves to reinforce the customer's perception of product quality.

KEY JIT PRACTICES

The four elements of JIT, elimination of waste, respect for people, continuous improvement, and focus on customer, are supported by 12 JIT practices. Understanding how waste occurs in the factory and the impact it has on operations is basic to the process of elimination of waste through "management by sight" or "visual control." Waste must be made visible so that everyone in the organization is aware of the problem, and new and creative ideas to solve these problems can be found. Key elements and practices of the JIT philosophy are illustrated in Figure 8–2.

JIT Production

Just-in-Time means producing exactly what the customer demands and delivering the good exactly when and where the customer wants. The objective of JIT is to "produce the right products, at the right quantity, at the right place, and at the right time" with the goal of achieving zero deviation from the assigned schedule. JIT production is a pull system, which refers to the "production of items only as demanded for use, or to replace those taken for use" (Cox et al., 1992). In a pull system, you produce exactly what you need, nothing more, nothing less. Simply stated, "If you don't need it, don't build it." The pull system works well for firms such as Toyota with high-volume repetitive production processes and well-defined material flows. With the pull philosophy, overproduction is essentially eliminated, and unnecessary inventories in the factory are minimized. Consequently, inventory turns will increase and holding costs will be reduced.

Toyota uses the *kanban* (Japanese for card or visual record) as a tool to implement JIT. Kanban is an information system used to control the production quantities in each process. The system is very simple, yet highly visible, and most importantly it is cost effective. Generally, there are two types of kanban used: withdrawal and production. A withdrawal kanban authorizes a container of parts to be withdrawn from the preceding process. A production kanban authorizes the processing of a container of parts. Figure 8–3 shows the use of these two kanbans to control the production flow.

To manage the workplace effectively by using the kanban system requires several operating conditions to be followed. These operating rules are

1. No defective items may be sent to the subsequent process. If a problem is identified, it should be solved to prevent its recurrence.
2. The subsequent process is allowed to withdraw only the exact quantity as required by the kanban from the preceding process, nothing more or less. No withdrawal can take place without a kanban, and a kanban must always accompany each container of parts withdrawn.
3. The preceding work station should produce only what has been withdrawn by the subsequent process. Production occurs in the sequence in which the cards are received.
4. The number of kanbans used should be a minimum. The maximum level of inventory is determined by the number of kanbans. Consequently, all attempts should be made to keep the number of kanbans as small as possible.

The formula for calculating the number of kanbans (K) required to support production of each part at a work center is provided in Decision Model Box 8-1. In general, the value of K seldom comes out as an integer and should be rounded up to the next whole

FIGURE 8-2 JIT Elements and Practices

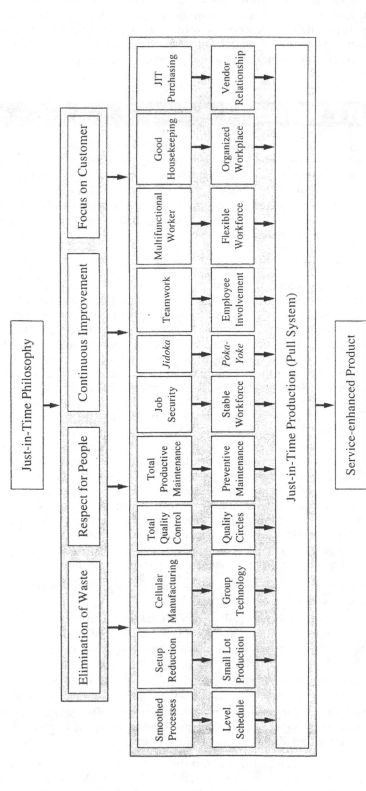

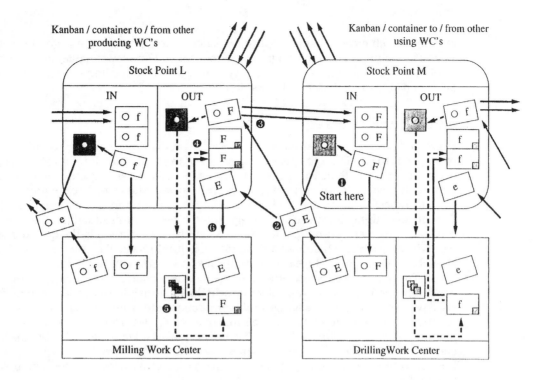

FIGURE 8-3 The Dual-Card Kanban and Container Flow Pattern

Key

Standard container	▭	Flow path	→	Kanban collection box	▨
Withdrawal kanban	O	Flow path	→	Work center "dispatch list" or box	▣
Production kanban	▨	Flow path	----►	E, e: Empty F, f: Full	

This example shows a milling work center supplying milled heads to a drilling center that drills bolt holes in them. Stock point L serves milling (and other nearby work centers); stock point M serves drilling (and other nearby work centers). The flows of parts containers and kanban between milling and drilling are labeled in upper case; other movements are labeled in lower case.

Parts for drilling are obtained as follows:

❶ A full parts container is about to be moved into drilling. Detach withdrawal kanban and place it in a collection box for stock point M.

❷ Attach withdrawal kanban from stock point M to container most recently emptied in drilling.

❸ Take empty container with withdrawal kanban to stock point L. Transfer kanban to a full container and take container back to stock point M.

This last act also triggers production activities as follows:

❹ The full container just taken had a production kanban attached to it. Before leaving stock point L, detach and place production kanban in a collection box.

❺ Take production kanbans (that apply to milling) to milling and place them in the dispatch box. The production kanbans are worked on in the order of receipt from stock point L.

❻ Place parts for each completed job into an empty container taken from stock point L. Attach the production kanban to the full container and move container to stock point L.

Reprinted by permission of Richard J. Schonberger, "Applications of Single-Card and Dual-Card Kanban," *Interfaces,* Vol. 13, No. 4, August 1983. Copyright 1983 the Operations Research Society of American and The Institute of Management Sciences, 290 Westminster Street, Providence, Rhode Island 02903.

number, which creates a small amount of safety stock. Therefore, it is good practice to start off the computation by assigning a zero value to V (policy variable) in the formula.

For JIT production to work effectively, it must be supported by the key practices described in the remainder of this section.

Smoothed Processes

Smoothed processes are the cornerstone for JIT production. The objective of smoothed processes is to eliminate the peaks and valleys in the work load. If we maintain capacity to meet peak rather than average demand, there is waste inherently embedded in the system. Such waste is in the form of slack associated with the work force, equipment, and work-in-process. The final assembly process is the most important starting point for production smoothing as it provides the signal for subsequent production at all preceding processes. By leveling production at final assembly, the variation in the quantity of each part withdrawn at each subassembly station is minimized. This then allows the subassembly stations to produce each part at a level rate in smaller daily lots.

At Toyota, the process for production smoothing involves first taking the total number of vehicles in the monthly production schedule and dividing it by the number of working days to determine the average daily production rate. Then, for each day, the goal is to produce in the same sequence the same mix of vehicles. Table 8-1 shows an example of a smoothed production schedule. Toyota also takes advantage of flexible machinery and reductions in production lead times to further smooth production. Reductions in lead time can be achieved with quicker setup times, improved layout, production in small lots, and so on.

Setup Reduction

High setup time promotes overproduction, since it necessitates production in large lots, which result in higher levels of inventory. Reducing the setup time would effectively increase machine capacity, eliminate overproduction, and reduce both finished goods as well as work-in-process inventories. In addition, setup reduction is a major requirement in promoting smooth production. Shorter setup times allow for small lot production, which reduces the production lead time and enables factory operations to become more flexible.

Suzaki (1987) suggests a three-pronged approach to improvements: simplify, combine, and eliminate. Thus, in any setup reduction program the goals are to: (1) simplify the process as much as possible; (2) combine several operations to reduce the number of steps; and (3) determine if any unnecessary steps can be removed. For example, Bumper Works achieved significant reductions in the setup time for dies on the stamping presses, not with new equipment but by making the alignment of the dies simpler and easier to carry out. The Japanese, with the assistance of Shigeo Shingo, developed SMED (Single Minute Exchange of Die), which means that all setups should be less than ten minutes. Similar terms that are often used are "single setup" or "one-touch setup." Examples are the following: Toyota reduced the setup time for a 1000-ton press from 4 hours in 1941 to 3 minutes in 1971; Hitachi's setup time for a die-casting machine decreased from 1.25 hours in 1976 to 3 minutes in 1983; Yanmar Diesel machining line's setup time was decreased from 9.3 hours in 1975 to 9 minutes in 1980 (Suzaki, 1987).

Cellular Manufacturing

In a JIT system, the layout of the plant is organized to minimize materials handling, transportation, work-in-process inventory, cycle time, and most importantly, to improve feedback of information. For these reasons, the Japanese prefer a product layout instead of a functional (process) layout (see Chapter 4). The problem with the process layout is that

DECISION MODEL BOX 8-1 Calculating the Number of Kanbans at Butler Bumper Co.

The Butler Bumper Company is using a kanban production system. The demand is 500 bumpers per day. Each container holds 25 bumpers. Typically, a container of bumpers requires 0.4 day for processing, and 0.1 day for wait time, which includes materials handling time. Compute the number of kanban sets to be authorized if the system is operating in an ideal environment free of external interference. If the operating system is exposed to external interference corresponding to 10% of daily demand, what is the number of kanban sets required and the level of inventory?

The formula for the number of kanban sets is

$$K = \frac{D(T_p + T_w)(1 + v)}{C}$$

where K = number of kanban sets

D = average daily demand for the part as determined by a uniform schedule

T_p = processing time including setup (decimal fractions of a day) for one container of parts

T_w = waiting time (decimal fractions of a day) in process and between process per container

C = container capacity (typically not to exceed 10% of daily demand)

V = policy variable set by management to reflect possible external interference (should be no more than 10%). This variable impacts the level of safety stock in the system.

Given $D = 500$, $T_p = 0.4$ day, $T_w = 0.1$ day, $C = 25$, and $V = 0$, then

$$K = \frac{500(0.4 + 0.1)(1 + 0)}{25} = \frac{500(0.5)(1)}{25} = \frac{250}{25} = \underline{10 \text{ kanban sets}}$$

Amount of inventory in the system = $KC = 10(25) = \underline{250 \text{ units}}$

If there is external interference, $V = 0.10$, and

$$K = \frac{500(0.4 + 0.1)(1 + 0.1)}{25} = \frac{500(0.5)(1.1)}{25} = \frac{275}{25} = \underline{11 \text{ kanban sets}}$$

Amount of inventory in the system = $KC = 11(25) = \underline{275 \text{ units}}$

Note that the system now has 25 additional units (safety stock) to cover contingencies.

similar machines are grouped together in such a manner that the material flow is not immediately visible. With this type of arrangement, consecutive processes could be some distance apart. Thus, the layout inhibits effective communication between workers at these processes, which makes it harder to ensure that the "next process is your customer." With a product layout, the processes are arranged in the sequence of production so that there is no confusion in terms of where the material is going next. Since the processes are placed close together, total travel distance for production is minimized, and communication between processes is significantly improved. Wastes and problems inherent in the process layout are eliminated and the result is a substantial improvement in the shop's performance.

TABLE 8-1 Example of an Ideal Smoothed Production Cycle for Toyota Camry

To smooth the production cycle for Toyota Camrys, production engineers calculate the monthly volume of each model and then define that volume in daily quantity and units per minute. These calculations are shown as follows:

Model	Monthly Quantity	Daily Quantity	Units per 9.6 Minutes
Sedan	8,000	400	4
Coupe	4,000	200	2
Wagon	2,000	100	1
	14,000	700	7

There are 20 working days per month and two 8-hour shifts per day.

$$\text{Cycle time} = \frac{(480 \text{ minutes}) (2 \text{ shifts})}{700 \text{ units}} = 1.37 \text{ minutes per unit}$$

The cycle repeats itself after 9.6 minutes (= 7 units × 1.37 minutes per unit). Sequence per 9.6 minute cycle: sedan-coupe-sedan-coupe-sedan-wagon-sedan.

In developing a product layout, the Japanese organize the production of parts or families of parts in a number of cells with U-shaped lines. This is called *cellular manufacturing,* where one or more workers are assigned to work on several machines in each cell dedicated to the production of a family of parts. Although cellular manufacturing has been equated with group technology, Goddard (1986, p. 20) says, "Technically, cellular manufacturing is the linking of machines and operations to produce a part, whereas group technology is primarily concerned with the production of like parts, grouped by design." The benefits of cellular layouts are discussed in Chapter 6. It is not uncommon to have a cell with several machines dedicated to the production of one part by a single worker. The worker starts processing on one part and, when it is completed, moves the part to the next machine for processing. Each worker has a route that is determined by the machines worked on. The worker is always handling and processing one part at a time. This is called *one-piece production.* Suzaki (1987) explained how a sporting goods factory on the West Coast reorganized its machines into U-shaped layouts to improve process flow. The benefits were a reduction of work-in-process inventories from 30 units to one unit, space savings of 50%, a big reduction in lead time, an improvement in labor productivity of 30%, and significant improvements in quality.

Total Quality Control and Quality Circles

Since JIT requires delivery of the right part at the right time, quality is extremely important. Bad parts mean that good parts are not available when needed. With pull production, small lot sizes, and small inventories, there is a strong possibility that the production line will be shut down if poor-quality parts are accepted for production. For JIT to work it must not only be "doing things right the first time" but "doing things right the first time and all the time."

The concept of total quality control (TQC) or total quality management (TQM) was originated by Armand Fiegenbaum, who defined it as "an effective system for integrating the quality development, quality maintenance, and quality improvement efforts of the various groups in an organization so as to enable production and service at the most economical levels which allow for full customer satisfaction." Fiegenbaum envisioned that TQC would be under the auspices of a management function devoted solely to product quality. The Japanese approach differed from Fiegenbaum's in that TQC activities are not the sole domain of QC specialists; all employees and divisions are deeply involved with studying and promoting QC. The goals of TQC are

1. Improving the corporate health and character of the company. Top management defines the goals, pointing out which part of the company's character requires modification, or which aspect must be improved.
2. Combining the efforts of all employees to establish a cooperative system.
3. Establishing a quality assurance system and obtaining the confidence of customers and consumers. Its primary goal is "quality first."
4. Aspiring to achieve the highest quality in the world; developing new products/services for that purpose.
5. Establishing a management system that can secure profit in times of slow growth and can meet related challenges.
6. Showing respect for humanity, nurturing human resources, considering employee happiness, and providing a cheerful workplace.
7. Utilizing statistical methods for QC (for example, statistical process control).*

Motorola believes that "to get people to care about quality, you have to care about them." Motorola invests heavily in employee training programs that respond to changing work environments. Employees are taught new creative skills, which enhance their sense of individual worth and well-being. The training programs show that Motorola is well aware of their employees' concern for personal development and advancement. Consequently, Motorola's employees can now reach a potential that was not though possible before. In 1988, Motorola received the Malcolm Baldrige National Quality Award in recognition of its commitment to quality.

The *quality circle*, a concept which originated in Japan in the early 1960s, is the cornerstone for implementing TQC. The Japanese Union of Scientists and Engineers (JUSE) (1987) reported that quality circle activities have spread to more than 50 countries worldwide. A quality circle is a small group of employees who voluntarily work together on areas of common concern such as quality, safety, communications, work environment, efficiency, and the like. The group meets on a regular basis, identifies problems, discusses potential solutions, and then forwards its proposals to management. The group is led by a facilitator rather than the traditional authoritarian decision maker. The facilitator's responsibilities include getting everyone involved, preventing domination by any one individual, dealing with negative comments, maintaining focus, keeping enthusiasm high, and managing conflict. At Toyota, the ultimate purpose of quality circles is to "promote a worker's sense of responsibility, provide a vehicle to achieve working goals, enable each worker to be accepted and recognized, and allow improvement and growth in a worker's technical abilities" (Monden, 1983, p. 132). The principles that justify the existence of quality circles are provided in Table 8-2.

One of the earliest reported attempts to introduce quality circles in the United States was made by Lockheed Missiles and Space Company in 1973 (Rieker, 1975). However, it was not until the late 1970s that quality circles became popular in the United States. Although quality circles are found in the United States and in Japan, there are some differences worth highlighting. In the United States, a quality circle is often initiated by management as a *formal* organization, while in Japan, it is an *informal* group among workers. There is full participation by Japanese workers due to group pressure, even though it is voluntary. Managers in the United States have to be more persuasive in convincing workers to join in quality circle activities. The frequency of turnover and layoffs in the United States makes it difficult form members to belong to the same circle for a long period of time, thus limiting the opportunity for consistent education on a long-term basis (Ishikawa, 1985).

---

*These seven goals are adapted from Ishikawa, *Total Quality Control: The Japanese Way* (translation by Lu), 1985, pp. 95–96.

Total Productive Maintenance

Just-in-time systems have very little work-in-process inventory, and any equipment break-down is very disruptive to production. The old adage of "don't fix it if it ain't broke," or breakdown maintenance, must be changed, since this approach promotes waste. The use of breakdown maintenance stems in part from the near-sighted focus of managers intent on putting off maintenance to improve short-term capacity utilization and profits.

Preventive maintenance is a proactive approach to making adjustments and repairs to equipment before problems occur, in order to eliminate unexpected downtime, eliminate processing variation, increase the life of equipment, avoid major equipment repairs, and ensure a smooth flow of products. The objective of preventive maintenance is to enable processes to be operable at the time they are needed. *Total productive maintenance or total preventive maintenance* (TPM) stresses achieving overall productive system effectiveness through preventive maintenance and total involvement of all employees in an organization. TPM is similar to TQC from the perspective of total employee commitment with the goals of improving quality and productivity. These ultimately lead to increased profitability of a plant. At the Mikuni plant, Washing Machine Division of Matshushita Electric Company in Japan there is a slogan associated with the TPM program that reads: "Maintenance for Profit" (Takatsuki, 1986).

Manufacturing personnel must be involved in the careful planning and scheduling of preventive maintenance to ensure that it happens regularly without disrupting production. There must be a spirit of cooperation between machine operators and the maintenance department. The machine operators should be trained to do routine maintenance such as machine cleaning, adding lubricant, bolt tightening, and the like to avoid premature deterioration of the machine. In addition, operators should be aware of early warning signs of machine degeneration by checking for excessive wear, oil leaks, listening for telltale sounds, and so on that suggest the onset of some serious problems. The job of maintenance personnel is to assist the operators with self-maintenance activities, repair broken equipment, specify machine operating procedures, determine machine design weaknesses, and take corrective actions.

Job Security and Stable Work Force

In Japan, employment is viewed as a "social commitment," while in the United States, employment is treated as a "contract." The lifetime employment system used by Japanese companies ensures that the company will have a reliable and stable pool of loyal, knowledgeable, and motivated workers. Workers benefit from the job security that the system guarantees. With lifetime employment, the company can invest in the long-term development of the individual without fear of the individual's being hired away by a competing firm. A comprehensive training program can be provided to mold the employee to best suit the needs of the company. Over time, the employee develops more and more capabilities. The premise is that an employee who has been with the company for ten years would have ten years of experience, and not ten times one year of experience. Although the ultimate objective is to provide lifetime employment for all employees in the company, a more realistic goal is to provide the highest level of job security that is possible for a core group of employees. In Japan, lifetime employment applies only to permanent workers, who represent only a portion of the Japanese work force.

In the "contract" system, a company hires when there is a position vacant. The applicant's qualifications must closely match the job's requirements. Basically, the individual is "selling" his/her skill, knowledge, and experience to the company. The employee does not feel obligated to the company and will switch jobs when he or she gets a better offer from another company. Turnover of employees in the workplace is higher with the contract system. According to Boyett and Conn (1991), an average American beginning a career in the 1990s will probably work for five or more employers and in ten or more jobs over the course of a lifetime.

TABLE 8-2 Principles of Quality Circle Activities

1. Quality circles should be initiated in the workplace on a voluntary basis. It is a group activity that accommodates everyone, not just the most capable, outgoing, or prominent workers. Sharing problems should be encouraged with participation according to individual capability.
2. Quality circle activities should occur during working hours—not before or after.
3. Quality circles should not be monopolized by either supervisors or management. Discussions should be entered into freely and frankly and seen as an opportunity for all members to listen with open minds. The goal is to bring harmony to the workplace.
4. Specific—not abstract—problems should be studied, beginning with immediate yet small, concrete issues. Solving problems should give members a feeling of confidence and accomplishment.
5. A stable, controlled operating environment should be established. Steps should be taken to stop recurring problems and to anticipate new ones. Problem-solving techniques require the application of quality control and industrial engineering methods, among others.
6. A work area is not simply a place for physical labor, but a place where the worker's creativity can be utilized. Workers are encouraged to think and generate new ideas.
7. Management should provide training to improve workers' skills.
8. Management should provide an environment where workers can find pleasure and meaning in life in their work.
9. Managers should be committed to giving guidance, training, and support, and to showing respect for people. Managers must reject their traditional distrust of shop workers.
10. Management should emphasize the spirit of give and take. Quality circles can help transcend corporate boundaries while still developing friendly rivalry.

Adapted from Akira Ishikawa, "Principles of QC Circle Activities and Their Effects on Productivity in Japan: A Corporate Analysis," *Management International Review,* Vol. 25, No. 3, 1985, pp. 33–40.

During the economic recession that started in 1991, U.S. corporations were forced to cut costs and downsize the work force. Announcements of layoffs have raised the anxiety level among U.S. workers about their job security. With downsizing, the danger is that employees feel demoralized and tend to work for themselves rather than providing the collaborative effort needed to meet corporate goals. This situation is bad for long-term competitiveness. For example, the announcement in December 1991 by General Motors that it plans to close 21 plants and lay off more than 74,000 employees over the next few years has sent shock waves through its rank and file. Although layoffs of such magnitude are rare in Japan, the deepening global recession has caused several Japanese companies to force managers into early retirement or to be transferred to lower-status jobs at subsidiary companies (Neff et al., 1993).

The fear of layoffs resulting from employee suggestions for improving the product or process should be allayed by management. Otherwise, it is unlikely that employees will make further suggestions for productivity improvement. Employees whose positions are made redundant should be moved to other areas that best suit their skills or should be retrained to develop new skills. Layoffs should be considered as the absolute last resort. Omark and Hewlett-Packard are U.S. companies that have a policy of no layoffs of their work force resulting from productivity improvements. At NUMMI, employees assisted the plant's assembly-maintenance crew in building a robot that eventually worked alongside humans doing the same work. The workers feel confident that no jobs will be lost even with the addition of more robots. The reason is a provision in NUMMI's agreement with the United Auto Workers union that states: "The company agrees that it will not lay off employees unless compelled to do so by severe economic conditions that threaten the long-term financial viability of the company." In addition, counter measures such as reducing the salaries of its officers and management will be taken before any layoffs can occur (Sheridan, 1990).

Jidoka

Toyota likes to refer to *jidoka* as "automation with a human touch," or *autonomation*. Most automated machines require operators to watch the machines run, and thus do not add value. In jidoka the machines are upgraded so that when an abnormal condition such as defects, tool breakage, or a shortage of parts occurs, the machine stops and gives a warning signal informing the operator to take the necessary action. The Japanese believe in "visual control" where abnormal conditions are made visible so that they can be eliminated. The jidoka concept can be extended to the production line. When an abnormality is found, both workers and machines must stop immediately. The andon light is a "visual control" used to signal problems on the line. When a problem occurs or the work cannot be completed in time, the operator pushes a button, which causes a yellow light to flash, signaling for help from the supervisor. If the supervisor cannot solve the problem after some time, the line is stopped and a red light comes on automatically. All efforts will be made to correct the problem and to prevent a similar recurrence.

Poka-yoke is Japanese for a "foolproof mechanism" that is incorporated into a machine to carry out 100% inspection and to provide immediate feedback when something abnormal occurs. Thus, poka-yoke is an example of a "visual control" tool which prevents defective parts from passing on to the next process and thus supports the goal of quality at the source. A warning signal is turned on when abnormalities occur, and the machine stops automatically. When this happens, the root cause of the problem is identified and solved to prevent it from recurring. Shingo (1986) describes numerous examples of actual poka-yoke devices installed in Japanese companies.

Teamwork

People learn best when they are given the opportunity to participate actively in decision making and problem solving. It is through active participation and involvement that people develop a sense of achievement and ownership through successfully solving a problem. This in turn creates the motivation and commitment necessary to attack and eliminate wastes at all levels in an organization. The idea behind the team approach is that synergy is created such that the "whole is greater than the sum of the parts."

The required traits of group consciousness and a sense of equality explain why the team approach to solving problems is extremely successful in Japan. Teamwork implies that all functions must work together for the common good of the company. Without people working together on the same team, the communications required to integrate the various elements of JIT will not be there. A team effort provides an environment conducive to generating more and better ideas for improvements than a group of individuals working independently. At Toyota, employees generate millions of suggestions annually, with over 90% of them adopted (Suzaki, 1987).

The teamwork approach is gaining increasing popularity in the United States. In 1985, NUMMI, the joint venture between GM and Toyota in Fremont, California, was formed to experiment with the JIT system, using unionized American workers and suppliers. According to Osamu Kimura, NUMMI president, the key to cultivating a team spirit is "to involve all team members in everything—that means quality, cost, safety, . . . everything. It is important to ask them to think and to make a plan by themselves. Nobody knows the situation—the problems—better than the team members. Management's role is to help and support them" (Sheridan, 1990). At GM's Saturn plant, teams are responsible for "hiring" workers, approving parts from suppliers, and handling administrative matters such as the team's budget, in addition to their regular assembly work (Woodruff et al., 1992).

Frank Ostroff and Douglas Smith of McKinsey & Company, envision a *horizontal organization,* where virtually everyone would "work together in multidisciplinary teams that perform core processes" to be more responsive to customers (Byrne, 1993). In moving toward this innovative form of "boundaryless" organization, companies such as Eastman Chemical, Lexmark International, Motorola, and Xerox are using cross-functional, self-directed teams to manage their operations horizontally. This concept fits nicely with the JIT philosophy.

Multifunctional Worker

The changing demands of the marketplace with shorter product life cycles bring about a need for manufacturing systems and workers that are sufficiently flexible to respond to the wide-ranging needs of the customers. Changing demands can cause the loads at work centers in the plant to change over time. To respond to these changes and use only the minimum number of workers may require workers to be transferred from one assembly area to another. Workers need to be cross-trained to be competent at a variety of processes in their work area. The objective is to develop a flexible work force with multiple skills.

The importance of a flexible and cross-trained work force becomes more apparent when companies use cellular manufacturing. Each worker basically operates several machines in the manufacturing cell and is responsible for setting up the machines, doing routine maintenance, and checking the quality of the parts. When a worker falls behind schedule, a fellow worker may be moved over to assist in restoring equilibrium. This requires workers to develop a variety of skills. To encourage employees to cross train, Toledo Scale instituted a "pay-for-skills" program. When a worker completes training and certification in a new skill, the worker's pay is increased by 18 to 22 cents per hour (Barnet, 1992).

Good Housekeeping and Organized Workplace

Housekeeping is more than just keeping shop floors clean and racks well organized. Housekeeping should not be considered as an expense item or an activity that could be avoided because "we cannot afford it." The benefits derived from good housekeeping far exceed the cost incurred. Clean floors and machines not only create an impression of good appearance but can expose problems such as oil leaks and surface cracks. These early warning signs lead to the detection of problems that can be corrected before major breakdowns can occur.

A clean and organized work environment improves workers' morale and instills in the employees a sense of pride in the workplace. An organized workplace also improves management–labor relations. The effort put into housekeeping is closely linked to the quantity of defective parts produced, the frequency of machine breakdowns, inventory level, number of employee suggestions for improvement, absenteeism level, number of accidents, and so forth. Thus we see how housekeeping can help reduce the cost of making a product. Housekeeping should be everybody's job because of its wide-ranging impact.

The Japanese place a high value on cleanliness and orderliness, and it is no coincidence that we find Japanese factories to be well organized, clean, and quiet. This philosophy extends even to Japanese factories in America. Any visitor to Honda's manufacturing facilities at Marysville, Ohio, will find a relatively quiet shop floor, employees dressed in clean overalls, aisles that are clearly marked and laid out, clean machines, floors, and rest rooms, and so on. As Hayes and Wheelwright (1984, p. 356) note: ". . . the personal attitudes of the Japanese worker, as impressive as they are, are not the major reason behind the almost total sense of order that is observed. Instead, it is more a reflection of the attitudes, practices, and systems that the managers of those plants have carefully put into place over a long period of time. The evidence of management ingenuity and hard work is everywhere."

JIT Purchasing

For JIT to work there must be a close working relationship with the suppliers. Buyers and sellers should develop long-term partnerships that are mutually beneficial. Instead of the traditional arms-length, adversarial relationship with suppliers, manufacturers should consider their suppliers as an extension of the factory. It has often been said that you are only as good as your suppliers. Companies should take advantage of supplier expertise to help with specifications, manufacturability, selection of materials, and the like. For example, Xerox now encourages their engineers to communicate with suppliers, where previously they had a policy of prohibiting this interaction. In addition, Xerox has a program that provides assistance to suppliers to improve their capabilities. There must be free flow of information between buyers and sellers. The benefit for Xerox is better quality and lower purchase prices. In the introductory case at the beginning of this chapter, Toyota provided assistance to one of its suppliers, Bumper Works, to implement JIT. During the implementation phase, things that went wrong were resolved by *open kimono* discussions between Bumper Works and Toyota. *Open kimono* implies that "there are no secrets" between the buyer and seller. The end result of this cooperative effort is that quality has improved and costs are coming down. Table 8-3 provides a comparison of conventional and JIT purchasing practices.

Companies are recognizing the need to have fewer but better suppliers. With fewer suppliers, companies are resorting to supplier certification to maintain high quality and to eliminate incoming inspections. For example, Ford Motor Company not only has a vendor certification program but gives a *Total Quality Excellence* award to the top echelon among Ford's suppliers in recognition of their "excellence and continuous improvement in quality, engineering expertise, delivery performance, and customer relations." Such recognition provides encouragement for the suppliers to continue their excellent work.

In a survey of JIT purchasing practices in the United States, Freeland (1991) identifies six dominant roadblocks to implementing JIT purchasing. The percentages shown for each of the factors represent the proportion of respondents who felt that the factor has impaired the company's ability to implement JIT purchasing. It should be noted that a respondent may select more than one factor as contributing to the problem.

1. Erratic end-user demand (70%)
2. Substantial distances between the company's facilities and available suppliers (43%)
3. Supplier quality (35%)
4. High frequency of product changes and updates (30%)
5. Wide variety of customer production options (30%)
6. Product that must be made to order (22%)

In Japan, major corporations have expanded the basic long-term supplier-vendor relationship and created a distinctive business practice known as *keiretsu*. Briefly, keiretsu is a long-term business alliance by which members are linked together through ownership of each other's stock and members enjoy preferential treatment in business transactions. Keiretsu can have either a horizontal or vertical orientation. *Horizontal keiretsu* is often referred to as *financial keiretsu*, where a bank, other financial institutions, and a giant trading company could link together with some unrelated companies, such as a consumer electronics manufacturer or brewery. Although keiretsu companies comprise less than 0.1% of all companies in Japan, they account for 78% of the value of all shares on the Tokyo Stock Exchange. The six major financial keiretsu of Mitsubishi, Mitsui, Sumitomo, Fuyo, DKB, and Sanwa have been responsible for nearly one-quarter of Japan's GNP (Rapoport, 1991). For example, the DKB group is comprised of major companies such as Dai-Ichi Kangyo (the world's largest bank), Asahi Chemical (the world's largest textile company), Fujitsu (the world's second largest computer company), Kawasaki Steel, Isuzu Motors, and cosmetics maker Shiseido.

Supply keiretsus are vertical alliances involving an interlocking network of suppliers dominated by a major manufacturer and are well entrenched in the auto, electronics, and

TABLE 8-3 Conventional and JIT Purchasing

Conventional Purchasing	Just-in-Time Purchasing
1. Large delivery lot sizes typically covering several weeks of requirements. Deliveries are infrequent.	1. Small delivery lot sizes based on the immediate needs for production usage. Deliveries are very frequent, e.g., several times a day.
2. Deliveries are timed according to the buyer's request date.	2. Deliveries are synchronized with the buyer's production schedule.
3. There are several suppliers for each part. Multiple sourcing is used to maintain adequate quality and competitive pricing.	3. Few suppliers are used for each part. Often, parts are single-sourced.
4. Typically, inventories are maintained for parts.	4. Little inventory is required, because deliveries are expected to be made frequently, on time, and with high-quality parts.
5. Purchasing agreements are short-term. Pressure suppliers by threat of withdrawing business.	5. Purchasing agreements are long-term. Pressure suppliers through obligation to perform.
6. Products are designed with few constraints on the number of different purchased components used.	6. Products are designed with great effort to use only currently purchased parts. Objective is to maximize the commonality of parts.
7. Minimal exchange of information between supplier and buyer.	7. Extensive exchange of information with regard to production schedules, production processes, etc.
8. Purchasing agent is the primary focus of communication with supplier.	8. Purchasing agent is the facilitator of many points of communication between design engineers, production engineers, etc.
9. Prices are established by suppliers.	9. Buyer works with supplier to reduce supplier's costs and thereby reduce prices.
10. Geographic proximity of supplier is not important for the supplier selection decision.	10. Geographic proximity is considered very important.

Reprinted with the permission of APICS, Inc., "A Survey of Just-in-Time Purchasing Practices in the United States," *Production and Inventory Management*, James R. Freeland, April–June 1991, p. 45.

machinery industries. The amount of intragroup trade in a supply keiretsu is strong; industry experts estimate that at least 30% of the business of member companies is carried out within the group. For example, Matshushita accounts for more than 20% of the Japanese VCR market, with its strongest domestic competitor, JVC, having just under 20% of the market. What is intriguing is that Matshusita owns 51% of JVC, which also designs many of Matshusita's products (Ferguson, 1990).

Keiretsu-like ties are emerging in the United States. When the Japanese automakers decided to set up manufacturing facilities in the United States, numerous Japanese parts suppliers were quick to emulate them. Since 1982, the Japanese have built eight auto assembly plants in the United States, mostly in the Midwest. Following closely on their heels were more than 250 Japanese suppliers (Rapoport, 1990). These suppliers are careful to locate close to the vendors' facilities so that delivery can be on a JIT basis. Environmentalists are concerned that the increased number of trips made to deliver purchased parts contribute to increased pollution and global warming. This concern must be balanced with improved efficiencies on the shop floor. Tougher standards set by the Environmental Protection Agency for auto manufacturers on fuel economy and emission control should help alleviate this problem.

FUNCTIONAL INTERACTIONS

Just-in-time necessitates that operations interact with other functions or departments such as marketing, design engineering, and accounting to support the concept of continuous improvement. Traditionally, each function operates within its narrowly defined territorial boundaries established by the organization. By focusing narrowly on functional or departmental efficiency without considering total organizational goals, local optimization results as opposed to the global optimization possible when all functional areas work together for the well-being of the organization.

Marketing Interface

The marketing function involves such activities as product management, sales, customer service, and marketing research. The marketing contribution to a successful JIT implementation is to obtain feedback from the customers in terms of their expectations and requirements in order to supply the information necessary to optimize the design engineering and production processes. Reduction of order processing time is another important area of support. A quick response with order-promise information can translate into a marketing competitive advantage. The process of order entry, credit checking, and other paperwork associated with the order must be streamlined and made error-free. Marketing must understand that customer orders provide the starting point for any operations activity. Customer orders are the vehicles that trigger the "pull" of the product through the factory.

Just-in-time is an excellent marketing tool, providing a company with a competitive edge over non-JIT competitors. A JIT manufacturer delivers products directly to the customer's assembly line, or on a more timely basis to the stocking point, without receiving inspection, which effectively reduces the customer's internal production costs. The sales department must seek out customers who want JIT goods or services and are willing to make long-term commitments with a reasonable amount of stability in delivery quantities and delivery dates. The sales policy should support JIT production, that is, the top priority for sales personnel is to secure firm contracts, since schedules are difficult to alter without major consequences and disruption to the production system. Marketing's support of the operations function in a JIT environment is summarized in Table 8-4.

Design Engineering Interface

The objective for design engineering is to design a product that not only meets customer requirements and needs but is also easy and cost effective to manufacture. The ability to meet customer requirements requires a close link to the customer. Marketing plays a critical role in providing inputs from the market in terms of customer requirements. Manufacturability of a product is important, because it determines the ease of fabrication or assembly of the product, the amount of scrap and defects generated, the type of inspection required, the level of production yields, and the production cost. Thus design engineering has a significant impact on the long-term cost, quality, and profitability of the product. At Hewlett-Packard's plant in Roseville, California, a "cost-of-complexity" analysis found that the selection of components for a printed-circuit assembly can impact the cost of production. One alternative, which involves inserting a part by using an automatic insertion machine, costs 15 cents. Another alternative, which adds the part after the wave-soldering operation (that is, backloading a part), costs $1.50. Chris Barmeir, the controller at HP, says, "If you can change a design to make a part auto-insertable and avoid the backload process, the process becomes less costly" (Sheridan, 1990). To design the 1990 Lincoln Town Car, Ford built more than 110 prototypes on the assembly line in the auto plant at Wixom, Michigan. Ford's workers helped to fine-tune the design to improve quality and ease of assembly. More than 2600 employee suggestions were incorporated into the final design (Sheridan, 1990).

An objective of product design is to reduce the number of parts used, because it has a major impact on cost and quality. With fewer parts, the benefits for the organization are wide-ranging: purchasing of parts is simplified; workload is reduced; finished goods and work-in-process are reduced; plant and warehouse storage space is decreased; fewer quality details have to be contended with; scheduling is simplified; and communication is simplified. For example, Texas Instrument's TI-25 calculators have been designed for ease of assembly with only seven components, the fewest number of parts in any scientific calculator in the world. The TI-25 calculators have five models, which are priced from $5 to $10. Production of these calculators at the Lubbock plant in Texas is approximately 2 million units per year (Sheridan, 1990).

Simultaneous or concurrent engineering has been suggested as a means of shortening the design-to-manufacture cycle time through the involvement of all functional areas in the design process. For example, Lee Iacocca announced in a recent TV commercial that it took Chrysler only two years to move from design to production of its sleek Viper sports car, using the teamwork approach involving personnel from engineering, marketing, and production.

Accounting Interface

Recently attention has focused on the appropriateness of traditional accounting practices in a JIT environment. Accounting plays an important role in providing valuable performance information. Japanese companies, like their American counterparts, must value inventory for tax and financial purposes. The difference is that the Japanese do not allow these accounting procedures to affect their measurement and control of organizational activities. Japanese companies do a better job of using their management control systems to augment and enhance their manufacturing strategies. In essence, there is a more direct link between management accounting practices and corporate goals.

Hiromoto (1988) notes that Japanese companies appear to utilize accounting systems as a means to motivate employees to perform in support of long-term manufacturing strategies rather than to provide senior management with precise data on costs, variances, and profits. Thus, accounting plays the role of an "influencer" rather than that of an "informer." For example, senior Japanese managers are less concerned about whether an overhead allocation system depicts the exact demands each product places on corporate resources than about how the system impacts the cost-reduction efforts of middle managers and workers on the shop floor.

Accounting in Japan has also exhibited an overwhelming commitment to "market-driven management." Japanese firms have long recognized that the design stage represents the most promising area for realizing low-cost production. The emphasis is on designing and building products that will satisfy the price predicted for market success. Many Japanese companies estimate costs of new products by making it a point not to rely solely on current engineering standards. Instead, they determine target costs based on competitive market price estimates. As a result, these target costs are normally much below prevailing costs, which are computed based on standard technologies and processes. Benchmarks are then set by managers to gauge incremental progress toward achieving

TABLE 8-4 Marketing's Support of Operations

Marketing Activity	Marketing's Support of Operations
Sales	Helps smooth production/service delivery schedules. Avoids end-of-period "hockey sticks" in orders. Develops a base of customers who want JIT goods or services and are willing to commit to long-term contracts with reasonably stable delivery quantities and dates.
Order entry and customer service	Reduces lead time in order processing.
Product/service management	Coordinates product/service strategy with operations in order to emphasize quality and on-time delivery.
Marketing research	Provides feedback to operations on quality variables relating to product/service quality.
Physical distribution*	Adheres to shipping schedules. Evaluates alternatives of warehouse location, fleet expansion and management, and third-party carriers. Increases visibility of customers' operations. Balance shipping loads with production batches for frequent deliveries. Coordinates customer carrier pickups. Implements pull system from warehouse.
Advertising and promotion	Coordinates promotions with operations to stabilize shop schedules.

*The distribution function is part of materials management in some organizations.
Adapted from R. Natarajan and J. Donald Weinrauch, "JIT and the Marketing Interface," *Production and Inventory Management*, July–September 1990, p. 43.

the target cost objectives. Hiromoto (1988) observes, "How efficiently a company *should be* able to build a product is less important to the Japanese than how efficiently it *must* be able to build it for maximum marketplace success." The lesson here is that accounting policies should be supportive of corporate strategy, not independent of it.

IMPLEMENTATION ISSUES

There is no ideal approach to implement JIT, since it depends to a large extent on the business environment and manufacturing processes involved. However, trying to implement all key JIT practices simultaneously would not be a wise decision. Management should be cautious not to bite off more than they can chew in the early process of JIT implementation. Wantuck (1989) suggests following the *ten-step game plan for change* to ensure success in designing a JIT implementation program.

1. *Top management leadership.* Management must not only provide leadership but also show visible commitment and involvement in the whole implementation process.
2. *Steering committee.* The steering committee is formed to formulate policy, select the pilot area, provide resources, and guide the project.
3. *Education program.* Widespread education is necessary, since JIT affects the entire organization. The objective is to get people to buy into the project.

4. *Pilot project planning.* The project team recommends the key JIT practices such as setup reduction, group technology, and smoothed production that are to be included in the pilot.

5. *Steering committee approval.* The project team makes a formal presentation to sell top management on the project with the goal of securing formal approval.

6. *Employee training.* After project approval, employees in the pilot area must be properly trained to enable them to understand the project. Employee participation and suggestions are extremely critical to the success of the project.

7. *Pilot implementation.* During implementation, progress should be monitored and recorded. Feedbacks should be used to revise the plan.

8. *Pilot post mortem.* A post mortem provides for an evaluation of the causes and effects of the project. An official report documents the major problems encountered and how they were solved.

9. *Feedback to steering committee.* Lessons learned from the post mortem are communicated to management. The presentation meeting marks the formal closeout of the project.

10. *Expansion to next project.* This step signals the beginning of the next project cycle. The process is ready to start over by building on knowledge gained so far.

Scott et al.'s (1992) empirical study at the Wilson Sporting Goods plant shows that levels of satisfaction tend to increase for production workers as their involvement with JIT practices increases. Inman and Brandon (1992) note that an undesirable effect of JIT is stress brought about by rapid changes in the workplace. Klein (1989) also argues that line operators experienced a higher level of stress under JIT. Unnecessary stress can be reduced by practicing better time management and having a good support system to attend to worker concerns. Ultimately, "Attitudes must change first. You have to accept the need for JIT, want it, believe you can do it, and commit that you will do it before it can happen" (Wantuck, 1989, p. 364).

JIT AND MRP

Just-in-time and material requirements planning (MRP) related systems are not incompatible with each other. The kanban pull system is relatively simple and cheap to operate, since it does not need a computer. MRP II (manufacturing resource planning) systems do an excellent job of planning and coordinating materials flow at higher levels and providing a common basis for communication among the various functional areas. Additionally, MRP systems can help managers better understand the impact of changes in the master production schedule and lot-sizing decisions on capacity and inventory. In a repetitive production environment with fairly steady schedules, effective production control can be achieved with a hybrid approach of MRP and JIT (Karmarker, 1989). In this environment, MRP works well, because frequent materials planning is not necessary. At the same time, the pull system performs well on the shop floor, keeping inventory to a minimum. Examples of hybrid systems are "synchro-MRP," "rate-based MRP II," and "JIT-MRP."

The Manufacturing Quality Assurance Organization (MQAO) at Kodak Park in Rochester, N.Y., provides services, such as product-quality information and test-development expertise, to Eastman Kodak's photographic supply chain. MQAO operates in an environment faced with increasing demand, costs of material, space, equipment, and labor. At the same time, MQAO's customers are demanding improved service quality, cost, delivery, and customer satisfaction. MQAO turned to JIT and MRP II to improve their operations. Reported benefits include reduced lead times, service costs, and space requirements (Wasco et al., 1991). MQAO's success shows that combining MRP II with JIT is doable and can lead to improved productivity and customer service.

JIT IN SERVICES

Just-in-time is applicable to services as well, because it emphasizes elimination of all types of waste. The seven types of waste identified earlier in the chapter can be found in service organizations as well. The second element of JIT, respect for people, is most obvious in a service environment, where contact between employees of an organization and customers is high. How well a firm manages its work force determines to a large extent the quality of service delivered. In essence, service quality is hard to "standardize," since it depends to a large extent on the provider of the service. Continuous improvement is another JIT philosophy that works in a service setting. There is always room for improvement in anything we do, be it manufacturing or services. The final element of JIT is the focus on customer, a concept that is widely practiced in the service industry. A point worth noting is that service sector productivity has been lagging behind that of the manufacturing sector. This indicates that there is plenty of room for improvement to be made in the service sector in terms of continuously eliminating wastes, by focusing on getting the maximum potential out of employees, and emphasizing meeting the needs of the customers.

Benson (1986) notes that service organizations such as banks and hospitals are applying the JIT philosophy. Application Box 8-1 shows how JIT is being used in hospitals. With health care costs soaring and insurance companies getting tougher on reimbursement of claims by hospitals, there is a need to control costs. Controlling spiraling costs through inventory reduction in the health care industry is where the JIT philosophy has its biggest potential. Inman and Mehra (1991) present three cases of JIT application for service environments: a telecommunication services corporation, a government contractor to the Department of Energy, and an overnight package delivery service company. Another example is the use of several key JIT practices by fast-food chains such as McDonald's, Wendy's, and Burger King to prepare and deliver "quality" burgers at an affordable price to customers on a timely basis. The banking industry with its repetitive, high-volume check processing operations and its electronic processes used to debit credit card purchases is another likely JIT candidate. Benefits resulting from JIT implementation for these service companies include improved quality, improved service, improved communication, lower costs, reduction in storage space resulting in the elimination of warehouse space, quicker resolution of problems, and decreased carrying costs. As Chase and Aquilano (1992, p. 298) state, "Once we start thinking of services as an organized system of production processes, we can consider the use of JIT-type concepts to re-engineer service delivery operations. The result will be consistent services of high quality and excellent value, produced with high productivity."

SUMMARY

Although many of the JIT concepts have been developed after World War II in Japan, many of the principles and practices work just as well in the United States. JIT requires people to challenge the way things have been traditionally done. JIT requires a new way of thinking, a new corporate culture, and a new philosophy. Continuous improvement is the cornerstone of JIT and world-class operations. Firms are continually looking for ways to eliminate waste. With continuous improvement comes continual change, which can be painful, but is absolutely necessary for the survival and growth of the business. This mindset must be conveyed to all employees and nourished through continual education, communication, feedback, and support. Continuous improvement requires the involvement of all employees in an organization. Respect for people is the key ingredient that enables a firm to extract the maximum potential from its employees. Ultimately, it is satisfying the customers' needs and requirements that provides the driving force behind the JIT philosophy.

APPLICATION BOX 8-1   JIT at St. Luke's Episcopal Hospital

In 1990, the nation's 6700 hospitals spent $15 billion on supplies such as disposable gloves and gowns, sutures, and therapeutic solutions. The major players in the lucrative hospital supplies market are Baxter International, Johnson & Johnson, and Abbott Laboratories. Baxter is the largest manufacturer of hospital supplies, with 29% of the market. J&J's share is 11% and Abbott Laboratories has about 10%. Baxter is also the leading distributor with 28% of the market.

Hospital supply expenditures only begin with the cost of the purchases. "For every dollar spent to buy a product, hospitals spend another dollar moving that product through the system," said David Cassak, hospitals editor for *In Vivo Business and Medicine Report*, a trade magazine. Hospitals are resorting to just-in-time (JIT) deliveries to cut down on the amount of inventories held at the stockroom. Expected savings accrue from reduced holding and handling costs as well as improved space utilization.

St. Luke's Episcopal Hospital, a 950-bed facility in Houston, has historically kept a high level of inventory of expensive medical supplies in its 20,000-sq-ft warehouse. Like all hospitals, St. Luke's cannot afford to run short of vital items, least of all in the operating rooms. Doctors at St. Luke's perform open-heart surgery on 3000 patients each year, using enormous quantities of supplies. However, the recent nationwide squeeze on health-care costs has put tremendous pressures on St. Luke's to control costs. As a result, St. Luke's shut its warehouse and sold the inventory to Baxter International.

Baxter runs a service called Valuelink at St. Luke's, which involves managing, ordering, and delivering products from Baxter as well as from 400 other suppliers. Initially, Baxter provided daily JIT deliveries to the hospital loading dock. The JIT supply method provided more frequent deliveries from the supplier and reduced inventory levels in the hospital's storeroom. Ultimately, the objective is to move towards a stockless supply system, where all inventory responsibilities are shifted from the hospital to the distributor, and deliveries are made daily. Baxter fills orders in exact quantities and delivers directly to the departments, including operating rooms and nursing floors, inside St. Luke's.

"We think we have saved $1.5 million a year since 1988 from just-in-time deliveries alone," said Randy Jackson, a St. Luke's vice president, "with another $500,000 likely once the stockless system is fully implemented. Annual savings of $350,000 are achieved with a reduction in staff and $162,500 from eliminating inventory. In addition, the hospital has converted storerooms to patient care and other income-generating use."

Materials drawn from Milt Freudenheim, "Removing the Warehouse from Cost-Conscious Hospitals," *New York Times*, March 3, 1991.

DISCUSSION QUESTIONS

1. What key elements of JIT are demonstrated in the introductory case describing Bumper Works' relationship with Toyota? How are key JIT practices used to support these key elements?
2. What are the key elements of JIT, and how does each contribute to improving productivity and quality?
3. Why is reducing setup times a key JIT practice, and what is the three-pronged approach to improvements suggested by Suzaki?
4. Define the term *poka-yoke*.
5. List some of the benefits of good housekeeping and an organized workplace.

6. Discuss the use of JIT in services in general and hospitals in particular.

7. What are the operating rules necessary to effectively use a kanban system?

8. What are the seven goals of total quality control (TQC)?

9. Define the concept of jidoka, or autonomation, and provide some examples of actual applications of the concept.

10. Discuss how a fast-food restaurant such as McDonald's, Wendy's, or Pizza Hut can make use of the principles of JIT to improve service.

11. Why is excess inventory "the root of all evil"?

12. Discuss the use of JIT in a continuous process environment, such as the beer and steel industries. Give some reasons for success or failure in such an environment.

13. Compare the differing attitudes toward employment in Japan and the United States.

14. There are two types of kanban. What are they and what is the purpose of each?

15. Define the term *open kimono* and describe how it relates to JIT purchasing.

16. JIT necessitates that manufacturing interact with other functions or departments within the company. Give three examples of interaction and explain the importance of developing cooperation among functions.

17. Discuss the human element of JIT and the resulting attitude toward mistakes.

18. Give another term for kaizen and discuss the basic philosophy underlying this concept.

19. Smooth production is a cornerstone for JIT production using kanban. What are the objectives and benefits of smooth production?

STRATEGIC DECISION SITUATIONS

1. The BiPed Bicycle Company is using a kanban production system. One part of the plant is dedicated to the production of bicycle seats. The demand is 100 bicycle seats per day. Each container holds four bicycle seats. Typically, a container of bicycle seats requires 0.03 day for processing, and 0.10 day for wait time, which includes materials handling time. Jay, the line supervisor at BiPed, has been assigned the task of computing the number of kanban sets to be authorized, assuming ideal conditions. What is the level of inventory in the system? Jay feels strongly that the materials handling system can be improved so that the wait time can be reduced to 0.05 day. Assuming this improvement can be carried out, describe the effects on the number of kanban sets required and the level of inventory in the system.

2. The Yopet Company manufactures three types of recreational vehicles: Yopet Gold, Yopet Silver, and Yopet Platinum. Yopet has determined the monthly demand as: Yopet Gold = 9000 units, Yopet Silver = 6000 units, and Yopet Platinum = 3000 units. The plant is working 20 days per month and three 8-hour shifts. Yopet is currently using the JIT method of production. Management would like to develop a smoothed daily production schedule for the recreational vehicles. What are the cycle time and an acceptable daily schedule?

REFERENCES

Barnet, D. Wolf. "Flexible Work Environment Improves Productivity," *Columbus Dispatch*. January 26, 1992.

Benson, Randall J. "JIT: Not Just for the Factory," *APICS 29th Annual International Conference Proceedings*. 1986, pp. 370–374.

Boyett, Joseph H., and Henry P. Conn. *Workplace 2000: The Revolution Reshaping American Business*. New York: Dutton, 1991.

Byrne, John A. "The Horizontal Corporation," *Business Week*. December 20, 1993, pp. 76–81.

Chase, Richard B., and Nicholas J. Aquilano. *Production and Operations Management: A Life Cycle Approach*, 6th ed. Homewood, Ill.: Irwin, 1992.

Chase, Richard B., and David A. Garvin. "The Service Factory," *Harvard Business Review*. July–August 1989, pp. 61–69.

Cox, James F., John Blackstone, Jr., and Michael Spencer, eds. *APICS Dictionary*, 7th ed. Falls Church, Va.: American Production and Inventory Control Society, 1992.

Dingus, V. R., and W. A. Golomski. *A Quality Revolution in Manufacturing*. Norcross, Ga.: Industrial Engineering and Management Press, 1988.

Ferguson, Charles H. "Computers and the Coming of the U.S. Keiretsu," *Harvard Business Review*. July-August 1990, pp. 55–70.

Freeland, James R. "A Survey of Just-in-Time Purchasing Practices in the United States," *Production and Inventory Management*. April–June 1991, pp. 43–49.

Freudenheim, Milt. "Removing the Warehouse from Cost-Conscious Hospitals," *New York Times*. March 3, 1991.

Gawronski, Francis J. "Toyota Suppliers a Key Component of Long-Term Strategy," *Automotive News*. April 1, 1991, p. 16.

Goddard, Walter E. *Just-in-Time: Surviving by Breaking Tradition*. Essex Junction, Vt.: Oliver Wight Limited Publications, 1986.

Hall, Robert W. *Zero Inventories*. Homewood, Ill.: Dow Jones-Irwin, 1983.

Hall, Robert W. *Attaining Manufacturing Excellence*. Homewood, Ill.: Dow Jones-Irwin, 1987.

Hayes, Robert H., and Steven C. Wheelwright. *Restoring Our Competitive Edge: Competing Through Manufacturing*. New York: John Wiley and Sons, 1984.

Hayes, Robert H., Steven C. Wheelwright, and Kim B. Clark. *Dynamic Manufacturing*. New York: Free Press, 1988.

Hiromoto, Toshiro. "Another Hidden Edge—Japanese Management Accounting," *Harvard Business Review*. July–August 1988, pp. 22–26.

Inman, R. Anthony, and Larry Brandon. "An Undesirable Effect of JIT," *Production and Inventory Management*. January–March 1992, pp. 55–58.

Inman, R. Anthony, and Satish Mehra. "JIT Applications for Service Environments," *Production and Inventory Management*. July–September 1991, pp. 16–20.

Ishikawa, Akira. "Principles of QC Circle Activities and Their Effects on Productivity in Japan: A Corporate Analysis," *Management International Review*. Vol. 25, No. 3, 1985, pp. 33–40.

Ishikawa, Kaoru. *What Is Total Quality Control?: The Japanese Way*, translated by David J. Lu. Englewood Cliffs, N.J.: Prentice Hall, 1985.

Karmarkar, Uday. "Getting Control of Just-in-Time," *Harvard Business Review*.September–October 1989, pp. 122–131.

Klein, Janice A. "The Human Cost of Manufacturing Reform," *Harvard Business Review*. March–April 1989, pp. 60–66.

Lu, David J. *Kanban: Just-in-Time at Toyota*. Stamford, Conn.: Productivity Press, 1985.

Melcher, Arlyn, William Acar, Paul DuMont, and Moutaz Khouja. "Standard-Maintaining and Continuous Systems: Experiences and Comparisons," *Interfaces*. May–June 1990, pp. 24–40.

Monden, Yasuhiro. *Toyota Production System: Practical Approach to Production Management.* Atlanta, Ga.: Industrial Engineering and Management Press, Institute of Industrial Engineers, 1983.

Natarajan, R., and J. Donald Weinrauch. "JIT and the Marketing Interface," *Production and Inventory Management.* July–September 1990, p. 42–46.

Neff, Robert, Neil Gross, and Larry Holyoke. "Japan: How Bad?" *Business Week.* December 13, 1993, pp. 56–59.

Rapoport, Carla. "Why Japan Keeps on Winning," *Fortune.* July 15, 1991, pp. 76–85.

Rieker, Wayne. "Trip Report for Study of Quality Control Circles in Japan," *JUSE Reports of Statistical Application Research.* Vol. 22, No. 2, 1975, pp. 33–48.

Schonberger, Richard J. *Japanese Manufacturing Techniques: Nine Hidden Lessons in Simplicity.* New York: Free Press, 1982.

Schonberger, Richard J. *World Class Manufacturing: The Lessons of Simplicity Applied.* New York: Free Press, 1986.

Schonberger, Richard J. "Applications of Single-Card and Dual-Card Kanban," *Interfaces.* August 1983, pp. 56–67.

Scott, Allan F., James H. Macomber, and Lawrence P. Ettkin. "JIT and Job Satisfaction: Some Empirical Results," *Production and Inventory Management.* January–March 1992, pp. 36–41.

Sepheri, Mehran. *Just-in-Time, Not Just in Japan: Case Studies of American Pioneers in JIT Implementation.* Falls Church, Va.: American Production and Inventory Control Society, 1986.

Sheridan, John H. "America's Best Plants," *Industry Week.* October 15, 1990, pp. 27–64.

Shingo, Shigeo. *Zero Quality Control: Source Inspection and the Poka-Yoke System,* translated by Andrew P. Dillon. Cambridge, Mass.: Productivity Press, 1986.

Suzaki, Kiyoshi. *The New Manufacturing Challenge: Techniques for Continuous Improvement.* New York: Free Press, 1987.

Takatsuki, Ryoichi. "Productivity and Quality Innovation with TPM (Total Productive Maintenance), in *Applying Just in Time: The American/Japanese Experience,* Yasuhiro Monden (ed.). Norcross, Ga.: Industrial Engineering and Management Press, 1986.

Wantuck, Kenneth. *Just-In-Time for America.* Southfield, Mich.: KWA Media, 1989.

Wasco, W. Calvin, Robert Stonehocker, and Larry Feldman. "Success with JIT and MRP II in a Service Organization," *Production and Inventory Management Journal.* October–December 1991, pp. 15–21.

White, Joseph B. "Japanese Auto Makers Help U.S. Suppliers Become More Efficient," *Wall Street Journal.* September 9, 1991.

Woodruff, David, James Treece, Sunita Wadekar Bhargava, and Karen Lowry Miller. "Saturn: GM Finally Has a Real Winner, But Success Is Bringing a Fresh Batch of Problems," *Business Week.* August 17, 1992, pp. 87–91.

CHAPTER 9

PRODUCTIVITY AND WORK FORCE MANAGEMENT

People are the catalysts that stimulate new productivity.
—William B. Werther, William A. Ruch,
and Lynne McClure

You lead, follow, or get out of the way. —Lee Iacocca

Objectives

After completing this chapter you should be able to:

- Define productivity and state several measures of productivity.
- Identify the contribution of people to productivity.
- State why management styles have recently moved toward increased employee empowerment.
- Describe the activities of workers, supervisors, and management in an empowered organization.
- Define and describe job design strategies and identify the advantages and disadvantages of those strategies.
- Identify factors that contribute to productivity and show how they are interrelated.

Outline

INTRODUCTORY CASE: INNOVATIVE WORK FORCE MANAGEMENT AT MCDONNELL DOUGLAS

In late 1991, John F. McDonnell, CEO of McDonnell Douglas Corporation,* was overwhelmed by the more than $36 billion of aircraft orders for its subsidiary, the Douglas Aircraft Company. While most CEOs would be pleased with such a situation, conditions at McDonnell Douglas were bleak. With defense orders down, the parent company had relied on the commercial business of its subsidiary for profits. But, the $36 billion in orders could not be filled on schedule, a common occurrence at the Douglas Aircraft Company.

Since 1975, Douglas had not reported profits due to inefficient manufacturing methods and poor management. Tired of such lackluster performance, in 1989 John McDonnell announced an innovative work force management system called the total quality management system (TQMS) program. More than 5200 vice presidents, general managers, and supervisors were stripped of their titles, though most remained with the company. Four levels of management were erased. Traditionally centralized departments, such as engineering, manufacturing, and customer relations, were decentralized. Though the company had created a new management structure, production methods were not changed. Those methods were based on a sort of "tribal knowledge." Because workers repeated

---

*Materials drawn from David Lynch, "Turbulence Dogs Douglas Overhaul," *Chicago Tribune*, September 9, 1991, Section 4, p. 1, and from James E. Ellis and Bruce Einhorn, "Gone Is My Co-Pilot?" *Business Week*, July 6, 1992, pp. 71–72.

the same tasks for each aircraft, they knew every operation from memory. They rarely consulted assembly instructions, even when the design changed. Thus, further down the line small mistakes required off-line correction, causing inefficiencies and risking other damage. Costs were increased and deliveries delayed.

By 1992, Douglas was expected to contribute 50% of the parent company's revenue and TQMS, an important component of the turnaround effort, was relied upon to change more than 20 years of abysmal financial performance. However, mass confusion resulted, which was perpetuated by the "Douglas salute" (crossed arms and index fingers pointing in opposite directions). Production workers did not know who was in charge, and the company's experienced, yet demoralized managers could not be consulted, since they were taking personality tests and doing role-playing exercises.

Ignoring years of employee experience, reassignments were based on handwritten essays, peer and subordinate evaluations, and behavioral tests. Employee average experience dropped from ten years to two. With more orders than it could handle, Douglas could not adequately train new workers; consequently, morale plummeted further and so did production. First-half losses in 1989 were $224 million. Though fourth-quarter profits were $25 million, the bottom fell out when first-quarter 1990 losses of $84 million were reported.

Seventeen months after the initial commitment, much of what had been taken apart began to be put back together. Because profitability had not been restored, the parent company opted for massive work force cuts during 1990 and 1991. Customer relations was recentralized after the company received complaints from customers who had to speak to a different Douglas executive for each Douglas aircraft they owned. Only the outlines of the program are now present at Douglas; however, its full collapse will likely not occur because, as John McDonnell said in a video mailed to employees in March, 1991, "I will not let TQMS collapse. . . . It is not just another initiative. It is here to stay because I want it to stay."

PRODUCTIVITY AS A SYSTEM

Productivity, broadly defined, is a way to measure the effectiveness of resource utilization for individuals, facilities, companies, and societies. Each of these must periodically find new sources of productivity. Those that do not, fail. For individuals, this means retraining or retiring; for facilities, this means redesigning or closing; for companies, this means restructuring or going out of business; for societies, this means social and political reorganization. Among the numerous examples of this process of loss and regeneration are individuals whose jobs (in the printing and metal-working industries, for example) have been automated, the many plants and companies in the electronics and automobile industries, and the social turbulence and rebirth in Eastern Europe and the former Soviet Union.

In addition to these several levels of evaluation, productivity results from the synergetic contribution of numerous factors. The operations function is to integrate these factors or resources efficiently and thus add value to the output in manufacturing, distribution, and service businesses. Productivity does not result from the management of only one resource or one factor; it is management's job to weave the components into an efficient transformation process. Thus, productivity is achieved through the management of a system, which functions at several levels and with numerous contributing factors.

This chapter initially defines productivity and the relationship of people to productivity, and then notes evolving labor-management practices. Individual aspects of productivity, such as work measurement and learning curves, are discussed in detail, followed by other more broadly defined contributors to productivity, including job design and work force structure. Finally, productivity management is described as a process of continuous improvement.

PRODUCTIVITY AND PEOPLE

Productivity is a people issue. Though productivity may be enhanced by technology and other tangible resources, it is the work force who are trained to use technology, it is the work force who must recognize and reduce wasted resources, such as materials, equipment, and capacity, and it is the work force as a synergy of labor and management that makes the operations system function. Labor has historically been suspicious of productivity improvement, expecting that productivity improvement would require more effort. Management counters that productivity improvement means working smarter, not harder—with benefits for all.

Numerous studies (Heizer and Render, 1991) suggest that of the roughly 2.5% average annual productivity increase in the United States over the past 100 years, 1.6% has resulted from management methods, 0.5% from labor improvements, and 0.4% from capital investments. Thus, people (labor and management) are responsible for 80% of the productivity gains during the past 100 years. Knowledge, a key component of management methods, is a major part of the people contribution, but training is also important, because labor must understand and apply the new methods, processes, and technologies. In fact, labor often understands the knowledge foundation of the production process better than does management. In either case, as highlighted by the introductory quote, "People are the catalysts that stimulate new productivity."

All companies have a labor-management style, supported by numerous explicit and implicit labor relations and human resource management policies. If the styles are not explicit (and often they are not), they are implicit in the standards and informal expectancies of both labor and management. These behaviors are likely conditioned by years of practice and tradition, and, in many cases, become corporate culture, but generally are not considered to be strategic in nature. Unfortunately, management styles directly affect worker expectancies, contributions, and demands, and labor responses affect management styles, all of which directly impact productivity. Because the human resource is so critical to productivity, operations strategy must include work force management as the central commitment and concern.

Productivity Defined

Productivity is generally defined as "an overall measure of production/service delivery effectiveness." It can be applied to individuals, work groups, plants, companies, and nations. More specifically, productivity is measured as a ratio of production or service outcomes and resources consumed to achieve those outcomes, or

$$\text{Productivity} = \frac{\text{output}}{\text{input}} = \frac{\text{production/service outcome}}{\text{input resources consumed}}$$

The difference between the output and the input of an operations activity is the value added, which occurs in the operations transformation. Because productivity is a measure of the amount of value added in the transformation process, it is a general indicator of the long-run viability of the company. Without productivity improvements in a competitive environment, operations of any sort are, or quickly become, irrelevant, as suggested by the quote of Lee Iacocca on the first page of this chapter.

Contribution of People

Wickham Skinner (1971) is among the first to identify the infrastructure contribution in American factories. He defines infrastructure as "organizational level wage systems, supervisory practices, production control and scheduling approaches, and job design and methods," or all of the "software" of the facility. Each of these work force-management contributors to the infrastructure directly affects the productivity of workers. The term "work force management" is defined here as "all activities that improve the match between individuals and the job." Though most organizations have a human resources staff function to administer specialized programs toward this end, work force management, in the generic sense used here, applies to the management practices such as work methods and performance measurement, job design and compensation, and creation of work environments.

Knowledge, both labor's and management's, is a key input in most businesses to the productivity equation. Management information systems provide many types of information to various users, but information, unless used, is wasted. To paraphrase Drucker (1989, p. 209), knowledge is data that are endowed with relevance; individuals give data relevance. To be a resource, knowledge must be applied toward the productivity goals of the firm. Thus, people with relevant data are the common element of productivity; or, stated in terms of the productivity formula, people with knowledge are the common denominator of all productivity measures.

In most organizations, as Drucker (1992) points out, the basis for the informal structure and labor productivity is the team. However, there are several different types of team. Some teams, such as baseball teams, have fixed positions staffed by specialist players. Though there is some synchrony, most of the teamwork is in a series of sequential actions, as in an assembly line. A second type of team, the football team, also uses fixed positions, but there is a simultaneousness of effort. The team, like an orchestra or a hospital emergency room team, operates in parallel. Finally, there is the tennis doubles team, like the work relationships of the GM Saturn plant, or the team of senior executives who form the office of the president of a firm. Though each team member has a fixed position, the positions are highly interactive—that is, they can cover for one another. Though each type of team has various characteristics and capabilities, as Drucker notes, team definition develops as an informal process. Management is beginning to learn more about how these decisions are made.

Several studies of top management teams have shown that the team composition is related to the firm's strategy. The demographic traits of teams were found to be significantly related to corporate strategy, while demographic diversity was not found to be related. Notably, firms involved in dynamic strategic change are more often managed by top management teams who have a lower average age, shorter organization tenure, higher team tenure, higher education levels, heterogeneous education specialties, and academic training in the sciences (Wiersema and Bantel, 1992). Other research (Michel and Hambrick, 1992) found significant relationships between the team attributes, such as tenure, functional homogeneity, and core function expertise, of the top management team and the diversification strategy of the firm. These studies suggest that, at least among top management teams, team composition is an important and related factor to strategy.

CHANGING FACE OF LABOR RELATIONS

Some managers view changes in workplace conditions with skepticism or contempt. To use Skinner's (1971) term, this is "anachronistic." The rate of change in most businesses is increasing. International competition, environmental concerns, openness of operations processes, and equity in work force management practices are driving and sometimes overtaking current change efforts. Equating these underlying factors to a short-lived economic downturn and suggesting that "this too will pass" is indeed short-sighted and risky. Further, rapidly developing technology requires changes in work force management styles. This section describes the emerging currents in work force management.

Emergence of Work Force Management

Management, as Drucker (1989) notes, is a rather recent phenomenon, dating in most business areas to the beginning of the twentieth century. Prior to that time, the smaller, more entrepreneurial and less differentiated production processes and service operations did not require extensive and formalized management, particularly as we understand the term today. Notable exceptions are early military, insurance, and church organizations and construction or transportation companies, such as railroads and shipping firms.

In the early twentieth century, however, ownership of a business became separated from the operation of that business. A bureaucracy was subsequently created to support the operation of the business. Though the 1960s and 1970s, management structures became increasingly differentiated as organizations sought to define responsibility and capabilities for different functions or to comply with different externally generated requirements, such as government regulation. More recently, availability and ease of use of the computer have made it possible to distribute knowledge rapidly throughout the organization, which has effectively empowered the diverse contributors of knowledge in the organization.

As early corporations and management grew in power, labor was organized as a countervailing force. Buffa (1985) argues that labor was organized only to the degree that management misused and abused its prerogatives. The industrial-relations staff was created to work with the developing labor unions, and, in the process, absorbed many of the functions and powers previously exercised by the operations function. Human resource staff specialists, often isolated from an operations perspective, viewed labor relations as a process of appeasing and mitigating. Matters of infrastructure and such key contributors to productivity as job design, work rules, wage rates, and organization structure were bargained and compromised. In the long run, according to Buffa, productivity was undermined.

As the unions became more powerful in the mid-twentieth century, their primary strategy was to organize most of the competitors in a market, then, through pattern bargaining, enforce a relatively uniform wage contract. This effectively eliminated labor costs from the competitive bargaining environment by establishing an industrywide standard wage. However, by the 1960s and 1970s, international competition and deregulation diminished the ability of businesses to pass through to customers the high costs of standardized union wages. Customers and businesses sought the lower-cost nonunion and foreign goods and services, effectively undercutting the power of the unions and companies with organized labor (Cappelli, 1986).

Future Directions of Work Force Management

The traditional model of labor relations, based on adversarial conflict and competition for resources, was necessary and effective in its time, but as the work force management environment has changed, that model has become increasingly counterproductive. Currently, in many industries, organizations must identify and emplace methods, structures, and management styles that encourage human resources toward continuously improving operations goals. These directions of work force management are apparent in the emerging information organization.

The information organization has subtly, yet explosively replaced the industrial organization. An early herald of the information-based organization was Bell (1969), followed by Toffler (1971), Naisbitt (1982), and Drucker (1989). Though each reflects a different perspective in defining the information-based organization, there are some striking similarities. The characteristics of the emerging information organization, compared with the traditional materials-based organization, are suggested in Table 9-1.

The displacement of capital and labor by information as the key strategic resource permits numerous efficiencies. Notably, because information is easily duplicatable, it can be distributed to many people and different activities simultaneously. Capital and labor (the key resources in earlier eras) usually are not directly or cheaply reproducible; thus their management and use as a resource was limited to a few individuals. But now, the reproducibility of information permits greater distribution and synchronous interaction of specialists. In the emerging information organization, decision making is based on more elaborate sharing and diagnosis of functional-area information, rather than individual

TABLE 9-1 The Emerging Information-based Organization

Characteristic	Traditional Materials-based Organization	Emerging Information-based Organization
Strategic resource	Capital or labor	Information
Locus of power	Management and, as delegated, staff	Technical specialists
Decision logic	Judgmental	Computational
Decisions based on	Experience, opinion	Diagnosis
Distribution of power	To a few	To many
Operations	Sequential, segmented	Synchronous, integrated
Strategy	Peripheral showpiece	Integrating overview
Organization design	Tall	Flat
Knowledge location	Support staffs	Line operations

opinions or experience. In the industrial organization, decision making is based on management judgment; strategy contributes only as a peripheral showpiece. Computational processes and diagnostic values aid decision making, and strategy provides an integrating overview in the information organization.

The knowledge of an organization today resides with diverse technical specialists; these individuals are primarily in operations activities and are more closely in touch with the value-adding transformation of the business. Specialists do not require layers of management to serve as information relays, which would likely only create communication problems. Instead, the few generalist managers facilitate an environment of trust and internalization of organization goals. The shift toward an information-based organization suggests a significant flattening of the organization design with fewer levels of hierarchy, with less direct supervision, and with a greater span of control for each supervisor. Drucker (1988) offers examples of a hospital or a symphony orchestra. In such organizations, specialists contribute their knowledge in clearly identified frameworks of organization structure. Communications among specialists are often lateral, developing a synergy that would be lost if interrupted by a supervisor's review.

Such organizations, according to Drucker, have four special management problems:

1. To reward specialists and identify career paths for them.
2. To ensure the training and preparation of top management.
3. To establish a unified vision of the organization.
4. To devise the structure to manage the organization.

Each of these four management problems is exacerbated by the nature of the information organization. Because management is not fully aware of the specialist's knowledge contribution, rewarding and projecting career paths is difficult. Correspondingly, traditional ways of providing for promotion to and preparation of top management through staff positions are less available. Management must function with increased visibility to ensure understanding of both formal and informal needs of the organization and internalization of those needs by diverse specialists.

Drucker's assessment is contested by Elliot Jaques (1990), who presents a strong case in support of the continued need for hierarchy. Though acknowledging that hierarchies involve potential problems and misuses, Jaques insists that the use of the hierarchy is the only way to define discrete categories of job complexity (vertical levels) and to differentiate types of mental activity (horizontal levels). Hierarchies emerged with the beginnings of social organization and have persisted in business organizations because they are uniquely able to provide these functions. A distinct difference in perspective is required by each level and each function of the organization, with a discontinuity of perspective from one level to the next and from one function to the next. Typically, for example, at the lowest level, the decision-making time limits of technicians and operators is one or two days, that of first-line management is three months, and so forth to the CEO, who may have a five to ten year perspective. The hierarchy, whether relatively tall or relatively flat, is thus inherent in social and business organizations. It is required because incumbents cannot rapidly shift their range of horizontal or vertical involvement. Management's function within the hierarchy is

1. To add value to subordinates' work.
2. To sustain a team of subordinates capable of doing the required work.
3. To set the direction and get subordinates to follow willingly.

Given that many organizations have upwards of 15 layers of vertical structure, both Drucker and Jaques concur on the need for downsizing. The flow of information must be enhanced through structures and infrastructures, requiring greater emphasis on understanding and trust. The management style of such organizations inevitably changes.

McGregor (1960) first differentiated the elements of theory X and theory Y management styles; he suggested that organizations were moving toward greater acceptance of theory Y. However, the coming information organization makes subordinate-centered theory Y processes absolutely necessary. Figure 9-1 elaborates the management style from boss-centered direction (generally theory X) to subordinate-centered involvement (generally theory Y). The downward movement on this continuum toward greater employee free-

FIGURE 9-1 Emerging Management Styles

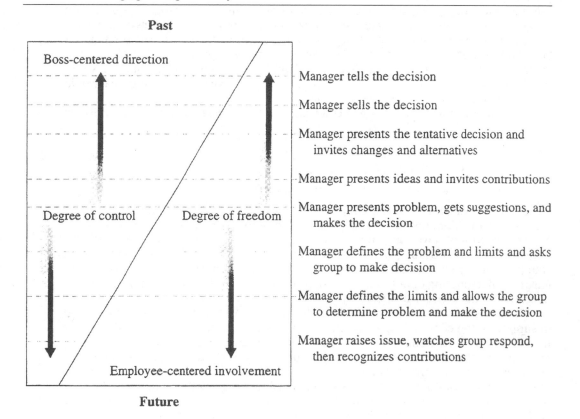

dom and employee-centered involvement is likely to continue for the foreseeable future for most types of organization. The positioning of management style on this continuum is a key management decision, one which directly affects productivity and which, as initially suggested by Figure 1-7, must be consistent with the internal and external factors of the environment.

When the formal and informal mechanisms of organization environment and values, communication, and individual responsibilities are changed, it is extremely important that both the old and new methods, and the reasons for change are understood. A method of visualizing the effects of the simultaneous pressures for change and resistance to change was expressed as field force theory by Lewin (1951). Change may be accomplished by either increasing the forces of change or by decreasing the forces of resistance to change. Schein (1984) suggests that the process of unfreezing, changing, and refreezing may be helpful in facilitating the change and minimizing discontinuities. An example of a management style change at Xerox Corporation is described in Application Box 9-1.

Employee Empowerment

The upshot of greater employee-centered management styles is employee empowerment. Empowerment is a natural extension of the long understood and practiced idea of delegating authority commensurate with responsibility. But empowerment is also multidimensional, resulting from increased integration of persons with diverse and specialized perspectives. Such individuals are likely, either as individuals or teams, to develop and implement varied and multidimensional responses to specific situations. Additionally, empowerment means "define and solve the problem," a much broader charter than offered by most delegation of authority. Employee empowerment is one of the most efficient ways to stimulate new productivity. This suggests a horizontal corporation of self-managing teams (Byme, 1993).

Employee empowerment may have developed as a way to incorporate Japanese management styles in American practices. Empowerment, for example, engenders the collective decision-making and holistic values that long have typified Japanese management styles. Though the further techniques of lifetime employment and long-term evaluation processes are not included in empowerment, they are implicit, because empowerment recognizes the value of the employee and thus the need to hire the right employee, and then retain and develop that individual (Bowen, 1991).

Little is understood about the characteristics of the empowered organization or about the activities and characteristics of the individuals at various levels in the empowered organization. Some vestiges of the traditional organization design are likely to remain. Indeed, as Jaques (1990) contends, they are inherent in organizations, though they will likely be less formal or apparent. At the highest level of the hierarchy, top management defines the culture and creates the vision. At the lowest level of the hierarchy, specialists are integrated with the organization communication system to achieve the necessary synchrony. The several layers of management or supervisory employees are primarily involved with process cost, quality, flexibility, and delivery, which reduce lead times and waste. These dimensions of the empowered organization are shown in Figure 9-2.

The new organization design, or strategic architecture, is more focused toward organization processes and the internal development of the firm, rather than toward external factors. This refocusing of the strategic architecture of the firm emphasizes organization learning, motivation, empowerment, and other internal growth activities (Kiernan, 1993).

Hall (1991) reports that plants with the best labor productivity gains are involved in a combination of quality improvement, lead time reduction, and employee involvement. These are formalized in programs to cut costs and improve quality, process flexibility, and delivery times. Despite this refocusing of the firm, measuring productivity improvement remains an important yet difficult function.

APPLICATION BOX 9-1   Changing Management Styles at Xerox

With the introduction of its first copying machine in 1960, the Xerox Corporation experienced growth and profits due to a near monopoly situation. Domestic competition did challenge Xerox during part of the 20 years following the product breakthrough, but only on service and reliability. It was not until Japanese companies entered the market in the mid-1970s with lower-priced equipment of comparable quality that Xerox was forced to compete on price and product innovation. Cost suddenly became paramount at Xerox; a companywide cultural change was mandated.

At the core of Xerox's reorganization was the altering of management styles. This meant adjusting from a highly technical management approach to a more employee-oriented style. Many changes had to be implemented; yet it was crucial to retain the commitment of Xerox's technology-oriented employees. The change process selected was the management style change strategy (Schein, 1984), consisting of three steps: unfreezing, changing, and refreezing. During "unfreezing," targeted areas are emphasized to unlock the "traditional ways of doing things." Next, managers are informed of the desired behaviors. Thus, "changing" of style occurs through identification and internalization of the modeled values, attitudes, and behaviors. Increased emphasis is placed on innovation and risk taking. An environment is developed to encourage employee participation. The final step is the "refreezing" of the newly defined management values, attitudes, and behaviors as the expected norm. Support mechanisms are put in place to reinforce the required changes, and organization rewards are implemented to further shape the behaviors of management.

Additionally, the company wanted an organizational climate conductive to motivation and change. The climate in which the employees operate directly affects the plausible methods of motivation. Lewin's field force theory views people performing in a field of restraining and driving forces. Typical examples of these two forces and their effects on the amount of productive effort are shown over time in the following diagram. These forces either limit or augment productivity. When the restraining forces are reduced or the driving forces are increased, the amount of productive effort is increased. The strength of the counteracting forces dictates overall actual behavior.

By dedicating itself to creating an employee-oriented work force, Xerox has been able to elevate some of the driving forces behind employee motivation. Such an overwhelming organizational transformation has allowed the copier giant to remain successful in a highly competitive market.

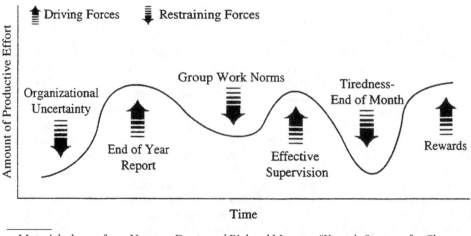

Materials drawn from Norman Deets and Richard Morano, "Xerox's Strategy for Changing Management Styles," *Management Review*, March 1986, pp. 31–35; Kurt Lewin, *Field Theory in Social Science*, New York: Harper and Brothers, 1951; and Edgar H. Schein, *Organizational Psychology*, Englewood Cliffs, N.J.: Prentice Hall, 1980.

FIGURE 9-2   The Structure of an Empowered Organization

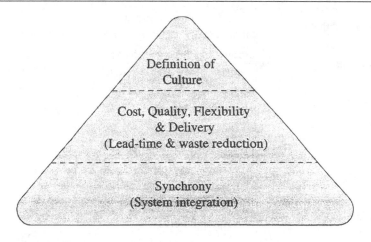

MEASURING PRODUCTIVITY

Despite far-reaching efforts and high levels of management support, productivity improvement has proven an elusive goal for many organizations, including McDonnell Douglas. Most productivity improvement efforts, as Skinner (1986) points out, have been directed toward labor efficiency, which is, in most manufacturing and many service situations, less than 20% of the total resource input. Without a coherent strategy, many innovations result in improvements in one area, but simultaneously incur problems and costs in other areas, resulting in limited, if any, gains. One difficulty is that businesses have long been guided by criteria of cost and efficiency, and managers draw conclusions based on these unidimensional measures and reject innovations that cannot satisfy cost or efficiency standards in the short run.

Productivity Evaluation

Often productivity measures, though computed with the best of intentions, exacerbate the situation. Few measures are constant, and few are unperturbed by external factors. For example, the automobile of the 1950s and 1960s is strikingly different from that of the 1990s. Emission control, gasoline mileage, available materials, and manufacturing technologies have all changed significantly. Consequently, the output measure of "one automobile" has changed from year to year—reducing its accuracy as a measure of yearly productivity. Further, a measured unit for one product may not be the same as for another product. A carburetor for an economy car is not the same as that for a performance sports car. Such difficulties prompted Vaughn Beals, president and CEO of Harley Davidson, to comment: "Measuring productivity is a total frustration. Any numbers I could quote, the accounting department might choke on. We have just looked at gross measures; we count all the motorcycles that go out the door, then count all the people working in the plants . . ." (Willis, 1986).

Measures of Productivity

Despite these difficulties, productivity is measured in a variety of ways at national and regional levels, at company and plant levels, and at work group and individual levels. The United States Department of Labor, Bureau of Labor Statistics measures and publishes the gross national product. Most companies compute a variety of productivity indexes (see Table 9-2), which are often used with an appreciation of their limitations. Vora (1992)

TABLE 9-2 Productivity Measures in Manufacturing and Service Activities

$$\text{Total factor productivity} = \frac{\text{output}}{\text{management} + \text{labor} + \text{capital} + \text{materials}}$$

$$\text{Productivity index} = \frac{\text{productivity for a specified period}}{\text{productivity for base period}}$$

$$\text{Labor efficiency} = \frac{\text{total units produced}}{\text{total labor hours}}$$

$$\text{Quality yield} = \frac{\text{total units produced } - \text{ rejected units}}{\text{total units produced}}$$

$$\text{Safety—lost time} = \frac{\text{productive time lost due to accidents}}{\text{total productive time}}$$

$$\text{Delivery—shipments} = \frac{\text{shipments or schedule}}{\text{total shipments}}$$

$$\text{Inventory turns} = \frac{\text{cost of sales/period}}{\text{average inventory investment/period}}$$

$$\text{Service application processing} = \frac{\text{number of applications processed correctly}}{\text{staff hours}}$$

$$\text{Service response efficiency} = \frac{\text{responses within specified time}}{\text{total number of responses}}$$

$$\text{Facility utilization} = \frac{\text{total hours of facility used}}{\text{total hour of facility available}}$$

$$\text{Facility occupancy} = \frac{\text{average seats occupied/period}}{\text{total available seats}}$$

Reprinted by permission from *Production and Operations Management* by Donald W. Fogarty, Thomas R. Hoffmann, and Peter W. Stonebraker. Cincinnati, Ohio: South-Western Publishing Co., 1989, Figure 1-9, p. 26.

finds that the productivity measures in use by a sampling of manufacturing and service firms varies widely; physical output, sales revenue, and profits are measured as outputs, while labor, capital, materials, energy, and space or land all are used as input measures. Top management primarily uses measures based on profit and sales per unit of capital input, and first-level management typically uses measures of physical output per unit of labor or material. Additionally, individual and group productivity measures were used for a variety of purposes, including compensation and performance appraisal. The accuracy and relevance of those measures is only as good, however, as the input and output information. As Beals suggests (Willis, 1986), they can be used as general measures to compare like activities or to evaluate performance of an activity over time.

Any measure of outputs over inputs may be used as a productivity measure or, if the output measure is compared to a base period, a productivity index. Improving productivity can be achieved by increasing outputs or decreasing inputs. The most common way to improve productivity is to increase inputs, in the hope that the outputs will increase at a greater rate. This is the rationale for economies of scale and scope, where an investment is made in technology in the expectancy that the increased productivity will be sufficient to permit higher volumes (scale) or greater variety (scope) and lower costs. Alternatively, a decrease in inputs that is greater than that of outputs also improves productivity. This approach is used during periods of recession, when layoffs and plant closings are used to reduce inputs (resources) faster than outputs (sales) and thus improve productivity.

FIGURE 9-3 An Input–Output Model of the Firm

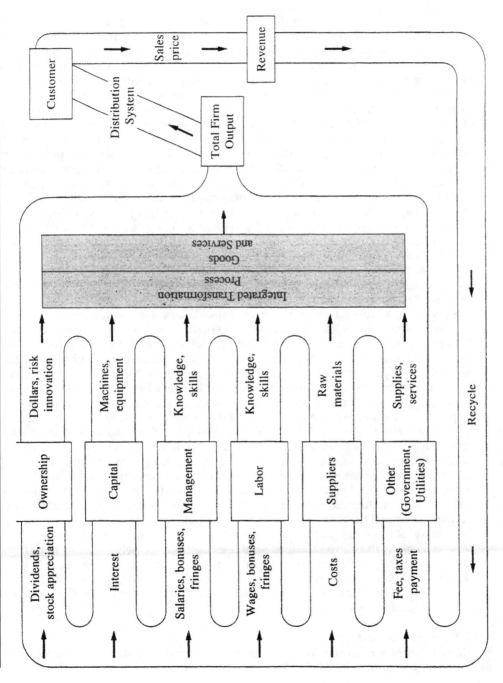

Adapted with permission from William A. Ruch and James C. Hershauer, *Factors Affecting Worker Productivity*. Tempe, Arizona: Arizona State University.

Multifactor Models

Though individual measures of productivity may be accurate, productivity is more useful when evaluated as a system of multiple factors. One example of a multifactor productivity model is the input–output model of the firm, developed by Ruch and Hershauer (1974). As shown in Figure 9-3, total productivity is a function of six general inputs: ownership, capital, management, labor, suppliers, and others, including government and utilities. However, those inputs are also constrained by the productivity of the firm, because the output is recycled as an input. This figure emphasizes why transformation must be a value-adding process. Productivity improvement is a dynamic and cyclic process, synergetically dependent upon the effects of numerous variables.

The input–output model of the firm can be related to the input–transformation–output cycle and to the logo-motif of this book. Productive resources are input from various sources, and transformed into products or services for customers. This generates revenue, which is then fed back into the system as an input. Of course, each resource is closely monitored for changes in cost, availability, and quality in each iteration.

The input-output model views productivity as an integrated, synchronous system. Few, if any, products in today's marketplace can be built with inputs from only one resource. Most products require the integration of several different contributors and, in fact, often benefit from the synergy of many different contributors. For this reason, measures of individual resource contributions, such as labor efficiency, may not be as relevant over time as an integrated multiresource measure, such as the total factor productivity measure (see Table 9-2). The individual factors do not reflect the synergy of input resource combinations. The individual labor measure would not, for example, reflect the failure or unavailability of other resource inputs, which would affect output. It is for this reason that many individual measures of productivity, such as the labor cost per unit, are flawed.

The significance of the input–output model of the firm is that it identifies the contributions and cost of each input resource, and the price of the transformed output, permitting the measurement of productivity at the facility or firm level. Productivity may be improved if less resource per unit is required from any of the contributors, or if the resource cost is reduced. For example, if labor is able to produce a greater number of units per hour or if compensation is reduced, productivity is improved. Similarly, if equipment costs less or if the interest rate paid on loans for that equipment decreases, the firm has made a productivity gain. Productivity is also improved if the price is increased. Again, however, the use of such individual measures to project expected productivity outcomes may be flawed. In this example, if compensation is reduced, productivity is improved only if labor stays on the job and continues to produce at the previous standard. From a broader perspective, the use of individual productivity measures to identify and eliminate cost-in-effective functions may be problematic because of the interactivity of the productive system (Skinner, 1986).

Of course, the real world is rarely so simple. Many such changes are occurring simultaneously and when a productivity gain is realized, it may be difficult to isolate the cause or causes. Even more fundamentally, it may not be possible to realize from week to week that productivity is changing. Additionally, because labor contributes a small and decreasing proportion of total productivity, cuts in labor (often the easiest factor to reduce) give little real benefit. Productivity measures thus are encumbered by numerous limitations. Though individual resource measures are easier to quantify, they may be less meaningful because of the synergy of multiple resources. Additionally, many resource contributors, particularly the more knowledge-intense contributors, defy accurate measurement because they frequently change or are inherently different, or because the activity itself (for example, thinking) does not lend itself to precise measurement. Productivity measurement must be used carefully to minimize these effects. Often it is used in conjunction with other evaluations or to provide a baseline.

Activity-Based Costing

The development of an activity-based costing (ABC) system assists in allocating overhead to specific cost bases, often defined as products or services. The conventional or traditional cost systems use direct material and labor consumed as the basis to factor overhead; they worked well as long as overhead activities were a small proportion of direct labor. However, because labor has been reduced by automation, overhead may now be several times the cost of direct labor. Thus, the use of direct labor as the primary apportioning mechanism can cause significant cost distortions and poor strategic decisions. ABC resolves this issue by identifying many more cost-allocation bases, including all operations resources. As such, the ABC approach is highly dependent upon accurate bills of material, routings, and work center data. The individual resource contributions are measured and aggregated in homogeneous cost pools, which are meaningful resource measures for management (Rhodes, 1992; Dhavale, 1992).

Methods of Work Measurement

With these reservations, work measurement is widely and successfully used to manage production systems and to identify areas of productivity improvements. Since the time of Frederick W. Taylor, industrial engineers have used methods, time, and measurement (MTM) studies to evaluate and categorize every type of work activity. Initially they studied the methods, time, and motions of industrial operations to determine the best way to do the job and define time standards. More recently, MTM has been used to evaluate service delivery options, such as telephone service inquiries, fast-food and full-service restaurant responsiveness, bank teller transactions, and retail checkout counter operations.

Work measurement techniques initially evaluate worker motions and collect time data to determine the best way to do a job. Numerous rules have been developed to govern efficiency of motion. These rules are helpful in placing the tools, parts bins, and other items in a work area. The work area should be designed to minimize human motion and to reduce the amount of effort required. Table 9-3 gives ten commonly used principles of motion economy.

After positioning the items in the work station, several work iterations should be practiced to ensure that the worker is familiar with the motions and setup. A particular task is usually broken down into several sequential subactivities, called *work elements*. Further adjustment and practice may be necessary before a specified work element becomes accepted. The importance of fitting the work environment to the human and to the task is directly related to performance, as the rapidly growing field of ergometrics suggests (Kroemer, 1993).

A time study measures the amount of time that each work element takes. For accuracy and convenience, the stop watches used in time studies often represent hundredths of a minute, rather than seconds. The continuous observation of several cycles of the task permits recording the continuous time for each work element. Subsequently, the individual

TABLE 9-3   Principles of Motion Economy

---

1. The two hands should begin and complete their motions at the same time.
2. The two hands should not be idle at the same time except during rest periods.
3. Hand and lower arm movements are preferred to upper arm and shoulder movements.
4. Arm motions should be simultaneous and made in opposite or symmetric directions.
5. The hand should be relieved of work that can be done by a jig, fixture, or foot-operated device.
6. Smooth, continuous motions are preferable to zigzag or irregular motions.
7. Rhythm is essential to smooth, automatic performance.
8. Tools, materials, and controls should be located close to and directly in front of the operator.
9. Gravity feed bins and containers should be used to deliver materials to the point of use.
10. Materials and tools should be located to permit the best sequence of motions.

Reprinted by permission from *Production and Operations Management* by Fogarty, Hoffman and Stonebraker, 1989, Figure 10-3, p. 346.

times of each work element are obtained by a series of subtractions. The continuous method has been traditionally preferred because it minimizes the measurement inaccuracies due to resetting a mechanical watch. However, more recently produced electronic watches and computers overcome this difficulty.

Time studies require completion of several steps. The average time is first computed for each work element, then adjusted through normalizing and standardizing. Adjustment to normalize the time is required, because a particular operator may be better or worse than "normal." Though controversial, experienced MTM evaluators have developed and published, through video tapes, normal performance rates for many work activities. Further, the normalized time must be adjusted for allowances, such as fatigue, personal needs, and unavoidable delay—for example, due to unavailability of materials. Adjustment of the normal time for allowances, usually by between 10% and 20%, gives the "standard time." An example of work measurement is shown in Decision Model Box 9-1.

In addition to the assumption of performance rates and allowances, which are often negotiated with union or labor groups, the key to work measurement accuracy is that the method has "stabilized" with low task and work element variance. Of course, changes in the employee motions, work place design, or in the technology of the job all affect the work performance. Such changes, if they result in productivity improvement, should be encouraged; however, the cost of a failed innovative method is likely a drop in productivity. Management may have to encourage innovation through explicit incentives or guarantees against loss if the innovation does not succeed.

Relevance of the Learning Curve

The learning curve measures the improvement in performance or productivity occurring over time. It may be used for evaluations of individual or group productivity improvement. If group performance is considered, cost measures are usually used, but if individual learning is considered, time measures are more common. The curve is based on the assumption that each time an operation is performed, the required time or cost decreases at a stable rate. When the number of units is doubled, the time or cost to produce one unit is reduced by 100 minus the learning rate. Experience or learning curves can be computed in many manufacturing or service environments for both individual or cumulative units produced. The curve is calculated by the following formula:

$$T_n = T_1 n^x$$

where
T_n = the time required to produce the nth unit
T_1 = the time for the first unit
n = the number of units produced

$$x = \frac{\text{natural log } L}{\text{natural log } 2}$$

L = the learning rate (in decimal)

Tables or computer programs may be used to get individual or cumulative unit times or resource costs. The learning rate (L) is initially calculated for the first several units. The measurement may be stated as the amount of time per unit or the number of units per period of time. For example, if the first unit time was 20 minutes and the time to produce the second unit was 18 minutes, the learning rate would be 18/20, or 90%. Alternatively, the improvement in units produced per day or week may be used. For example, the first-week (40 hours) production of 40 units and the fourth-week production of 62.5 units would be converted to per-unit-times, respectively, of 1 hour and 0.64 hour, which is an 80% ($1 \times 0.8 \times 0.8$) learning curve.

Commonly encountered learning rates are 75%, 80%, 85%, and 90%, where 75% means that when the number of units is doubled, the processing time of the later unit is 75% of that of the earlier unit. This, of course, is a faster learning rate than, for example, is 90%.

The learning curve is useful (1) to estimate production costs of custom jobs, (2) to assess the duration of the start-up stage for a new process, (3) to determine how long it will

DECISION MODEL BOX 9-1   Work Measurement at the Mid-Continental Bank

The Mid-Continental Bank wants to evaluate the times of several teller transactions. One task, the crediting of cash to an account, has been studied and a description of standard motions and five work elements has been developed. The bank's security camera film was used as a source of time data, because it is less intrusive or disruptive than a work measurement engineer with a stop watch. Continuous time data are observed for 10 complete cycles of work. The continuous data are adjusted to unit times through a series of subtractions. For example, the work element unit time of cycle 1, element 2 is 0.156 minute, computed as $0.408 - 0.252 = 0.156$.

Cycle Number	Work Element Continuous Times (min)					Cycle Number	Work Element Unit Times (min)				
	1	2	3	4	5		1	2	3	4	5
1	0.252	0.408	0.591	0.690	0.808	1	0.252	0.156	0.183	0.099	0.118
2	1.049	1.214	1.386	1.488	1.601	2	0.241	0.165	0.172	0.102	0.113
3	1.854	2.016	2.191	2.296	2.415	3	0.253	0.162	0.175	0.105	0.119
4	2.655	2.813	2.990	3.090	3.204	4	0.240	0.158	0.177	0.100	0.114
5	3.449	3.610	3.788	3.889	4.006	5	0.245	0.161	0.178	0.101	0.117
6	4.253	4.412	4.594	4.694	4.809	6	0.247	0.159	0.182	0.100	0.115
7	5.060	5.217	5.394	5.498	5.614	7	0.251	0.157	0.177	0.104	0.116
8	5.860	6.018	6.197	6.299	6.416	8	0.246	0.158	0.179	0.102	0.117
9	6.660	6.819	7.000	7.103	7.216	9	0.244	0.159	0.181	0.103	0.113
10	7.466	7.626	7.806	7.906	8.021	10	0.250	0.160	0.180	0.100	0.115
						Avg.	0.2469	0.1595	0.1784	0.1016	0.1157

The data then are adjusted for performance ratings and total allowances by using the formulas:

Normal time = average time × performance rate (a measured or bargained value)

Standard time = normal time × percent allowances (18% is assumed here)

The standard time is computed for both work elements and tasks. Because there may be some variances and possibly error in the measurement of each work element, the number of required cycles to observe for confidence in the stability of the data is computed. That evaluation uses the formula:

$$n = \frac{Z^2 S_x^2}{e^2}$$

where Z = the standard score of the confidence interval (for example, 2 for 95%, 3 for 99%)

Sx = the sample standard deviation for a small sample, the formula for which is

$$S_x = \sqrt{\frac{\Sigma(x_i - \bar{x})^2}{(n-1)}}$$

e = the acceptable measurement error

If the acceptable error in measuring task times is 0.003 minute (which is 0.18 second or about one-fifth of a second error for activities that average from 6 to 15 seconds) and the confidence interval is 99%, the necessary cycles to measure for this data are shown.

Work Element	Average Time	Performance Rating	Normal Time	Standard Time	Standard Deviation	Necessary Cycles
1	0.2469	0.95	0.2346	0.2768	0.0043	18.5 ≈ 19
2	0.1595	1.10	0.1755	0.2071	0.0025	6.3 ≈ 7
3	0.1784	1.00	0.1784	0.2105	0.0032	10.3 ≈ 11
4	0.1016	0.90	0.0914	0.1079	0.0019	3.6 ≈ 4
5	0.1157	1.05	0.1215	0.1434	0.0020	4.0 ≈ 4

The analyst would conclude that the task standard time is just less than one minute, or about 63 tasks per hour. Based on the 99% confidence level and the range of acceptable error of 0.003 minute, the work elements would require between 4 and 19 cycles of observations, as indicated. Because in this case the standard deviation of the work element unit times is small, other measures can be relatively tight ($Z = 3$; $e = 0.003$) and the necessary cycles to measure remains quite small. In fact, all elements except 1 and 3 would require less than the ten cycles already measured.

take to train or certify a new employee on a piece of equipment, and (4) to evaluate individual or organization productivity improvement over the long run. Improvements may be due to any of several factors, including the use of better methods, increased familiarity with work motions, more labor effort, and changes in the technology, such as the use of a mechanical assist. Motivational effects, such as might result from the presence of a study team, cannot be evaluated by using the learning curve method. Early studies cited by Hirschmann (1964) show stable improvement in learning rates in a variety of applications, including petroleum refining production, repetitive maintenance operations, construction of new units of heavy equipment, and in steel and electricity output. These studies consistently showed roughly the same rates over as much as 55 years. An example of the use of the learning curve is shown in Decision Model Box 9-2.

However, there are limitations of the learning curve. The most apparent limit is that the learning rate may change, either by leveling off or by toeing down, as a result of a change in the technology, work methods, incentives, or other resource inputs. Additionally, projecting the curve too far into the future may be very risky. If such future projections are necessary, conservative improvement rates might be selected, and regular reevaluation of the learning rates should be considered.

There is, however, another more subtle problem with the learning curve. Technology and innovation do not typically change at a constant rate. Rather, rates of change are often quite stable for long periods of time, then irregularly punctuated by significant technological developments. Additionally, if workers do not do a task for a period of time, they may forget and would be slower when they return to the task. Further, the learning curve may encourage a short-term perspective by rewarding ways to achieve minor improvements that ensure the accomplishment of limited improvement goals, but avoid the potentially risky and costly transitions to major new technologies. This perspective, elaborated by Abernathy and Wayne (1974) and Bell and Burnham (1989), can result in missing the chance to implement the periodic major improvements or technological innovations. The outcome is a likely decline in the technological innovation and long-term productivity and competitiveness.

Work measurement evaluates the fit of the individual with the physical activities of the task or, if the tasks are sequential and repetitive enough, a job. Work measurement techniques are difficult to use with knowledge contributions and are best used after the task has stabilized—that is, after learning improvements have ceased, or have become relatively small. Learning curves measure the amount of improvement in job performance. Though some of these improvements may be caused by working harder or faster, most improvements, particularly over the long run, result from improved methods, technological assists,

DECISION MODEL BOX 9-2   The Learning Curve—Product and Process Costing at The Wadsworth Garage

The Wadsworth Garage has been asked to bid on a required farm implement modification. It is estimated that 100 units will be modified in the first year. Experience with similar jobs indicates that Wadsworth mechanics have a roughly 80% learning rate for the first 50 units; but for estimation purposes, the company assumes no further improvement. Engineers estimate that the first unit will take 30 hours. The bid should be based on labor costs of $24/hour, parts costs of $15 per unit, overhead of $10/unit, and a 10% profit margin.

The learning curve table suggests that, with an 80% learning rate, the first 50 units will take 30 × 20.122 (the first unit time multiplied by the cumulative learning rate factor, a table value) or 604 hours, and that subsequent units will take 30 × 0.284 (the first unit time multiplied by the per-unit learning rate factor, a table value) or 8.520 hours each. Note that any learning rate may be evaluated by dividing the hours per unit for a designated period by the hours per unit for the first period and finding the table value for that designated period which most closely corresponds to the calculated value. Costing for the first 50 units is:

Labor	Materials	Overhead		Total	
30 × 20.122 × $24	$15 × 50	$10 × 50			
$14,487.84 +	$750 +	$500	=	$15,737.84	
			× 0.10	1,573.78	margin
				17,311.62	

For each subsequent unit:

Labor	Materials	Overhead		Total	
8.250 × $24					
$204.48 +	$15 +	$10	=	$229.48	
			× 0.10	22.93	margin
				252.41	

The unit and cumulative learning curves are given below.

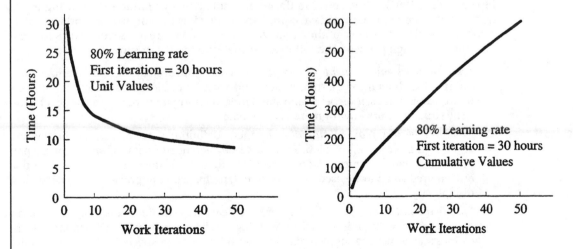

CHAPTER 9   PRODUCTIVITY AND WORK FORCE MANAGEMENT   275

and knowledge contributions. This was also suggested by the 100-year productivity improvement data cited at the beginning of the chapter. These techniques are generally most accurate when used to evaluate individual or possibly small group productivity, though they can be used with care in applications with larger work teams, shifts, plants, and companies. Work measurement and learning curve analysis provide the initial baseline measures for productivity studies.

JOB DESIGN

Job design efforts define and integrate the activities of an individual worker with those of other team members and with the rest of the organization. Though job design does focus on one job, or on a class of jobs, it is also concerned with identifying the source of all inputs to the job and the use of all outputs from the job. This information about the inputs and outputs of a job permits specification of the interactions required by the job with other jobs and functions.

Job Design Process

Job design is a multistep process of assessing the work environment and the job, and then enumerating the specific knowledge, skills, abilities, effort, and working conditions required of the job. Subsequently, the hiring activities design a "rite of passage" to reinforce the person–organization fit. This process reaffirms the employment decision (Bowen et al., 1991). Concisely, job design is a consciously planned structuring of the work effort to define what task is accomplished, how it is accomplished, and with what standards, within the fabric of the organization. Though there are several ways to organize the job-design process, the following three sequential steps are often used:

Assess the work environment—the systematic collection, evaluation, and organization of information about the work environment and activities of a job. This job analysis process uses questionnaires, interviews, and standardized information formats to gather and initially structure work environment and job data.

Infer the type of employee required—the concise definition of the responsibilities, duties, and working conditions of a job. This job description document is often the formal part of the employment contract; it defines the individual performances and interactions that are required and may be used for recruitment, performance appraisal, and, if necessary, disciplinary actions.

Specify the individual job—the further specification of the demands of a job, in terms of knowledge, skills, abilities, effort, working conditions, and other factors. Job specifications may be used to supplement job descriptions for very specialized jobs or for training or reinforcement purposes.

Figure 9-4   A Historical Perspective of Job Specialization

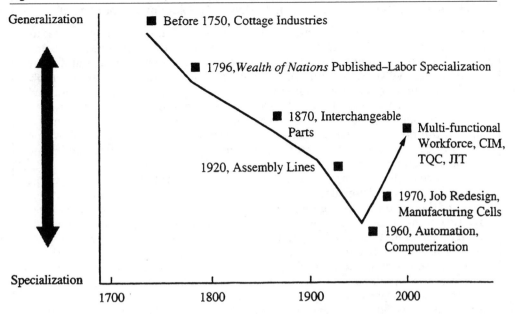

Some organizations ask newly hired employees to write or rewrite their own job descriptions, a technique which ensures that the employee is familiar with the job requirements and facilitates internalization of those requirements, but gives an employee the opportunity to suggest innovative ways to perform the job. Historically, over much of the past 200 years, jobs have become increasingly specialized; however, several recent developments suggest a reversal of that direction. The historical growth of specialization in job design is shown by Figure 9-4.

Early production was very generalized. That is, a worker did all or most of the tasks required to produce a finished good. That same worker also performed the distribution and retailing functions. Adam Smith may have been the first to formally identify the benefits of labor specialization in the *Wealth of Nations*. Work became increasingly specialized as the efficiencies of standardized parts and standardized assembly processes became apparent. With job redefinition, the work contribution of an individual to the total product became smaller and more specialized. Mechanized and power assists to production, work automation, and early computerization furthered this trend toward specialization; however, automation and computerization also permit redesigning jobs toward more generalized skills. Computer-integrated manufacturing systems and distributed information systems define a greater range of individual tasks required for a job and more generalized labor contribution. The emergence of JIT, CIM, TQC, and the multifunctional work force suggests that this trend will continue, if not increase.

Generalization Versus Specialization

There are likely limits to the amount of specialization that labor can tolerate. Job redesign was suggested in the late 1950s as a way to enrich the breadth and depth of the content of the job, thus increasing the scope of a specialist's activities. It was seen as a way of countering the increasing boredom and more serious symptoms of labor resistance to faster job cycles and increasingly specialized, repetitive jobs. Application Box 9-2 describes job redesign efforts at Volvo.

There are advantages of both specialization and generalization. Advantages of specialization include increased productivity due to repetition, lower skill requirements and

APPLICATION BOX 9-2   Work Teams at Volvo: An Experiment That Failed

In August 1988, Volvo began manufacturing cars with a humanistic approach at its plant in Uddevalla, Sweden. This was Volvo's second redesigned manufacturing plant. The Kalmar plant was redesigned in the late 1970s to build trucks and some sedan models. Volvo was the first large-scale manufacturer to abolish the assembly line from its production process and to shape its factory jobs to be more generalized and team-oriented. At Uddevalla the team of workers spent an average of two to three hours building a car. This is drastically different from the traditional assembly-line environment, where specialization of jobs drives each worker to repeat the same task throughout an eight-hour shift and spend between thirty seconds and three minutes on each passing car.

Plagued by the highest turnover and absenteeism rates of the developed nations, Volvo executives envisioned that by encouraging Swedish workers to increase their range of skills and thus giving them more control over their jobs, working in a car manufacturing factory would become less monotonous and more personally rewarding. This generalization of jobs would result in increased productivity due to satisfaction and less absenteeism, tardiness, and turnover. The team approach necessitated the elimination of many of the middle management and supervisor jobs, plus the installation of revolutionary materials-handling methods.

The Uddevalla facility consists of two complexes with three small assembly plants, which are connected by an L-shaped building. Painted car bodies and parts are carried on an electric transporter through the L-shaped structure, where the larger components, such as exhaust systems, fuel tanks, and axles are assembled. The 650 to 700 required car parts are transported to the assembly teams by other electric carriers. In the middle of each complex, a shared area exists for the three small assembly plants to test assembled cars. The last stop before distribution is the L-shaped building, where the paint receives a final inspection, and rust protection and grease are added.

A total of eight teams, consisting of eight to ten highly skilled workers, work in each of the six assembly areas. With three or less people working on a car, each team builds four cars at one time. The 48 teams were expected to manufacture 40,000 cars per year. However, because the factory has used only 35 assembly teams and those teams took longer than expected to develop their individual production pattern, the 1990 production total was a mere 16,100 cars.

Volvo's executives have claimed that the quality of work life at Uddevalla has been augmented and the plant's 900 workers seem more content. Unfortunately, dismal productivity levels have caused top management to periodically reevaluate the team approach. For the first time in a decade, in 1990, Volvo's car division posted a loss; further losses occurred in 1991 and for 1992. In late 1992, Volvo president Sören Gyll announced that the company will close the Kalmar and Uddevalla plants. Even though some advantages of generalized job tasks have been evident, the company cannot be successful in the long term with factories that are not competitive. Unfortunately, the Kalmar and Uddevalla plants may be regarded by management historians as interesting but unprofitable social experiments. It appears that there are limits to the amount that a production process can be adjusted.

It is interesting to note that the General Motors Spring Hill Saturn Plant has retained the moving assembly line, but has incorporated a variety of team and group tasks. Clearly, the interaction of teams in monotonous task situations reduces boredom and improves productivity. The production process, however, also must be economic. Companies are expected to continue to search for the combination of human resources and technology that best facilitate profitable labor.

Materials drawn from Steven Prokesch, "Kinder, Gentler Plant a Failure," *Chicago Tribune*, July 14, 1991, p. 5, and from Richard A. Melcher, "Volvo and Renault: Marriage May Be the Only Answer," *Business Week*, November 23, 1992, p. 50–52.

thus lower wage costs, and simpler management processes due to routinization. Labor issues in such an environment would be likely to be simpler to define. However, the disadvantages of greater specialization include employee dissatisfaction, the boredom of repetitive work cycles, and the corresponding higher levels of absenteeism, tardyism, and turnover. Higher grievance rates and low-quality work due to lower employee incentives, motivation, and accountability, and less operations flexibility due to more narrowly defined jobs would likely also result. These disadvantages of specialization correspond to the advantages of more generalized jobs.

These pure job-design strategies identify a range of job-redesign options, but the actual strategy would likely be some combination of specialization and generalization. One approach is to design the job to fit the needs of the work force, as Volvo has attempted at Uddevalla and Kalmar. The alternative strategy is to reassert the engineering and scientific management goals of fitting people to the job. Redesigning the job to fit employee needs tends toward the employee-centered involvement style noted in Figure 9-1; fitting the people to the job more closely corresponds to the boss-centered direction style in that figure. Many compromise alternatives have been developed, including the Saturn plant work teams. In each environment, in each job and task, and with each employee, the management function is to get the best fit of job requirements, employee needs, and management style. This fit is the basis for an ongoing discourse between management and labor.

JOB REDESIGN FOR QUALITY OF WORK LIFE

Quality of work life (QWL) programs were developed in the 1970s as a systems approach to job redesign. QWL was expected to integrate various individual, structural, environmental, and technology factors in the job-redesign process. These programs go by a variety of names, including employee involvement, participative management, and team building. QWL can be more concisely defined as "processes by which an organization attempts to unlock the creative potential of its people by involving them in discussions affecting their work lives" (Guest, 1979).

Components of Quality of Work Life Programs

This very general definition reflects the highly individualized nature of QWL programs; each of the thousands of successful programs have been situationally defined. Though there is no set formula for a QWL program, the following characteristics are commonly encountered.

Job Redesign and Participative Management.   Job-redesign initiatives often define jobs toward more general tasks and greater participation in the decision-making processes of the job. Job redesign enhances the perceived job freedom and potentially increases involvement and internalization of job functions and tasks by employees. Decisions about how to do the job are done by those who, because they are closest to the situations, are best able to make the decision. This can be a positive motivator and, with appropriate work force training, can reduce one or several layers of management. Greater participation in the decision-making processes, however, ensures greater inherent employee training and commitment.

Innovative Rewards and Compensation Structures.   Innovative rewards and compensation structures may be designed to more directly measure productivity and identify and reward contributions to productivity and overall firm performance. Individual and group incentive plans quickly emerged after work activities were shown to be measurable in the 1920s and 1930s. Initial methods tied productivity to pay through sometimes complex mechanical formulations. More recent plans have included cafeteria benefits programs and flexible work schedules. Lincoln Electric, an excellent example of the productivity effects of gain-sharing methods, incorporates peer evaluation to define the proportion of the annual bonus received by each employee. Lincoln Electric has survived for more than 60 years, partly because of the effectiveness of its gains-sharing plan, which pays more in annual productivity bonuses than in annual salaries (Hillinger, 1983).

Enhancing a Climate of Workplace Democracy. The mechanisms of workplace democracy include employee ownership, employee stock ownership plans, worker self-management, and participative or empowered work environments. Stock ownership plans have been quite successful, with participation ranging from 15% to 35% of the outstanding stock ("Labor's Voice . . . ," 1984). However, worker self-management efforts have been resisted due to the feeling that employee groups are not able to manage themselves. Participative theory Z (Ouchi, 1981) work environments, because they facilitate trust and consensual, participative decision-making, have been widely sponsored, though they may give more aura of participation than substance. Certainly, QWL programs, however defined, have the potential to be major contributors to productivity improvement efforts, but such efforts must be carefully planned to achieve consistency and fit of the worker with the job, and by extension, with the environment.

Developing a Productivity Improvement Program

Clearly, productivity improvement is a multifaceted, difficult-to-measure, and continuous management task. Most managers would concur with Vaughn Beals' statement, quoted earlier, that productivity measurement "is a total frustration." Because of the vagueness and difficulty of measurement, the dynamics of the variables involved, and the continuous and cyclic nature of the process, most managers regard models of productivity with well-deserved skepticism. Yet, simultaneously, the skeptics are not able to offer reasonable alternatives, and at the end of the month, quarter, or year, management must be able to show measured improvement relative to prior performance or relative to the competition. Thus, productivity measurement is accepted for corporations or plants because performance must be measured, if only to avoid surprises and to permit early planning of necessary corrective actions. Additionally, performance measures must be tied to strategic objectives. Perhaps the best approach is to develop the most inclusive, interactive, and accurate measure possible, and then to recognize and understand its limits. The productivity paradigm, shown in Figure 9-5, reflects these limitations of productivity models. The paradigm shows a general model of the interaction of some of the more recognized contributing variables to productivity in a continuous improvement cycle.

Six general factors are depicted, each with several subfactors. The diagram moves from smaller-scale individual factors at the top to broader-scale corporate and external factors at the bottom. Though an effort has been made toward succinctness and to avoid elaboration and duplication, certainly other factors and subfactors could be included, particularly in specific applications. Productivity results from the synergy of all factors and most, if not all, subfactors. That is, each factor simultaneously makes a contribution which, when grouped with the others, achieves its effect. Correspondingly, the failure of any factor, such as the reward or material use, will very quickly, though often subtly, result in a decline of overall productivity. The productivity paradigm is related to the productivity formula and the input–transformation–output motif, because each of the factors is an input to the transformation process. This representation emphasizes both the central contribution of people to productivity and the simultaneous contribution of other factors. Productivity management necessitates regular vigilance over all input resources. As Davis (1991) notes, the main reasons for productivity improvement failure ultimately can be ascribed to ineffective integration of people and knowledge.

Figure 9-5 The Productivity Paradigm

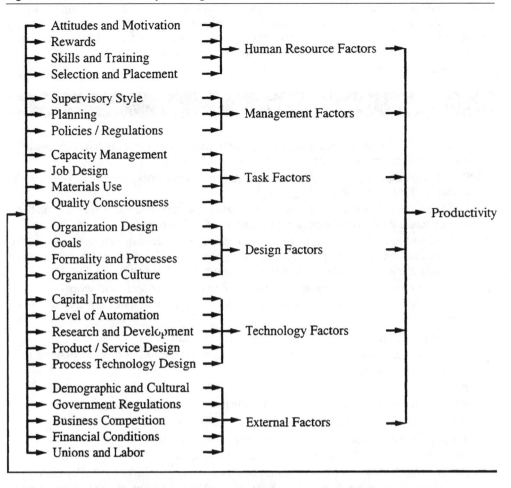

SUMMARY

Productivity is about transforming inputs into outputs; in the process, in the process, value is added to those outputs. Productivity may be evaluated by any of several measures of output divided by inputs, though such measures must be used carefully. Because people are direct contributors through labor to productivity, and indirect contributors to capital, materials, knowledge, and other resources, people are the most important contributors to productivity and to new sources of added value. As labor has become increasingly specialized over the past 200 or more years, management has increasingly moved toward a style of empowerment, a technique that encourages innovation.

Productivity ultimately must be viewed as a system; the manipulation of one variable will likely have little effect, unless accompanied by corresponding changes in other variables. This is the productivity paradox (Skinner, 1986). Because of the synergistic nature of operations processes and productivity improvement, management efforts should not be directed toward squeezing more work out of labor, but rather toward total system improvement and fit. Work measurement and productivity improvement due to worker and team experience are described, and the limitations of these methods are noted. Job design and redesign methods can make a contribution to productivity, but even those techniques are probably best used as part of a QWL program.

The productivity paradigm summarizes the dilemma by representing some of the variables that can be incorporated in a specific productivity improvement program, the interactivity and synergy of those variables, and the iterativeness of productivity efforts. Though technology, capital, and external factors all contribute to productivity, ultimately, as noted in the introductory quote, "People are the catalysts that stimulate new productivity."

DISCUSSION QUESTIONS

1. From your work experiences, give examples of management, labor, and/or capital methods used to increase productivity.
2. Productivity equals production outcome divided by resources consumed. Give several examples of each component.
3. Briefly describe how the information organization has replaced the industrial organization by relating this transformation to a business familiar to you.
4. Identify and describe an organization that consists primarily of diverse specialists. Then give the four management problems which, according to Drucker, are inherent in such organizations and apply those ideas to the organization that you have selected.
5. How does productivity fit into the rationale for economies of scale and scope?
6. Explain why the transformation stage of the input–output model must be a value-added process.
7. What is the significance of the input–output model of the firm?
8. From your work experiences, briefly describe a job that applies some or all of the principles of motion economy.
9. What can the learning curve accomplish in service management organizations?
10. Why is it risky to project the learning curve more than several units or months into the future?
11. List and define the three sequential steps of the job-design process.
12. Identify the advantages of specialization versus generalization.
13. From your own experiences or readings, describe a quality of work life program.
14. List and briefly describe the six general factors included in the productivity paradigm. Describe a specific work situation and relate the six factors to productivity in that situation.

STRATEGIC DECISION SITUATIONS

1. The Riverside Campus of Central State University has been required to reorganize due to budget cuts. The dean of the College of Arts and Sciences must manage the reduction of the number of departments from 13 to eight. Several departments are very small; thus, the consolidation would reduce overhead (department chair positions). But the dean expects resistance from the faculty, many of whom are tenured. The dean also desires to use the normal events in the university calendar as driving forces to implement the change. Identify the restraining and driving forces and relate those forces to the university calendar.
2. The Global Health Care Corporation manufactures surgical instruments and packages them in kits that are designed for specific types of operations. For disease prevention and sterilization reasons, the kits are disposable, even though some components could be sterilized and reused. The Deerfield Surgical Instrument Manufacturing Facility produces most of the nonplastic components (primarily some form of blade or scissor) for such kits. To improve efficiency, a major portion of the facility will be redesigned from a

line process to a U-shaped work center design. Previous work measurement of the line found that for 60 work elements (one for each employee on the line), the production time was 0.52 minute per instrument, with minor variations in time due to different instrument configurations. The facility was able to produce roughly 500 instruments per day. In prototype demonstrations, the production manager showed the following times for five consolidated work elements of the U-shaped facility. The plant manager is considering the use of either three or four such five-person U-shaped production centers. If 18% total allowances are used, and the performance rating for all activities is 1.05, and the acceptable error is 0.005 minute (0.3 second), with a 95% confidence interval, evaluate the U-shaped design in the following ways:

a. Advise the production manager on the number of U-shaped cells that should be designed.

Cycle Number	Work Element—Continuous Times (min)				
	1	2	3	4	5
1	1.235	1.681	2.406	2.639	3.454
2	4.723	4.953	5.501	5.855	6.210
3	7.589	8.255	8.862	8.964	9.672
4	10.649	11.382	11.978	12.151	12.802
5	14.004	14.692	15.462	15.562	15.881
6	17.458	17.742	18.473	18.543	19.205
7	20.273	21.098	21.704	22.156	22.563
8	23.635	24.258	24.872	25.225	25.987
9	27.469	27.586	28.394	28.909	29.200
10	30.505	30.873	31.713	32.382	33.303

b. The corporate vice president of operations, a rather traditionally oriented manufacturing type, has expressed concern over the potential ramifications of this redesign. Provide comments that will place this action in perspective.

3. The Triquest Development Corporation plans to build a meat processing plant in the Tver Valley of the Russian Republic (roughly 100 miles northwest of Moscow). Local stock will be improved by the import of chickens, pigs, and heifers from the American heartland, and three separate slaughterhouse operations will be designed in one factory based on American models. Plans call for the plant to be built in the spring of 1995 and for operations to begin in August. Technology will be improved and training upgraded regularly, and distribution will be accomplished through privatized stores and Russian Orthodox Church charities. The following average daily production per week is expected during initial start-up.

Stock	Number of Employees	Week			
		1	2	3	4
Chickens	10	500	650	750	800
Pigs	10	100	130	150	200
Heifers	10	50	70	80	90

Hint: the data are most useful for learning curve analysis if they are converted to hours per unit of production per employee, and learning is considered from work to work.

a. Calculate the learning rates for chickens, pigs, and heifers.

b. Use learning curve analysis to project the daily production of the plant per week (assume 40 hours per week) in each commodity for the eighth week (end of November), sixteenth week (mid-January), and thirty-second week (early May).

c. Discuss some of the limitations of this analysis.

REFERENCES

Abernathy, William J., and Kenneth Wayne. "Limits of the Learning Curve," *Harvard Business Review*. September–October 1974.

Albin, Peter S. "Job Design, Control Technology, and Technical Change," *Journal of Economic Issues*. September 1985, pp. 703–730.

Andrew, Charles G. "Motivation in Manufacturing," *Production and Inventory Management*. April–June 1986, pp. 133–142.

Bell, Daniel. *Toward the Year 2000, Work in Progress*. Boston, Mass.: Beacon Press, 1969.

Bell, Robert R., and John M. Burnham. "The Paradox of Manufacturing Productivity and Innovation," *Business Horizons*. September–October 1989, pp. 58–64.

Bowen, David E., Gerald E. Ledford, Jr., and Barry R. Nathan. "Hiring for the Organization, Not the Job," *The Executive*. Vol. 5, No. 4, 1991, pp. 35–51.

Buffa, Elwood S. "Meeting the Competitive Challenge with Manufacturing Strategy," *National Productivity Review*. Spring 1985, pp. 155–169.

Byrne, John A. "The Horizontal Corporation," *Business Week*. December 20, 1993, pp. 76–81.

Cappelli, Peter. "The Changing Face of Labor–Management Relations," *Management Review*. March 1986, pp. 28–30.

Chakravarthy, Balaji S. "Measuring Strategic Performance," *Strategic Management Journal*. Vol. 7, No. 5, 1986, pp. 437–458.

Davis, Tim R. V. "Information Technology and White Collar Productivity," *The Executive*. Vol. 5, No. 1, 1991, pp. 55–68.

Deets, Norman, and Richard Morano. "Xerox's Strategy for Changing Management Styles," *Management Review*. March 1986, pp. 31–35.

Dhavale, Dileep. "Activity-Based Costing in Cellular Manufacturing Systems," *Industrial Engineering*. February 1992, pp. 44–46.

Drucker, Peter F. "The Coming of the New Organization," *Harvard Business Review*. January–February 1988, pp. 45.

Drucker, Peter F. *The New Realities: In Government and Politics/in Economics and Business/in Society and World View*. New York: Harper and Row, Publishers, 1989.

Drucker, Peter F. "There's More Than One Kind of Team," *Wall Street Journal*. February 11, 1992.

Ellis, James E., and Bruce Einhorn. "Gone Is My Co-Pilot?" *Business Week*. July 6, 1992, pp. 71–72.

Fogarty, Donald W., Thomas R. Hoffmann, and Peter W. Stonebraker. *Production and Operations Management*. Cincinnati, Ohio: South-Western Publishing Co., 1989.

Guest, Robert H. "Quality of Work Life—Learning from Tarrytown," *Harvard Business Review*. July–August 1979, pp. 76–77.

Hall, Robert W. "Empowerment: The 1990s Manufacturing Enterprise," *APICS—The Performance Advantage*, July 1991, p. 26.

Hayes, Robert H., and Steven C. Wheelwright. *Restoring Our Competitive Edge: Competing Through Manufacturing*. New York: John Wiley and Sons, 1984.

Heizer, Jay, and Barry Render. *Production and Operations Management*. Boston, Mass.: Allyn and Bacon, 1991.

Hillinger, Charles. "Big Bonuses at Lincoln Electric Get Big Results," *Professional Trainer*. Winter 1983, p. 1.

Jaques, Elliot. "In Praise of Hierarchy," *Harvard Business Review*. January–February 1990, pp. 127–133.

Kiernan, Matthew J. "The New Strategic Architecture: Learning to Compete in the Twenty-first Century," *Academy of Management Executive*. Vol. 7, No. 1, 1993, pp. 7–21.

Kroemer, K. E. H. "Fitting the Workplace to the Human and Not Vice Versa," *Industrial Engineering*. Vol. 25, No. 3, March 1993, pp. 56–62.

"Labor's Voice on Corporate Boards: Good or Bad?" *Business Week*. May 7, 1984, pp. 151–153.

Lewin, Kurt. *Field Theory in Social Science: Selected Theoretical Papers.* New York: Harper and Brothers, 1951.

Lynch, David J. "Turbulence Dogs Douglas Overhaul," *Chicago Tribune.* September 9, 1991, Section 4, p. 1.

McGregor, Douglas. *The Human Side of Enterprise.* New York: McGraw-Hill, 1960.

Melcher, Richard A. "Volvo and Renault: Marriage May Be the Only Answer," *Business Week.* November 23, 1992, pp. 50–52.

Michel, John G., and Donald C. Hambrick. "Diversification Posture and Top Management Team Characteristics," *The Academy of Management Journal.* Vol. 35, No. 1, 1992, pp. 9–37.

Naisbitt, John. *Megatrends.* New York: Warner Books, 1982.

Ouchi, William. *Theory Z: How American Business Can Meet the Japanese Challenge.* Reading, Mass.: Addison-Wesley, 1981.

Prokesch, Steven. "Kinder, Gentler Plant a Failure," *Chicago Tribune.* July 14, 1991, p. 5.

Rhodes, Philip. "Activity-Based Costing," *APICS—The Performance Advantage.* August 1992, pp. 29–31.

Ruch, William A., and James C. Hershauer. *Factors Affecting Worker Productivity.* Tempe, Arizona: Bureau of Business and Economic Research, Arizona State University, 1974.

Schein, Edgar H. *Organizational Psychology*, 3rd ed. Englewood Cliffs, N. J.: Prentice Hall, 1980.

Skinner, Wickham. "The Anachronistic Factory," *Harvard Business Review.* January–February 1971, pp. 61–70.

Skinner, Wickham. "The Productivity Paradox," *Management Review.* September 1986.

Stonebraker, Peter W. *Exercises and Problems in Human Resource Management: Using the Microcomputer:* New York: McGraw-Hill, 1989.

Toffler, Alvin. *Future Shock.* New York: Bantam, 1971.

Vora, Jay A. "Productivity and Performance Measures: Who Uses Them?" *Production and Inventory Management Journal.* January–March 1992, pp. 46–49.

Werther, William B., William A. Ruch, and Lynne McClure. *Productivity Through People.* St. Paul, Minn.: West Publishing Co., 1986.

Wiersema, Margarethe F., and Karen A. Bantel. "Top Management Team Demography and Corporate Strategic Change," *The Academy of Management Journal.* Vol. 35, No. 1, 1992, pp. 91–121.

Willis, Rod. "Harley Davidson Comes Roaring Back," *Management Review.* March 1986, p. 20.

CHAPTER 10

Developing a Manufacturing Strategy—Principles and Concepts

Companies invest in a wide range of functions and capabilities to make and sell products at a profit. Consequently, the degree to which a company's functions are aligned to the needs of its markets will significantly affect its overall revenue growth and profit. The appropriate investment in processes and infrastructure in manufacturing is fundamental to this success and a lack of fit between these key investments and a company's markets will lead to a business being well wide of the mark. If a company could change its manufacturing capabilities without incurring penalties such as long delays and large reinvestments, then the strategic decisions within manufacturing would be of little concern or consequence. However, nothing could be further from the truth. Many executives are still unaware "that what appear to be routine manufacturing decisions frequently come to limit the corporation's strategic options, binding it with facilities, equipment, personnel, basic controls, and policies to a noncompetitive posture, which may take years to turn round."[1]

---

[1] W. Skinner, "Manufacturing—Missing Link in Corporate Strategy," *Harvard Business Review*, May-June 1969, p. 13.

The compelling reasons to ensure fit are tied to the very nature of manufacturing process and infrastructure investments, which are invariably large and fixed. They are large in terms of the size of the investment ($s) and fixed in that it takes a long time to agree, sanction, and implement these decisions in the first instance and even longer to agree to change them. Companies having invested inappropriately cannot afford to put things right. The financial implications, systems development, training requirements, and the time to make the changes would leave the company, at best, seriously disadvantaged. To avoid this problem, companies need to be aware of how well manufacturing can support the marketplace and be conscious of the investments and time dimensions involved in changing current positions into future proposals.

FUNCTIONAL STRATEGIES

In most companies, corporate strategy statements are a compilation of functional strategies and nothing more. They are derived independently both of one another and the corporate whole (see Figure 10-1).

Charged with developing strategies for their own parts of a business, functions such as research and development, marketing, manufacturing, and engineering prepare their strategy statements independently. The result is a comprehensive list of functional statements that are then put together as the strategy for the corporate whole. However, companywide debate rarely concerns how these fit together or assesses their support of agreed markets. Congruence is assumed and is given credence by the use of broad descriptions of strategy that, instead of providing clarity and the means of testing fit, wash over the debate in generalities.

Through debate and challenge, functional strategies must be developed that support agreed markets with consistency between the various parts of a business. Only in this way can coherent strategies be forged that align all functions to support the business. Thus, corporate strategy is the outcome of functional strategies and can only be achieved by integration across the functional boundaries; corporate strategy, then, is both the binding mechanism for and the end result of this process (see Figure 10-2). Thus, all the functions within a business need to be party to agreeing on the blueprint of corporate strategy. They are then party to the debate and its resolution that facilitates the identification of the individual strategies necessary to support agreed direction and for which each function takes responsibility.

FIGURE 10-1 Functional Strategies Are Developed Independently of One Another and the Corporate Whole

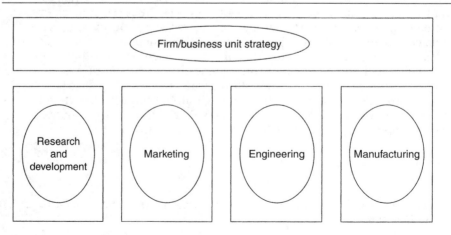

FIGURE 10-2 Integrating Functional Strategies and Forging the Corporate Strategic Outcome

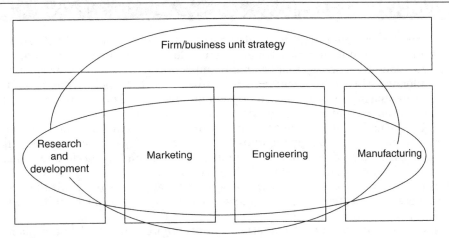

STRATEGIES VERSUS PHILOSOPHIES

Strategies concern supporting markets. Therefore, functions that have the principal or shared responsibility for providing the needs of markets have to develop a strategy to undertake those tasks. Many companies, however, have failed to recognize this link. Consequently, all functions (irrespective of whether or not they have responsibility for directly supporting a company's markets) have been asked to provide strategic statements as an input into the overall strategy of the firm. Companies have failed to distinguish between strategies (actions to directly support markets) and philosophies (preferred ways of accomplishing tasks or approaches to elements of management).

This approach has added to the confusion. Philosophies have been mixed in with strategies. For example, R&D's strategic inputs may concern issues such as product design and material substitution; marketing's issues may include branding, pricing, and customer relations; manufacturing's may include delivery reliability, price, and quality conformance; and engineering's may include process development and technical support. However, other functions do not have a strategic role per se.

For example, human resources, accounting, and finance provide essential inputs to a business, but invariably, they have neither the principal nor shared responsibility for any factors in a company's markets and consequently would not have a strategic role. However, their role is not insignificant. On the contrary, their inputs are essential and far reaching. They are, though, in the form of philosophical statements about approaches that enhance the overall ability of a company to undertake and fulfill its operational and strategic tasks.

Why argue for this distinction? The reason is to increase a company's awareness of what strategy is, which functions are responsible for providing the relevant dimensions, and the key role of other functions to help in this task. Until companies sharpen their awareness of the necessity to understand markets, identify the functions with prime responsibility for providing relevant market needs, and harness the support of the whole organization in that provision, they will continue to be disadvantaged in a world where the level of competition continues to increase. Without this level of distinction, strategy will continue to be expressed and explained in a broad, generic manner, fail to give direction, and give functions no option other than do what they think best. Motherhood and apple pie have good attributes in themselves but are not necessarily strategic in their origins or orientation.

FUNCTIONAL DOMINANCE WITHIN CORPORATE STRATEGY

In broad terms, the changing world demand/capacity balance has brought with it a change in the fortunes of different functions. Up to the mid-1960s, many industries had enjoyed a capacity/demand relationship that favored manufacturing's position in the sphere of strategic influence. This factor, together with postwar growth, helped create the dominance of the manufacturing function in many corporations. As the demand/capacity balance began to even out and selling into existing and new markets became more difficult, the power base of corporate influence began to swing away from manufacturing, heralding the rise of marketing. Then by the mid-1970s, the impact of recessions and energy crises had, in turn, opened the door to the influence of accounting and finance. These varying fortunes, however, rarely seemed to be based on what was best for the total good of the business but more on which functional perspective appeared to provide the key to corporate success or salvation. As a result, those functions out in the cold themselves were left without due corporate influence.

These events reinforced the functional bias within corporate strategy debate explained in the last section. The independent formulation of functional strategies and the failure to cross-relate them continues to be the order of the day. This failure to debate strategy has led to essential perspectives and contributions of key functions being left out of strategic outcomes.

However, the existence of increasing world competition, overcapacity in many sectors of manufacturing industry, increasing scarcity of key resources, and decreasing product life cycles make it all the more logical for businesses to incorporate the key functional perspectives when determining policy decisions. Why then, does this not happen? In many organizations, manufacturing adopts or is required to take a reactive stance in corporate strategy discussions. Yet how can the perspectives of the function that controls such a large slice of the assets, expenditure, and people, thus underpinning the very welfare of a company, be omitted?

REASONS FOR MANUFACTURING'S REACTIVE ROLE IN CORPORATE STRATEGY

The importance of manufacturing's contribution to the success of a business is readily acknowledged. The prosperous nations of today owe their success to their wealth-creating sectors, of which manufacturing is a key part. Why then do manufacturing executives typically adopt a reactive role within strategic debate? Why doesn't this situation improve?

How Production Executives See Their Role

A prime reason that manufacturing's strategic contribution is reactive is that production managers view their strategic role as requiring them to react as well as possible to all that is asked of the production system. They feel that they must

- Exercise skill and experience in effectively coping with the exacting and varying demands placed on manufacturing.
- Reconcile the trade-offs inherent in these demands as best they can.

Rarely do they see as an integral part of their role the need to contribute appropriately to corporate decisions that will affect the demands on manufacturing and its ability to provide the necessary market support.

They do not explain the different sets of manufacturing implications created by alternative policy decisions and changes in direction. By not contributing at the corporate level, they fail to help the company arrive at decisions that embrace all the important business perspectives.

How Companies See Manufacturing's Strategic Contribution

Companies themselves often reinforce production executives' emphasis on the short-term operational aspects of manufacturing. They too see manufacturing's role as involving the day-to-day operations and signal this orientation through discussion and required contributions.

Companies also reinforce such an orientation by the way in which they develop managers within manufacturing. Many companies typically promote operators to supervisors, supervisors to managers, and managers to executives, with scant regard for the change in emphasis that needs to take place. Firms provide little help to make this transition a success. One major company, recognizing the important corporate contribution to be made by its manufacturing executives, instituted a series of tailor-made programs in manufacturing strategy. During the first of these, 16 plant managers reflected that as a group their aggregate company service exceeded 300 years, yet the collective training they had received to help them prepare for their manufacturing executive roles was less than 30 days.

The outcome is that the short-term, "minding the store" role is reinforced by corporate expectations. Thus the accepted and required contribution of manufacturing executives tends to be confined to daily events, and the reactive role in strategy decision making continues to be the reality.[2]

Too Late in the Corporate Debate to Effectively Influence Strategic Outcomes

Manufacturing executives are typically not involved, or do not involve themselves, in corporate strategy decisions until these decisions have started to take shape. Before long, this point of entry into the strategy debate becomes the norm. The result is that manufacturing has less opportunity to contribute and less chance to influence outcomes. As a consequence, production managers always appear to be complaining about the unrealistic demands made of them and the problems that invariably ensue.

Failure to Say No When Strategically Appropriate

The "can't say no" syndrome is still the hallmark of the production culture. But this attitude helps no one. Manufacturing executives tend to respond to corporate needs and difficulties without evaluating the consequences or alternatives and then explaining these to others. Any senior executive, including those in manufacturing, must be able to say no from a total business perspective and with sound corporate-related arguments. In typical situations, production managers accept the current and future demands placed on the systems and capacities they control and then work to resolve them. In this way, they decide between corporate alternatives but only from a narrow functional perspective of what they believe to be best for the business. This situation must change. Resolving corporate-related issues in a unilateral way is not the most effective method to resolve the complex alternatives at hand. This resolution needs corporate debate to ensure that the relevant factors and options are taken into account so an appropriate corporate decision can be concluded.

---

[2] Also, refer to W. Skinner, *Manufacturing—The Formidable Competitive Weapon* (New York: John Wiley & Sons, 1985). The section titled "Wanted: A New Breed of Manufacturing Manager" provides insights on developments in production management from 1980 to 1984 and the changing task to meet, among other things, the strategic role in manufacturing.

Strategic decisions need to encompass the important trade-offs embodied in alternatives that have their roots in the process and infrastructure investments associated with manufacturing and are reflected in the high proportion of assets and expenditures under its control.

Lack of Language to Explain and Concepts to Underpin Manufacturing Strategy

On the whole, production managers do not have a history of explaining their functions clearly and effectively to others in the organization. This is particularly so for manufacturing strategy issues and the production consequences that will arise from the corporate decisions under discussion. On the other hand, marketing and financial executives are able to explain their function in a more straightforward and intelligible manner.[3] By talking about how strategic alternatives will affect the business, they can capture the attention of others regarding the issues at hand and their strategic outcomes.

However, the reasons for this difference in perspective and presentation are not solely attributable to manufacturing executives. The knowledge base, concepts, and language essential to highlighting corporate relevance and arresting attention have not been developed to the same level within manufacturing as within other key functions. Consequently, shared perspectives within manufacturing, let alone between functions, are not held, which contributes to the lack of interfunctional understanding.

For evidence of this last point, compare the number of books and articles written and postgraduate and postexperience courses provided in the area of manufacturing strategy to those for the other major functions of marketing and accounting/finance. Relatively few contributors address this fundamental area. The result is that manufacturing executives are less able to explain their essential perspectives. Hence executives from other functions are less attuned to the ideas and perspectives that form the basis for understanding manufacturing's strategic contribution.

Functional Goals versus Manufacturing's Needs

In many organizations, the managers of different functions are measured by their departmental efficiency (an operational perspective) and not overall effectiveness (a business perspective). Furthermore, their career prospects are governed by their performance within a functional value system. As a consequence, managers make trade-offs that are suboptimal for the business as a whole. Typically, the performance of these specialist departments is measured by their own functionally derived goals and perspectives rather than those of line management and hence the requirements of the business itself. Getting adequate and timely resources committed to manufacturing's needs normally proves difficult.

Competing in different value systems, being measured against different performance criteria, and gaining prominence and promotion through different departmental opinions of what constitutes important contributions has gradually fragmented the functions making up a business. It has created a situation in which shared perspectives and overlapping views are left to individual accomplishment and endeavor rather than in response to clear corporate direction.

Figure 10-3 illustrates this dichotomy. An accountant or salesperson, when receiving a customer order, will typically look at one figure as being the most significant measure of business relevance—the total value ($s) of the order placed.

Given the same document, manufacturing managers will look at the order makeup. For them, the business relevance of an order is not its value, but the product mix, volumes, and delivery requirements it embodies. This aspect determines the ease with which an

---

[3] This argument was put forward in T. J. Hill, "Manufacturing Implications in Determining Corporate Policy," *International Journal of Operations and Production Management* 1, no. 1, p. 4.

FIGURE 10-3 Dichotomy of Business Views Illustrated by the Different Figures Included on Typical Customer-Order Paperwork

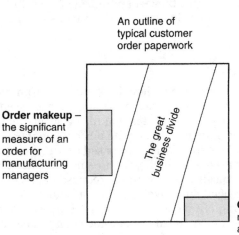

An outline of
typical customer
order paperwork

Order makeup –
the significant
measure of an
order for
manufacturing
managers

The great
business divide

Order value – the significant
measure of an order for
accountants and salespersons

Source: T. Hill, *Manufacturing Strategy: The Strategic Management of the Manufacturing Function* (New York: Macmillan, 1993, p. 30 (with permission).

order can be made in terms of the process configurations already laid down and the process lead times involved. It will reflect manufacturing's ability to meet the cost base and delivery schedule of the product(s) ordered and hence the profit margin and delivery performance that will result.

Where marketing executives are measured by the level of sales revenue achieved, each dollar of sales in their value system will carry the same weight as any other dollar of sales. Hence all sales are deemed equal. In reality, all orders are not of the same value to a business. The more that anticipated product mix and volumes match actual sales, the more that target profit levels will normally be met. Product costs based on one level of volumes, process configurations or product mix are rarely, if ever, realigned with actual incremental volume and mix changes. Even the costing base that underpins initial forecasts is rarely, if ever, adjusted each time the market picture alters. A great business divide, therefore, separates the two realities of marketing and manufacturing. The simplistic measure of total sales value disguises those actual market characteristics so essential to manufacturing's ability to sustain cost and profit-margin structures in a business and other order-winners that create long-term growth.

Length of Tenure

Since the mid-1960s, there has been a growing practice to reduce the length of tenure for job incumbents. Introduced under the umbrella of executive development, it has been seen as a way of broadening perspectives and signaling the company's level of regard for an executive's future within the corporation. However, the significant drawbacks of this trend have gone largely unnoticed. Managerially and strategically this trend goes against the overall corporate good. It militates against executives developing the area of responsibility within their control and contributing to the essential long-term strategic requirements of a business. For without the necessary level of continuity to see through developments and without sufficient understanding of the essential functional perspectives within the strategic debate, executives are discouraged from taking the longer-term corporate view. In fact, to start developments in key areas without the time frame to see their completion is arguably irresponsible.

The result is an inclination to maintain the status quo and to meet functional goals above all else. In times of change, neither of these promotes the corporate good. Instead, managers will make decisions that are based on how they will politically affect themselves in the future, rather than how the decisions will affect the business's competitive position.

Top Management's View of Strategy

The authors of business plans and corporate marketing reviews look outward from the business. Top executives associate themselves with these activities, seeing them as essential components in developing corporate strategy. The result is that they give adequate and appropriate attention to the external environment in which the business operates.

Manufacturing plans address stated business needs and are based on the internal dimensions of the processes and capabilities used to meet these. Top executives usually do not take part in developing these plans. Typically, top executives request and receive a manufacturing strategy statement without becoming involved in its structure, development, or verification. They see manufacturing as not having an external dimension and assume, therefore, that the corporate strategy debate need not embrace these perspectives. Rather, they focus on such manufacturing outcomes of strategic alternatives as capacity and costs.

But manufacturing plays a vital role in supporting a company's chosen markets. Assessing the investment and time required for such support and which markets to grow is fundamental to strategic debate and agreed upon outcomes. In many companies, however, top management has abdicated the key task in corporate strategy of linking markets and manufacturing or is not even aware that such a linkage should be made.

THE CONTENT OF CORPORATE STRATEGY

The failure of companies to incorporate functional perspectives into their corporate strategy debate stems in part from the approaches to strategy development as advocated by leading researchers and writers in the field. The training of both executives charged with strategy development and specialists who provide relevant support reinforces such failure. This problem is apparent in the content of corporate strategy statements and manifests itself in a number of ways.

Strategy Statements Are General in Nature

Since strategy is general in nature, using all-encompassing statements to express it is deemed appropriate. The result is that expressions of strategy typically use words with more than one meaning. This broadbrush manner assumes that these general perspectives are universal in nature and relevance. But what typifies markets today is difference not similarity. Thus general statements are inaccurate and misleading. By ignoring the differences within markets, functional strategies become general in nature and driven by their own rather than a business perspective.

General statements may underpin theory, but strategy, like management, is applied. The key to understanding a business is to determine the ways in which it competes in its different segments. And of this you can be sure, segments will require functional strategies to reflect these differences.

Strategy Debate and Formulation Stops at the Interface

Functional strategies are typically not linked to one another. Most companies require each function to provide a strategic statement but fail to integrate them. The result is that corporate strategies stop at the interface between functions.

This approach is also reenacted in many large corporations at the next level. Often, multinationals seem unable or unwilling to incorporate individual company statements into a strategy for the whole group. This failure to link, either by default or intent, is a consistent and comprehensive weakness in strategy formulation. The result is that in increasingly dynamic and competitive markets, companies systematically fail to realize their strategic potential and consequently are outperformed.

Furthermore, this apparent lack of need to integrate strategies is paralleled in the literature. A review of books on strategic marketing and corporate strategy will confirm that the link between the marketing-related dimensions of strategy and those of manufacturing is not made. The implication is, therefore, that it is unnecessary. Or if necessary, its impact is of insufficient consequence to be an integral part of the review process.

Articles and books on marketing strategy were recently reviewed. Of the 1,250 pages covered by the nine articles and three books, less than 1 percent concerned manufacturing. A similar review of 10 books in the field of corporate strategy revealed that of the 4,000 pages written, only 2 percent concerned manufacturing. Thus strategy formulation as advocated and undertaken by leading researchers in the fields of corporate and marketing strategy also stops at the interface. Methodologies are put forward that lead companies into making major decisions and committing a business for many years ahead without requiring essential interface.

The consequences are enormous. First, the risks associated with such approaches in today's markets are substantial. The high level of risk is not a result of the uncertainty of future markets and the unknown moves of competitors but of the process of internal strategy formulation. Second, such approaches consistently result in the failure to create the type of strategic advantage that comes directly from embracing key functional perspectives and arriving at commonly agreed and understood corporate directions.

Whole versus Parts

The underlying rationale for these advocated and adopted methodologies appears to be based on the assumption that corporate improvement can be accomplished by working solely on the corporate whole. Although reshaping the whole is an important facet of strategic resolution, the necessary links to constituent parts and the role of those parts in bringing about agreed directions and change is fundamental. Unless companies forge these links when choosing what is best for business and agreeing on directions to pursue, they are unlikely to arrive at appropriate decisions essential for their growth and prosperity over time.

Typical Outcomes

The results of this lack of integration are documents and statements that have the trappings, but not the essence, of corporate debate. With functional strategies independently derived, the nearest they get to integration is that they sit side by side in the same binder. The title "corporate strategy" for most companies is a misnomer. In reality, the strategy is no more than a compilation of functional strategies separated, as in the binder, one from another.

Furthermore, even a department's presentation of its strategy is not intended to and does not, in fact, spark corporate-based discussion. Those companies that justify this procedure on the grounds that it requires executives to engage in rigorous, functionally oriented debate are not only guilty of false rationalization but also are missing the point. In today's markets, companies that fail to harness the resources of all facets of their business will be seriously disadvantaged. Not only will they miss out, they may well be in danger of missing out altogether.

Companies require a strategy not based solely on marketing, manufacturing, or any other function, but one that embraces the interface between markets and functions. Thus what should and must be the link between functional strategies is the markets a business serves or intends to serve. One illustration is the link between marketing and manufacturing. Both functions must have a common understanding and agreement about company markets. Only then can the degree of fit between the proposed marketing strategy and manufacturing's ability to support it be known at the business level and objectively resolved within corporate perspectives and constraints.

For this step to take place, both the relevant internal information explaining a company's manufacturing capabilities and the traditional marketing information that is primarily concerned with the customer and the market opportunities associated with a company's products need to be available within a business. However, it is not sufficient that such information should be available—and often it is not. To be effective, the ownership of its use must be vested in top management. As with other functions, manufacturing strategy is not owned by manufacturing. It requires corporate ownership. Senior executives need to understand all the strategic inputs in the corporate debate, for without this understanding the resolution between conflicting or nonmatching functional perspectives cannot be fully investigated and resolved. Without this understanding individual functions must handle the trade-offs involved as best they can.

Typically, top executives inappropriately delegate this task. But leaving it to others borders on being irresponsible. Developing and agreeing on strategy is top management's key task. In fact, it is the one task that cannot be delegated. If it is, top executives will find themselves able to exercise control over decisions only in a global, after-the-event way.

Strategic Integration—Linking Manufacturing to Marketing

There is no shortcut to moving forward. There are, however, five basic steps that provide an analytical and objective structure in which the corporate debate and consequent actions can be taken, as shown in Figure 10-4.

These are, in one sense, classic steps in corporate planning. The problem is that most corporate planners treat the first two as interactive with "feedback loops" and the last two as linear and deterministic. While each step has substance in its own right, each also affects the others—hence the involved nature of strategy formulation. This process is further exacerbated by the inherent complexity of manufacturing and the general failure to take account of the essential interaction between marketing and manufacturing strategies. What is required, therefore, is an approach that recognizes these features and yet provides an ordered and analytical way forward.

FIGURE 10-4 Steps to Help Link Manufacturing to Marketing within Corporate Strategy Development

Steps	1. Define corporate objectives.
	2. Determine marketing strategies to meet these objectives.
	3. Assess how different products qualify in their respective markets and win orders against competitors.
	4. Establish the appropriate process to manufacture these products (process choice).
	5. Provide the manufacturing infrastructure to support production.

FIGURES 10-5 Framework for Reflecting Manufacturing Strategy Issues in Corporate Decisions (step involved)*

Corporate Objectives	Marketing Strategy	How Do Products Qualify and Win Orders in the Marketplace?	Manufacturing Strategy	
			Process Choice	Infrastructure
Growth	Product markets and	Price	Choice of alternative	Function support
Survival	segments	Conformance quality	processes	Manufacturing
Profit	Range	Delivery	Trade-offs embodied	planning and control
Return on investment	Mix	Speed	in the process	systems
Other financial	Volumes	Reliability	choice	Quality assurance
measures	Standardization versus	Demand increases	Role of inventory in	and control
	customization	Color range	the process	Manufacturing
	Level of innovation	Product range	configuration	systems
	Leader versus follower	Design	Make or buy	engineering
	alternatives	Brand image	Capacity	Clerical procedures
		Technical support	Size	Compensation
		After-sales support	Timing	agreements
			Location	Work structuring
				Organizational
				structure

*Although the steps to be followed are given as finite points in a stated procedure, in reality the process will involve statement and restatement, for several of these aspects will impinge on each other.

The suggested approach to linking manufacturing with corporate marketing decisions is schematically outlined in Figure 10-5. It is presented in the form of a framework to help outline the stages involved. A glance at the exhibit will reveal a gap between columns 2 and 3. This gap is to indicate the fact that the corporate objectives/marketing strategy interface that typically takes place as part of a firm's corporate planning procedure does so often as a separate corporate exercise. Column 3 highlights the need for companies to understand their markets (the criteria listed here are typical of some that may relate to a firm's various markets) as this understanding forms the basis of manufacturing's task to support the needs of agreed on markets. And just as there are typically different markets, there will be different tasks that call for different strategies. The approach provides the key to stimulating corporate debate about the business so as to enable manufacturing to assess how it needs to and the degree to which it can support products in the marketplace and to identify the developments and investments it needs to undertake as part of its strategic role. This approach has been researched and tested successfully in many industries and business of different sizes.

How It Works

How to use the methodology outlined in Figure 10-5 will be covered in two sections of the book. The following sections will overview the basic steps. Chapter 11 will cover the methodology to be followed when undertaking these types of analyses. Specifically, it will

- Provide background for analyzing the cases included in this text by explaining what data are reviewed and why.
- Give an approach for students to follow if their course requires an in-plant review.
- Help executives undertake reviews of this kind within their own businesses.

The objective of using this framework is to produce a manufacturing strategy for a business (steps 4 and 5). In all instances this approach will include a review of existing products plus a review of proposed product introductions. Furthermore, the review will be based on current and future market expectations because manufacturing needs to support a product (i.e., with after-sales service and supply) over the whole and not just a part of its life cycle, and hence the business needs to address this total decision. As product requirements change, so will manufacturing's task. The range of support requirements, therefore, will invariably affect the choice of process (step 4) and infrastructure (step 5) considered appropriate for the business over the whole life cycle of each product or product family. Levels of investment will also need to reflect this total support, and the varying degrees of mismatch over the life cycle between the product requirements and manufacturing process and infrastructure capability will need to be understood and agreed on. In this way, the business will make conscious decisions at the corporate level. It will exercise its due responsibility for resolving trade-offs between the investment required to reduce the degree of mismatch and the ramifications for the business by allowing the mismatch to go unaltered.

However, to get to steps 4 and 5 the three earlier steps need to be taken. With some understanding of what is to be achieved in a manufacturing strategy statement, it is now opportune to go through each step and then to explain how the necessary interrelations between these parts come together as a whole to form a corporate strategy for a business.

Step 1—Corporate Objectives

Inputs into corporate strategy need to be linked to the objectives of a business. The essential nature of this link is twofold. First, it provides the basis for establishing clear, strategic direction for a business and demonstrates both the strategic awareness and strategic willingness essential to corporate success. Second, it will define the boundaries and mark the parameters against which the various inputs can be measured and consistency established, thus providing the hallmarks of a coherent corporate plan.

For each company, the objectives will be different in nature and emphasis. They will reflect the nature of the economy, markets, opportunities, and preferences of those involved. The important issues here, however, are that they need to be well thought through, hold logically together, and provide necessary direction for the business.

Typical measures concern profit in relation to sales and investment, together with targets for both absolute sales growth and market-share growth. Businesses may also wish to include employee policies and environmental issues as part of their overall sets of objectives.

Step 2—Marketing Strategy

Linked closely to the provision of agreed corporate objectives, a marketing strategy needs to be developed and will often include the following stages:

1. Market planning and control units need to be established. Their task is to bring together a number of products that have closely related market targets and that often share a common marketing program. This will help to identify a number of manageable units with similar marketing characteristics.

2. The second stage involves a situational analysis of product markets that includes

   a. Determining current and future volumes.
   b. Defining end-user characteristics.
   c. Assessing patterns of buying behavior.
   d. Examining industry practices and trends.
   e. Identifying key competitors and reviewing a business's relative position.

3. The final stage concerns identifying target markets and agreeing on objectives for each. This step will include both a broad review of how to achieve these and the short-term action plans necessary to achieve the more global objectives involved.

In addition, a company should agree on the level of service support necessary in each market and assess the investments and resources needed to provide these throughout the business.

The outcome of this process will be a declaration to the business of the product markets and segments that the strategy proposes and the identification of the range, mix, and volumes involved. Other issues pertinent to the business will include the degree of standardization/customerization involved within each product range, the level of innovation and product development proposed, whether the business should be a leader or follower in each of its markets, and the extent and timing of these strategic initiatives.

Step 3—How Do Products Qualify and Win Orders in the Marketplace?

Manufacturing's strategic task is to meet the qualifiers* for which it is responsible and provide, better than the manufacturing functions of competitors, those criteria that enable the products to win orders in the marketplace. The debate initiated by this methodology is iterative in nature and is both appropriate for and fundamental to strategic resolution. Thus the company as a whole needs to agree on the markets and segments within those markets in which it decides to compete.

In no way can these critical decisions be the responsibility or prerogative of a single function. Typically, however, most companies develop strategy through a marketing perspective (see steps 1 and 2). Although the marketing debate is preeminent in corporate strategy procedures, the problem is that the debate ends here.

As a function, marketing will have an important and essential view. But it is not the only view and in no way should it be allowed to dominate corporate strategy resolution. Functional dominance, no matter of what origin, is detrimental to today's business needs and must be avoided. One essential perspective of a firm's markets has to come from manufacturing. This perspective is established by determining those order-winners and qualifiers that manufacturing needs to provide. The procedure is, in reality, to ask the marketing function questions about markets that require manufacturing answers. This step, therefore, forms the essential link between corporate marketing proposals and commitments and the manufacturing processes and infrastructure necessary to support them (see Figure 10-6).

However, not only are the relevant order-winners and qualifiers of differing levels of importance in different markets, but the degree of importance will also change over time. The procedure to be followed and the important issues to be addressed are covered in some detail later in this chapter.

Step 4—Process Choice

Manufacturing can choose from a number of alternative processes to make particular products. The key to this choice is volume and the order-winning criteria involved. Each

Figure 10-6 How Order-Winners Link Corporate Marketing Decisions with Manufacturing Strategy

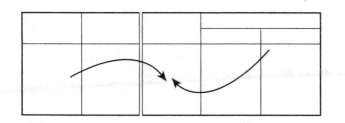

---

*Suffice here to say that qualifiers get and keep companies in markets, but do not win orders.

choice, therefore, needs to reflect the current and future trade-offs involved for the various products. The issues embodied in these trade-offs are both extensive and important. Chapter 12 is devoted to process choice and examines in detail the implications embodied in this fundamental decision.

Step 5—Infrastructure

Manufacturing infrastructure consists of the nonprocess features within production. It encompasses the procedures, systems, controls, compensation systems, work-structuring alternatives, organizational issues, and so on within manufacturing. Chapter 14 discusses and illustrates some of the major areas involved.

Although these five steps constitute the elements of manufacturing strategy development, this book treats the first two steps in a somewhat superficial way—they are dealt with rigorously in other textbooks.[4] The purpose of including them is both to demonstrate the integral nature of strategy formulation and to reinforce the interactive nature of the procedures involved. The remaining three steps are all dealt with extensively in later chapters. Step 3, which concerns the order-winners and qualifiers of different products, is now discussed in general terms.

ORDER-WINNERS AND QUALIFIERS

Some order-winners do not fall within the jurisdiction of manufacturing. For example, after-sales service, being the existing supplier, technical liaison capability, brand name, and design leadership are features provided by functions other than manufacturing. Whether or not to allocate resources to provide one or more of these particular features is, therefore, a corporate decision. However, within the mix of order-winners over a product's life cycle, manufacturing-related criteria will normally be the most important.

The rationale for establishing the order-winners for different products is to improve a company's understanding of its markets. The following section describes some important characteristics and issues involved to give essential background and context for this procedure.

Define the Meaning

To understand a business requires relevant discussion that leads to outcomes that are both comprehensive and clear. As mentioned earlier, many companies perceive strategy to be broadly based and are content with arriving at all-embracing but essentially unclear statements. Given that difference rather than similarity characterizes today's markets, a company must understand its markets to achieve adequate and clear outcomes from strategic discussion. A prerequisite is that the dimensions that characterize a company's markets are clearly defined and agreed. Using words that convey more than one meaning will only lead to misunderstanding and an inadequate base on which to establish agreed direction.

Therefore, companies that use descriptions of the success factors in their markets such as *customer service* are poorly served. Customer service can mean any number of things. The key is to agree which dimension of customer service is the important criterion. The reason is simple. Without this level of clarity, executives will walk away from a strategy debate with their own idea of which dimension of a particular factor is the most

---

[4]These include D. A. Aaker, *Developing Business Strategies*, 5th ed. (New York: John Wiley, 1998); P. J. Below et al., *The Executive Guide to Strategic Planning* (San Francisco: Jossey-Bass, 1987); B. Houlden, *Understanding Company Strategy*, 2nd ed. (Basil Blackwell, 1996); G. Johnson and K. Scholes, *Exploring Corporate Strategy*, 4th ed. (Englewood Cliffs, N.J.: Prentice Hall, 1997); and J. Quinn et al., *The Strategy Process*, 2nd ed. (1993).

critical to the business. Furthermore, reviewing the importance of the same factor in the different markets served by a company can also embody similar misunderstandings. Most, if not all, companies today are selling products in markets characterized by difference and not similarity, and these essential insights need to be clearly identified as a prerequisite for sound strategy making.

Two words illustrate these points: *quality* and *delivery*. It is essential, for instance, to separate the word *design* from *quality* conformance. Although the dimensions are related, the former concerns creating a product specification, and the latter describes the task of meeting the given specification. Although one is the task of the design function, the other is a distinct manufacturing task. While the perspectives are interrelated, the essential reason for clarity is that the tasks form part of different functional offerings.

Similarly, take the aspect of *delivery*. Separating the issue of "on time" from that of "short lead times" is an essential part of understanding the key dimensions of a market. Describing both under the one word *delivery* will hide essential insights.

Strategy Is Time- and Market-Specific

It is not appropriate to discuss strategy as a set of stereotypes. To do so may simplify the process but will confuse the outputs. To be relevant, strategy debate needs to be time- and market-specific. Recognizing this fact will prevent stereotypes from being applied and will help to create and sustain the essential dimension of clarity emphasized earlier.

Definitions of Order-Winners and Qualifiers

The last two sections have emphasized the need to distinguish differences as part of strategy formulation. To this end, an essential part of manufacturing's task is to recognize and apply the concept of order-winners and qualifiers.

- **Qualifiers** are those criteria that a company must meet for a customer to even consider it as a possible supplier. For example, customers increasingly require suppliers to be registered under the ISO 9000 series. Suppliers, therefore, who are so registered have only achieved the right to bid or be considered. Furthermore, they will need to retain the qualification to stay on the short list or be considered as a competitor in a given market. However, providing or attaining these criteria do not win orders.
- **Order-winners** are those criteria that win the order.

Order-Winners versus Qualifiers

Part of sound strategy formulation is based upon recognizing the essential difference between the two dimensions of order-winners and qualifiers and their respective roles in a market. To provide qualifiers, companies need only to be as good as competitors; to provide order-winners, companies need to be better than competitors. However, qualifiers are not less important than order—winners-they are different. Both are essential if companies are to maintain existing share and grow.

The following example highlights the need to distinguish between criteria that win orders in the marketplace and those that qualify the product to be there. When Japanese companies entered the color television market, they changed the way in which products won orders from predominantly price to product quality and reliability in service. The relatively low product quality conformance and reliability in service of existing television sets meant that in the changed competitive forces of this market, existing producers were losing orders through quality to Japanese companies; that is, existing manufacturers were not providing the criteria that qualified them to be in the marketplace. By the early 1980s, manufacturers that lost orders raised quality conformance so that they were again qualified to be in the market. As a result, quality conformance and reliability in service became qualifiers again and the most important order-winner in this market reverted to price.

Manufacturing, therefore, must provide the qualifiers to get into or stay in a marketplace. But these alone will not win orders. They merely prevent a company from losing orders to its competitors. Once the qualifiers have been achieved, manufacturing then has to turn its attention to the ways in which orders are won and ideally to provide these better than anyone else.

Also, if price is not the predominant order-winner, it does not mean that a company can charge what it wishes. Although it needs to recognize that it does not compete on price and, therefore, should exploit this opportunity, the company has to keep its exploitation within sensible bounds. Failure to do so will result in the increasing loss of orders to those who are more competitively priced. Hence, in this situation, a company can turn a qualifying criterion (i.e., a product highly priced within some limits) into an order-losing criterion when the price becomes too high.

CHAPTER 11

DEVELOPING A MANUFACTURING STRATEGY—METHODOLOGY

The preceding two chapters introduced the concepts and principles underpinning the development of a manufacturing strategy. They also discussed the key strategic task of developing a clear understanding of how a company competes. This chapter addresses the question of how to develop a manufacturing strategy.

Functions manage, control, and develop the resources for which they are responsible at both the operational and strategic levels. These roles are the two sides of the same coin. The operational tasks concern managing and controlling the day-to-day, short-term aspects of a business. The strategic task concerns investing in and developing those capabilities to provide the qualifiers and order-winners that relate to agreed upon current and future markets. Figure 11-1 provides an overview of what is involved in developing a manufacturing strategy.

Knowing how a firm competes in relevant markets is a prerequisite for sound strategy development. Without this knowledge, functions may pursue good practice but not necessarily sound strategy. They will, in terms of strategic direction, be simply working in the dark. That today's markets are different from each other rather than similar has been stressed through the early chapters. A basic task is to determine what these differences are so that appropriate context and direction can be established and on which functional strategies can be based.

That companies must support their markets is clearly acknowledged. What constitutes markets, however, is inadequately established by most companies. As clearly understanding markets is a prerequisite for functional strategy development, a detailed and comprehensive review of a company's current and future markets is the first step in sound strategy formulation.

FIGURE 11-1 From Markets to Manufacturing Strategy

Markets	How do you qualify and win orders?	Manufacturing's		
		Strategic task	Current Performance	Strategy
Agree on the current and future markets in which a company competes	Determine the order-winners and qualifiers for each market segment	Translate the relevant order-winners and qualifiers into the equivalent manufacturing tasks	Assess how well manufacturing currently provides the order-winners and qualifiers for which it is solely or jointly responsible	Prioritize the investments and developments to better support the needs (order-winning and qualifying criteria) of current and future markets for which manufacturing is solely or jointly responsible

Why then do companies typically not provide this essential clarification? One common reason is that most companies undertake and work with general reviews of markets that typically provide descriptions (for example, the standard industrial code of a company or geographic regions are commonly used methods of segmenting customers) but do not address the question, How do you qualify and win orders in that segment or customer group? The result is that companies do not know any other way and are unable to undertake reviews that identify the competitive factors within different segments.

GENERIC STRATEGIES: TODAY'S VERSION OF THE ALCHEMIST'S STONE

Academics, consultants, and other third-party advisers seek generic strategies in much the same way as those who sought to change base metal into gold. Perhaps this quest will be set aside only when firms realize that, despite best intentions, the reality they need to manage embodies a diversity and dynamism that makes categorization impossible and hence irrelevant.

That markets are inherently and increasingly different leads to a simple conclusion: By definition there cannot be some way of overlaying this diversity and its dynamic nature with a process that seeks the selection and application of one or more generic options.

What, then, is the alternative? If markets are dissimilar, then strategies need to match this diversity. Consequently, functions have to develop different strategies to match the needs of their different markets. Arguing for generic strategies not only is inappropriate by being simplistic in nature and origin but also results in the failure to align strategies to a firm's various markets.

> *Niche, low cost, core competence-type arguments are seductive in their apparent offerings. The promise of uniformity is appealing to those with the task of developing strategies for businesses which are typified by difference not similarity. In fact, such approaches purport to identify a corporate similarity which, though desirable, is inherently not available. The alternative is to recognize difference and develop multi-strategies to address these separate needs . . . For strategy is not a process*

leading to generalisations . . . It is a distillation process with the task of identifying the very essence of what comprises a business.[1]

THE NATURE OF STRATEGY: DIRECTIONAL AND ITERATIVE

To assume or believe that companies can forge strategic understanding to the point that it will not require development and/or adaption is unrealistic. Strategy is directional. It points the way and, assuming that the debate is rigorous, involves relevant functional perspectives and has opinions challenged and verified by data analysis, then it gives sound insight and direction. However, the dynamic and changing nature of today's markets and the need to adjust and readjust to meet change introduces an iterative and emerging dimension to the way in which strategy unfolds over time. However, the emergent element concerns the nature of strategy. It does not imply that firms should follow an approach that is largely without direction at the start and gradually evolve a strategy as one emerges. The essence of strategy is to provide direction, but does not imply that the chosen direction is correct. It may be wrong (in whole or part) in itself or need adjustment as markets change and/or opportunities/threats emerge. However, both direction and the ability to recognize the need to change as markets are better understood and in response to the changes inherent in the nature of today's business environment are essential to sound strategy. The task, then, is to discuss, check, and agree on markets on a continuous basis.

With these thoughts in mind, let us now return to the approaches to follow when undertaking the development of a manufacturing strategy.

CHECKING MARKETS

To gain the essential understanding of markets requires a detailed review. Only analysis of this depth will yield the insights essential to fulfilling this task. Given that corporate strategy and its constituent functional strategies are the result, a company should not have to justify giving adequate time, attention, and resources to undertake the task. Strategy is hard work, often painstaking in its execution, and needs top management's full attention. Furthermore, it is an ongoing task. Simply, without this commitment, firms take risks, especially in difficult environments. The need is obvious. Who would thank an airline crew that did not plan its route with care? Corporate recognition of this need is not well established, and its execution is, therefore, often lacking.

Substituting Customer Behavior for Customer Voice

The purpose of collecting data and verifying the nature of a customer's orders is best summed up as moving from a recognition that the nature of markets is not what a customer says it is but to how a customer actually behaves (see Figure 10-10). I have yet to have a customer declare that the agreed on price for a product is too low or that the nature of the business on offer will be fraught with problems and difficult to support. The reality is not known until the demands placed on a supplier by a customer's orders unfold. Unless these are checked, the nature of the business on hand (and what functional strategies have to support) will not be known.

---

[1]Taken from T. Hill *The Strategy Quest* (AMD Publishing, 1998), pp. vi and vii. This book, written in the form of a novel, addresses the issues within this chapter.

The Most Important Orders Are the Ones You Turn Down

Once a company identifies its markets and their characteristics, it starts to gain control of its strategy. Then it is able to judge whether a piece of business fits its strategic direction. Thus, from there on in, the most important orders are the ones which a company turns down. These mark the boundaries by declaring the segments of a market in which a company decides it does not wish to compete. Without this level of clarity, all orders are deemed to be equally attractive. By definition that cannot be. But without a mechanism for knowing how to judge, appropriate decisions cannot be made.

Form and Nature

An introduction to the form and nature of market reviews was provided in Chapter 10 together with the examples given in Figures 10-7, 10-8, and 10-9. It will help now to discuss these three different applications to illustrate the form and nature of these outputs.

U.S. Graphics Company. The example given in Figure 10-7 shows the order-winners and qualifiers for two customers in one of this company's markets. At the time of the analysis the sales revenue derived from Customer A was four times that of Customer B. As you will guess, the company supplies to a whole range of customers that, in turn, are in different markets themselves. The market review, therefore, would need to establish the order-winners and qualifiers for all customers in all markets. Very often, customers will have similar order-winners and qualifiers, a fact that must be clearly established as part of the analysis. The grouping together of customers with like order-winners and qualifiers is then completed at the next stage. Assumptions on the likeness of segments must be avoided. Analysis will establish the level of similarity or difference that exists in a company's markets, and approaches to strategy formulation based on analysis and verification need to replace the broad-brush overviews that characterize current practice.

What then does Figure 10-7 reveal? Without adequate discussion and analysis, companies tend to work on the assumption that the needs of customers are the same. However, Figure 10-7 shows that there are marked differences. For Customer A, the predominant order-winners concern the technical offering of the company and the proposed strategy is to increase this emphasis in the future such that in two years after this analysis was completed, the product specification and R&D support would constitute the only order-winners. Throughout, price has remained a qualifier (i.e., the company enjoys high margin business with Customer A) and support for Customer A's short lead time requirements is clearly recognized. In addition, part of its manufacturing strategy is to create a capability where this becomes a prerequisite for doing business with this customer.

Customer B on the other hand is distinctly more price sensitive than Customer A, a factor signalled by the 40 point weighting given at the time of the analysis. Equally, the importance of the technical dimension of design and R&D support is much lower than with Customer A. However, a glance forward shows how the company intends to change Customer B's view of this business to bring it more into line with Customer A. In this way, the company is moving from being market-driven to being market-driving, and thereby capitalizing on the strengths of its research and development (R&D) and technical support functions. Manufacturing's strategic role will increasingly be to support the key qualifiers of price, delivery reliability, delivery speed and quality conformance.

European Battery Company. Figure 10-8 shows the order-winners and qualifiers for two products. Companies may assume that products of the same type (in this instance, batteries) will win orders in a similar way to one another. The analysis completed here shows how very different they are for these two selected products. The current and anticipated price sensitivity of Product Type 10A is in marked contrast to that of Product Type C80. The role of design reflects the non-price sensitive nature of sales at the time the analysis was completed and the high margins they attract. However, as competitors match the

C80 design price is expected to become an increasingly important order-winner. Delivery speed remains an order-winner while on-time delivery is an order-losing sensitive qualifier in both instances with both forming part of manufacturing's strategic task. Finally, the aspects of quality conformance for C80 reflects in manufacturing's capability to make this product to specification and is recognized as forming part (with design) of the technical dimension being offered. For Product Type 10A, making to specification (i.e. quality conformance) is a qualifier and constitutes a process capability that is not in any way unique to the company.

European Engineered Sealing Systems Company. This company supplies engineered sealing systems to a range of customers throughout the world, three of which are given in Figure 10-9. The examples again illustrate how segments can differ from one another. In fact, in this instance, the company wins orders from these customers in very different and sometimes opposing ways. In 1999, price ranged from a qualifier for customer C to being the dominant order-winner for Company B. Similarly, the role of design was markedly different for customer C compared to customers A and B, as was the importance of delivery speed in winning orders from customer A compared to the other two customers. While the criteria delivery reliability, quality conformance, technical support and brand name are more similar to all three customers in terms of role and weighting.

These three examples bring out a number of important points to bear in mind while reading the following sections that describe the methodology to use when undertaking this work.

1. Markets are characterized by increasing difference. The key to understanding markets lies in being able to identify and highlight these differences so as to be able to develop functional responses to support them.

2. Marketing segments markets from the point of view of identifying differences in customer buying behavior. The examples given as Figures 10-7 to 10-9 illustrate how different order-winners and qualifiers may be present within a given marketing segment. Reversing the segmentation process by identifying manufacturing-related differences is, therefore, an essential first step in developing a manufacturing strategy.

3. Order-winners and qualifiers invariably change over time. Hence strategy is both time- and market-specific, and this duality necessitates identifying differences both today and tomorrow.

4. The process of identifying the order-winners and qualifiers relevant to a company's markets involves all functions as well as appropriate analysis with which to test initial opinions and assumptions. Only by sound, in-depth discussions will the essential characteristics of a company's markets be revealed. In this way, functions are required to explain their perspective and, once determined, the essential support from manufacturing and other functions (e.g., design and marketing) is clearly identified. This detailed analysis forms the basis on which functional strategies need to be developed, leading to greater coherence within a business and the essential support for agreed on markets and customers.

The key to all these points is the in-depth discussion that needs to take place, a style very different from the form and nature of today's strategic debate in many firms. Only by statement, explanation, analysis, and reexplanation will more accurate and better understood strategic insights be shared by all concerned. Without this process, companies will invariably revert to functionally based strategic alternatives, that will typically pull a business in different directions.

Reviewing Relevant Order-Winners and Qualifiers

Let us now turn to how discussions are structured and the types of analysis needed to test views and to help distinguish essential differences within a company's chosen markets. To facilitate the strategy debate, it is necessary to start with some stated view of the market as a focal point for discussion. And the best place to start is to seek the views of marketing. To do so, marketing should be asked to

- Segment the market from a marketing point of view and choose products or customers that represent each chosen segment.
- Establish for each segment appropriate future planning horizons that reflect the relevant time scales involved. Normally, this is given as two future time periods similar to the examples in Figures 10-7 to 10-9.
- Select and weight the order-winners and qualifiers for each segment for both the current and future time periods, using the products and customers that represent each segment as part of this step.

Marketing's inputs then form the basis for discussion and are challenged by

- The opinions of other functions.
- The data collected to test the initial views on how a company wins orders in its markets.

Using the initial views of marketing as the inputs to and focus of debate, other functions express opinions, ask questions, and seek clarification of why segments work the way marketing suggests. The outcomes include an improved understanding between functions and a revised understanding of the markets in which a company competes, and may alter the weightings attributed to particular order-winners and qualifiers or change them altogether.

The more significant inputs into this important debate come from collecting the data and completing the analyses relevant to the markets under review. The purpose of this step is to enable companies to replace opinions with facts. The inclusion of data and analysis helps the strategic debate reach sound conclusions based on the needs of the overall business rather than being unduly swayed by the forceful arguments of individual functions. The discussion also seeks to identify the further analysis necessary to verify the opinions and views expressed as part of a continuous evaluating process.

Throughout it is important to use functional opinions within the strategy debate not as sets of arguments and counterarguments, but as a means of directing analysis. When functional views are raised, the next question should be, "What analyses and data need to be provided to check whether or not these views are correct?" Only in this way can companies move to a level of debate that provides the essential quality and yields the necessary insights on which to make sound strategic decisions.

A review of some of the necessary analyses follows. The principal purpose is to explain the approach and its underlying rationale to enable this way of working to be transferred to other areas of analysis and to other companies.

General Issues

As explained earlier, when a company undertakes the initial review of its markets, it asks marketing to identify products or customers that represent each chosen segment. Subsequent analysis is based on these, as analyzing representative products or customers equates to analyzing the relevant segment. The assumption underlying the concept of segmentation is that everything that falls within the selected groupings is similar. The purpose of the analysis is to test this perception, not only as a checking mechanism but also to

- Improve a company's understanding of its markets.
- Allow it to review its markets or parts of them.
- Change its decisions on the relative importance of these parts.
- Form the basis of functional strategies by prioritizing investments and developments.

The outcomes affect all parts of the business as would be expected and as emphasized earlier.

Analyses to Be Completed

What follows is a list of analyses that will provide key insights. However, in using them there are two points to bear in mind.

1. The analyses will not be of equal value in all situations. Some may be difficult to undertake because of data availability, while others will not identify differences that will give further insights.
2. The checks listed below will sometimes overlap. Thus undertaking a customer-related review may duplicate (in part) the analysis involved in one of the manufacturing-related checks.

Though these points are not significant in themselves, being aware of these issues is useful background. Often analysis leads nowhere but still needs to be completed, as knowing this outcome is important in its own right.

Manufacturing-Related Analyses

The key role of analyzing markets in strategic debate has been stressed throughout. As mentioned earlier, however, many companies confine their review of markets to the perspectives held by marketing and consequently limit their analysis to customer surveys, statements on the size and share of current and future markets, competitor analyses, SWOT* reviews,[2] and other classic marketing-oriented approaches.

The purpose of these manufacturing-related analyses is to review markets from a manufacturing perspective in terms of the stated order-winners and qualifiers. Thus the market review moves from an external customer perspective to an internal one that considers what actually happens in the business. This internal review supplements the more subjective judgments of customers and externally oriented marketers by adding perspectives based on the reality of the orders placed by customers and the demands these make on the organization. This process then allows companies to verify functional views and modify them on the basis of analysis rather than opinion.

Finally, when undertaking this investigation, it is essential that the customer orders and/or contracts reviewed are chosen and verified by the executives involved. Seeking their knowledge of what is representative is essential to ensure that the findings are relevant and usable. The next step is to complete the following analyses. This section covers all the criteria that relate to manufacturing. Which ones to undertake in a particular company will reflect the criteria that are relevant to that firm's markets. Similar analyses would need to be undertaken to test other non-manufacturing-related criteria, the provision of which is the responsibility of functions other than manufacturing.

Price. Where price is a criterion, companies need to review the actual costs and margins associated with the orders involved. In many instances, companies use their own form of standard costs as the basis for reviewing margins and making comparisons between one customer or order and another. However, these cost calculations are invariably inaccurate, distorting the decisions based on them. It is essential, therefore, that companies analyze the actual costs incurred in completing the orders under review. Also, in many instances they should increase the order sample being checked to provide a wider basis for comparisons.

---

*A SWOT analysis determines the strengths, weaknesses, opportunities, and threats relating to a company in its chosen markets.

[2]The limitations of SWOT analyses are questioned in T.J. Hill and R.K. Westerook's article "SWOT Analysis: It's Time for a Product Recall," *Long Range Planning* 30, no. 1 (1997), pp. 46–52.

The inaccuracies that result from assumptions are thus exposed. For example, Figure 11-2 compares the actual contribution for a representative group of products to the weighting given to price as an order-winner and shows the noticeable inconsistency between these two related factors.

Similarly, Figure 11-3 compares the estimated contribution for a number of representative products to the actual contribution recorded when orders for these products were made on relevant processes.

More accurate cost information provides fresh insights and essential detail on the relative value of different customers or orders. The data given in Figure 11-2 and 11-3 result from summaries of such analyses and give an overview of the differences that typically exist between actual and estimated contributions and between reality and opinions. A company would use the individual data entries and, where necessary, would complete further analyses to verify different perspectives and trends before reaching a decision.

To improve the quality of cost data, a company must identify direct costs other than labor and materials wherever possible; for example, delivery charges where a direct delivery service is provided. In addition, it is important to supplement the analysis to give further critical insights where possible. For example, where different orders are processed on the same equipment and where this is a scarce resource, an additional calculation should be made to identify the contribution earned per machine hour. Contributions as a percentage of the selling price does not give the best insight into the relative value of orders as it assumes that all other nondirect factors involved are of the same relative importance.

Contribution per machine hour, or other scarce resource, relates the contribution earned to the use made by each order of a given process, where, in effect, a company is selling available machine capacity. As illustrated by Figure 11-4, the two analyses give very different insights into the worth of these orders. Whereas contribution as a percentage of price gives one rank-order listing, contribution per machine hour gives another.

As highlighted previously, the segmentation of markets from a marketing perspective implies that the customers/orders within each segment are similar. From a marketing

FIGURE 11-2 Comparison of Actual Contribution for a Group of Representative Products to the Order-Winner Weighting Given to Price

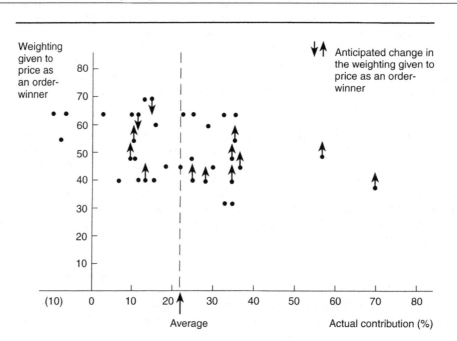

FIGURE 11-3 Actual versus Estimated Contribution for a Number of Representative Products

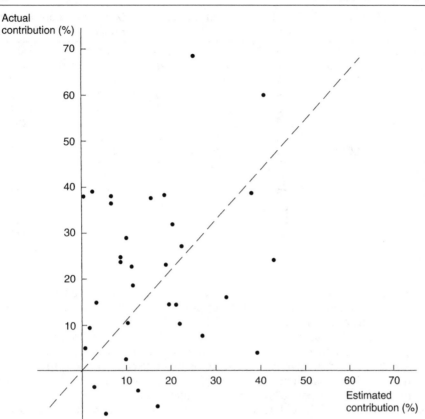

perspective this is so; it is the very premise on which the principle of marketing segmentation is built. But companies lacking other insights extend this similarity concept to other pertinent dimensions of the business, more through a lack of rigor than an overt statement. The key step in manufacturing strategy is to add those missing dimensions that are relevant to manufacturing. By so doing this step checks how orders are won and the uniform nature of relevant criteria within each segment. Without this review, functional strategies will be pursued that typically are not consistent with how orders are won for different subsegments or customers.

Part of this clarifying process tests perceptions of markets, as shown in Figures 11-2 and 11-3. Figure 11-5 goes one step further. In addition to testing initial perspectives, it also checks on the level of consistency within a segment. As the data show, customers within a segment yield markedly different levels of contributions.*

From a marketing point of view, the segments chosen remain valid as they reflect essential marketing differences that are clustered together. From a manufacturing view, however, the segments do not constitute the same level of similarity. These fresh insights challenge the initial views of segment groupings and the level of company awareness of what constitutes above-and below-average business from a contribution-earning point of view. Again, the contribution percentage of sales and contribution per machine hour analyses provide essential and often different insights into this strategic discussion. Thus

---

*Further analyses can also be completed that test the level of consistency within a customer's portfolio of orders.

FIGURE 11-4 Contribution Percentage and Contribution per Machine Hour Comparisons for Representative Orders*

Order Reference	Price	Direct Costs	Contribution		Machine Hours	Contribution per Machine Hour
631	$ 220	$ 44	$176	80%	1.5	$117
205	568	114	454	80	3.9	116
216	1,246	269	977	78	11.2	87
470	244	56	188	77	4.0	47
298	1,960	462	1,496	77	9.3	161
607	3,612	830	2,782	77	13.3	209
512	134	32	102	76	1.5	66
483	4,010	1,004	3,006	75	21.5	140
658	166	42	124	75	0.7	107
313	1,134	306	828	73	5.7	145
284	864	246	618	72	2.1	294
182	724	65	159	71	4.7	14
573	1,066	320	746	70	3.1	240
417	3,345	1,140	2,205	66	7.9	279

*All data are actuals.

decisions on which market segments, customers, or orders should receive priority in terms of growth, development investment, and support can now be made at a more informed level and on a corporate rather than distinctly functional basis.

The need to collect actual data has been stressed throughout. Shopfloor records are often kept outside the formal system. These records need to be sought, and where they do not exist, a once-off arrangement needs to be made to capture the actual labor, materials, and other direct costs incurred in completing an order or making a given quantity of relevant products. With price known, the calculations are straightforward and the outcomes then form part of the debate on a particular segment or the business as a whole.

Quality Conformance. Many analyses within companies are completed in a general format. Typical of these is the measurement of conformance quality. However, while its overall effect on costs is relevant, the external dimension of quality is not general but is

FIGURE 11-5 Contribution Percentage of Sales and Contribution per Machine Hour for Representative Orders for Two Segments

Customer	Actual Contribution*	
	% Sales	Per Machine Hour
Segment 1		
Hulton	41.8	918
Avis Robins	24.6	431
MKC	8.6	288
Clairelle	12.4	152
Aristé	30.7	714
Segment 2		
Pelpac	14.0	243
JRR	8.6	186
Sheuks	16.1	115
Dells	(1.0)	(64)
Avenols	22.3	408

* Customer data is the average for a representative sample of orders.

particular to a customer. Thus the key dimension here is not average conformance quality level but the actual customer level provided.

Reviewing quality conformance by product, order, or customer yields essential insights. Such analyses will also build into the direct material dimension of costs addressed in the preceding section.

Delivery Reliability. As with quality conformance, on-time delivery (OTD) tends to be measured in aggregate, if at all. Not only does this form of assessment fail to distinguish the importance of individual customers, it also fails to identify the differing delivery needs of customers.

What constitutes on-time cannot be covered by a simple definition. Customers' needs can range from given hourly slots on a stated day to any day within a given week or even longer period. Others may not want delivery before a given time but will accept delivery any time thereafter, within stated limits. Furthermore, delivering the perfect order also includes providing all line items on the order at the correct quantities. Moreover, the dimensions of on-time delivery, order-fill accuracy, and error-free shipments are inter-linked in terms of the level of overall delivery reliability. Being 95 percent on time with an order-fill rate of 90 percent and an error-free rate of 98 percent results in an overall delivery performance of less than 84 percent.

The task of checking delivery reliability, therefore, must be preceded by defining what constitutes OTD, and the other dimensions that need to be measured. Measurement of delivery reliability should reflect performance by customer and segment and relate to its perceived role in winning orders. In most companies, delivery reliability will be a qualifier rather than an order-winner; in many, it will be an order-losing sensitive qualifier. Knowing what to measure and its relative importance are as critical as the performance record itself. Where OTD is a relevant criterion, companies should define and measure it as discussed above. Tracking actual orders provides the dimension of reality in the discussion on markets.

Delivery Speed. The definition of delivery speed was given earlier. Assessing its presence in markets involves comparing the total lead time normally required by all relevant stages of the process—order processing, material/component purchasing, material/component delivery, manufacturing, assembly, packing, and shipping—against the lead time given by the customer (i.e., the time between order placement and required delivery).

In some instances, customers will accelerate the required delivery date part way through the process. Companies must identify how such an action affects delivery speed in only part of the process by comparing the remaining elements of lead time to the revised customer lead time.

Many companies have consistently responded to the growing importance of delivery speed in their markets by shortening lead times through actions such as reducing setups, eliminating delays, and investing in inventory ahead of time. When checking the extent of delivery speed within its markets, a company should note the level of ongoing investment within the business that is a direct result of its response to meeting the demands of this criterion. Such continuing costs should then be set against relevant customers and form part of a company's overall evaluation.

Once again, only by checking specific orders and customer requirements can the reality of markets be exposed. This increased understanding provides a more informed view of a business and the reality of how it competes.

In terms of performance, checks on the overall lead time from receipt of customer order to the point of payment (the cash-to-cash cycle) give key insights. Checks between the start and end of the overall process then need to be made. Comparing actual processing time and overall lead time at each step identifies the extent and size of delays and highlights the areas where actual processing needs reviewing and delays need to be eliminated. (These reviews should adopt a business reengineering approach to ensure that the whole as well as the parts are reviewed, and will lead to the best opportunity to reduce the time and costs involved.)[3]

Other Criteria.   There are many other order-winning and qualifying criteria besides those addressed above. Checks on the extent of their provisions and the level of ongoing performance achieved will take, in principle, a form similar to the approaches outlined in more detail for the four criteria addressed here. However, this selection does not imply that some criteria are more important than others. The ones chosen are typically present more often in markets, are related specifically to manufacturing, and provides suitable illustrations of general approaches to follow. Knowing the dimensions to look for and using orders as the basis of analysis will yield the essential insights that companies need to have to succeed in today's competitive environment.

Customer- and Product-Related Analyses

As explained in the preceding section, very often the purpose of the analyses is to give insights concerning products, ranges of products, and customers. As the earlier examples in the chapter illustrate, products within a range and customers within a segment differ. Also, orders from the same customer are often significantly different from one another. Sometimes the variance occurs because orders are received from different parts of a customer's total business, although in other instances difference still exists even though the orders come from the same customer source.

---

[3]Several books and articles are available on the topic of business reengineering. They include T. H. Davenport and J. E. Short, "The New Industrial Engineering: Information Technology and Business Process Redesign," *Sloan Management Review* 31, no. 4 (Summer 1990), pp. 11–26; T.H. Davenport, *Process Innovation: Reengineering Work through Information Technology* (Cambridge, Mass.: Harvard Business School Press, 1993); M. Hammer and J. Champy, *Reengineering the Corporation: A Manifesto for Business Revolution* (New York: Harper Business, 1993); H. J. Johansson, P. McHugh, J. Pendlebury, and W. A. Wheeler III, *Business Process Reengineering* (New York: John Wiley, 1993); D. C. Morris and J. S. Brandon, *Reengineering Your Business* (New York: McGraw-Hill, 1993); E. Obeng and S. Crainer, *Making Reengineering Happen* (London: Pitman Publishing, 1994); and J. Champy, *Reengineering Management—The Mandate for New Leadership* (New York: HarperCollins, 1995).

CHAPTER 12

PROCESS CHOICE

The way a business decides to make its products is a choice many executives believe to be based on the single dimension of technology. As a consequence, they leave this decision to engineering/process specialists on the assumption that they—the custodians of technological understanding—are best able to draw the fine distinctions that need to be made. The designation of those specialists as the appropriate people to make such decisions creates a situation in which the important manufacturing and business perspectives are at best given inadequate weight and in many instances omitted altogether.

Manufacturing is not an engineering or technology-related function. It is a business-related function. Whereas products need to be made according to their technical specifications, they also have to be supplied in ways that win orders in the marketplace. This business dimension is the concern of manufacturing. When making decisions, therefore, concerning which processes to invest in, companies need to satisfy both technical and business perspectives. The former is the concern of engineering; the latter is the concern of manufacturing.

This chapter describes the manufacturing and business implications of process choice; in so doing, it highlights the importance of these issues when making investment decisions. In this way, it helps to broaden the view of manufacturing currently held by senior executives[1] and provides a way of reviewing the manufacturing implications of marketing decisions, hence facilitating the manufacturing input into corporate strategy. This approach ensures that the necessary marketing/manufacturing interface is made and that the strategies adopted are business rather than functionally led.

---

[1]One reason for manufacturing's reactive role in corporate strategy is discussed earlier in Chapter 10.

PROCESS CHOICE

When choosing the appropriate way in which to manufacture its products, a business will take the following steps:

1. Decide on how much to buy from outside the company, which in turn determines the make-in task.

2. Identify the appropriate engineering-technology alternatives to complete the tasks embodied in each product. This check will concern bringing together the made-in components with the bought-out items to produce the final product specification at the agreed on levels of quality.

3. Choose between alternative manufacturing approaches to undertaking the tasks involved in making those parts or whole products to be completed in-house. This will need to reflect each market in which a product competes and the volumes associated with those sales. The present processes in many existing factories often are not ideal. This issue is dealt with later in the chapter after the important insights into process choice have been covered.

The choice of process concerns step 3 in this procedure. It will need to embody the decisions made in the other two steps and recognize any constraints imposed by them. However, while these constraints alter the dimensions within the decision (for example, what is involved), they do not alter its nature. The essence of the choice is linked to the appropriate way to manufacture, given the market and associated volumes involved.

Having stressed the optimal nature of process choice, we must now consider certain constraints that have an overriding impact on this decision. What these are and how they limit business options are explained in the next section.

The Manufacturing Function

The principal function of the manufacturing process is to convert inputs (materials, labor, and energy) into products. To complete this function, a business usually must choose between different modes of manufacturing. It chooses one or, as is often the case, several ways. The fundamental rationale for this decision must be that the chosen process is the one best able to support a company competitively in the marketplace. Several important perspectives must be taken into account. Each choice of process will bring with it certain implications for a business in terms of response to its markets, manufacturing capabilities and characteristics, level of investment required, unit costs involved, and the type of control and style of management that are appropriate. To help understand these, it is necessary to review the process choices available.

There are five generic types of manufacturing processes: project, jobbing, batch, line, and continuous processing. However, in many situations, hybrids have been developed that blur the edges between one process and the next. What these hybrids are, how they relate to the classic types, and what they mean for a business are also discussed in this chapter.

Before going on to describe the process choices involved, it is worth noting here that two of them (project and continuous processing) are associated with a particular product type (civil engineering and foods/liquids, respectively), a point addressed later in the chapter. A firm may find that in reality it has little option but to choose the one appropriate process (for instance, oil refining and continuous processing are for all intents and purposes inextricably linked). However, the company must be clearly aware of the precise nature of the business implications involved in the choice it is "forced" to go along with and that the trade-offs associated with these dimensions are fixed.

An important factor to note at this time is that a company does not invest and reinvest progressively as demand increases as, say, in line with product life cycles. Doing so is simply too expensive. Neither will a company wish to reinvest as demand decreases later in the cycle.

The Generic Types of Process Choices

Project

Companies that produce large-scale, one-off (i.e., unique), complex products will normally provide these on a project basis. Examples include products involved in civil engineering contracts* and aerospace programs. A project process concerns the provision of a unique product requiring the coordination of large-scale inputs to achieve a customer's requirement. The resource inputs will normally be taken to where the product is to be built, since it is not feasible to move it once completed. All activities, including the necessary support functions, will usually be controlled by a total system for the duration of the project. Resources allocated to the project will be reallocated once their part of the task is complete or at the end of the project.

The selection of project as the appropriate process is based on two features. First, the product is a one-off, customer-specified requirement; second, it is often too large to be moved or simply cannot be moved once completed. The second criterion is such an overwhelming facet of this decision that products of this nature will always be made using the project choice of process. However, businesses will also be concerned with determining how much of the product to make off-site and how best to provide the parts or sections that go into the structures made on-site. These components will, in turn, often be produced using a different choice of process. These decisions need to be based on other criteria, which will become clear in the descriptions that follow.

Some confusion arises in the use of the word *project*. It commonly refers to a one-off complex task and/or the managerial style used to control such an event. This meaning needs to be distinguished from its use here, which identifies a distinct process of making a product, the very characteristics of which (e.g., moving resources to and from a site) are detailed above.

Jobbing**

A jobbing process is used to meet the one-off order requirements of customers; for example, tooling made in line with the specific requirements of a customer. The product involved will be of an individual nature. This requires the supplier to interpret the customer's design and specification and apply relatively high-level skills in the conversion process. A large degree of this interpretation will normally be made by skilled employees, whose experience in this type of work is an essential facet of the process. Once the design has been specified, one skilled person—or possibly a small number of them, if

---

*The construction of standard housing (where price would be an order-winner) would be completed by using a combination of project and batch processes: projects in that resources need to be brought to the site and reallocated to other sites once their part in the task is complete or at the end of the building program while batch processes would also be used as several houses would typically be built in parallel. This approach is feasible as the houses are standard (basic structures with a list of options) and their construction known ahead of time. This combination of processes is desirable as it shortens building lead times and reduces labor costs. For batch processes to be used, the construction of a house is broken down into a number of steps. Each step is then completed on several houses before the next step in the program starts.

Hence the foundations and footings would be completed on several houses and then the next step would be commenced and so on. Completing the same stage of a number of houses at the same time or within the same period increases the utilization of both the skilled workers involved and any equipment necessary at a particular stage. In the same way, the level of prefabrication (e.g., roof timbers, walls and partitions, doors, door frames, and windows) will be maximized to reduce both the material and labor costs involved in constructing this phase of a house.

**Also, sometimes called unit or one-off.

the task is time-consuming—is assigned the task and is responsible for deciding how best to complete and carry it out. This responsibility may also include scheduling, liaison with other functions, and some involvement with arrangements for outside, subcontracted phases, where necessary.

The one-off provision means that the product will not again be required in its exact form, or if it is, the demand will tend to be irregular, with long interludes between orders. For this reason, investment in the manufacturing process (e.g., in jigs, fixtures, and specialist equipment) will not normally be warranted.

Jobbing versus Job Shop.   It is worth noting here that confusion often arises around the terms *jobbing* and *job shop*. While the former refers to a choice of process as explained above, the latter is a commercial description of a type of business. For example, a small printing business may often be referred to as a job shop or even a jobbing printer. This is intended to convey the nature of the business involved or market served; that is, it describes that the printer undertakes work, typically low-volume in nature, that meets the specific needs of a whole range of customers. However, printing is, in fact, a classic example of a batch process, which is explained in the next section. Thus, from a commercial standpoint, such a firm takes on low-volume orders (hence the term *job*) from its customers but, from a manufacturing perspective, uses a batch process to meet these requirements.

Special versus Customized versus Standard Products.   Finally, it is also important to distinguish between special, customized, and standard products. The word *special* is used to describe the one-off provision referred to earlier in this section—that is, the product will not again be required in its exact form or, if it is, the demand will be irregular, with long interludes between orders. The phrase *standard product* means the opposite—the demand for the product is repeated (or the single customer order is of such a large volume nature) and thus warrants investment.

The word *customized* refers to a product made to a customer's specification. However, the demand for a customized product can be either special (i.e., not repeated) or standard (i.e., repeated). An example of the latter is a container of a particular shape and size, as determined by a customer. Although customized, the demand for such a container (e.g., Coca-Cola or other soft drink products) will be high and of a repeat nature. The appropriate choice of process will, therefore, be determined by volume and not the customized nature of the product.

Furthermore, some businesses are by their very nature the producers of customized products. The earlier example of the printing firm is such a case. Here, products will normally be customized in that the printed material will comprise the logo, name, product, and other details of the customer in question. However, a printer will find a significant level of similarity between the demands placed on manufacturing of the different customer orders. In fact, the differences will be provisioned in the plate containing the specific images and writing and the ink colors and paper size in question. To manufacturing, therefore, these customized jobs are not specials (as defined earlier) but standards. Thus, it will select a process other than jobbing to meet the requirements of the markets it serves. In the printing example, this would be batch, and the rationale for this and what is involved become clear in the next section.

Batch

A company decides to manufacture using batch processes because it is providing similar items on a repeat basis, usually in larger volumes—quantity $\times$ work content—than associated with jobbing.* This type of process however, is chosen to cover a wide range of volumes, as represented in Figure 12-1 by the elongated shape of batch, compared to the

---

*Companies do manufacture order quantities of one on a batch basis. In this instance, what underlies their process decision is the repeat nature of a product, not the size of an order quantity.

FIGURE 12-1 Process Choice Related to Volume*

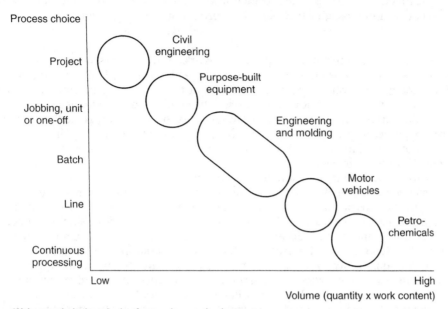

*Volume on the horizontal axis refers to order-quantity size.

Source: T. Hill, *"Operations Management: Strategic Context and Managerial Analysis"* (Basingstoke, UK: Macmillan, 2000), Chapter 4.

other processes. At the low-volume end, the repeat orders will be small and infrequent. In fact, some companies producing very large, one-off items will adopt a batch rather than a jobbing process for their manufacturing. In this case, the work content involved will be high in jobbing terms, while the order quantity is for a small number of the same but unique items. At the high-volume end, the order quantities may involve many hours, shifts, or even weeks of work for the same product at one or more stages in its designated manufacturing route.

The batch procedure divides the manufacturing task into a series of appropriate operations, which together will make the products involved. The reason is simply to determine the most effective manufacturing route so that the low cost requirements of repeat, higher-volume markets can be best achieved. At this stage, suitable jigs and fixtures will be identified to help reduce the processing times involved, the investment in which is justified by the total product output over time.

Each order quantity is manufactured by setting up that step of the process necessary to complete the first operation for a particular product. The whole order quantity is completed at this stage. Then the next operation in the process is made ready, the total order quantity is completed, and so on until all the stages required to make a product are completed. Meanwhile, the process used to complete the first operation for the product is then reset to complete an operation for another product, and so on. Thus capacity at each stage in the process is used and reused to meet the different requirements of different orders.

Examples (in addition to printing mentioned earlier) include molding processes. Here the mold to produce an item is put into a machine. The order for that component or product is then produced, the mold is taken off, the raw materials may have to be changed, a mold for another product is put into the machine, and so on. Similarly, in metal-machining processes, a machine is set to complete the necessary metal-cutting operation for a product, and the whole order quantity is processed. When finished, the machine is question is reset to do the required metal-cutting work on another item while the order quantity of the first product goes on to its next stage, which is completed in another part of the process. At times, an order quantity may have more than one stage completed on the same machine. Here the same principle applies, with the process reset to perform the next operation through which the whole order quantity will be passed.

Line

With further increases in volumes (quantity × work content), investment is made to provide a process dedicated to the needs of a single product or a small range of products. The width of the product range will be determined at the time of the investment. In a line process (see Figure 12-1), products are passed through the same sequence of operations. The standard nature of the products allows for this to happen; hence changes outside the prescribed range of options (which can be very wide, for example, with motor vehicles) cannot be accommodated on the line itself. The cumulative volume of the product range underpins the investment.

As explained in a later section, it is important to clearly recognize the fundamental differences in what constitutes volume. In a car assembly plant, for instance, customer order quantities are normally small. The eventual owner of a car orders in units of one, which the dealership passes onto the assembly plant as an order for a single car or cumulates with one or more other orders for single units. In manufacturing terms, however, all orders for single cars are for products that the production process interprets as being the same product. Hence the order quantity of a car assembly plant comprises the cumulative volume of all orders over a given period. This fact constitutes the high-volume nature of this business, making line the appropriate process.

Normally, the wider the product range, the higher is the investment required in the process to provide the degree of flexibility necessary to make these products. Where the options provided are very wide and the products involved are costly or bulky, the company is more likely to make them on an order basis only. For example, there will normally be a longer delay when purchasing an automobile (especially if several options are specified)* than, say, a domestic appliance. The underlying reason is the different degree of product standardization involved. The automobile will be made against a specific customer order, and the domestic appliance to stock.

In summary, in a line process all products (irrespective of the options involved) are perceived to be standard. Thus the process does not have to be stopped to meet the requirements of the products made on the line. However, to accommodate another product in batch (which, for example, may involve only a different color), the process has to be stopped and reset.

Continuous Processing

With continuous processing, a basic material is passed through successive stages or operations and refined or processed into one or more products. Petrochemicals is an example. This choice of process is based on two features. The first is very high volume demand; the second is that the materials involved can be moved easily from one part of the process to another; for example, fluids, gases, and foods.

The high-volume nature of the demand justifies the very high investment involved. The processes are designed to run all day and every day with minimum shut-downs, due to the high costs of starting up and closing down. Normally, the product range is quite narrow and often the products offered are purposely restricted to enhance volumes of all the products in the range. For example, oil companies have systematically restricted the range of octanes offered and hence increased the volumes of all those grades provided. Another feature in continuous processing is the nature of the materials being processed. Whereas in line there are manual inputs into the manufacture of the products as they pass

---

*Whereas this case is typical in Western motor vehicle plants, Japanese automakers schedule their manufacturing plants on the basis of sales forecasts and make-to-stock rather than order-backlog, make-to-order principles.

along, in continuous processing the materials will be transferred automatically from one part of the process to the next, with the process monitoring and self-adjusting flow and quality. The labor tasks in these situations predominantly involve checking the system and typically do not provide manual inputs into the process as they would on a line.

Choices of Processes within a Business

The five generic processes have been described separately because they are discrete choices. However, most businesses will select two or more processes as being appropriate for the products they manufacture, a fact that reflects the different volume requirements of components, subassemblies, and products. An illustration of this concept is the use of batch processes to make components and line processes to assemble those components into final products. This choice of two different processes occurs because although the quantity required in both operations may be the same (and frequently it is larger in the first, as two or more of the same component are often required for each assembly), the work involved in making a component is much smaller than that in building the final product. The result is that the volume requirements (quantity × work content) for components is insufficient to justify the level of investment for a more dedicated process such as line.

Markets and Product Volumes

As emphasized throughout the preceding sections, the underlying factor in choosing which of the five processes is most appropriate to manufacturing a product is volume (i.e. quantity × work content). The link between the demand for a product and the investment in processes to complete this task is fundamental to this decision. It is important, therefore, to clearly define the term *volume*.

Though companies express forecast sales in terms of a period (typically a year), manufacturing does not make annual volumes—it makes order quantities. Thus contracts based on agreed to total sales in a given period, but not the size of actual orders (or call-offs), can be very misleading. On the other hand, manufacturing often cumulates orders from different customers (using order-backlog/forward-load principles) or decides to make products for finished goods inventory to be sold in the future as a way to enhance volume. The choice is restricted by the degree of customization of the product and factors such as current forward load, seasonality of sales, and lead times in supplying customers' requirements. Hence the horizontal axis in Figure 12-1 concerns order quantities placed on manufacturing. In project and jobbing, products are always made to customer order. In batch, decisions to cumulate demand, or make to inventory, relate to appropriate volumes for the process investments in place and the actual sales-order volume required.

The term *flexibility* is used to describe several different requirements. Two of these relate to volume. One concerns demand increases, and the other alludes to the ability of a process to manufacture low quantities at required levels of cost. In turn, the latter concerns the relationship between setup and process time. Thus, where a company experiences reducing order volumes but has already invested in a high-volume process designed to manufacture products at fast output speeds, it will need appropriate investment to ensure that it can keep setup times sufficiently short to maintain this ratio at an acceptable level. Current research work in many manufacturing companies provides numerous illustrations of where annual sales for a product may be similar to those in the past but actual order quantities (or call-offs) have reduced significantly. The link between this section and the previous one is fundamental in terms of process investment.

Technical Specification versus Business Specification

As volumes increase, the justification for investing in processes dedicated to make that product increases. High plant utilization underpins the investment. Similarly, if processes will not be highly utilized by one product, they need to be chosen so that they can meet the manufacturing and business needs of other products. Therefore, firms when choosing processes, need to distinguish between the technology required to make a product and the way the product is manufactured. On the one hand, the process technology choice concerns the engineering dimension of providing a process that will form, shape, cut, and so forth a product to the size and tolerances required (the technical specification). On the other hand, the manufacturing dimension concerns determining the best way to make a product. This decision needs to be based on volumes and relevant order-winners and qualifiers, (the business specification)—see Figure 12-2. As volumes rise, the appropriate choice will change, as illustrated in Figure 12-1.

When companies invest in processes, they typically specify the technical requirements. This task is recognized as fundamental, and appropriately so. However, companies typically fail to specify the business requirement the process investment has to meet. But this requirement is crucial to the success of a business. In the past, manufacturing has failed to develop these critical, strategic arguments and insights. The consequences for many companies have been serious, leading to premature reinvestment of a considerable size or even the closing down of parts of the business. Leaving the choice of these investments to be made against the single dimension of the technical specification has led to inappropriate decisions, set against the narrow base of technology. Manufacturing's failure to realize that it is the custodian of these decisions has indirectly supported this approach.

The choice of process needs to be understood, not in engineering terms (the technical specification), but in terms of manufacturing constraints and other dimensions of the business specification. Understanding how well a process can support the order-winning criteria of a product, the implications of the process for a company's infrastructure, and other relevant investments is fundamental to this strategic decision. These issues are dealt with in the following section.

BUSINESS IMPLICATIONS OF PROCESS CHOICE

It has already been explained that market characteristics (order-winners and qualifiers) and product volumes are the underlying factors in choosing the appropriate process. In addition, the nature of the product is also a factor in this decision in terms of the two extremes in Figures 12-1 and 12-3, namely, project and continuous processing.

Hence the procedure used is to first assess the market-volume dimension. This assessment then forms the basis for choosing which process is appropriate to best meet these critical business needs. The engineering dimension provides the initial set of alternatives concerning the ways to meet the requirements of the product. However, at this juncture the engineering dimension finishes, and the manufacturing and business dimensions start. Phase 1 links the market volumes to the process choice (the manufacturing

FIGURE 12-2 Constituents of Customer Orders When Choosing Processes and Function Responsible for Their Clarification

Specification	Responsible Function
Technical specification—the functional requirements of a product including its physical dimensions	Research and development or engineering
Business specification—the order quantities and relevant order-winners and qualifiers of the markets in which a product will compete	Manufacturing

dimension, which also takes into account the engineering dimension described earlier)—
A1 and B1 in Figure 12-3. Phase 2 automatically picks up the corresponding point on each
of the various manufacturing and business implications given in Figure 12–4, A2 and B2
respectively in Figure 12-3. However, many companies recognize the engineering dimension but not the manufacturing and business dimensions. The engineering proposal currently underpins the major part of process investment decisions, which in turn are based
on the forecast market volumes that form part of the corporate marketing strategy. The
manufacturing and business implications embodied in a proposal are given scant recognition. But it is these issues that bind manufacturing and regulate its ability to respond
to the business needs. Once the investment is made, the processes as well as the whole
of the manufacturing infrastructure are fixed. The result is that this decision dictates
the extent to which manufacturing can support the needs of the marketplace, the essence
of business success.

When phase 1 in Figure 12-3 is completed, the choice of process is designated. However, at the same time this decision stipulates the position on the vertical dimensions,
which will accrue as a result. Hence, phase 2 is inextricably tied to phase 1. Therefore,
the decisions in phase 1 cannot be taken in isolation. The choice has to embrace both
phase 1 and phase 2. Only in this way will an organization avoid falling into the cyclopean
trap from which it will take years to extricate itself. Only in this way will a business take
into account the short- and long-term implications that emanate from the decision to
manufacture, using one choice of process as opposed to another.

To help explain the business implications of process choice, the perspectives involved
have been placed into four categories—products and markets, manufacturing, investment
and cost, and infrastructure. Furthermore, the issues for illustration and discussion have
been chosen on the basis of their overall business importance. However, many other issues

FIGURE 12-3 Engineering, Manufacturing, and Business Dimension Phases Involved in
Process Choice

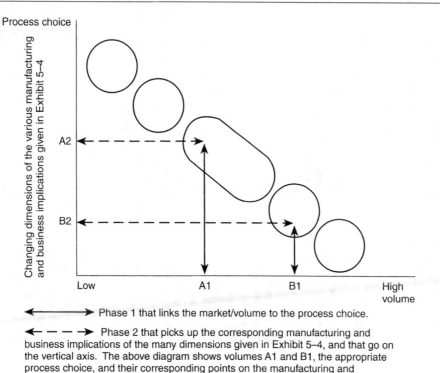

Phase 1 that links the market/volume to the process choice.

Phase 2 that picks up the corresponding manufacturing and
business implications of the many dimensions given in Exhibit 5–4, and that go on
the vertical axis. The above diagram shows volumes A1 and B1, the appropriate
process choice, and their corresponding points on the manufacturing and
business implications dimensions, A2 and B2.

FIGURE 12-4 Selected Business Implications of Process Choice

Aspects	Typical Characteristics of Process Choice				
	Project	Jobbing	Batch	Line	Continuous Processing
Products and Markets					
Type of product	Special/small range of standards	Special	↑	Standard	Standard
Product range	Wide	Wide	↑	Narrow: standard products	Very narrow: standard products
Customer order size	Small	Small	↑	Large	Very large
Level of product change required	High	High	↑	Low and within agreed on options	None
Rate of new product introductions	High	High	↑	Low	Very low
What does the company sell?	Capability	Capability	↑	Products	Products
How are orders won?					
Order-winning criteria	Delivery speed/unique design capability	Delivery speed/unique capability/design	↑	Price	Price
Qualifying criteria	Price/on-time delivery/conformance quality	Price/on-time delivery/conformance quality	On-time delivery/conformance quality	Design/on-time delivery/conformance quality	Design/on-time delivery/conformance quality
Manufacturing					
Nature of the process technology	Oriented toward general purpose	Universal	↑	Dedicated	Highly dedicated
Process flexibility	High	High	↑	Low	Inflexible
Production volumes	Low	Low	↑	High	Very High
Dominant utilization	Mixed	Labor	↑	Plant	Plant
Changes in capacity	Incremental	Incremental	↑	Stepped change	New facility
Key manufacturing task	To meet specification/delivery schedules	To meet specification/delivery dates	↑	Low-cost production	Low-cost production

Investment and Cost					
Level of capital investment	Low/high	Low	→	High	Very high
Level of inventory					
Components/raw material	As required	As required/low	Often medium	Planned with buffer stocks/low	Planned with buffer stocks
Work-in-process	High*	High*	Very high	Low	Low
Finished goods	Low	Low	→	High†	High‡
Percent of total costs					
Direct labor	Low	High	→	Low	Very low
Direct materials	High	Low	→	High	Very high
Site/plant overheads	Low	Low	→	High	High
Infrastructure					
Appropriate organizational					
Control	Decentralized/centralized	Decentralized	→	Centralized	Centralized
Style	Entrepreneurial	Entrepreneurial	→	Bureaucratic	Bureaucratic
Most important production management perspective	Technology	Technology	→	Business/people	Technology
Level of specialist support to manufacturing	High	Low	→	High	Very high

Notes: *Depends on stage payment arrangements.

†However, many businesses here only build their products in response to customer schedules or on receipt of a customer order.

‡The finished-goods inventory in, for instance, oil refining is stored in the postprocessing stages of distribution and at the pont of sale.

are equally important to understand, and these have distinct operational rather than strategic overtones.[2]

The critical issue embodied in Figure 12-4 is how each perspective reviewed changes between one choice of process and another. Thus when a company decides to invest in a process, it will at the same time have determined the corresponding point on each dimension within these four categories. It is necessary for companies to understand this relationship, and be aware of the trade-offs embodied in that choice.

Figure 12-4 contains many generalized statements that are intended to relate the usual requirements of one type of process to the other four. In almost all cases, an arrow is drawn between jobbing and line. This arrow indicates that as a process moves from jobbing to low-volume batch to high-volume batch through to line, the particular characteristic will change from one form to the other. The reason for this approach is to help explain the implications of these choices and examine the consequences that will normally follow.

Companies selling products typically made using the project process will need to make decisions on how much is made away from the site and transported in. Today, for instance, many parts of a civil engineering structure are made off-site by jobbing, batch, or line processes and then brought in as required. Similarly, products with the fluid, semifluid, or gaseous characteristics necessary to avail themselves of continuous processing may also be made on a batch process basis. Thus the changing business characteristics displayed in Figure 12-4 illustrate the sets of alternatives embodied in these choices as well.

Finally, Figure 12-4 has been arranged to illustrate the linked relationship between jobbing, batch, and line choices as opposed to the more distinct process-product relationship existing in project and continuous processing, described earlier. The section that follows adopts this division.

---

[2]Many of these additional issues are illustrated and discussed in T. Hill, Basingstoke, UK *Operations Management: Strategic Context and Managerial Analysis* (Macmillan, 2000), Chapter 4

CHAPTER 13

PRODUCT PROFILING

A company needs to have a comprehensive understanding of how well manufacturing can support its business as alternative processes are chosen. The size of and time scales involved in these process investments create issues that must be addressed in the corporate strategy debate. Chapter 12 discussed the implications of process choice, provided insights, and outlined some of the blocks on which to build manufacturing's strategic dimension. Assessing how well existing processes fit an organization's current market requirements and making appropriate process choices to meet future needs are critical manufacturing responsibilities, owing to the high investment associated with the outcomes of these decisions.

When companies buy processes, however, they often fail to appreciate the business trade-offs embodied in those investments (see Figure 12-2). Product profiling enables a company to test the current or anticipated level of fit between the characteristics of its market(s) and the characteristics of its existing or proposed processes and infrastructure investments (the components of manufacturing strategy—see Figure 10-5). The purpose of this assessment is twofold. First, it provides a way to evaluate and, where necessary, improve the degree of fit between the way in which a company wins orders in its markets and manufacturing's ability to support these criteria (i.e., manufacturing's strategic response). Second, it helps a company move away from classic strategy building characterized by functional perspectives separately agreed to, without adequate attempts to test the fit or reconcile different opinions of what is best for the business as a whole (as illustrated in Figures 10-1 and 10-2).

In many instances though, companies will be unable or unwilling to take the necessary steps to provide the degree of fit desired because of the level of investment, executive energy, and time scales involved. However, sound strategy is not a case of having every facet correctly in place. It concerns improving the level of consciousness a company brings to bear on its corporate decisions. Living with existing mismatches or allowing the level of fit to deteriorate can be strategically sound if a company is aware of its position and makes these choices knowingly. Reality can constrain strategic decisions. In such circumstances, product profiling will help increase corporate awareness and allow a conscious choice between alternatives. In the past, many companies have not aspired to this level of strategic alertness.

THE NEED TO EXPAND MANUFACTURING STRATEGY'S LANGUAGE BASE

Manufacturing has had difficulty expressing important perspectives in a manner that provides for corporate debate and discussion. Unless it can do this, other business functions will find difficulty in embracing the issues on hand and, in turn, being party to their resolution. Intuition, experience, and gut feeling must give way to business-related concepts and explanations. This is not to imply that the former are of little value. On the contrary, they form an integral part of sound management practice. However, at the strategic level perspectives based on intuition must be explained in a way that other executives can understand, so allowing these views to become part of the on-going corporate debate and strategic outcomes. In fact, one of the key tests for the usefulness of management theory is whether or not it crystallizes the intuitive insights of experienced executives. In this way, it contributes to the essential intellectual nature of the management debate—intellectual not in the sense of theory, but in reflecting the complex and applied nature of the management task.

Each business will require its own approach and resolution. The examples described in the following sections met the specific needs of those businesses to which they relate. They should not be considered universally applicable. The conceptual base on which these analyses rest, however, can be transferred and used to prepare similar analyses that will yield their own profiles.

PRODUCT PROFILING

Inconsistency between the market and the capability of the manufacturing process to support the business specification of its products can be induced by changes in the market or process investment decisions, or a combination of the two. In all instances, the mismatch results from the fact that while manufacturing investments are inherently large and fixed (once a company has purchased them, it will have to live with them for better or for worse for many years), markets are inherently dynamic. In addition, corporate marketing decisions can often be relatively transient should a business so decide. The inherently changing nature of markets and a company's ability to alter marketing perspectives to allow for change and repositioning are in opposition to manufacturing decisions that bind a business for years ahead. A company must reconcile these differences which requires strategic awareness, recognition, and action.

Product profiling is a way to ascertain the level of fit between the choice of processes that have been or are proposed to be made and the order-winning criteria of the product(s) under review. The sections that follow describe situations and, to some extent, different levels of the same problem.

Levels of Applications

Product profiling can be undertaken at the level of either the company or the process. Company-based applications provide an overview of the degree of fit between all or significant parts of a business and existing manufacturing facilities or its proposed manufacturing investments and developments. Process-based applications provide a check of the fit between the products that the equipment under review is to provide.

Procedure

The procedure used in product profiling is outlined below. This outline details the basic steps to follow, but the essential direction of the analysis needs to reflect the match/mismatch issues within the whole or parts of a business. Remember, the purpose of profiling is to draw a picture to help identify the current or potential problem, hence allowing discussion of and agreement on what steps should be taken to improve the company's strategic position.

1. Select relevant aspects of products/markets, manufacturing, investment/cost, and infrastructure as outlined in Figure 12-4. This choice must meet two overriding requirements.
   a. The criteria selected must relate to the issues on hand and reflect the strategic dimensions of relevant markets. Thus dimensions other than those given in Figure 12-4 will often be selected, as the examples that follow illustrate.
   b. The number of criteria selected must be kept small enough to allow the picture illustrating the issues to show through. Choosing too large a list will blur the essential clarity required and detract from the facilitating role that this approach plays within strategic formulation.
2. Display the trade-offs of process choice that would be typical for each criterion chosen in (1) above. The resulting diagram provides the backdrop against which the product or products can be profiled.
3. The purpose of profiling is to provide comparison. The next step then is to profile the products, product groups, or companies involved and is done by positioning the selected product(s), group(s) of products, or companies on each criterion selected. Remember, you are using a comparative technique; therefore, you want to show the relationship of one product to another, compare a company today with what it was (or would be) in a selected earlier (or later) period, or review one business with another. The purpose is to test the correlation between market requirements and manufacturing's current or proposed response to their provision. Thus the profiling (the position on each chosen dimension where what is being reviewed is placed) is to display a comparative picture and not become an issue of exactness.
4. The resulting profile illustrates the degree of consistency between the characteristics of the market(s) and the relative provision of the processes and infrastructure within manufacturing. The more consistency that exists, the straighter the profile will be. Inconsistencies between the market and manufacturing's inherent ability to meet these needs will result in a dogleg-shaped profile.

   Remember throughout that the purposes of a profile are to display the issues relevant to a business and to enable a company to review the degree of alignment that exists. This pictorial representation of those dimensions relevant to a business allows the executives responsible for strategic decisions to recognize the issues, their origins, and the corrective action to take.

   The examples that follow illustrate the points above and afford the opportunity to discuss particular applications.

COMPANY-BASED PROFILES

Inducing Mismatch with Process Investments

As emphasized in the last chapter, all process choices include fixed business trade-offs that can be changed only by further investment or development. Thus a company's investment in a process embodying trade-offs inconsistent with part or all of its markets induces mismatches between process and market unless the company changes its markets. These would correspond to the relative size and importance of the process(es) involved and the associated level of reinvestment.

A company producing a range of cartons, for example, decided to invest $6 million in part of its processes, which was core to a range of its products accounting for some 30 percent of total sales revenue. Based on the current level of activity, the investment would have been paid back in 5.5 years. However, to meet the parent group's return-on-investment four-year norms, the company needed to increase the output of these products by some 50 percent.

For some time, the company's marketing strategy had been to position itself in the higher-quality end of all its markets. However, to gain the larger volumes necessary to justify this process investment, the company had to go for business won on price. Soon the company had almost 15 percent of its total business with distinct low-cost needs while having to meet the schedule-change needs of a further 30 percent. The consequences were significant and the ramifications substantial. Within a short space of time, the process investment had introduced manufacturing conflict in a large part of its total business.

Product profiling can draw attention to the sort of mismatches involved here by graphically representing key marketing and manufacturing differences that the single set of processes had to accommodate (see Figure 13-1).

In this example, the $6 million process investment was, in terms of its point on the jobbing-batch-line continuum in Figure 13-1, consistent with its existing processes and chosen to support its existing business. However, the additional price-sensitive business required different process and infrastructure support. The straight-line and dogleg relationships in the exhibit reflect this.

FIGURE 13-1 Product Profile Illustrating Mismatch between the Market and Manufacturing Induced by Process Investment

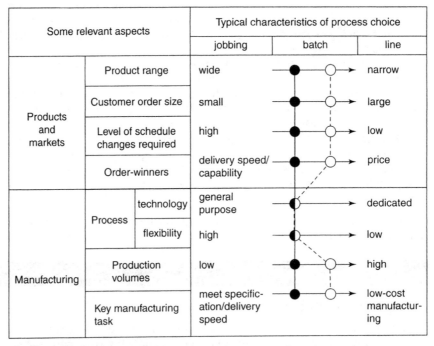

● ◑ Position of existing products on each of the chosen dimensions and resulting profile _____

○ ◑ Position of new products on each of the chosen dimensions and the resulting profile _____

Applying the Same Manufacturing Strategy to Two Different Markets

The first example concerned the impact of a process investment on the fit between a company's market and its manufacturing capability. Without a well-developed manufacturing strategy, the company was unconsciously driven by other functional (in this instance, finance) norms and arguments into an inappropriate major investment. Failure to recognize that investment decisions need to be based on strategy, and not on functional perspectives and prerequisites, is a common contributor to poor corporate performance.

However, an equally important source of inappropriate investment decisions is the assumption that to meet different corporate requirements a similar manufacturing strategy approach can be applied. Typically, this happens where specialists' views form the basis of initiatives, rather than a manufacturing strategy formulated to the requirements of individual markets. Again, product profiling can provide a graphic description of the resulting mismatch and help explain these differences.

Faced with a decline in markets and profits, a company undertook a major internal review of its two manufacturing plants. To provide orientation for its business, it decided to manufacture different products at each of its two sites; each plant, then, manufactured distinct products and associated volumes. Four or five years later, the number of product types handled by plant B was eight times as many as plant A, and, as one would expect, product volume changes were reflected in this decision. While in plant A, average volumes for individual product rose by 60 percent, in plant B they decreased by 40 percent. In addition, to redress the decline in profits, the company embarked on major manufacturing investments at each plant, involving identical process investments and infrastructure changes. Figure 13-2 illustrates how these changes fitted plant A's markets, while they led to a significant mismatch for plant B.

The procedure followed is similar to the one outlined in the previous section. Again, the first step is to describe, in conceptual terms, the characteristics of product/markets, manufacturing, investment/cost, and infrastructure features pertinent to the business. The dimensions selected for these two plants are detailed in Figure 13-2. First the characteristics that reflect the change between jobbing, batch, and line need to be described. Thus the product range associated with jobbing is wide and becomes increasingly narrow as it moves through to line, whereas customer order size is small in jobbing and becomes increasingly larger as it moves through to line and so on. These dimensions represent the classic characteristics of the trade-offs embodied in process choice. Plant A's profile shows a straight-line relationship between the products and markets and the manufacturing and infrastructure provision. However, plant B's profile shows a dogleg because of the difference in markets, compared to the similar process and infrastructure investments made in each of the two plants.

Based on Figure 13-2, Figure 13-3 provides a further illustration and additional insights into the extent of the mismatch brought about by applying the same manufacturing strategy to plants A and B described here. Whereas plant A had appropriate process investments in line with its product volumes, plant B did not (referred to as "Profile mismatch 1" in Figure 13-3). As a consequence, whereas plant A was appropriately positioned on each dimension on the vertical axis (see Figure 13-2 and Figure 13-3), again plant B was not (referred to as "Profile Mismatch 2" in Figure 13-3).

Incremental Marketing Decisions Resulting in a Mismatch

For many companies, changes in market needs happen over time, and these incremental changes are more typically the source of mismatches in a business. Product profiling provides an important way of describing these changes and their overall impact on a company.

As highlighted earlier, while markets are inherently dynamic, manufacturing is inherently fixed. This is not, however, a result of attitudes or preferences—markets will simply change over time whether or not a company so desires, whereas the manufacturing

FIGURE 13-2   Product Profile Illustrating the Level of Match and Mismatch between
Two Plants and Their Respective Markets Induced by Applying the Same Manufacturing
Strategy to Both Plants

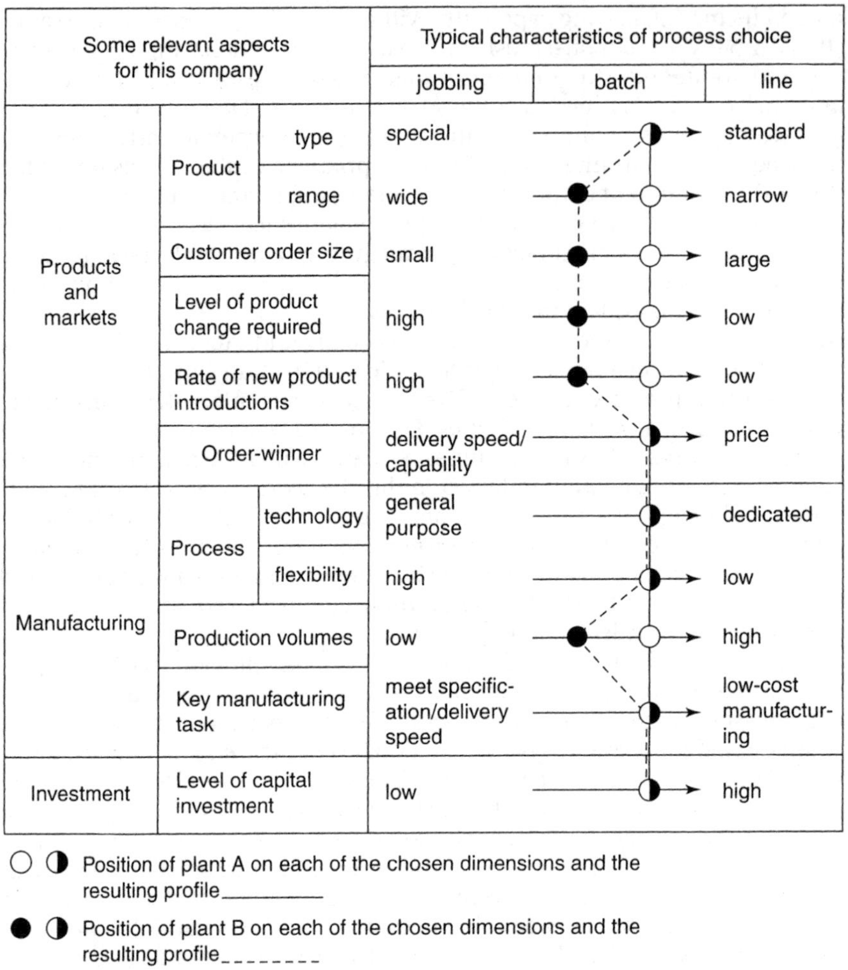

Some relevant aspects for this company			Typical characteristics of process choice		
			jobbing	batch	line
Products and markets	Product	type	special		standard
		range	wide		narrow
	Customer order size		small		large
	Level of product change required		high		low
	Rate of new product introductions		high		low
	Order-winner		delivery speed/capability		price
Manufacturing	Process	technology	general purpose		dedicated
		flexibility	high		low
	Production volumes		low		high
	Key manufacturing task		meet specification/delivery speed		low-cost manufacturing
Investment	Level of capital investment		low		high

○ ◑ Position of plant A on each of the chosen dimensions and the
      resulting profile _____

● ◑ Position of plant B on each of the chosen dimensions and the
      resulting profile _ _ _ _ _ _ _

investments will stay as they are unless deliberately changed by development or further investment.

Product profiling is a way of mapping the fit between the requirements of current markets and the characteristics of existing processes. The key to identifying these differences lies in the recognition that while the needs of the market may have changed, the characteristics of the manufacturing process and infrastructure investments will not. These, as emphasized in Chapter 12, will remain fixed, unless there is further, appropriate investment.

To illustrate, let's consider a European-based business that was finding itself under pressure from its U.S. parent company to grow sales and profits. Its response was to adopt a marketing strategy to broaden its product range. Process investments had already been updated, and there was excess capacity over and above current sales levels. Supporting the required sales growth would consequently not incur significant investments. As the strategy developed, the product range widened, while the customer order size decreased and the number of production schedule changes increased. Now, several years into their marketing strategy, the company is experiencing problems in terms of manufacturing's

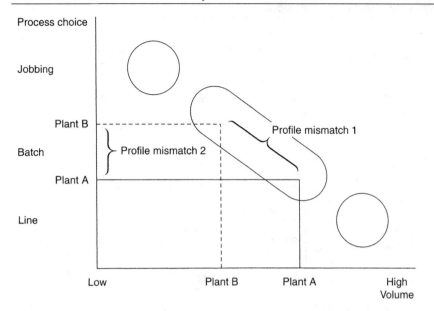

ability to support current markets and provide required levels of profit. To explain the causes of this problem it is necessary to compare the current year with the year in which its manufacturing process and infrastructure investments were made. The reason is because a company when it invests in processes does so to reflect the characteristics of its markets as perceived at that time. As shown in Figure 13-4, in the period before the marketing strategy change, there was a match between the characteristics of the company's products and markets, manufacturing, and infrastructure. The incremental marketing changes in the ensuing period had the cumulative effect of moving to the left the company's position on several, relevant dimensions under the heading "products and markets" detailed in Figure 13-4. The implications for manufacturing of the incremental marketing changes in these years are revealed when drawing the equivalent profile for the current year. Again, the profile mismatch illustrates that manufacturing had become increasingly less able to support the changing marketing trends, which the dogleg profile illustrates (see Figure 13-4).

Reallocation of Products Due to Downsizing

Companies faced with a reduction in overall demand often decide to downsize total manufacturing capacity as a way of meeting future profit expectations. This decision involves the reallocation of products from one plant to another, thereby enabling one to downsize or close while improving current machine utilization in the other. Debates of this kind are based on two checks:

- A technical specification fit between the products to be made and the process.
- The financial implications of the different decisions.

Often, however, companies fail to check whether the business specifications of the products to be transferred match the process. There were many illustrations of this source of mismatch in the 1990s. The resulting profile is similar to that in Figure 13-4 but is due to stepped rather than incremental changes. It results from the failure to recognize that

FIGURE 13-4 Product Profile of a Company's Mainstream Products to Illustrate the Impact of Incremental Marketing Decisions

Some relevant aspects		Typical characteristics of process choice		
		jobbing	batch	line
Products and markets	Product range	wide	●──○→	narrow
	Order size	small	●──○→	large
	Frequency of changes — product	high	●──○→	low
	Frequency of changes — schedule	high	●──○→	low
	Order-winners	delivery speed/ capability	◐→	price
Manufacturing	Process technology	general purpose	◐→	dedicated
	Production volumes	low	●──○→	high
	Ability to cope with change — product	easy	◐→	difficult
	Ability to cope with change — schedule	easy	◐→	difficult
	Setups — number	many	●──○→	few
	Setups — expense	inexpensive	◐→	expensive
Infrastructure	Engineering orientation	Product introductions	●──○→	Process improvements

○ ◐ Company's original position on each of the chosen aspects and the resulting profile _____

● ◐ Company's current position on each of the chosen aspects and the resulting profile _ _ _ _ _ _ _

The current-year profile illustrates the dogleg shape, which reflects the inconsistencies between the high-volume batch processes and infrastructure purchased in the past, and the current market position.

different units of capacity, though meeting similar technical specifications, do not have the same business specifications (see Figure 12-2).

Internal Sourcing Decisions Based on Unit Costs

Often within a group of companies the same product will be manufactured in two or more locations. Executives with profit responsibility for a region will understandably look to sourcing costs as a major factor in profit performance. Where two or more plants make the same product, differences in unit price will attract some sister companies within the group to place their business with the least cost company. A North American multinational was under pressure to maintain its record of profit performance; the various parts

334 CHAPTER 13 PRODUCT PROFILING

of the business were required to match or even improve their own performance. The result was that executives switched their internal source of product on the basis of lowest unit cost as an important way of maintaining or improving their own individual profit performance. Within a short time, however, the least-cost plant found that it could no longer maintain its previous cost levels. Attracting volumes of differing (often low) levels and other market requirements led to its best plant grossly underperforming. A product profile showed why, with reasons similar to those described in the last two examples, although with different origins.

PROCESS-BASED PROFILES

Company-based profiles help reflect changes at the corporate level and identify the varying degrees of match or mismatch that exist or will exist if market needs and characteristics are not reflected in manufacturing. Process-based profiles provide similar insights but concern the review of a single process (or group of similar processes) in relation to the products produced on it (them). More than one process-based profile can be completed within a single plant.

A prime reason why mismatches develop is that as demand for a product(s) changes, capacity is released. The typical result is that companies will allocate other products to that process on the basis of a technical specification check but not a business specification check. These may be either derivations of products already made in that process or new products. In both instances, the product range widens, overall individual order quantities decrease, and the process stops and starts more often.

The outcome is that the process will increasingly be required to support the business specification of two or more products that have different order-winners or other market characteristics. Profiles based on a format similar to those given earlier will help explain this problem to a business so that decisions are changed or expectations realigned.

A U.S.-based pharmaceutical company located the manufacture of a major new product in its Kansas City plant. The initial sales of this product justified forecasts, and following this initial success the company introduced product variants to maximize total sales revenue. These variants took the form of dosage, package size, and labels/leaflets in several languages. Sales continued to grow, and the company purchased further packaging equipment, similar to the existing processes, to meet increased capacity requirements. Variants continued and so did total sales. Though not competing on price (brand name was an important factor for this product in winning orders), margins deteriorated. Furthermore, as competing products entered the market and price levels were revised, overall profit levels fell short of expectations.

The profile in Figure 13-5 helps explain why. A mismatch between marketing and manufacturing resulted from engineering and manufacturing's orientation shifting away from exploiting the potential cost advantages associated with volumes toward that of product introductions necessitated by the variations strategy. The process investment and manufacturing orientation were misaligned with the needs of the market and the profit potential associated with reducing costs. Consequently, profit margins were short of the level necessary to support the high R&D expenditure essential to secure future growth and market penetration in pharmaceutical markets.

USING PRODUCT PROFILING

The examples given in this chapter illustrate the role product profiling may play in helping a company to check its existing product and process choice relationship and allow, where relevant, comparisons to be made between similar applications, or to measure trends over time. However, the reviews given were based on hindsight, not on the forward-

FIGURE 13-5 Profile of the Product Variants Completed on a Number of Similar Packaging Lines

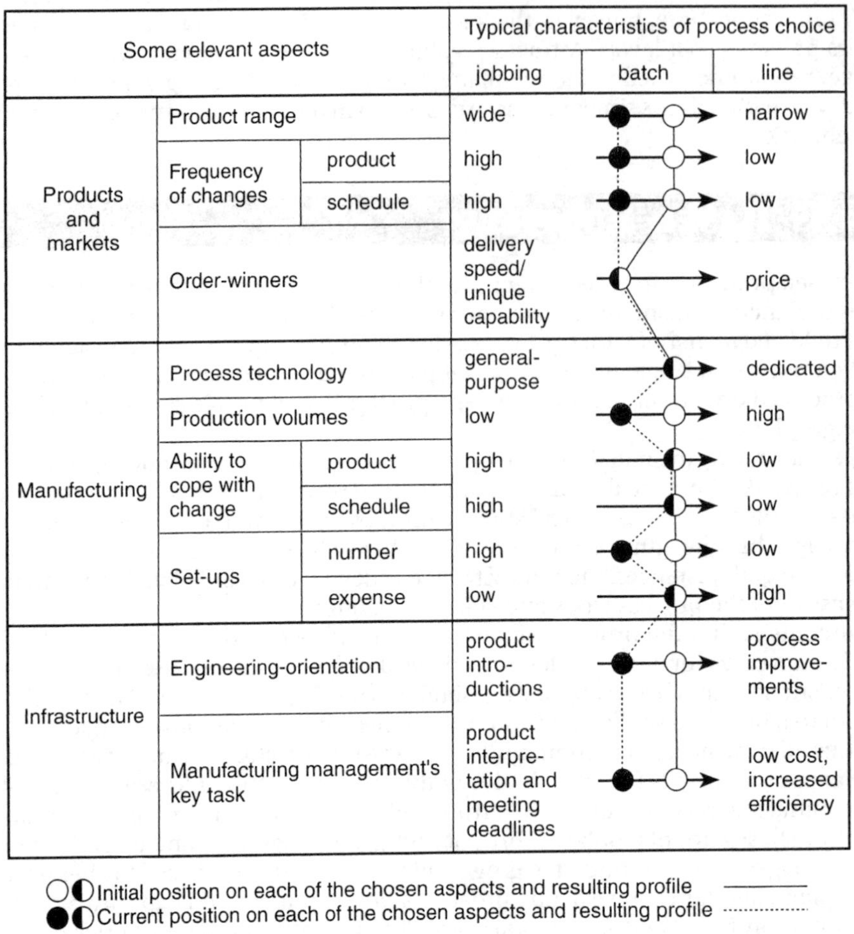

Some relevant aspects			Typical characteristics of process choice			
			jobbing	batch	line	
Products and markets	Product range		wide			narrow
	Frequency of changes	product	high			low
		schedule	high			low
	Order-winners		delivery speed/ unique capability			price
Manufacturing	Process technology		general-purpose			dedicated
	Production volumes		low			high
	Ability to cope with change	product	high			low
		schedule	high			low
	Set-ups	number	high			low
		expense	low			high
Infrastructure	Engineering-orientation		product introductions			process improvements
	Manufacturing management's key task		product interpretation and meeting deadlines			low cost, increased efficiency

○◐ Initial position on each of the chosen aspects and resulting profile ————

●◐ Current position on each of the chosen aspects and resulting profile ⋯⋯⋯⋯

looking characteristics of strategy. When a company is able to illustrate current positions and future alternatives, it can discuss alternatives and determine which strategic direction best meets the needs of the business. In this role, product profiling helps companies determine the business perspectives of manufacturing.

However, companies that are, for whatever reason, experiencing a mismatch between their current market needs and existing manufacturing processes and infrastructure face a number of alternative choices. These are

1. Live with the mismatch.
2. Redress the profile mismatch by altering the marketing strategy.
3. Redress the profile mismatch by investing in and changing manufacturing and its infrastructure.
4. A combination of (2) and (3).

Alternative 1 affords companies the opportunity to consciously make a decision on the trade-offs involved and may be the correct strategic choice. Such a decision brings a company's expectations more in line with reality, makes a company aware of the real costs of being in different markets, changes the measures of performance used by distinguishing between those based on business-related decisions and those based on functional achievement, and raises the level of corporate consciousness about the overall consequences of maintaining product profile status quo or the decision to improve or widen any *mismatch* that may exist. Furthermore, future decisions concerning new products are now more able to incorporate these essential perspectives; such decisions reconcile the diverse functional perspectives under the mantle of what is best for the business overall.

Alternatives 2 and 3 concern ways of straightening existing—or consciously avoiding the widening of existing or creation of new—mismatches. These decisions may be taken independently or in unison. Alternative 2 involves influencing corporate policy through changes or modifications to existing or proposed marketing strategies. In this way, the implications for manufacturing of marketing decisions are addressed and included as an integral part of the corporate strategy debate. Thus manufacturing is able to move from the reactive stance it currently takes to a proactive mode, so essential to sound policy decisions.

Alternative 3 involves a company's decision to invest in the processes and infrastructure of its business either to enable manufacturing to become more effective in its provision of the order-winning criteria and support in the marketplace for existing products or to establish the required level of support for future products. Like alternative 2, alternative 3 enables manufacturing to switch from a reactive to a proactive response to corporate marketing decisions. Thus, by receiving pertinent inputs at the strategic level, the business becomes more aware of the implications involved and is able to arrive at strategic options based on the relevant and comprehensive inputs necessary to make sound judgments at the strategic level.

CONCLUSION

The reasons companies fail to incorporate the manufacturing perspectives into the strategy debate are many. For one, manufacturing is traditionally presented as a technical or engineering-related function. This approach not only creates barriers to discussion but also misrepresents the key perspectives a company needs to address. A major thrust within manufacturing strategy is to reorient its contribution from a technical/engineering to a business perspective. This change opens the debate by providing meaningful insights and introduces those manufacturing perspectives that can contribute to the success of a business. In this way, the change to a business perspective helps create the link between manufacturing and other functions by using the common denominator of the market to create interest in and highlight the relevance of its corporate contribution to other functions. The results are business-based discussions leading to essential strategic outcomes.

Product profiling is one such development. By translating process investments into business issues, companies are able to assess the fit between these major resources and the markets they are required to support. In addition, being able to explain trends, mismatches, and options in picture form enhances the power of the illustration and increases its role in corporate understanding and debate. Thus, product profiling helps lead to sound strategy developments by enabling functions to explain themselves in corporate terms and provides a language to enhance essential discussion and agreement.

CHAPTER 14

Manufacturing Infrastructure Development

The need for a business to resolve the issues of process choice in line with the manufacturing strategy requirement has been paramount in the book so far. To reiterate, companies must clearly understand which manufacturing processes can best meet the needs of the marketplace, or how well existing processes provide the order-winners for products in different segments. However, the task facing manufacturing is not simply to choose the process and necessary hardware. Once this has been analyzed and the trade-offs reconciled, the emphasis shifts. It must now ensure that the structure and composition of the component parts, or functions, that provide the necessary systems and communications within a company are also developed in line with the manufacturing strategy requirement. Process choice concerns the features of hardware, the tangible ways in which products are manufactured. But the task is more than this. The supporting structures, controls, procedures, and other systems within manufacturing are equally necessary for successful, competitive manufacturing performance.

These structures, controls, procedures, and other systems are collectively known as the *manufacturing infrastructure*. It comprises the inner structure of manufacturing and necessarily includes the attitudes, experience, and skills of the people involved. Together, they form the basis of the manufacturing organization, charged with the task of providing the necessary support to the areas of responsibility involved.

As illustrated in Figure 10-5, manufacturing strategy comprises both processes and infrastructure. Getting one in line with market needs and not the other will lead to inconsistencies similar to the levels of mismatch illustrated in Chapter 13. Aligning process characteristics with market needs is insufficient in itself. The impact of infrastructure investments on sound manufacturing strategy provision is as critical as process choice and, in some companies, more so.

Infrastructure developments are also characterized by their high level of investment and their fixed nature. These decisions are as binding as their hardware

FIGURE 14-1 The Inexorable Link of Components of Manufacturing Strategy with Each Other and with the Market Needs of a Business

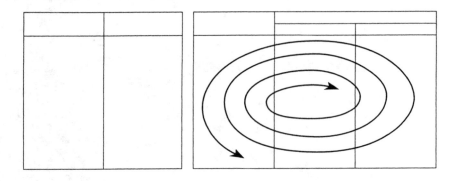

counterparts and must be made with the same clear link to the needs of a company's markets. If not, problems will arise that are identical to those already highlighted for process decisions. Furthermore, companies need to parallel continuing market changes with appropriate development in manufacturing. The inherently fixed nature of manufacturing infrastructure is often coupled with an inertia for change stemming in part from corporate reviewing procedures built on functional goals and perspectives. Often, those responsible for the realignment of the essential components of manufacturing infrastructure are unaware of or unable to respond to the growing need to make the necessary and appropriate changes. One underlying message in Peters and Waterman's *In Search of Excellence* is that success depends on awareness.[1] Building and developing infrastructure on a manufacturing strategy base does just that. It gives appropriate direction and allows a choice to be made between alternative sets of trade-offs. In this way a company has a shared awareness of what is required in manufacturing if it is to best support the current and future needs of the business, and the necessity of linking manufacturing to the marketplace through its process hardware and organizational software is also highlighted. Thus the components of manufacturing strategy must be inexorably linked to give them coherence and synergistic purpose, as illustrated in Figure 14-1.

Infrastructure represents part of the complexity inherent in manufacturing. To develop an appropriate infrastructure to support manufacturing effectively, a company must recognize two important dimensions. The first concerns the way the company is structured internally and why it has evolved that way. The second involves recognizing the key perspectives to be taken into account when developing the important areas of infrastructure.

By themselves, most elements of infrastructure do not require the same level of investment nor do they have the same impact on manufacturing's strategic role as does process choice; but taken collectively they do. Together, their importance in providing the strategic support for the business cannot be overstressed. Similarly, the difficulties experienced through the interaction of inappropriate systems and the costs involved in effecting major changes can be of the same magnitude as those decisions involving manufacturing hardware. Transforming over time the support for the marketplace into an appropriate collection of facilities, structures, controls, procedures, and people comprises the manufacturing strategy task. As Hayes and Wheelwright conclude:

> *It is this pattern of structural* [process] *and infrastructural decisions that constitutes the "manufacturing strategy" of a business unit. More formally, a manufacturing strategy consists of a sequence of decisions that, over time, enables a business unit to*

---

[1]T. J. Peters and R. H. Waterman Jr., *In Search of Excellence: Lessons from America's Best-Run Companies* (New York: Harper & Row, 1982).

achieve a desired [market related] *manufacturing structure* [process choice], *infra-structure, and set of specific capabilities.*[2]

In relation to corporate strategy, they recognize that "the primary function of a manufacturing strategy is to guide the business in putting together the set of manufacturing capabilities that will enable it to pursue its chosen competitive strategy over the long term."[3]

MANUFACTURING INFRASTRUCTURE ISSUES

Manufacturing infrastructure comprises a complex set of interacting factors. Western companies have traditionally coped with this by breaking their infrastructures into appropriate sets of responsibilities or functions and deploying people to provide the necessary support. To work effectively this structure requires a high degree of coordination linked to manufacturing's strategic tasks. However, reality does not bear out the theory. Typically, these parts or functions are managed separately and come together primarily at the tactical or operational interface. Developments within the infrastructure are given the level of detailed attention they require at the points of application. It is at these levels where meaningful, in-depth discussion takes place, no doubt stimulated by the real need to make the particular area of infrastructure development work effectively. However, the merits of the individual parts and how they fit together are rarely encompassed by any strategic overview. For this reason, piecemeal developments, propounded in the main by specialists, lead to an uncoordinated approach to infrastructure design.

It is essential that the basic parts of the organizational framework reinforce and support the manufacturing task. This enables a company to get away from functionally based perspectives of what is appropriate and important. The only way to achieve this change is to orient discussion on the requirements of the business, that is, to replace functional argument by a corporate resolution between alternatives and to replace unilaterally stimulated argument of what is best for the business by corporate-based argument of the same. Such a change in orientation then provides a base on which to develop a comprehensive, coordinated, and directed infrastructure to meet a firm's current and future needs, by enabling a company not only to get its orientation right but also to avoid a situation of being saddled with functions that are no longer required or are inappropriately influential when related to the business needs. Changing the *status quo* is difficult unless the firm knows why and how it wants or has to change. Only then is it able to move from subjectively-based to objectively-based analyses and decisions. This change requires a very clear statement of what constitutes the manufacturing task—the manufacturing strategy appropriate to the company. Once functional managers understand and appreciate this, a company can reshuffle the *status quo*. It is then in a position to avoid situations where vested interests argue for the retention or growth in capabilities and budgets for their own sake rather than for their relative contribution to the current and future success of the business.

Questions stemming from these views concern why functions hold on to their current level of size and why they argue for their own retention and growth. In many instances, they do so because it is the best perspective they have. Only when a business orients functions toward the outside (i.e., what the market requires) can it provide the opportunity for alternatives to be measured against corporate-related criteria. The provision of a common, relevant base enables functional arguments to be put into perspective. It shifts the evaluation of proposals from the use of subjective to objective criteria. It gives appropriate direction to which all infrastructure development must aspire while also providing detailed checklists against which developments can be evaluated. In this way, these costly

---

[2]R. H. Hayes and S. C. Wheelwright, *Restoring Our Competitive Edge: Competing through Manufacturing* (John Wiley & Sons, Inc., 1984), p. 32.

[3]Ibid., p. 33.

developments will meet manufacturing strategy requirements rather than functional or specialist perspectives. Furthermore, by looking outward and forward, developments will be made with a knowing eye on future competition and thus become more likely to incorporate the manufacturing needs of tomorrow.

If the functions charged with making effective infrastructure provision are not given strategic direction, there is the real possibility that specialist support functions will pursue their own points of view, a problem many businesses experience today. Firms need the functional and specialist capabilities to make sense of the complexity. Without these inputs, they cannot reach the level of effectiveness necessary to meet today's competitive pressures. The difference between an infrastructure based on a number of specialist views and one coordinated to meet the needs of a business by an appropriate strategy is significant for most firms and critical for many.

The review and incremental development of infrastructure within the strategic context of manufacturing is equally important—it concerns altering the balance or changing the focus of development so that it is in line with the manufacturing task, and hence forms an integral part of manufacturing strategy. A firm's ability to backtrack on its decisions is also important at times. This activity, however, is often thwarted by the difficulties presented by specialists who are typically highly analytical people capable of arguing their case with great clarity and strength and protecting their own views and areas of responsibility in a vacuum. The existence of a manufacturing strategy provides the parameters for analysis and debate to either reconcile arguments or views or redirect development activity.

INFRASTRUCTURE DEVELOPMENT

Strategy comprises the development and declaration of a shared view of business direction. Unless a business regularly updates its strategy in response to market change, deviations from supporting market needs will go unnoticed, and individual interpretations of strategy, rather than the strategy statement itself, will become fact. In both instances, fragmentation will occur, and the necessary coherence will diminish.

The successful development of infrastructure requires care. Many companies have adopted a piecemeal approach by resolving one facet at a time, as often stimulated by the apparent need of the moment as by a carefully selected priority. Picking off one area makes

FIGURE 14-2 Companies Need to Determine the Level of Manufacturing Complexity before Developing Appropriate Infrastructures.

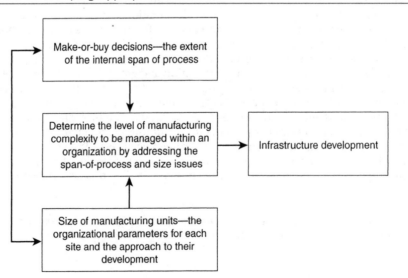

sense as a way of coping with the complexity involved. However, many organizations even in these situations do not undertake sufficient analyses before determining the area to be developed. This preliminary analysis need not become a complex debate; Figure 14-2 points to the essential issues—the need to determine the make-or-buy decision and define the size of the manufacturing units. Thus, rather than investing money, time, and effort in resolving the current complexity, a company should define the level of complexity it wishes to handle. Only then is it able to decide how best to manage the chosen level, and only then is it able to develop the infrastructure appropriate to its needs. For once a company understands its manufacturing task and the organizational makeup involved (its *organizational profile*), the direction and content of any infrastructure development will become clear and comprehensible.

Many companies in the past have pursued the economies of large scale without fully evaluating the net gains involved. A classic approach to achieving these apparent gains has sometimes been to centralize at corporate and plant levels. This had led to centralized functions being created throughout the organization. Primary counterarguments concern the increased complexity involved in large organizations and the difficulties of reshaping them in times of change. In many instances, the anticipated gains of centralized functions have become an organizational El Dorado.

The chapter so far has emphasized the importance of appropriately developing manufacturing infrastructure and its significant contribution to providing the necessary manufacturing support to the marketplace. Before discussing some of the key areas of infrastructure design, it will be worthwhile to highlight practical, but general considerations.

- It is most important to determine and agree on the important areas of infrastructure within manufacturing. A discretionary approach to change is essential to ensure that scarce development resources are used in those areas that will yield the best returns. The approach to change must reflect those areas that will have the most strategic impact, a point emanating from the concept of the 80/20 rule.[4]

- As with process choice, it is necessary to establish and then choose between sets of trade-offs that go hand in hand with each decision. The criteria, however, against which to measure the trade-offs must be concerned with manufacturing's strategic role.

- The essence of sound infrastructure design is that it must respond to the dynamics of reality. Although some areas will require major change, much of the necessary change can be achieved incrementally. After drawing this distinction, the company must regularly review areas of manufacturing infrastructure to effect the necessary developments, including the simplification and even withdrawal of controls, systems, and procedures. It is most important, on the other hand, to avoid major change wherever possible. In many instances, the need for major change reflects the degree of mismatch between requirement and provision that has developed incrementally over time within the relevant area of infrastructure. Often, sizable and lengthy disruptions are required to put things right.

- Linked to the issue of avoiding situations of stepped change is the decision of what constitutes the job of work and what is the role of specialists within an organization. Although addressed later in the chapter, it is important to emphasize here that continuous development is easier to bring about where the responsibility for identifying and implementing improvements is locally based. Employee involvement creates conditions where changes are brought about by incremental developments. On the other hand, control through specialists can result in the need for changes being undetected or unattended. In such circumstances, the requirements for change will often be set aside, and when eventually addressed, developments and tasks involved tend to be large.

---

[4] The 80/20 rule reflects the implied relationship between two sets of data or consequences. In this instance, it illustrates that 80 percent of the total strategic benefits to be gained from infrastructure development will arise from 20 percent of the areas of application. The use of the figures 80 and 20, however, is illustrative of the relationship implied in the selected phenomenon and not intended to be definitive.

Important Infrastructure Issues

A company that fails to develop its infrastructure, as part of its response to meeting the needs of its marketplace, is likely to experience two linked consequences:

1. The business position may worsen because, among other things, the systems and controls will fail to give executives accurate and timely indicators to help them manage the business and initiate the necessary developments.

2. The key components of infrastructure necessary to help reshape or rebuild the business may not be in place when they are most necessary and most urgently required.

The approach to developing the separate parts of a manufacturing company's infrastructure involves two integrated steps. The first is determining the market-place or competitive requirements; that is, each aspect of infrastructure must be built around the way products win orders. The controls, systems, procedures, attitudes, and skills involved will then be oriented toward those manufacturing tasks pertinent to the order-winning criteria of different products. The second is ensuring that the necessary level of coherence and coordination exists in the various but related parts of manufacturing infrastructure. In this way all the software pulls in the same, appropriate direction and the company releases the synergy inherent in this substantial investment. In addition, those involved feel the consequential facilitating and motivating benefits of coherent direction.